LIVES OF SPIRIT

In proud and loving memory of my parents:

Herbert William John Hallett (1907–2004)
Dorothy Lucy Cecilia Hallett (née Maiden) (1922–1998)

Lives of Spirit
English Carmelite Self-Writing of the Early Modern Period

NICKY HALLETT
University of Kent, UK

ASHGATE

Published by
Ashgate Publishing Limited
Gower House
Croft Road
Aldershot
Hampshire GU11 3HR
England

Ashgate Publishing Company
Suite 420
101 Cherry Street
Burlington, VT 05401-4405
USA

Ashgate website: http://www.ashgate.com

British Library Cataloguing in Publication Data
Lives of spirit : an edition of English Carmelite auto/biographies of the early modern period.
– (The early modern Englishwoman, 1500-1750. Contemporary editions)
1. Carmelites – Biography – Early works to 1800 2. Nuns – Belgium – Antwerp – Biography – Early works to 1800 3. English – Belgium – Antwerp – Biography – Early works to 1800
I. Hallett, Nicky
271.9'71'0092242

Library of Congress Cataloging-in-Publication Data
Lives of spirit : an edition of English Carmelite auto/biographies of the early modern period / Nicky Hallett.
  p. cm. — (The early modern Englishwoman, 1500-1750. Contemporary editions)
  Includes bibliographical references and index.
  ISBN 978-0-7546-0675-8 (alk. paper)
  1. Discalced Carmelite nuns—Biography. 2. Carmelites—Biography. 3. Monastic and religious life of women. 4. Monasticism and religious orders for women—Biography. 5. Church history—17th century. 6. Church history—18th century. I. Hallett, Nicky.

  BX4308.Z7L58 2007
  271'.971023210492—dc22

2006036044

ISBN-13: 9-780-7546-0675-8

Printed and bound in Great Britain by MPG Books Ltd, Bodmin, Cornwall.

Contents

The Early Modern Englishwoman 1500–1750: Contemporary Editions General Editors' Preface

Foregrounding women and gender has created a genuine revolution in the way we construct the early-modern period, and the aim of 'Contemporary Editions' (like its sister series, 'The Early-Modern Englishwoman, 1500–1750: A Facsimile Library of Essential Works') is to encourage and perpetuate this revolution by making available the texts that in so many ways have generated it.

'Contemporary Editions' shares with the facsimile series a desire to recover neglected or unknown texts as well as to make more readily available texts that the feminist rereading of the period has now brought to light. Apart from the inherent differences in editorial methodology between the two series, the format of the new series permits a fuller response to the wide range of writings of and about women. 'Contemporary Editions' is designed to provide distinguished editions, in both modernized and old-spelling format, of writings not only by but also for and about early-modern women. Volumes include long, interpretive essays and range widely in format from anthologies to single texts.

We hope that this series will capture the energy of the many scholars who are engaged in the reinterpretation of the early modern period, and that 'Contemporary Editions' will in time become, like its sister project, 'a library of essential works' for the study of early modern women and gender.

Acknowledgements

I wish to express affectionate gratitude to the Carmelite communities at Lanherne (now joined with St Helens) and Darlington for permission to produce editions of these manuscripts and for allowing me generous access to their archives. In particular I would like to thank their Prioresses – Reverend Mother Margaret Mary, of Lanherne; Reverend Mother Teresa, of St Helen's; the late Sister Margaret, of Darlington, and her successor, Sister Frances Thérèse. The warmth of their welcome and support has made this a journey of pleasure.

Mother Margaret Mary's enthusiasm for this project was based on the words of her seventeenth-century predecessor, Mary Frances Birkbeck, the Prioress at Antwerp who wrote of her incentive 'to collect ... the many remarkable things which [otherwise] by ... neglect will ever be buryed in oblivion'. It has been an inspiration to uncover these 'remarkable things', and to work now with her successors.

In addition, I wish to thank the University of Kent for allowing me Study Leave to pursue this work, and the AHRB for funding Research Leave to advance it more quickly. Special tribute should go to Peter Brown, Andrew Butcher, Lyn Innes, Jan Montefiore, and other staff and students of the School of English and the Centre for Medieval and Tudor Studies for their continuing inspiration.

I should also like to thank Johan Bergström-Allen of the Carmelite Projects office in York, and Father Antony Lester, Prior Provincial of the British Province of Carmelites for inviting me to take part in the *Cum Nulla* symposium and celebration in York in May 2003 and for their discussion of my work.

Caroline Bowden and Elizabeth Clarke, through their invitations to speak at conferences on women religious at St Mary's College, London, and the Perdita symposium at St Hilda's, Oxford, both in 2002, gave me the opportunity to air ideas at an early stage; and Liz Stanley's invitation to a colloquium at the University of Manchester in 2003 enabled me to present work on testimony and witness. Along with Derek Pearsall and Felicity Riddy, they have all generously discussed or read work in progress at various stages.

Thanks, too, to Sister Winefride and to Margaret Harcourt-Williams, the meticulous archivists at the Darlington convent; to Sister Constance Fitzgerald of the Carmelite Convent in Baltimore; to library staff at the British Library, London, and at the Universities of Kent and Sheffield; to Pat FitzGerald for her expertise in preparing camera-ready copy; and, most especially, to the General Editors of this series, Betty S. Travitsky, Patrick Cullen and Anne Lake Prescott whose wise interventions and timely advice improved and informed the final text. Erika Gaffney at Ashgate has guided this project throughout, with insight, tact and refreshing directness: the best of commissioning editors.

Not least, huge personal thanks, as ever, must go to Rosie Valerio.

Contents

The Early Modern Englishwoman 1500–1750: Contemporary Editions General Editors' Preface

Foregrounding women and gender has created a genuine revolution in the way we construct the early-modern period, and the aim of 'Contemporary Editions' (like its sister series, 'The Early-Modern Englishwoman, 1500–1750: A Facsimile Library of Essential Works') is to encourage and perpetuate this revolution by making available the texts that in so many ways have generated it.

'Contemporary Editions' shares with the facsimile series a desire to recover neglected or unknown texts as well as to make more readily available texts that the feminist rereading of the period has now brought to light. Apart from the inherent differences in editorial methodology between the two series, the format of the new series permits a fuller response to the wide range of writings of and about women. 'Contemporary Editions' is designed to provide distinguished editions, in both modernized and old-spelling format, of writings not only by but also for and about early-modern women. Volumes include long, interpretive essays and range widely in format from anthologies to single texts.

We hope that this series will capture the energy of the many scholars who are engaged in the reinterpretation of the early modern period, and that 'Contemporary Editions' will in time become, like its sister project, 'a library of essential works' for the study of early modern women and gender.

Acknowledgements

I wish to express affectionate gratitude to the Carmelite communities at Lanherne (now joined with St Helens) and Darlington for permission to produce editions of these manuscripts and for allowing me generous access to their archives. In particular I would like to thank their Prioresses – Reverend Mother Margaret Mary, of Lanherne; Reverend Mother Teresa, of St Helen's; the late Sister Margaret, of Darlington, and her successor, Sister Frances Thérèse. The warmth of their welcome and support has made this a journey of pleasure.

Mother Margaret Mary's enthusiasm for this project was based on the words of her seventeenth-century predecessor, Mary Frances Birkbeck, the Prioress at Antwerp who wrote of her incentive 'to collect … the many remarkable things which [otherwise] by … neglect will ever be buryed in oblivion'. It has been an inspiration to uncover these 'remarkable things', and to work now with her successors.

In addition, I wish to thank the University of Kent for allowing me Study Leave to pursue this work, and the AHRB for funding Research Leave to advance it more quickly. Special tribute should go to Peter Brown, Andrew Butcher, Lyn Innes, Jan Montefiore, and other staff and students of the School of English and the Centre for Medieval and Tudor Studies for their continuing inspiration.

I should also like to thank Johan Bergström-Allen of the Carmelite Projects office in York, and Father Antony Lester, Prior Provincial of the British Province of Carmelites for inviting me to take part in the *Cum Nulla* symposium and celebration in York in May 2003 and for their discussion of my work.

Caroline Bowden and Elizabeth Clarke, through their invitations to speak at conferences on women religious at St Mary's College, London, and the Perdita symposium at St Hilda's, Oxford, both in 2002, gave me the opportunity to air ideas at an early stage; and Liz Stanley's invitation to a colloquium at the University of Manchester in 2003 enabled me to present work on testimony and witness. Along with Derek Pearsall and Felicity Riddy, they have all generously discussed or read work in progress at various stages.

Thanks, too, to Sister Winefride and to Margaret Harcourt-Williams, the meticulous archivists at the Darlington convent; to Sister Constance Fitzgerald of the Carmelite Convent in Baltimore; to library staff at the British Library, London, and at the Universities of Kent and Sheffield; to Pat FitzGerald for her expertise in preparing camera-ready copy; and, most especially, to the General Editors of this series, Betty S. Travitsky, Patrick Cullen and Anne Lake Prescott whose wise interventions and timely advice improved and informed the final text. Erika Gaffney at Ashgate has guided this project throughout, with insight, tact and refreshing directness: the best of commissioning editors.

Not least, huge personal thanks, as ever, must go to Rosie Valerio.

General Introduction

This book is a study and a selected edition of the life-writing of around sixty Catholic nuns, most of them English, living in Carmelite convents in the Low Countries between 1619 and 1794. It presents largely unpublished material drawn from papers compiled by women who, in the words of one, 'came out of England in time of the persecution on account of Religion, that they might with more quiet and liberty serve God' (*A1*, 30). Succeeding generations continued to travel to continental Europe right through the time of the Civil War, during which 'fresh persecutions sprang up every day' (*L3.30F*), eventually returning to England when, as Basil Whelan colourfully put it, 'the devoted nuns were driven by the blasphemous frenzy of the French Revolution back to their now hospitable native shore' (1936, 3). Certainly, when the women re-established their convents in England, they did so in a more accommodating atmosphere of religious cohabitation, albeit within a situation of Protestant pre-eminence.

These papers offer new and beguiling sources for the study of female experience in early modern Europe. They show, through narratives that reflect both changing circumstance and continuity with earlier styles of spiritual self-writing, from positions of expatriate enclosure, that the religious women were able to shape distinctive devotional identities within the reforming church. Most of all, the papers are characterized by their immediacy of encounter and reveal intimate moments of body or soul: this is at once a deeply stylized and uninhibited autobiography in which the nuns occupy each other's waking, dreaming, dying lives.

This General Introduction seeks to provide background for a reading of the Lives[1] that follow, describing the intricacies of the situation within which the women wrote, during periods of social and religious upheaval in early modern Europe. It begins with a brief account of the cultural conditions that affected the reception of such papers, and then discusses how these and other contexts may have shaped the nuns' original writing.

---

[1] Throughout this book, 'Life', 'Lives' or 'self-writing' are used in preference to 'autobiography' or 'biography' since these last two terms are generally associated with generic preconceptions that do not always apply to personal spiritual testimony. For example, notions of autobiography as a 'unified, retrospective first-person narrative [which] uniquely totalizes its subject as both author and hero' (Mascuch, 1997, 23) are inapplicable to women's devotional life-writing which often has multiple authorship, a divine rather than human focus, and does not seek to chart the progress of a personality. 'Life' and 'Lives' in this context are capitalized to differentiate from '(a) life' or 'lives'.

Early Modern Historiographic and Catholic Contexts

The Carmelite women featured in this book produced a remarkable set of papers. That these have been so long overlooked is part of the heritage of an English religious historiography which has frequently discarded experience that does not appear to contribute to a sense of putative national enlightenment. It is now well recognized that 'Protestant hostility towards Catholicism functioned as a constitutive element in the emergence of nationalistic and imperial ideology' (Tumbleson, 1998, 11), and that this hostility had a concomitant effect on a construction of Catholics as deviant, enemy, foreign, other. However, there has been less attention given to the discursive treatment of enclosed and exiled women within this proscribed religion. Here the languages of nation and of gender appear to coalesce to particular effect. Just as some post-Reformation artists employed Marian iconography to portray Elizabeth I as inviolably chaste, so the country itself became an emblem of impermeability that sought to exclude the very women from whom the language itself was drawn: 'The state, like the virgin, was a *hortus conclusus*, an enclosed garden walled off from enemies' (Stallybrass, 1986, 129). The Carmelite papers naturally offer a different view: here Catholics represent themselves as true patriots, praying for the 'poor, distressed country of England', and it is the apparently marginalized who occupy positions of perceived centrality, claiming continuity within a pre-lapsarian spatial poetic, their 'paradise upon earth' (see p. 117, note 4).

Male-orientated literary criticism with its attendant ideas of genre has also until recently tended to neglect female writing, and particularly spiritual self-writing, which it has often construed to be at the peripheries of the significant. As a result, texts by many women in early modern Europe have largely gone unread, and historians have provided little sense of the role of nuns in cultural debates said to be central to emergent modernities. Discussion has been '... predominantly concerned with affairs inside England's borders. The nuns have only ever been mentioned as incidental to both the English mission and the seigneurial Catholicism of gentry households' (Walker, 2003, 4).[2] It is clear from the Carmelite papers, as from other sources, that women assumed positions of religious leadership in conventual life as well as in lay circles, and that from their situation in exile the nuns were able, to some extent at least, to influence English Catholic perceptions of religious renewal.

---

2   Claire Walker, in her own excellent study of English convents in France and the Low Countries (2003), notes exceptions in the work of Bowerbank, 1986; Crawford, 1993; Grundy, 1992; McNamara, 1996; Norman, 1975/76; Warnicke, 1983; as well as in literary studies by Crawford and Gowing, 2000; Latz, 1989; Travitsky and Cullen, 2000; Weller and Ferguson, 1994 – to which should be added, amongst others, studies that have augmented cultural perceptions of religious women, such as those by Aers and Staley, 1996; Ahlgren, 1996; Bell, 1995; Carlson and Weisl, 1999; Magray, 1998; Schutte, 1996; Walsh, 2002; Weber, 1990. Walker's own book focuses on a range of religious Orders, for the most part specifically excluding discussion of the Carmelites. Many of her general points about conditions within early modern female monasticism are borne out by my own study, however, and I remain indebted to her work.

Early Modern Carmelite History: the English Foundations in the Spanish Netherlands

The convents from which the papers in this book originated were part of the proliferation of Catholic monastic foundations in seventeenth-century Europe within what has been seen as a 'renaissance' of female religious activity (Walker, 2003, 9). During this resurgence, a significant number of Carmelite convents were established. These were initially founded by the companions and immediate successors of Teresa de Jesus (Teresa Sánchez de Cepeda y Ahumada, of Avila: 1515–82) who was beatified in 1614 and canonized in 1622; and they were part of the reformed, Discalced (that is, 'unshod') Order developed by St Teresa, by the time of whose death there were some 17 flourishing Carmels in Spain. Having arrived in Paris in 1604, these women moved across France, via Mons, to Antwerp where, in 1611, they founded what has since become known as the 'Spanish Carmel'. In 1619 a further convent specifically for English women was established in the Hopland area of the city, the lay founder of which was Mary Roper, Lady Lovel. Her negotiations with ecclesiastical authorities continued for several years from around 1608, during which time she considered entering or establishing convents from various religious Orders (Hardman, 1936, 3, 31).

During the 1619–1794 period covered by this book, the Hopland convent saw some 129 professions under 21 Prioresses, and other Carmels were founded in the region to accommodate increasing numbers – at Bois-le-Duc (1624), Bruges (1625), Cologne (1630), Alost (1631), Düsseldorf (1643) and – most importantly for this study – in 1648, at Lierre, a small town some 20 miles or so from Antwerp. Another English Carmel was established in 1678 at nearby Hoogstraeten.

This edition draws on material written by nuns and lay sisters from the English Carmels at Antwerp and Lierre. The Lierre community was established by religious from Antwerp, and strong links and some rivalry continued to exist between the two convents.[3] It is clear from their papers that the nuns were acutely aware of the political situation outside their convents. Their foundations were closely observed by English Protestant authorities, who were mindful of the ways in which religious communities formed conduits of influence between European Catholicism and families in England. Accounts of Mary Lovel's activities, for example, appear in correspondence from Thomas Edmonds, an English agent in Brussels, who considered her to be the 'most passyonate besotted poore woman that ever was' (cited Walker, 2003, 116). Such attitudes are informed by Protestant representations of the religious being, like Mary Lovel herself, 'unstable' or 'silly women … muzzled in blindenesse' (Robinson, 1622, 18), in thrall to Jesuits or other clerics, if not literally imprisoned by them. Certainly the attention of English agents at particular times successfully hampered the flow of crucial revenue to the religious houses. The papers show, too, how individual nuns

---

3   In general in this book, the English Carmel is referred to simply as 'Antwerp', unless it is being specifically differentiated from the Spanish Carmel in the city, in which case 'Hopland' is used.

were affected by the fluctuating fortunes of their families in England and placed in personal predicament during their journeys to Antwerp at a time of civil war.

Despite, and in some cases because of, such political conditions, the Carmels pursued particular paths in their devotional development. Their original foundation is clearly part of a wider Catholic regeneration following the Council of Trent (1545–63), contributing to a re-evangelizing mission within northern Europe that was in turn influenced by forces within and outside church reform (Harline, 1995; Walker, 2003, 8–42). The movement of women to these Carmelite convents from 1619 onwards continued a Catholic migration from England that had seen successive stages from the sixteenth century, for example following the dissolution of the monasteries or after the 1569 Rising of the North. Within the Spanish Netherlands, a region approximating present-day Belgium, the rule of Isabella and Albert (1598–1621)[4] was particularly conducive to the foundation movement (Guilday, 1914, 21). This era followed a stage of prolonged religious and social unrest when, after various uprisings and the eventually successful Dutch revolt against Philip II, the Low Countries were divided, the northern region becoming the United Provinces (or Dutch Republic), and the southern area continuing to be governed by Spain until 1713.

Throughout this period, Antwerp was a busy commercial city, comprising around 85,000 citizens by the mid-sixteenth century. Though its prosperity fluctuated, when blockades of the Scheldt compromised trading routes, for example (Israel, 1995, 744), the Carmelite papers show that the city continued to serve as a transit route for travellers to and from Catholic centres of northern Europe and that Antwerp remained a useful base for individuals who sought to re-establish fortunes or maintain a flow of religious revenue from England under cover of business. Several of the women featured in this book indeed used such commercial networks to deliver funding; and some were themselves from families that had settled in the region or that had visited nearby cities for commerce or education.

The papers give a strong sense of the nuns' lives in a region with a precarious religious history, one within which internally displaced Catholics and Protestants had moved as various regions changed allegiance. Just 30 or so years before the English foundation at Antwerp, for instance, in the few years following 1585, Protestants (until then comprising an estimated half of the population) left the city to live in northern Netherlandish towns (Israel, 1995, 219). If the southern region offered relative security for Catholics, this nevertheless remained a time of political turmoil during which nuns in the convents variously expressed their concern and vulnerability. Clearly, if these Carmels were havens for women in exile seeking to pursue a contemplative life, they were by no means isolated from the turbulent politics affecting the early modern Continent, and the Carmelite papers illustrate the rich interchange of letters, alms, ideas and individuals, at this crossroads of Europe.

---

[4] Isabella Clara Eugenia (1566–1623), the daughter of Philip II (1527–98) of Spain, married to Albert of Austria (1559–1621).

English migrants came and went within the region according to the fluctuating political situation of their home-land: several families of the Antwerp and Lierre nuns arrived, for example, during the aftermath of the Titus Oates 'Popish Plot' of 1678 (see Chapter 31E). The Carmels at various times gave shelter to 'distressed cavaliers' (see p. 186), and the religious appear to have been well aware of the intricate politics of the court in exile during the English Civil War. Indeed, some women who joined the convents had direct knowledge of the situation: for example, Mary Constantia of the Assumption of the Blessed Virgin (Laura Bulstrode: 1680–1752) came to Brabant when her father, Sir Richard Bulstrode, 'follow'd King James ye 2d out of England, & by him was knighted; & he remaind with him at St Germans a long time'. She professed at Lierre, and 'cou'd give a pritty account of ye King, Queen, Princes & Passages of court during her residence there; she was a good mimic & cou'd be very diverting to ye Community' (*L13*.7, 297). Such evidence challenges modern notions of claustration and complete female withdrawal from the world that have so often infused discussion of convent life.

In other papers, too, the personal and political appear in close proximity, even within the same palimpsest manuscript. This is the case in material attributed to Anne of the Ascension (Anne Worsley: 1588–1644) who was the first Prioress at Antwerp. She compiled a series of notes on religious life, writing on fragments of used paper, including her 'meanes to mortification' listed on the back of a letter addressed to her as 'La Mere Anne de l'Ascension Prieure de Carmelines Angloises' from 'John Rogers' in Brussels (*L1.6.K*, 1; see p. 41). Her thoughts on 'tasiturnity' appear on the reverse of a further scrap of correspondence from 'Thomas Wriget', who mentions a battle and had originally enclosed a 'map to see w[h]ere all thees exploits were effected'. Here the nun writes '... the first and princypall effect of silence is to be more willing to hier others speech then ourselues as more estiming thir thoughts and affections then our owne' (*L1.6.J*, 1). From her professed and initially unsettled émigré position she says 'first as trees diply rooted bare seueralle branches which make them diper in yt ground so voluntary pourty chastyty and obedience ar as trees diply rooted ...' (*L1.6.I*, 1).

Such papers underline both the nature and the context of the nuns' life-writing. Descriptions of devotional discipline appear alongside accounts of events that seem unlikely to be conducive to contemplation, and in such situations the religious needed to be adept in order to maintain their meditative focus whilst managing transactions with people outside the convents. Different nuns wrote or communicated in English, varieties of Dutch, French, Spanish, and on occasion German, as well as in Latin. In this last language, distinctions are often made between basic liturgical use and a more advanced understanding of non-familiar phrases: in her own effort to learn, Mary Xaveria of the Angels (Catherine Burton: 1668–1714) was helped by her name-saint, whilst her widowed sister Anne Maria Joseph of St Xaveria (Anne Woolmer: 1662–1740) never succeeded despite all support (Chapters 20, 28). Several documents attest to the general fluency of some nuns while others struggled: if Anne of the Ascension moved with ease between several languages without even noticing it during a conversation with an English merchant (Chapter 2), a Dutch lay sister gave much amusement to other nuns in trying to acquire new English vocabulary (Chapter 39). For practical reasons, some young women at the pre-entrant stage were sent to live with local families in order to learn new languages: Mary Warren (Chapter 35), for example, was 'placed abraud for her improuement, perticulaly to learn ye languiss of ye cuntrey, a quality most nessisary for our house … It was resouled to put her in a Douch scoule, wher in a short time she spooke Duch parfectly well'.

Such linguistic and other skills were essential for conducting daily and strategic business. Carmelite letters show that the religious were often required to deal skilfully with ecclesiastical and secular powers, to ensure a continuing flow of alms, for example, especially since authorities in the Spanish Netherlands had insisted that the English convents were not to be a burden on their local communities. The nuns, particularly the Superiors, needed business acumen to maintain income, and they often relied on outside agents to collect rents, pursue payment of dowries and maintain investments – such as those held in the 'India and South Tea Company', discussed in a letter of 1727 to the Prioress at Antwerp.[5] Although often the papers attribute the convent's financial survival to miraculous intervention, it is clear that the nuns themselves were also responsible for the continuing existence of their communities at critical times in their history.

Early Modern Carmelite History: Ecclesiastical Controversies and Issues of Female Authority

Within post-Tridentine Catholicism, Carmelite women were able to shape a distinctive contribution to devotional change. The form that this took was derived in part from the origins of the Order within the reforming church in Spain. Gillian Ahlgren has argued that, because Spanish orthodoxy placed authority firmly with the clergy and clearly outlined relative male and female spiritual roles, sixteenth-century figures such as Teresa de Jesus were necessarily involved 'in the construction of a gender ideology' (1996, 7). Whilst such views inform Ahlgren's claim for a specific 'politics of sanctity' in early modern Spain, her general observations translate more widely within Europe. Certainly the later female Carmelites appear to have inherited the rhetoric of Teresa de Jesus' struggle if not her precise position, and internal Carmelite history during the period remained relatively turbulent. Just as the saint had striven to establish and then maintain the rules of her reformed Order, so succeeding generations of Discalced nuns continued to feel sorely tried by the Carmelite friars, particularly concerning questions of male and female authority vested in the constitutions. The papers of Anne of the Ascension describe in some detail the heated exchanges between the two groups (see Chapter 2), and this is a recurring theme throughout the papers as a whole. Many of the women are represented as defenders not only of the true faith but also of Teresian reform, and it is repeatedly stressed that they received their authority directly from Teresa de Jesus through Anne of St Bartholomew (1549–1626), in whose

5   Unclassified manuscript, now at St Helens Carmelite convent.

arms the Saint was said to have died, and who in turn chose Anne of the Ascension to accompany her to Antwerp. It is a measure of the effectiveness of their assertion that commentators even hundreds of years later repeat so exactly these details of spiritual succession (for example, Anson, 1949, 200; Guilday, 1914, 358).

In 1621, within two years of the Antwerp foundation, the nuns faced a serious challenge when they were ordered to destroy their constitutions and adopt new ones that gave the local Provincial power to appoint their confessors. Under the leadership of Anne of the Ascension, the religious fiercely resisted the move, considering the freedom to choose their own confessor to be a central tenet of Teresian reform. Widespread argument ensued, and controversy extended beyond both the Order and the Low Countries with consequential loss of crucial income as potential new novices were deterred from entry. Eventually the matter was referred to Rome, and the issue was resolved in the nuns' favour in March 1623 when the Antwerp Carmel was placed directly under the jurisdiction of the Bishop (Guilday, 1914, 364–66). The repercussions of the dispute continued, however, and successive Prioresses note the consequences and ongoing suspicion between male and female Discalced.

Beyond the Carmelite Order, there seems to have been a wider political imperative at the heart of this disagreement, relating to the relationship between religious women and their male spiritual directors that had resulted from the contemporary stress placed on the importance of confession. Patricia Ranft considers that 'The development of the confessor-director figure had a particular impact on women. The emphasis on compatibility between confessor-director and directee gave women a great deal of leverage in a penitential system where they previously had none' (2000, 108).

What might seem a merely local fracas within the Carmelite Order has, therefore, a wider significance relating to male anxiety concerning female spiritual autonomy. Again, this is reflected in Teresa de Jesus' own writing in which she clearly relies on good relations with her confessor for her ideas to be heard. In her *Book*[6] she continually appears to defer to him, and her careful handling of matters of authority is indicative of a situation in which her Carmelite successors continued to find themselves similarly challenged.

The Carmelite Papers from Antwerp and Lierre: Issues of Authorship

Unlike the Renaissance 'virgins of Venice' whose Lives were 'embedded in the records forged by male officials … when nuns were denied access to pen and ink'

---

6   Elizabeth Rhodes argues for the use of this title instead of the more widely adopted *Vida* or *Life,* which derived from the 1588 version of the work, use of which she says 'inscribes an isomorphic relationship between Teresa's historical person and the text's narrative persona and thereby invites positivistic readings …'. 'Naming the text her *Life,* and subsequently reading it through the lens of autobiography, effectively canonizes Teresa's life for posterity devoid of almost all of her public activity and without any of her other writings in it' (2000, 80, 84).

(Laven, 2002, xxx), the Carmelite women at Antwerp and Lierre composed a vast array of personal writings during the course of some 150 years. These comprise letters, devotional diaries and meditative papers, as well as more or less sustained autobiographical or biographical accounts contained either in individual Lives or in official histories and necrologies. Some personal papers were used by later nuns to write a 'biography', perhaps for the purpose of an obituary or for the convent annals (that is, the official convent chronicles). There are, then, three main sources for these Lives that can be categorized as *institutional* (constitutions, rules, liturgies), *conventual* (annals, necrologies, formal documents) and *individual* (personal papers, such as copies of devotions, spiritual testimonies, written confession, life-histories in whole or in part). Sometimes, of course, such categories overlap: personal accounts were drawn upon in official chronicles, for example, and part of the fascination of reading this material is in reconstructing cross-references, establishing 'veracity' (or doubt) by checking for accuracy of detail.

The process of narrative restoration is occasionally complicated by the convents' system of storage and dissemination of material. Sometimes personal papers were simply bundled together after the death of their author, read for edification by succeeding nuns or left in archives, perhaps destroyed (which compilers frequently lament), or regathered in the face of dramatically enforced or voluntary moves to other convents. The effect is diasporic: not only do individual Lives relating to one particular person sometimes exist in various locations, but the women themselves also often express a sense of dissipated selfhood that derives in part from mnemonic systems practised within a contemplative tradition that aspired to self-forgetfulness. The nuns' expressions of self-doubt are sometimes couched, therefore, in terms of questioning about their capacity to write or even to act as authorities about their own experience. If these concerns have a particular Carmelite and early modern quality to them, such tensions are of course inherent in ideas of the 'Author' at the heart of earlier female writing, especially that within a spiritual sphere, where

> The concept of authority (*auctoritas*) in its theological, political and literary senses, was thoroughly male. The supreme and highest *auctor* ... was God himself who in the Middle Ages was indisputably male ... In medieval Latin *auctor* also means 'writer' ... female [Biblical] figures, however exalted, were not represented in art or literature as engaging in literary composition ... (Barratt, 1992, 6).

To some considerable extent Carmelite women derived a sense of authority to write from Teresa de Jesus herself, who in turn drew on the earlier example of Catherine of Siena (Ahlgren, 2000, 53). Both saints wrote their Lives within circumstances in which female mysticism was regarded as suspicious, and the Carmelite papers frequently refer to their texts as highly influential: generations of women writers within the Order felt justified by their authorial example.

From her earliest visual representation, Teresa de Jesus was shown in the act of writing, often in rapture, under divine inspiration: 'In the uncertain theological climate of the late sixteenth century Teresa defended herself, as her earliest iconographers had envisioned, not only with the palm branch of her personal virtues but also with the golden pen of her rhetoric' (Weber, 1990, 5). Her own texts were central to the foundations, and many early modern female Carmelites implicitly or explicitly defended their own reading and writing by reference to them, drawing, too, upon the saint's rhetoric of reluctant authorship. While some religious continued to employ techniques adopted by earlier women writers,[7] the Carmelites were for the most part able to overcome the strictures that some critics have claimed existed for women within early modern culture, in which 'Silence, the closed mouth, is made a sign of chastity' (Stallybrass, 1986, 127).[8]

Amidst debates over femininity and female speech, the position of nuns as writers was complex. If some later historians have thought that 'the literature of female chastity is the literature of textual oppression and misogyny, of the containment of women and their absence from history' (Wogan-Browne, 1994, 24), the Carmelite texts reveal the varied nature of female religious influence. From situations of enclosure, the nuns derive authority and inspiration precisely because 'their exile from the sexual community, real or figurative, accompanied by their special access to the divine, created spaces for self-articulation' (Carlson and Weisl, 1999, 5).

Principles of Compilation: the Original Papers

The nuns' particular conditions, in which spiritual and somatic experience converged, significantly informed their life-writing during the seventeenth and eighteenth centuries. Indeed, the Antwerp papers were most probably compiled directly as a result of dramatic events that unfolded in 1716 following the discovery in the convent crypt of the incorrupt body of Mary Margaret of the Angels (Margaret Wake: 1617–78), who had died some 38 years before. This find attracted such huge interest that the nuns were forced to close their doors to the public who flocked to the convent (Hardman, 1939, 157); and the significance of this discovery appears to have motivated the Prioress at Antwerp, Mary Frances of St Teresa (Mary Birkbeck: 1674–1733; Chapter 15), to commission Lives of the religious. Aware of a lack of written records of nuns at the Carmel since its foundation, she later ordered the individual Lives of Margaret Wake and of Catherine Burton (see Chapters 28, 29) and also the composite, sequential Lives of all the other religious from 1619 onwards, to be contained in the annals so 'that what we found and knew of might not be forever lost' (*A1*, x; see p. 37).

---

[7] In the early modern period, some female writers continued to use strategies that Alexandra Barratt has identified for medieval women – circumventing male authority by writing anonymously; appearing to embrace silence and submission; attaching themselves to men as translators [or, in the Carmelite cases in this book, allowing – or appear to concede – an editorial power to their Confessor]; or claiming the authority of experience as a means to 'bypass the human, male, authority of the Church on earth and claim to be instruments of a higher, divine authority' (1992, 7–20).

[8] See also Beilin, 1987; Hannay, 1985; Hull, 1982; Wiesner, 1993, 24.

Within all these Lives, principles of spiritual progress clearly govern selection and treatment of material. Since their emphasis is upon epiphanal devotional moments and contemplative ideals, individual narratives were not necessarily written in the manner of traditional secular biography, chronologically from birth to death. This is partly because the women wrote from a post-profession position in which temporal structures were themselves challenged by emphasis on the eternal rather than the quotidian, and in which the usual parameters of life-narrative are extended, to include after-death experiences or aspirations.

Chronology is affected, too, by the system of compilation that operated in the convents at that time. The religious wrote autobiographical texts at various stages in their lives, often in the form of spiritual testimonies which drew upon the tradition of Teresa de Jesus in a mode of written confession supplied to a spiritual director (see 1946 ed., Volume I). In the Carmelite papers these accounts were sometimes incorporated within a later, third-person Life of a nun, often written immediately after her death. On occasion, the compiler clearly had vivid personal knowledge of a religious (and this is particularly the case at Lierre); otherwise she used entirely written sources to produce the Life. At Antwerp, composition of the annals began over 100 years after some of the incidents occurred, and so the compiler relied heavily on the nuns' own autobiographical material, especially during the earlier stages of her work.

The Antwerp compiler herself actually remains anonymous until the point in the narrative at which her own Life appears, some 26 years after she began, when it emerges that she is Mary Joseph of St Teresa (Mary Howard: 1688–1756; Chapters 1, 21). She had originally arranged the material in order of profession of the religious at the convent. However, on reaching the Life of an individual who was still alive, her system foundered and, with marvellous self-awareness and some humour, she switched editorial horses midstream, and began to organize her chronicle in order of the dates of death of her subjects:

> ... but now coming in order of profession to our dear Sr Winifred of St Teresa[9] who, Blessed be God, is all present in perfect health and as quick in her understanding and senses as ever, only finding in some things the effects of old age, and this to the great advantage of this work, since it could not have been brought so far but by her help and knowledge ... [she has lived 53 years] in this house, in what follows I will place them according to the time of their death and not as before of their profession ... (*A1*, 524–5).

The Lierre annals, begun at an earlier stage soon after the foundation of that convent in 1648, are organized by this necrological system from the outset. They have an immediacy based on personal witness, whereas the earliest Lives in the Antwerp annals were invariably second- or third-generational given the time-span operating there, and they often appear to draw on repeated hearsay as well as on the ostensibly accurate. The process of accretion that underlies this life-writing system is illustrated, amongst

---

[9]   Elizabeth Lingen: 1662–1740 (Chapter 19).

others, by the Life of Sister Winifred herself, which contains details 'she used to tell us' (p. 109), and also by that of Mary of the Holy Ghost (Mary Wigmore: 1622–91), which draws upon oral as well as written testimony: after her death it emerged that she had put her papers in the hands of her spiritual director, '… who assured us that her life was full of supernaturall favours … and took one little paper which he had there in his pockett and read which ran thus: "On such a day an angel appeared to me with a beautiful crown in his hand …"' (*A1*, 418).

Some nuns made rather different decisions and destroyed their papers. In those cases, elements of self-consciousness leave an impression by their absence when traces of the very act of obliteration are in themselves revealing of personal circumstance. Beatrix of St Teresa (Beatrix Aurelia Gelthoff: 1664–1729) left little evidence of her life except a beguiling memento: 'upon the cover of a few papers concerning her soul wch she desired might be burnt she left writt these words, "adue my beloved sisters till in eternity, pray for me"' (*A1*, 538). Other records suggest the nature of what was once disclosed: Anne of the Ascension (Catherine Keynes: 1619–78) 'by orders of her Directors writ her own Life, which was full of extraordinary favours, but they being removed she burnt it a little before her death which we now lament' (*A1*, 331). Agnes of Jesus (Elizabeth Cavill: 1626–82) also 'a little before she dyed … burnt all the papers that concerned her interior; so that we are ignorant of the favours Allm: God was pleased to do her' (*A1*, 394).

Personal and external pressures clearly affected some such decisions: Beatrix of Jesus (Alice Chantrell: 1709–82) 'lost her reason … [and] disposed of all her private papers before she quite lost her senses, so that all I know of her interiour is that Our Lord recompensed her fidelity' (*A2*, 323). As the hostile situation around the convent worsened in 1794, the religious realized that they needed to escape the advancing French revolutionary forces. Mary Teresa of St Ann (Alexandra Maria Howard: born 1726) at this point burnt some of her own documents, just as, soon afterwards 'every one at ye desolution of ye convent disposed of all superfluous papers, that they might not fall into Commissurys hands: we had at that time had all reason to expect ye same doom …' (*A2*, 339).

The loss of such papers is lamented by some compilers, and the resulting entries are sometimes chronologically confused or have inconsistencies in them, with writers bolstering their position by drawing openly on witness testimony or quoting other sources. In this weaving together of strands, the annals typify much auto/biographical endeavour by communities which record themselves through corporate, layered memory in which apparently 'competing' truths are synthesized to reveal a sense of 'a social self lodged within a network of others' (Stanley, 1992, 194).

Community Relationships

This sense of female community living is not feminist fantasy or utopics but is expressed by the women themselves. They describe the various choices available to spinsters of their different classes – perhaps to go into service at Court, become a companion to a noble woman or establish independent businesses. Some of the women were previously employed; one in an Antwerp coffee-house, while others had been servants and had come with their mistresses to join the convents as lay sisters or professed nuns. Many give reasons for their choice of monastery or Order, sometimes based on chance (visiting a sick brother in the city, passing through on a coach, buying the wrong ticket), sometimes contrived (their families deliberately sending them to acquire a taste for religious life), sometimes inspired (hearing of Teresa de Jesus or reading her works), frequently driven by a sense of vocation, maybe in determined opposition to their families, even in one case breaking into the convent to the surprise of the nuns inside (Chapter 8).

Such narratives unsettle the belief that 'The history of female monachism is at least in part the history of female imprisonment' (King, 1991, 86); and that female choices were determined by the either/or of marriage or nunnery when '... a holy life permitted the vile daughter of Eve to transform herself into the immaculate daughter of Mary. ... [Catholicism] gave women a choice between sanctity and procreative marriage as an appropriate life course. Protestantism gave them only procreative marriage' (Stimpson, 1991, x).

Although several of the women did resist secular marriage, the situation is complicated because rituals of profession themselves employed marital metaphors which seem simply to translate normalized relationships from a temporal to a religious life. It is true that, in theory, 'Although she was a virgin, the *sponsa Christi* was subject to male authority: her father, her bishop, her spiritual father' (Zarri, 1998, 208). For some, however, 'Chastity was important chiefly insofar as it could lead to a woman's escape from patriarchal proprietorship' (Jordan, 1990, 30). It is thus too simple to consider that the women traded one set of compulsory heterosexual conditions for another, either inside or outside the convents; and the Lives provide a fine sense of the varieties of emotional relationships available both before and after profession. If some nuns display frustration at the tensions of community life, others express great affection for each other, sometimes in a style that suggests 'particular friendships' (Raymond, 1986, 91–8; and see Ballaster, 1994; Faderman, 1981; Traub, 2002). These special relationships were forbidden by the constitutions, and Teresa de Jesus had warned her religious away from them because they potentially damage the cohesion of the wider group: 'These intimate friendships are seldom calculated to make for the love of God; I am more inclined to believe that the devil initiates them so as to create factions within religious orders' (1946 ed., *II*, 30–31). Some of the Lives (see pp. 48, 188, for example), indeed, specifically seek to deter nuns from such associations, recounting events in a manner that echoes incidents in Teresa de Jesus' *Book*: 'Once when I was with one person ... the Lord was pleased to show me that such friendships were not good for me ... Christ appeared before me, looking most severe ... and giving me to understand that there was something about this that displeased Him ...' (1957 ed., 53).

Other Lives include details that seem intense beyond the ordinary: Anne of the Ascension gives a moving description of her enforced separation from Anne of St Bartholomew (see Chapter 2), and other women are particularly distraught at the deaths of beloved Sisters.

That these details are included in papers written by the women themselves or by their biographers suggests that apparent signs of same-sex passion should be read with sensitivity: had the compilers construed the relationships to be within a prohibited realm then presumably they would have either omitted the details or, as some writers do, shown the nun to be reformed thereafter. Their inclusion suggests that the nature of these relationships was for the most part acceptable, and that a wide range of personal associations allowed special interactions within community living (such as those between Bridget Howard and Anne Holm: Chapter 22).

Family and Nation: Early Modern Geographies

The papers also give insight into extended and immediate family relationships: some of the women, for example, spent their childhoods with their grandmothers in domiciles where several generations cohabited, while others managed households from an early age, sometimes as young as 12, following the death of a parent, even bringing up their younger siblings. Ann of Jesus (Ann Gerard: *c*.1678–1743), for instance,

> was the eldest child of 11 children when her mother died, and was then only about 17 years of age. Her father who found himself left with so great a charge of children, and many of them very young and one 6 weeks old, was in greatest desolation, but this his dear daughter comforted him with so much prudence and goodness … which made him call all his children together and told them to look upon this their sister and obey her as their mother … They truly loved and respected her as a real mother. [She] taught them all her self to read writ work & c. so that their father never spent one penny on their education, and yet no ones children behaved more prittly, nor read, writ, nor worked better, then they did …. (*A1*, 161; and see Chapter 17)

Mary Teresa of Jesus (Anna Maria Parnham: born 1716), a native of Virginia, received her education 'with some very devout ladys' in Maryland:

> … there she also learned plain work & embroidery & had an excellent hand at both. At 13 years of age her Father placed her at the head of his family of which … she had the sole management, cut and shaped all her family's brothers and sisters linin … (*L13.8*, 5)

Overall, some startling childhood stories are recalled – of a thwarted abduction, of an infant saved from malnutrition at the hands of an aberrant wet-nurse, of loving care or family strife in the face of extreme persecution (Chapters 14, 26). Many of the Lives describe early signs of piety or extraordinary childhood devotion (vows of chastity, establishing hermitages); and some of the women arrived at the convents with friends with whom they had engaged in just such 'games' (see Chapter 10). Others, such as the Mostyn family (Chapter 31), the Bedingfields (Chapter 32) or the Downes (Chapters 30, 35), chose the convents because they already had relations there, sometimes over several generations, or, indeed, because they did not, to avoid unnecessary distractions: a religious who came from Antwerp, Teresa of Jesus (Jonna Catharna Murs: 1630–55) 'was wont to say a chiff reason wch caused her to make

joyces of this Monasterie [at Lierre] was that, being in an othere towne, she should
not be troubled wth many vssetts of her frinds, and kindered ...' (*L13.7*, 12).

From numerous home backgrounds – relatively richer and poorer, from various
parts of England, Ireland and Wales, as well as from northern continental Europe
and North America – the women travelled to the Spanish Netherlands. Some came
from slave-owning families in Maryland, and the language they employ to describe
social relationships reveals perceptions of class, race and national identity (see
Chapter 23). Many described their journeys in dramatic detail: their arrival in strange
cities after tempests, shipwrecks, falling from carriages, being besieged by English
parliamentary forces (see Chapters 31A, 40) – and hence they provide a sense of early
modern geographies, not only giving detail of the actual places themselves but of the
conceptualizations such women had of them. England and Wales are generally, and
understandably, construed to be heretic lands, full of danger for these women and
their families, quite unlike the safe places portrayed within Protestant discourse. For
example, the Life of Monica of St Laurence (Anne James: 1606–78), who professed
in 1641 as a lay sister, describes an incident from her childhood in Monmouthshire:

> When very young she understood that her father was going to compound for his estate,
> which was ready to be seized upon on the account of religion. And she, fearing he should
> do any thing contrary to his conscience, called all her little br[other]s and sisters to her
> and bid them do as she did, and going with them to the place where her father was takeing
> horse, they all knelt down with her, holding up their little hands, and she beged him in
> the name of them all that he would do nothing against his conscience for their sakes, for
> that they were all prepared and well content to go a begging to maintain their religion.
> (*A1*, 388)

Though this description may be felt to owe something to more literary genres, clearly
there were ever-present physical as well as economic dangers for Catholics. Teresa of
Jesus Maria Joseph (Mary Poole: 1696–1793) was said to have been born prematurely
because of trauma brought about by such pressures:

> ... at seven months her mother falling suddenly into labour from the alteration she
> was seized with on seeing her husband hurry'd off in the night to prison, it being then
> very troublesome times in England which gave Catholick familys much to suffer; in
> consequence of this premature birth, she was so very small and delicate ... (*L13.8*, 18)

Risks are similarly illustrated in a posthumous account of Teresa of Jesus Maria (Jane
Bedingfield: 1617–42) who had entered the convent in June 1634, having travelled
from Suffolk to Antwerp under an alias:

> ... A while after [her] death ... there came a secular gentlewoman and desired to speak
> to the Superior, and told her that one of her religious had been with her that night ... and
> desire'd her to tell them [the community] so, but she [the gentlewoman] answer'd 'Who
> shall I say you are?' She reply'd 'Jane Long', upon which the Superior said, there had
> bene none of that name in the house ... Our first dear Mother [Anne of the Ascension],
> in time of recreation, told this story to the community ... upon which a relation of hers

who came over with her, said with great surprise 'Dear ma mere … she took the name of Jane Long in the ship when she came over', whereupon our dear Mother caused several devotions to be offer'd for her …. (*A1*, 294)

Anne of the Ascension herself was urged to be cautious in addressing her letters to England for fear of exposing their recipients to danger (see Appendix 3A; Hallett, 2002b); and the Life of Margaret of Jesus (Margaret Mostyn: 1625–79; Chapter 31A) suggests the perils of travel during a time of civil and religious war.

If England was described as dangerous and sinful, and Wales was experienced as alien by an American woman almost shipwrecked there on her way to Antwerp (Chapter 40), other European regions were represented as uncivilized, and the manners of their inhabitants as 'coarse', particularly in terms of diet. Amidst this, the convent is portrayed as a kind of ex-patriot haven, the enclosure embraced as liberating, with descriptions given of various personal gestures (such as kissing the gates in thanksgiving) or community rituals to secure cultural as well as devotional containment (Chapters 24, 7).

The papers also provide spatial details of the various convents in which the women lived. Not only do layouts remain fairly static, with formal plans reflecting a monastic history of space,[10] but the texts often provide sufficient detail for a reader to envisage the physical relation of rooms, stairways, windows overlooking gardens, garrets, corridors, particular chapels and the frequently mentioned dead-cellar or crypt. Lives, after all, are played out within designed spaces, the construction and conception of which reveal much about notions of the self and its relationship to others in that same location. It is within such elements of fixity and fluidity – spatial and temporal – that varieties of religious experience are so sharply exposed.

We can, then, derive here a sense of the complexities of inner/outer, private/public spaces, and their relationships to bodily configurations. The nature of enclosure protected the religious from outside intrusion, and after 1563 particularly, clausura was strictly enforced by statutes as well as by architecture (Walker, 2003, 50). Breaches – whether literal, or by showing one's face without a veil or talking unnecessarily to outsiders – were regarded very seriously, with severe penalties imposed. Visitors, including confessors,[11] were expected to meet with the nuns through a system of metal grids or grates that separated them, either at the entrance itself or in the speakhouse, the parlour where meetings between nuns and seculars took place. Accounts by some visitors indicate the nature of exchanges. In 1687 Thomas Penson visited Antwerp, where he met a novice at the grate:

---

[10] Detailed plans survive of successive houses in Lierre, from the mid-seventeenth century (*L5.52*; and see van der Linden, 1984): these are extremely similar to those of many other religious houses, before and since (see Gilchrist, 1994).

[11] 'In noe case ye Confessour ought not to enter … if it be not to confesse ye sicke when ye phision [physician] shall say yt it is necssary' (see Appendix 1).

There soon appeared (as an angel of light) a delicate, proper, young, beautiful lady, all in white garments and barefaced ... And having paid my respects and fed my greedy eye a short moment on this lovely creature, I thus spoke: 'Madam, may heaven bless and enable you in your undertakings, which to us that are abroad in the world seem so hard and difficult. For we account it no less than being buried alive to be immured within the confines of these walls.' To which she answered: 'Sir ... I would not change conditions with any princess or noble lady in the world'. (van Strien, 1991, 500)

On all such occasions a religious was to be accompanied by two companions (even at confession, at some distance away). Touching of any kind was forbidden, and the 'turn' (a rotating barrel-like device, with a vertical half-division) was used to convey small items in and out of the convent without revealing the face of the nun inside. It was in the turn that one young woman who aspired to be a religious crammed herself, with some physical difficulty, to gain illicit entry to the convent in disobedience to her family (Chapter 8): her dramatic arrival and subsequent reluctant meetings with her angry relations through the grates reveal much about ideas of personal bodily integrity and threats from without.

Teresa de Jesus had stressed the dangers to which unenclosed nuns were exposed (*Book*, 51), yet these papers suggest just how often enclosure was 'broken' – for building maintenance, or when seculars (especially royal, noble or well-connected ones) entered to meet with the nuns. Some such encounters are surprising: the Duke of York, for instance, 'came to the King [Charles II] and told him, if he had a mind to see a pritty woman he must go to the Infirmary which he did, where dear Sr Tecla was ...' (Chapter 10); and the Duke of Perth appears to have been a regular visitor to the convents, with special favourites among the nuns at Antwerp, including Margaret of St Ignatius (Margaret Andrew: 1641–1716): 'he alwayes call'd her "his deare Mistress", and when ever he entered within the inclosier, he would always [go] to find her, whether in the kitching or doeing other labours, and would sometimes stand an hour by her discourseing of spirituall things, finding in her a hidden treasure ...' (*A1*, 489). He visited Bruges in 1694, and was entertained at the grate of the Augustinian convent 'with a fine collation of milks, fruits and sweetmeats' by the daughters of the duke of Norfolk, and at the Franciscan cloister by a nun who 'sung the best of any woman I have heard in these Countries' (Jerdan, 1845, 43, 44; Walker, 2003, 109, 170),

Vocation and Entry

Several of the religious describe their dilemmas about which Order to join, making particular mention of choices between the Carmelites, the Poor Clares at Graveline and the Augustinians at Bruges. Some, indeed, had trials in other convents before they joined the Carmel. For example, Joseph Frances of the Blessed Trinity who professed in 1709, one of several Howard family sisters in the Order (see Chapters 21 and 22), had allways a great devotion to St Bennet [Benedict] and designd the imbracing that Order, but passing by our monastery she was extreemly taken with our observance … in so much that she own'd she, with great force, kept St Bennet before her eyes that she might not see St Teresa and so compell'd her self to make a short tryall in his order, but St Teresa proved stronger and brought her here …. (*A1*, 585)

Some felt they had a clear calling specifically to Antwerp, if only in retrospect: Jane of the Cross (Jane Rutter: 1704/10–81) joined the Carmel as a lay sister in 1736, following Ann of Jesus (Ann Gerard: *c*.1678/85–1743; see p. 13), for whose family she had worked as a nursery maid:

> She told me she had seen all the nuns of this convent some time before she left England, either in a dream or she knew not how, but when she came to this house [she] perfectly rememberd all their faces. One of the religious happend to be absent whom she mist, but meeting her afterwards, knew her also …. (*A1*, 321)

Having decided on which Order to join, several of the women then faced other issues. Choir nuns were required to supply a dowry, and while some of the entrants had sufficient personal or family wealth to pay this fee, even if their flow of income was occasionally disrupted during periods of war or persecution, other religious mention their attempts to obtain sponsorship (from the Spanish Infanta, for example: Chapters 2, 3), and poorer women sometimes came in 'upon the fortune' of another, in some cases part of an entourage of entrants (see Chapter 12). Throughout their professed lives some of the nuns retained close links with royal or noble patrons, and such well-placed connections had important political and economic benefits the communities.

Age at entry varied. Though the constitutions do not allow admission below the age of 17 years, and though most religious seem to have professed in their early-to-mid-20s, a few were permitted to go in at unusually early or, indeed, late stages (Chapters 6, 13). Generally, the women entered directly from their family home or from education at another convent, though some had longer secular careers and a few were widows; in these latter cases the Superiors occasionally express misgivings about the entrants' capacity to adapt, having been so long used to 'the ways of the world'.

New entrants were required by the constitutions to be 'healthfull of body, having a good understanding': some women, or their families, clearly successfully concealed their infirmities until after profession. One nun, apparently unaware that she needed to declare it, afterwards revealed that she was blind in one eye (Chapter 37), while several others had 'want of understanding'. Constantia of the Holy Ghost (Constantia Vekemans: 1623–93), from Antwerp,

> had so great a vocation to this order and house that wn she apprehended, upon the account of her not having a perfect understanding and capacity, they would dismiss her, as in effect the community had some thoughts (and therefore defered her profession), she would follow our first dear Mother [Anne of the Ascension] and the religious in all placess, often creeping upon her knees most earnestly begging them not to turn her out … (*A1*, 391; and see p. 25)

Ursula Maria of St Xavius (Ursula Short: 1688–1750), came to the Carmel after a period at Louvain: 'She was a vertuous, good soul, but was a person of very small capacity wch made those religious [at Louvain] unwilling to admit her to her profession, tho they kept her some years in quality of novice' (*A2*, 229).

Generally rules restricting entry were designed to safeguard communities from unscrupulous families and against the financial or domestic strains of providing for the needy, so when the religious were aware of personal situations, they weighed up their capacity to support potentially fragile entrants. Even allowing for the fact that official chronicles are likely to show a community in a good light, there is much other evidence that the nuns were compassionate towards the infirm, caring for them over many years of protracted physical and mental illness.

The first ceremonial for a new arrival was one of clothing: this rite was surrounded by nuptial imagery and involved acts of symbolic re-dressing, underlining a move from a secular to an espoused, religious life. Actual style of dress varied, mostly according to wealth: some entrances were modest; others gave occasion for a show of worldly prosperity. Anne of the Angels (Anne Somerset: 1613–51; Chapter 11), from a noble English family, was 'cloathed in black velvett almost covered with pearl', and the entrance of Mary Teresa of St Anne (Alexandra Maria Howard: born 1726), who professed in 1748, was accompanied by kettledrums and trumpets.

After clothing, the Lives generally provide details of the nuns' inductions, their education and discipline under Novice Mistresses, and the ease or struggle of their transition in adapting to a new diet and to the austerities of religious life. Frequently the English women's Lives mention the 'crudeness' of Spanish manners and the Dutch diet, and often they announce, too, the new nuns' joy at leaving behind earthly concerns, their espousal of poverty freeing them to focus on matters of the spirit.

Education, Reading and Writing

Some of the nuns arrived with a fair degree of education: richer novices, in particular, had often been taught at home or had, from their youth, been pensioners at other convents, receiving training 'appropriate to their status' in languages, music, reading and writing. Some of the less wealthy entrants mention that they were educated, to some extent at least, by their mistresses in the noble households where they had been previously employed.

For several, a sense of vocation was intimately associated with the act of reading, one of which had resulted in conversion from Protestantism (Chapter 18). Many nuns of this period (and since) describe coming to religion via books, especially those written by Teresa de Jesus, or receiving spiritual insight or comfort through bookish connections. In 1681, for example, Teresa de Jesus (Catherine Wakeman: 1636–98), one of five sisters from her family to join the Carmelites, was temporarily away from her convent:

> In that time of her being at Hooghstracte [Hoogstraeten], as she was one day sitting alone and, as it were, overwhelmed with darkness and dejection of mind, she found herself

suddainly transported into the liberary of Antwerp with her hand upon a book, which she took up and red the title of the book which was, *The Love of Our Lord Jesus Christ, to his Beloved Spouses of Anwerp*. And in confidence of her being one of these spouses, all her disolations vanished. (*A1*, 484).

Her sister, Teresa of the Holy Ghost (Teresa Wakeman: 1641–1702), who professed in 1671, like other religious was confirmed in her vocation by reading 'St Francis Sales book intitled *The Love of God*' (*A1*, 499).

Frequently, spiritual books are placed in direct opposition to secular texts; and 'romances', linked by Teresa de Jesus in her *Book* to earthly vanities, are contrasted to saints' lives, to the extent that overreliance on the former is directly linked to extended periods spent in Purgatory. This was said to be the fate of the grandmother of Margaret Mostyn, punished because she lured her granddaughter away from an early vocation:

> When she [Margaret Mostyn] was about 11 years of age, having a cousin in the house who was mightily addicted to the reading of idle histories such as Sir Philip Sidney's Arcadia[12] & c: her grandmother would have her read them also, so that she might learn language & divert herself from a desire to [enter] religion …. (*L3.31*; see Hallett, 2007)

Other religious could neither read nor write, and some came into the convent as lay sisters: their Lives often place great emphasis on their 'holy simplicity'. Some women, however, like Winifred of St Teresa (Elizabeth Lingen: 1622–1740; Chapter 19), actively chose this role though they would have been able to join as choir sisters, having the necessary training in Latin and liturgy, so it is clearly incorrect to correlate lack of formal education with a lay profession.

Daily Life

Almost uniquely within the realm of life-writing, for those in a religious Order we have exact information on the shape of daily lives: the rhythm of the liturgical hours is closely prescribed and readily discoverable, to the extent that we can compare the list of daily devotional readings to a nun's journal entries, for example, to see how far particular passages affected her personal thinking. Sometimes, indeed, individuals reflect in some detail on their distractions or doubts, and from such sources we may feel we know much about the women's moment-by-moment routines and inner preoccupations. The papers of Anne of the Ascension, for example, discuss her struggle with prayer over several years, and her writing echoes ideas from various instructional manuals, including those by Francisco de Ribera and Alfonso Rodríguez, which she is known to have read (see Chapter 2). By considering the nun's own writing alongside

---

[12] Sir Philip Sidney (1554–86). His early version of *Arcadia*, a prose romance, was completed in 1581, and a second version in 1585.

the texts that influenced her, it is possible to see the role and affect such reading had, and to see how it supplemented the rhythms circumscribed by the rules within which an Order lived (Appendix 1). If routines set down in the constitutions may be thought to indicate ideals rather than reality, then one advantage of a confessional tradition is that the religious themselves supply great detail about their perceived shortfalls and dilemmas. Certain papers, too, indicate the disciplinary frameworks that operated within the convents, outlining what steps should be taken to rectify personal problems – such as a Superior's notes about how to instil obedience in the convent (Appendix 2).

In addition, the Lives describe offices held within the community. A range of roles are included – Portress (in charge of the turn and main entrances); Infirmarian (responsible for caring for the sick, either in their own cell or, more commonly, in the convent infirmary); Discreet or Depositary (acting as treasurer or bookkeeper); Sacristan (looking after the church, calling the nuns to confession); Monatrice (observing and reporting faults of other religious); Novice Mistress (educating the new entrants); Subprioress (taking care of the choir, deputising in the absence of the Superior); and Prioress (responsible for the overall governance of the convent).

Beyond these offices, the papers also provide information about daily occupations, such as gardening, sewing, spinning, making the spargatts (the nuns' footwear): even after she had been partially paralyzed by a severe stroke, one religious still did beading with her able hand, while other women were said to carry their knitting wherever they went, to avoid wasting time when they opened the turn or received visitors. Teresa of Jesus Maria Joseph (see p. 14),

> tho blind she was always occupy'd, wou'd trim beads, thread purl combe ... silk, weave strings ... wholy by guess custome and attention of mind; and when no longer able to do these kinds of things she wou'd stich spargets for the lay sisters and do other coarse work. (*L13.8*, 21)

Other documents describe the general routine of lay sisters (Chapters 19, 37, 39), so we do not only have information on the choir nuns here, but descriptions of most roles within the convent.

It is also possible to derive information about matters such as diet: some chose the Order because the religious did not eat meat; others expressed extreme aversion to eggs (a central part of the menu), or habitually ate leftovers or scraps; one nun lived for months on only oranges, and another complained about flat beer. A range of eating disorders or dietary-related illnesses can be discerned from this information, as well as a sense of how the consumption or denial of food functioned as an expression of piety.

Modes of entertainment also feature strongly: the religious prepared poems or devotional dramas for feast days, danced, sang or read to each other (the last of these on a daily basis, at recreation). Some, like Margaret Mostyn, were particularly praised for their capacity to 'recreate' the community, with their reading or dramatic style.

Various Lives tell of their subjects' mortifications and the daily meditative or disciplinary systems the nuns used, with or without permission from their spiritual directors. Routines might involve physical discomfort (such as praying on the edge of steps, kneeling for long hours, sleeping on a board), self-flagellation or wearing a chain, fasting or eating unpalatable food. Mary of the Holy Ghost (see p. 11),

> When she found difficulty in any thing she could never rest till, for the love of God, [she] had overcome her self in it ... and in mortification her passion was so great that it often defeated her tender body and putt her sometimes into a feaver, and once to that degree her Mistress found her att night all covered with red spotts. ... (*A1*, 407)

Other forms of mortification include extreme obedience to the letter of a command: Mary of St Albert (Mary Trentam: 1607–29), the first religious to die in the Antwerp Carmel,

> ... was so simple in obedience that her Superior must well heed what she said to her, for if she had spoken to her of any thing, tho it was out of reason, yet she would not have put in execution as she show'd in divers occasions – as for example, once her Superior said, 'Stay & I will come to you again', and forgeting her she remained there some hours tho it was in such an incomodious place, where she was wett with the snow, yet would have stay'd there all night if she had not been missed & call'd away ... (*A1*, 213)

Similarly, Monica of the Holy Ghost (Anne James: 1606–78),

> ... being sent into a garret with a spoon to emty a wash tub sett there to receive the rain comeing thro, she continued some hours to fling out the water with the spoon att the window, without haveing the thought of any difficulty or strangness of the command, but was wholy taken up with the consideration of the will of God. In like manner she sought for a needle she had lost in the ashes and persevered till she had found it ... (*A1*, 389)

Another religious drank her own urine, in obedience to what she took to be a literal command (Chapter 26). Mary Xaveria was severely tested and at times bewildered by conflicting instructions (Chapter 28), while Elizabeth of the Visitation (Elizabeth Emery: 1617–70), 'euen in her great weaknes [when] she sometimes was forgotten to be bidden sleep, or the like, she would expreess so much joy that it seemed her content was in being neclected ...' (*L13.7*, 24).

Whatever secular attitudes to such behaviour might be (and some of the more extreme acts evidently led to illness or recurring health problems), the aim of these religious was to reduce dependence on physical comfort and needs, to assert the pre-eminence of spiritual concerns. The bodily, as ever, coexisted, sometimes in precarious relation, with matters of the soul.

Lives of Spirit

The religious describe in vivid detail their spiritual experiences, whether in daily devotions or in more dramatic 'supernatural' encounters: there are numerous examples here of favours (visions or inner knowledges of saints, angels, divine revelation, miraculous cures) and of troubles (ghosts, apparitions, hauntings, demonic visitation), showing the continuum of physical and extra-physical phenomena that was perceived to exist within their lives, before and after entry.

When she was a child, for example, Francisca Tereca of the Passion (Frances Turner: born *c*.1629)

> ... had such a violent fevour that her life was dispared of, and her mother, being much afflicted, took her recourse by perticular devotion to Blessed Aloysius then newly beatify'd[13], and goeing in ye morning to see her, the child said 'O Mother I am quite well, and have not the least pain'. She asked how she came to yt suddain change; the child answered 'A litle man in black came & put his hand upon my head and took away all my pains'. The mother, full of joy, brought her severall pictures & amongst the rest that of Blessed Aloysius, which she presently pointed to, saying 'O that is he yt cured me' ... (*A1*, 430)

Other nuns had premonitions of their own or other's deaths:

> Sister Margarett of St Ignatius [Margaret Andrew: 1641–1716] said that she dreamt that, passing by our dead celler, she saw it all in light and our Venble Mother Mary Margt of the Angels [Margaret Wake: 1617–78] in the midst of it, who gave her to understand that one of this community was soon to dye and that they must prepare for it, adding 'Quickly, Quickly, Quickly' ... This happened about 10 days before Sister Mary of the Blessed Trinity [Mary Cotton: 1629–94] dyed who, as soon as she heard it, believed it was for herself ... And the same night, it pleased God she should see certain rayes of light in her cell, two or three different times, which confirmed her in ye thought and made her diligently prepare her self for death, and a day or two after she was seased suddainly in ye night so that she could not rise nor call to any body and would have dyed had not one accidently come and raised her upp. (*A1*, 480)

Sudden demise presented potential posthumous peril, since the nun might not have been fully prepared for death. On some such occasions, as with Teresa of Jesus Maria (see p. 14), this lack of spiritual readiness apparently resulted in their reappearance as an unquiet spirit which prayers afterwards sought to allay. Martha of Jesus (Anne Baccus: 1626–84), ill in the infirmary, asked another religious to pray with her

> ...and towards the end of it Sister Martha slipped down upon her knees and dyed upon the spott, never speaking a word more, tho her heart was found to beat when she received the last absolution ...

> [Lady Reingrave[14] said the next morning to the Superiour that she had seen a religious] all in light and heard a voice which said 3 times 'Martha, Martha, Martha'. This was the more remarkable because she had never seen her nor knew her name ... (*A1*, 475)

---

13   Aloysius Gonzaga (1568–91) cared for plague victims in Rome, and died of the disease. The beatification process had begun shortly after his death, and he was canonized in 1726.

14   She was the temporal founder of the Hoogstraeten Carmel and was closely associated with the religious at Hopland.

In such accounts, the 'marvellous' is generally contained in the language of the everyday, indicating just how embedded were ideas of the supernatural. Elsewhere, the women often describe the ease of direct speech between holy and human figures, slipping between discourses that otherwise might seem to operate in separate realms. Teresa de Jesus, within a mystic tradition of communion, had herself laid emphasis on such immediacy and on the mysteries of different spiritual states: she instructed her religious in meditative techniques, to 'Imagine that this Lord himself is at your side' (1946 ed., *II*, 106). From such imaginative states, it is not difficult to envisage how a sense of real presence could ensue and a dialogue could develop between human and divine figures within a scheme of affective piety.

In descriptions of this kind of devotion, geographies of the soul bridge physical and spiritual divides, and diffuse mind/body distinctions. When a religious 'sees' the Blessed Virgin, for example, she asks herself if she does this with the eyes of her body (actual revelation), mind (imaginary) or soul (mystical); the style of her self-questioning indicates how freely she moves between these zones, how untroubled (except by questions of orthodoxy) such transitions were. Dreams accordingly feature strongly in the papers, and there is much discussion about their nature and whether they reflect earthly realities or indicate holy intervention or premonition – just as there is also a questioning of the sources of various favours. More unusually, the Life of Mary Xaveria (Chapter 28) gives an example of spiritual substitution when she exchanges her own tranquil state with another nun who was experiencing extreme despair. Apart from the misery caused by the exchange itself, this does not seem to have been a particularly questionable act, not open to those doubts expressed by Teresa de Jesus about whether her own apparent favours came from godly or diabolical roots. These, for some of St Teresa's successors, continued to be troubling questions.

The Carmelite papers describe several incidents when devils were said to appear to the nuns. If these events and others thought to be associated with witchcraft were not conceptually unsettling, they still caused drama in the convents. Some cases of bewitchment were said to relate to the effects of sorcery that occurred before a nun entered the convent, the symptoms of which only became manifest after her arrival: Francisca of the Blessed Sacrament (Elizabeth Osmund: 1669–1720), for example, was enchanted by a woman claiming to be a Countess whose spell was destroyed only after the nun had burned the paper on which it was written (Chapter 14). Other effects were less easy to dispel: Margaret and Elizabeth Mostyn (Chapter 31) were both bewitched by would-be suitors, and after the women had professed they became seriously ill and were repeatedly afflicted by appearances of the devil. Eventually, the two nuns were thought to be possessed, resulting in their exorcism in 1651 when some 300 demons were withdrawn (see Hallett, 2007).

The closeness of medicinal, clerical and miraculous discourses in relation to such phenomena indicates how interconnected these systems were, and, equally, just how easy it was to interpret or confuse cause and cure. When Elizabeth Lingen was revived as a child by an old woman who massaged her seemingly dead body, the outcome might easily have been ascribed to witchcraft had events turned out differently (Chapter 19; and see Tausiet, 2001). Margaret of Jesus (Chapter 31A) was given the crushed bones of a martyr in her wine, and was immediately cured of a urine stoppage, while outside the convents at this time other women were persecuted for similarly administering food or drink, especially when the result was less positive (Briggs, 2001, 166; Robinsheaux, 2001, 197; Roper, 1991). Context, motive and outcome, as ever, were crucial in such matters; and bodily and spiritual health were closely connected.

The Body

Within these lives of spirit there is, accordingly, a tremendous emphasis on matters of the body. Partly this is an organizational hazard: many of the Lives were written soon after the death of the Sister concerned, so they were likely to be preoccupied with her last phase. More than this, in a culture concerned to prepare for the afterlife, the religious were ever-watchful for signs of an approaching death, sitting in vigil with the sick to ensure that last rites were duly administered. Their descriptions of bodily care constantly probe the relationship between medicine and faith. If, as so frequently happened, a doctor failed to diagnose or effectively treat a nun, the priest or the Sisters (sometimes simultaneously with the physicians, sometimes in contradiction) administered other cures, using relics or visits to shrines instead of, or in parallel with, medical solutions.

The papers provide rich details on beliefs about the body, as well as about individual treatments used for certain diseases. Some accounts vividly and movingly describe the community care of particular nuns suffering from, for example, severe mental illness, gangrene, smallpox, cancer or leprosy. The nuns also describe cases of sudden or accidental death, including one in which Martha of Jesus (Rose Fisher: 1600–c.1640), was

> seased with a violent faver and the Infirmarian gave her, by mistake (as she found afterwards), a glass of vinegar in place of beer, which she drunk up without saying one word. Whether this had any bad effect or no, we cannot judge, but many of the sisters used to call her the martyr of mortification ... (*A1*, 300).

Teresa Joseph Maria of the Heart of Jesus (Catherine Howard: 1722–75) died on 26 July 1775 as a result of a particular misfortune:

> Her last sickness & death was occasiond by an accident from the fumes of sulpher. Going on Ascension Eve into the garden, with a chasing dish in one hand and brimstone in the other, she threw the sulpher on ye hot coles under a tree, to destroy by the fume the catterpillers which were that year in great abudance. And altho she used this dangerous experiment with precausion, the smoke enterd her mouth & fill upon her breast; of which tho in that moment she did not find any bad effect, nor thought she any more of it till a shortness of breath & faintings insued, for which no cause could be assignd; she then reflected on the sulpher. Her sufferings were terible, the doctors declared that her stomack was drawn & shrivelld up, like a peece of parchment curled by the fire. In fine a deep dropsy joynd to this illness finishd her cours .... (*A1*, 307)

There is information, too, about various types of treatment: as well as the standard use of bleeding or blistering, various nuns travel to spa baths or move through Europe in search of cures; another wears an iron bodice and callipers; there is a bogus female doctor – all details that give a clear sense of early modern medicine and diagnoses. Given the alarming medical remedies proposed for various ailments, and the evidence of acute suffering at the hands of physicians, it is perhaps not surprising that several of the nuns, like Constantia of the Holy Ghost (see p. 17), 'bore many illnesses with great patience and suffered very great pains in her last sickness, and a very little before she dyed she said that for the love of God she pardoned the chrurgeon [surgeon] who she beleived had shor[te]ned her life' (*A1*, 392).

In some cases there are surprisingly detailed descriptions of the physicality of nuns – identifying extraordinary strength or stature, obesity or severe under-weight, or remarkable personal beauty: one Sister is startlingly described as a 'nymph', and another was openly admired by the Duke of York (Chapters 37, 39, 10).

There is only one account here that features a male subject, the Life of Edmund Bedingfield (Chapter 32A) who was confessor to the Lierre convent for many years; and this has interesting features, differing from the female Lives in its emphasis. Not one of the many more numerous accounts of women mention the possibility of sexualized relationships after profession, though some refer to potential suitors before that stage, to note their rejection; and there is no evidence of speculation or teasing about the nuns having amatory interests. Edmund Bedingfield, on the other hand, is construed to be self-denying in his sexuality, and the annals light-heartedly mention his interaction with secular women and his possible attractiveness to them. Unlike the religious women, he is conceived to be potentially active within his celibacy: their chastity is never referred to, and nor is their choice of convent, in the 'meanest of conditions', though many of the women, like him, could easily have led comfortable lives elsewhere in more ostensibly sparkling careers. When the ships that they sail on are attacked, the women pray and put their trust entirely in the Blessed Virgin or their Saint (Chapter 31A): Edmund Bedingfield loads guns and helps the captain defeat the Turkish assailants. The male body in these narratives operates in a different sphere.

The Mind

It is, indeed, in discourses of the body that beliefs about the mind become apparent. Nuns are often described as being 'present to themselves on all occasions', and this is especially important when last rites are being administered. Conversely, those who lose their mental health are sometimes said 'never to return' to themselves. This language is revealing, suggesting that there are 'spatial' elements to intellectual stability attained by a repeated rehearsal of oneself, a literal 'grounding', the continuities of which make self-writing possible.

There are challenges here, as well as correlations, to Cartesian ideas of mind/ body division and to the continuum of mind/body/spirit: mnemonic suppression, a 'continual leaving and denying' of oneself in physical terms, effects a spiritual state beyond mind and body, and yet relies upon both for that transition itself. 'Scinking in to our senter' (Anne of the Ascension's words: Appendix 3C) depends upon having a centred self in which to sink, and it is not surprising that a contemplative discipline committed to 'continuall vigilance ouer our selues' (*L1.6.*K, see p. 42) results in an elevated state of consciousness as a stage towards eventual personal negation. However much this self-denial appears to place value on a self for which similarity to others is of overriding importance, personal characteristics still drive the means to the end. Accordingly, the Carmelite papers reveal much about intricacies of various transitive states and the early modern philosophies that surround them.

Afterlife

In a tradition organized around notions of intercession, care did not, of course, cease at death. Not only did the religious attend to the corpse of the deceased – laying it out, washing, dressing, exposing it and collecting relics of particularly blessed sisters for the devout – but they also ministered to her soul. The papers provide details of both physical and spiritual rituals, including prayers, masses and funeral ceremonies, describing the care taken to expedite the delivery of a soul from Purgatory. In one case, a body continued to sweat after death to the consternation of the community, who continued with the public burial and afterwards privately retrieved the body to be sure the nun was indeed dead (Chapter 40).

Frequently, dead religious appear to their Sisters – either as they were in life or in clouds or dreams (Chapters 4, 9, 17, 28, 35). Although individuals who see such apparitions are sometimes initially alarmed, for the most part appearances were not conceptually disturbing and ghosts, spirits and revelations are discussed as part of the everyday.

Much emphasis is placed in the papers on the dead-cellar, the crypt where the bodies are placed in individual 'ovens' or vaults. Frequently, the nuns visit this area, to pray or investigate, sometimes searching for, and on occasion finding, incorrupt bodies. This activity was not without its own dangers: a lay sister, Frances of St Ignatius (Margaret Downs: 1598–1650) 'was one day particularly inspired to make very clean & put in order ye cellars and especially the dead cellar, saying perhaps it may be for my self ... [later] she immediately was seased with a violent feaver wch rendered her uncapable of any thing ...' (*A1*, 206).

Some descriptions of bodies are vividly detailed: the religious come across 'rotten moist bones' and 'slimy, wet' remains and express their joy when they find intact parts or whole bodies. The discovery of one particular body, at the Carmel in Newburgh in 1727 – that of Magdalen of St Joseph (Magdalen Bedingfield: 1620–83) – is revealing about the process of burial, including the use in this case of lime on the body:

> For want of place for burying our deceased religious, it was necessary to open some graves in our dead vault ... of those who had been the longest deceased, amongst which number there was the body of our most Reverend Mother Magdalene of St Joseph, foundress of our convent who had been dead 44 years pas'd. In opening her

coffin, we found her body wholly incorrupt ... The master of masons who open'd the graves was extreemly astonished, and said immediately that it was a supernaturall thing, first because there was upon the body two messures of lime which was yett also white and new as if but just putt in ... Prince Electorall of Palatin, Philip William, our founder,[15] judging that in time when her body should be found intire and incorrupt with such a quantity of lime, her sanctity would shine so much the greater ... (*A1*, 309).

Here, as elsewhere within the Carmelite and wider Catholic tradition, the notion of intactness was never far from one of canonization: the body of St Teresa herself had also been found to be preserved, and the iconography of the incorrupt body and early modern Carmelite claims for purity of narrative tradition and female authority run hand-in-hand within the Antwerp papers, crucially informing ideas of life-writing within the convent.

Carmelite Self-writing and Early Modern Autobiographics

The traditions of self-writing that operated at Antwerp and Lierre were drawn from a contemplative discipline in which the nuns' experience before profession was 'shelved', even actively forgotten, then recalled for the purpose of spiritual testimony. Here mnemonic practice is based on notions of self-effacement that relate to focussed meditative states in which a nun is engrossed in pursuit of a contemplative union with God.

Many women write of the agonies of their progress to self-forgetfulness, aspiring to break from human bonds or emotion: Mary Xaveria (Chapter 28), for example, describes in moving detail the death of her father and of her Superior, both of whom she loved, after which she seeks to 'break all human ties'. Other women demonstrate the delicate coexistence of earthly and spiritual caring, as nuns nurse each other in sickness, attend to physical and devotional needs whilst refraining (more or less successfully) from special attachment. In some narratives, they suspend their faculties of recollection, or revive them for particular purposes: Anne of St Bartholomew (Anne Downs: 1593–1674), for example, 'desired leave of ye Superiour to call to mind some passages of her former life to recreate the Community' (Chapter 5).

The Lives are constructed, therefore, in a context of concentrated mental discipline in which past lives are less significant than present meditative concerns – and yet these 'pasts' are sometimes revisited to explain that present: how a nun came to be at Antwerp, how certain pious practices were lifelong. Habitual self-forgetfulness coalesces with conscious recollection; and individual memories are sometimes reshaped in the light of previous or subsequent realizations, or explained in the face of dialogue with other religious or with spiritual directors. Mary Xaveria (Chapter 28), for example, frequently glosses passages she has previously written, rewriting

---

[15]   See pp. 73, 74.

her experience with explanations from orthodox practice: 'what I said concerning my seeing these angels is not meant to be meant yt I saw them with the eyes of my body …' (p. 145). Paradoxically, then, from narratives based on supreme self-effacement there emerge highly self-conscious accounts of personal transformation and epiphany: communities that engage with ideas of personal diminution naturally enough focus on an enlarged sense of self in order to dispel it.

On occasion, the 'correctives' may seem to distort the Life itself, redressing experience in such a way as to appear intrusive, even falsifying. What notions, after all, are being established or challenged by a system of life-writing in which individuals base their own narratives on other people's biographies or in which an exemplary life is closely mirrored by a later one, in a reiterative, rather than originating tradition? Some of the nuns quite transparently base their accounts on Teresa de Jesus' *Book*, for example, and she, in turn, had quite clearly modelled hers on other writers such as Catherine of Siena (see p. 185; Ahlgren, 2000).

The intricacies of self-patterning that these papers expose clearly challenge those precepts of later modern post-Enlightenment autobiography that privilege the 'conscious awareness of the singularity of each individual life' (Gusdorf, 1980, 29). They also indicate continuities in self-construction across some 400 years or so, pre-dating and traversing periods of philosophical change in which it has often been claimed that the medieval and supposedly unselfconscious self had been discarded.[16] If it is possible to see continuities – to some extent rhetorically exaggerated – in female self-writing from at least Catherine of Siena (1347–80), through Teresa de Jesus (1515–62) and Margaret Mostyn (1625–79) to Catherine Burton (1668–1714), then these continuities may appear to challenge paradigms of autobiography that are based on individuation within an Hegelian structure of struggle and loss.[17] These Carmelite Lives demonstrate how much 'community' (literally and metaphorically) is central to personal construction, and how narratives of interrelationship abut, succeed, merge with accounts of a predominant self in which 'the individual does not oppose herself to all others … but [is] very much *with* others in an interdependent existence' (Friedman, 1988, 41).

Ideas of a reiterative, relational self are at the heart, of course, of a biblical interpretive typology of fulfilment and salvation in which successive selves co-exist with others in a figurative, teleological framework founded on Christ as the second Adam. They are therefore naturally central to the mimetic tradition this in turn draws upon – of Christians mirroring their Saviour in exemplary lives, and of later devout

---

16   Many commentators, from Burckhardt (1860) onwards, identify a crucial growth of individualism occurring in the Renaissance. Gusdorf, for example, locates the emergence of 'the modern subject' at the beginning of the seventeenth century (see Marcus, 1994, 156; Porter, 1997, 1–14; Burke, 1997).

17   'Thus the relation of two self-conscious individuals is such that they prove themselves and each other through a life-and-death struggle … It is only through staking one's life that freedom is won' (Docherty, 1996, 5, citing Hegel, 1977, 114).

individuals following a saintly precursor. However, there were also particular pressures relating to the internal dynamics of the Carmelite reform that explain some of the ways in which this imitative pattern and individual spiritual autobiography co-related to give particular features to the genre within the Order.

Teresa de Jesus' *Book,* written around 1562, was circulated among friends from around 1565. In 1572–73, the Inquisition confiscated the manuscript and never returned it: later versions were published, translated and widely read, increasingly so after Teresa de Jesus' canonization in 1622. During her lifetime, despite developing general support, her spiritual favours and insights were regarded by some authorities as highly suspect and a potential threat to received orthodoxies. As such, her reputation and the reception of her writing remained in doubt for some years within a context of continuing suspicion of female mysticism and authority, and of charges of witchcraft and blasphemy made against other contemporary women.[18] In such a situation, it was no wonder that she presented herself in her *Book* so carefully, cannily, warily and wittily, modelling herself on already-accepted figures within normalized protocols of devotional life-writing; ideas of uniquely originating blessedness were not necessarily feasible in a context in which insistent individuality might be fundamentally suspect, and where personal and female experience of God were felt to unsettle the boundaries of faith. To survive in such a situation, and to achieve an evangelizing mission, one route available for female writers was to stress how similar they were to others in the already-approved determining orthodoxy – yet how different they were in personal spiritual favours, rocking the cradle of belief without appearing to tip it over.

Accordingly, succeeding generations of Carmelites continued to shape themselves in literary as well as spiritual terms to their saintly authorial prototype, including in their autobiographies a 'profusion of self-depreciatory remarks' which is said by Alison Weber to characterize Teresa de Jesus' *Book*: the Saint, she claims, adopted a 'rhetoric of femininity … which exploited certain stereotypes about women's character and language', writing 'as she believed women were *perceived* to speak' in order to avoid censorship (1990, 11).

Teresian echoes in the early modern texts arise, then, partly from the influence of the wider religious reiterative tradition, and partly from a Carmelite history of autobiographics that had a particular historical exigency in seventeenth-century foundations. Faced by successive challenges from the friars of the Order, the Discalced women consistently restate their rights in a line of succession from the Saint. Here the personal is political even in matters of the soul, and narratives framed within what may appear to be an intensely conservative mode (repetitive, consolidatory) reveal deeply radical female imperatives.

---

[18] For the relationship between the reputation of Magdalena de la Cruz, a nun who was persecuted for her 'suspect mysticism', and the problems of Teresa de Jesus, see Weber, 1990, 44.

Editorial Note

The papers from the Antwerp and Lierre Carmels are relatively dispersed. Whilst some documents are well organized and self-contained by nature of their genre (transcribed and arranged sequentially in the books of annals, for example), other manuscripts are on loose fragments that may have been miscellaneously gathered by later nuns. Although papers relating to a particular religious are now sometimes held in different locations, I have arranged them in this edition by their subject, and have grouped documents from various sources around the main Life.

Various dilemmas presented themselves when I was editing these papers, particularly concerning the order in which they should appear. Organizationally, after all, that which appears later on in the original chronology should come first – since finding the body of Margaret Wake seems to have led to the Antwerp Lives being commissioned. Yet the account of that discovery comes in documents written after 1716, whilst the earlier Antwerp Lives use material from 1619 onwards even though these were only drawn together much later. The creative springboard is, therefore, towards the end of the narrative organization. If this 'reverse ordering' represents an exemplification of the canonizing process in which the facts of death lead forward to a Life, it also makes for a complicated editorial process.

There were other alternatives available: the papers could have been presented by date of the nuns' birth, but this would have been confusing too since in the original manuscripts they appear, in part, ordered by date of death. Organization by theme was another possibility, but several Lives would have belonged naturally in several sections and, most importantly, this process would have involved introducing categories that might reflect twenty-first century rather than early modern preoccupations, and that organization therefore seemed unduly intrusive.

In the end, the simplest solution seemed to be the best one: to adopt the same organizational principles as the first compilers and to present material more or less in the order in which it appears in the original documents. This decision has the key advantage of minimizing editorial interventions to allow voices to speak for themselves. It also preserves the sense of community, which is so evident in the original papers, the elaborate interconnectedness of the daily lives of women living together within shared histories and spaces.

If many of the Lives are drawn together by a single compiler, behind her there may have been multiple authors. One of the pleasures of such heterogeneity is that the writers' voices are varied: although the Antwerp annals had one main compiler for the 1619–1730 papers, the Lierre annals appear to have been written by successive Prioresses, so changes occur more frequently. In order to retain the integrity of these individual voices – whether the original, primary autobiographer, the secondary biographer or the tertiary compiler – I have presented the material with minimal changes.

Spelling remains by and large as it was in the original manuscript. Personal names and place names are mostly standardized, those in the Low Countries to the form most commonly used by the nuns themselves, though there are variations between texts: so – Antwerp (not Antwerpen), Bruges (not Brugge), Ghent (not Gent), Lierre (not Lier), Louvain (not Leuven), Mechelen (not Malines), Ypres (not Ieper). Familiar contractions (such as 'Sr' for Sister; 'Rev' for Reverence; 'wch' for which; 'yt' for that) are left untouched, though more obscure ones are expanded or glossed in square parentheses. For the most part, punctuation remains as it is in the original text, though on occasion I have broken up extremely long sentences, signalling changes in a footnote. Quotations within the text are now shown by punctuation ('…'), whereas systems vary in the original, or often give no indication at all except through the sense; and where first and third person voices often merge, I have tried to differentiate between them by layout or by notes.

Selection was inevitable, and some Lives have simply been omitted. I have tried to be representative whilst avoiding repetition (many of the texts have similar features, especially in listing the virtues and devotions of their subject in a relatively impersonal manner) and providing a sense of the varieties as well as commonalities of religious experience. Inevitably, many nuns' accounts relate to others in the convent, showing a complex interconnectedness within the community, before and after death: I try to identify in each case the religious who is mentioned, generally within square parentheses in the text.

A few Lives have been grouped together: whilst I rejected an overarching ordering by theme, I have nonetheless combined some narratives in one chapter (for instance, where two religious were lifelong friends, or arrived as part of another Sister's entourage, or where they nursed each other, or died on the same day). Some others are grouped by family (such as Mostyn and Bedingfield) to show how different careers were shaped from similar beginnings, how personal characteristics varied or were similar.

Some accounts are inevitably longer than others. To a large extent this reflects how they appear in the original texts: some religious have only a few paragraphs in the annals, yet their entries seemed important to include for the wider picture they provide of Carmelite and more general female experience. Catherine Burton, Margaret Wake and Margaret Mostyn, on the other hand, each had lengthy single-subject biographies. Some of these longer texts have previously been published in whole or in limited part (Hunter, ed. Coleridge, 1876; Hardman, 1937, 1939; Booy, 2002, 285–90), but earlier editions are largely selective, hagiographical and long-since unavailable; neither do they present material within the context of other Carmelite writing. In consequence, because the original sources are so rich, I have included longer extracts.

In the text, square parentheses indicate an editorial intervention or gloss, added for clarity, while three dots (…) and no line-break indicates short omissions from the original manuscript, generally of only a few words; gaps of up to around 10 lines are also signalled by a line-break. When omissions are longer, this is indicated in a footnote that describes the extent and sometimes the nature of the material excluded. Notes also explain more obscure references, for example to liturgy or a particular person the first time they occur in the book as a whole: the index shows where in the text the first reference appears.

The chapter titles and subheadings are editorial additions unless otherwise specified or it is obvious by the context or spelling; and such editorial headings are used to suggest features of the Life included in that section, to reflect something of the spirit of the woman herself, her characteristic verve, idiosyncrasies and faith. Each chapter has its own introduction, giving background to the religious and to aspects of their texts that appear to require particular explanation, together with reference to the manuscript from which the extract is drawn, codicological descriptions of which appear in a note on sources at the end of this section. The Lives are in the order in which they appear in the original documents unless otherwise stated, and the index suggests ways of following alternative routes through the papers.

The appendices provide additional background information. A seventeenth-century copy of the constitutions and 'Rule of St Albert' is included (Appendix 1) to show the governing systems so central to the nuns, informing their aspiration if not perfect practice. Similarly, the notion of obedience was at the heart of community living, so a copy of a Superior's notes on this subject is also included (Appendix 2): read in conjunction with the Lives, it is clear how deeply habitual certain aspects of its practice became. Several letters are also included (Appendix 3) to show some of the wider political frameworks and relationships between various religious.

Throughout this book I use the term 'Life' to refer to an autobiographical or biographical text, capitalized to differentiate it from 'the life of a nun'. I do this because 'autobiography' may infer generic conditions that do not always apply to early modern women's self-writing (see General Introduction, note 1); because many of the texts are actually a combination of autobiography and biography, making it awkward to refer to them accurately and concisely; and because many of the texts do not have a title as such.

In general discussion, a nun is referred to by her birth name before profession and by her religious name subsequently. Her personal details are given in brackets the first time she is mentioned, and a shortened version of her professed name is mostly used thereafter. Personal details are only repeated if the discussion at a later point relies on precise knowledge (for example, of date of death); otherwise page numbers or chapter details are given for cross reference. Occasionally, however, even after profession, a religious may be called by her family name: this happens for ease of style or for variety (if she has been mentioned just previously, or if she appears in a list otherwise ordered by birth name). If two nuns have the same religious name, the family details are repeated to avoid ambiguity. When a nun who is mentioned in the General Introduction also has a full Life in a separate chapter, her full details are again given there.

St Teresa of Avila is mostly referred to as 'Teresa de Jesus'. Her 'autobiography' – variously styled by critics as *Life* or *Vida* – is here consistently called *Book* (see General Introduction, note 6).

Sources and Abbreviations

The Antwerp Manuscripts

The Antwerp papers, abbreviated in references throughout to '*A*', include the Lives of nuns and lay sisters written during the period 1619–1794. They comprise two main books of convent annals that were compiled from *c*.1731 onwards, drawn from personal autobiographical and biographical writings by individual nuns from the foundation of the convent until they returned to England during the French Revolution.

The first volume of the annals is referred to here as *A1*. This book, with two clasps and a white leather cover, measures 18.5 cm × 23.5 cm, and it is written in various hands, having five preliminary sheets (i–v), and pages numbered 1 to 602. Folio 2v has an ink drawing of Anne of the Ascension. The second volume, *A2*, is also written in various hands, and is only around half filled. This book has two clasps and a brown cover, and measures 18.5 cm × 23.5 cm, with four preliminary sheets (i–iv), and pages numbered 1 to 344.

Extracts are also included from two further volumes of Antwerp papers. The Life of Catherine Burton is designated *A3*. It is written in the same hand throughout, and is contained in a book with a brown cover. It measures 18.5 cm × 23.5 cm, and has two blank pages, an unnumbered preface (i–xii), and pages numbered 1 to 490, an index (unnumbered, six pages, two blank). Folio 2r has an ink with wash shading drawing of Catherine Burton in three-quarter length. After page 457 (unnumbered) there is a one-page, full-length, horizontal, ink drawing of the body of Margaret Wake. This book was commissioned in 1723/24 (see p. 135).

The Life of Margaret Wake is designated *A4*. This book has dark brown cover, coming away at the spine, and it measures 18.5 cm × 23 5 cm. A glued-in frontispiece has a pen and ink drawing of Margaret Wake, which is a simplified version of that within *A3*. Preliminary pages are unnumbered, and include a title page and preface (i–xviii), and a list of contents (xix–xx); the Life itself is on pages numbered 1 to 306, with the numbering corrected from page 110 onwards. The book appears to have been written between *c*.1716 and 1730, if it is the same book referred to in the preamble of *A1* ('your last work of our Venble Mother Mary Margaret of the Angels' [Wake]) which was started *c*.1731–33 (see p. 36).

The four volumes, with other belongings, were transported from Antwerp to Lanherne in Cornwall, the place where the religious resettled for some 200 years on their return to England. The material is now housed in the archive of St Helens Carmelite convent in Merseyside, following the amalgamation of the Lanherne and St Helens communities.

The Lierre Manuscripts

The Lierre annals and associated papers contain the Lives of nuns and lay sisters written from 1648 when the convent was established to 1794 when the nuns returned to England. The papers now housed in the Carmelite convent at Darlington, County Durham, where they have been comprehensively catalogued by their archivist. They include the composite Lives contained in the annals, as well a numerous other documents and loose papers, some of which are drawn on for this edition. I have designated material from this archive with '*L*' for Lierre; otherwise the reference system is that given by the archivist, the first number indicating the box in which the documents are stored, followed by the number of the bundle within this. On occasion, when referring to individual sheets within a group of loose papers, I have added a letter to the numbering to differentiate between manuscripts – hence Box 1, document group 6, sheet A is referenced as *L1.6.A*, followed by the page number.

Primarily material is from *L13.7*, the Lierre annals of this period, contained in a book measuring 20cm x 32cm, with a pale cover over card, no clasps and the remains of an original tie. Pages are numbered 1 to 325, written in various hands. These Lives appear to have been compiled soon after the death of each religious by the Prioress at the time. A few details are drawn from *L13.8*, 'a continuation of the summary or relation of the deceased religious' (f2r), the annals that contain the Lives of nuns who died between 1779 and 1877. This book is also 20 cm × 32 cm; it has 453 pages, written in different hands, and is broken inside at the spine.

Supplementary material is drawn from other papers in the archive, referenced as they arise. These include a seventeenth-century copy of the constitutions (*L3.34*: Appendix 1), a Prioress' notes on mortification (*L3.5*: Appendix 2) and papers relating to Anne of the Ascension (*L1.6*: Appendix 3).

Chapter 1

The Inspiration to Compose: Burial in Oblivion and the Miraculous Discovery of an Incorrupt Body

The annals of the Antwerp Carmel were commissioned by Mary Frances of St Teresa (Mary Birkbeck: 1674–1733; Chapter 15). It was in 1716 during her time as Prioress that the incorrupt body of Mary Margaret of the Angels (Margaret Wake: 1617–78; Chapter 29) was discovered in the dead-cellar of the convent. This inspired Mary Frances to 'procure the writeing' of various Lives to commemorate the religious from the foundation of the convent in 1619, and in particular to stress their line of authority from the immediate followers of Teresa de Jesus.

The opening of the first volume of the annals (*A1*) contains a dedication to Father Percy Plowden (1672–1745),[1] spiritual director of the convent at the time of the discovery of the body, who himself had written a Life of Margaret Wake at the Prioress' suggestion. In her introduction, Mary Frances mentions that the compilation of the annals has been neglected 'for this hunder'd and a 11 years'; and she addresses Plowden as rector of the English College in Rome, an office he held from 1731–34. This means that we can date the beginning of the compilation of the Antwerp annals with some precision to between 1731 and 1733 (when Mary Frances herself died).

Mary Frances' preface is framed within a formula of female modesty and obedience, familiar from other texts such as Teresa de Jesus' Book 'written by herself at the command of her confessor', to whom she constantly defers, claiming she is 'too stupid to express or convey in a few words something which is so important' (*Book*, 21, 93). Just as Teresa de Jesus wrote 'I have almost to steal time for writing' (*Book*, 74), so Mary Frances blames 'shortness of time' as well as lack of ability for her neglect of this work; and just as Teresa de Jesus asks her confessor to burn her text if it is not consistent with the truths of the church (*Book*, 75), so Mary Frances

---

[1]   Thomas Percy Plowden (1672–1745), the youngest son of Edmund and Penelope (née Drummond) of Plowden Hall in Shropshire, was a member of the Society of Jesus from 1693, and Rector of the English College at Rome from 1731–34; Superior at Ghent, 1735–39; and Rector of St Omers, 1739–42. He was spiritual director at the Hopland Carmel for several years (*Catholic Encyclopaedia*; Hardman 1939, 14).

asks Plowden to 'scratch out' any part of the annals that is contrary to doctrine.

The Prioress' own introductory section is followed by another preface, composed by the nun initially delegated to write the annals, the first stages of which she compiled from *c*.1731–1750. This religious remains anonymous until her own Life appears, posthumously, in the second volume, when she is named as Mary Joseph of St Teresa (Mary Howard: 1688–1756: Chapter 21). In her preamble to *A1*, she sets out her editorial method and her reasons for writing, a system which falters at a later stage (see p. 10).

This extract includes the text of both Mary Frances' and Mary Joseph's introductions; the heading appears at the opening of the original volume.

[*A1*, v–x]

Short Colections of the Beginings of Our English Monastery of Teresians In Antwerp with some few Particulars of our Dear Deceased Religious

To the very Reverend Father Percy Plowden, Rector of the English College at Rome

It may seem an unpardonable presumption in me to dedicate this imperfect colection to the person of so great judgment and learning of which your Rec[torship] has given to the world most convincing proofs by your excellent agreable pen: your last work of our Venble Mother Mary Margaret of the Angels has to the highest degree edifyd and charmd us all ... but remembering that parents are accustomed to take more pleasure in the imperfect expressions of their children then in the most accomplished discourses of riper understandings, I find myself inclined to present this to your Rec as to a true Father of this Community (who are most sensible of your being such) the more because it was upon your Rec's own advice and order that I undertook to colect the little we had or knew of, repaireing as much as in our powers, the many remarkable things which by this neglect will ever be buryed in oblivion, and tho it be done in a poor and silly manner yet I hope the goodness and substance of the matter will in time move some friendly pious hand to put it into a more advantagious light, least the poorness of the style and want of meathod may lessen its intended effect tho only design'd for our private Instruction and incouragment.

However I please myself to think that amongst your Recs more serious and weighty imploys it may sometimes make you smile at its simplicity and nonsense, which I can easily find out myself, but have not the witt to mend it. If it gives your Rec this little devertion I shall be truly glad to have thus exposed my ignorance, which is allready so well known that you cannot wonder at this new proof of it tho by the by I ingeniously owne I have some little vanity to bring thus far a work, which has been for this hunder'd and a 11 years neglected and yet successively wish'd and aimd at, by all that has gone before me, and which if not now done could never have been repared by those who follow.

I could justly make a thousand excuses, in regard of the shortness of time, for so great & intricate a work, my want of health and capacity, the imperfect knowledge of many particulars & c. tho I have endeavour'd to say nothing but upon very good grounds, and the informations I had from several of our Monasterys, if your Rec finds any thing contrary to true doctrine or edification I beg you will please to scratch it out, as you read it, which will give more authority to what remains.

In fine the knowledge and experience I have had of yr Recs Fatherly goodness, makes me confide you will take all in good part, from one that is with more esteem affection and gratitude then can be express'd very Rd Father yr Recs most obedient humble servant and poor unworthy child M[ary] F[rances][2]

Jesus Maria Joseph Teresa[3]

Finding on severall occasions great inconveninces from the not having register'd the beginings of this Monastery, and the particulars of our dear deceased religious which we have little knowledge of, only in loose papers in comparison of the much that might justly be said of them, our present Reverand Mother, Mary Frances of St Teresa, order'd this little colection, that what we found and knew of might not be forever lost, to the end that those present and those who follows may be animated with the primitive spirit and fervour couragiously to follow the examples of these their predecessors, who successively have by their heroick vertues maintained the first observance of our glorious Mother St Terese and render'd this Monastery singularly remarkable for love, charity and union amongst themselves, great tenderness and affection towards the sick, obedience, submission and loving respect to Superiours, aversion to the least propriety, intire dependence on divine providence, and preseverant constancy in the practices of our Holy Mother even to the least things, all which our first Superiour Rd Mother Anne of the Ascension took from the companions of St Teresa under whom she was professed and lived several years with, as will be seen afterwards.

It will also show the wonderful providence Almighty God, from the beginning, had had over this house, by so many particular and miraculous favours shewd in its regard both as to spirituals and temporals for this 100 and a 11 years, as allso in the choice of such fitt members wholly unthought of, as we still experience, shewing us that his kind and mercyfull hand is not yett shortend which ought still, more and more, to rase our confidence in his goodness and make us with a new gratitude and love fervourously to persue our happy course. Praised be God for all and may he be still more glorifyd in his Saints.

---

[2] One page of the original text is blank at this point: it resumes with an introduction by the compiler, Mary Joseph.

[3] This opening invocation, sometimes abbreviated to 'JMJT', is common throughout the papers.

Chapter 2

Anne of the Ascension, First Prioress at Antwerp

Anne Worsley (1588–1644) was the first Prioress of the English foundation at Antwerp, and her Life accordingly is the first within the annals (*A1*, 1–77). It has clear strategic as well as spiritual importance for the convent because of her credentials in a direct line of authority from Teresa de Jesus herself through Spanish religious, and because she made a spirited defence of the Teresian constitutions in the face of challenge from friars of the Order. The Life includes copies of documents felt by the compiler to be important evidence of the substance of Teresa de Jesus' reform, upon which subsequent claims for relative autonomy are founded.

For the most part, the text appears to be based on Anne of the Ascension's own papers, which are characterized by spiritual enquiry and struggles towards self-effacement. The Life, one of several versions in existence, is organized in the annals into four main sections, reflected in this extract's subdivisions. The first part, headed in the original 'A short account ... written by her self', includes information about the nun's early secular and religious life at different convents, with details of her struggles with the friars and of her illness. After various gaps in the manuscript, presumably left for other details to be added, and some third-person commentary, a second part continues with a 'manifestation of conscience', again in the first person, copied from personal 'loose papers'. A third section deals with aspects of her later life and death, and a fourth gathers material that supports Teresian reformist claims.

In the early part of her Life, Anne of the Ascension describes the choices she thought available to an unmarried woman of her status with relatively limited means – service with a Lady or a religious vocation. She felt herself to be at a special disadvantage since her family was in exile, without appropriate connections to promote her career. Like her sister, Elizabeth Worsley (Chapter 3), she sought support from the Spanish Infanta governing the region, who she hoped would pay her dowry to the convent. Her call to a religious vocation, like others described in the annals, was underlined by a mystical encounter, in her case by seeing 'a monstrous great head' that alarmed her greatly.

The subsequent narrative describes her early religious life, including details of her attachment to Anne of St Bartholomew, her first Superior, the intensity of which appears surprising given the directives against 'particular friendship' within the Order. It gives a moving account of their enforced separation under obedience to a spiritual director whom Anne of the Ascension had thwarted in his plans for constitutional change. At one stage, the bereft nun is consoled by the appearance of Christ, who urges her to turn her affection towards him instead. Similar corrective redirections away from intense human association occur in the Life of Teresa de Jesus herself, as well as in that of Ursula of All Saints (Elizabeth Mostyn: 1626–1700) (see pp. 12, 188).

This Life, too, exposes the potential tension between the nuns and their founders. Anne of the Ascension describes with tact and ever-increasing frustration her dealings with Mary, Lady Lovel (see p. 3), as well as her encounters with the Carmelite friars, details which together with letters (Appendix 3) shed light on her dilemmas, role and relationships.

Her 'manifestation of conscience' reveals her sense of interiority and shows the influence of particular styles of devotional reading and practice. These inform an understanding of other Carmelite Lives and for this reason they are discussed in some detail here. Anne of the Ascension writes, for example, of 'recollection', a central tenet of contemplative devotion that Teresa de Jesus herself had described:

> For it appears that just as the soul has exterior senses it also has other interior senses through which it seems to want to withdraw within, away from the outside noise. So, sometimes this recollection draws these exterior senses after itself, for it gives the soul the desire to close its eyes and not hear or see or understand anything other than that in which it is then occupied, which is communion with God in solitude. In this state none of the sense or faculties are lost, for all are left intact. But they are left that way so that the soul can be occupied in God ... From this prayer there usually proceeds what is called a *sleep of the faculties*, for they are neither absorbed nor so suspended that the prayer can be called a rapture ... (*Spiritual Testimonies*, 1976 ed., 426; and see *Way of Perfection*, 1946 ed.)

Both women repeatedly differentiate between variant types of mysticism. In *c.*1557 Teresa de Jesus had experienced her first locution and rapture, followed later by imaginative visions and revelations, and she writes of their relative status as steps towards union of the soul with God (*Book*, Chapters 25–9). She constantly glosses her own experience in the light of church authority – for example: 'One day when I was at prayer – it was the feast day of the glorious St Peter – I saw Christ at my side – or, to put it better, I was conscious of Him, for I saw nothing with the eyes of the body or the eyes of the soul ...' (*Book*, 187).

Such Teresian influence is clearly evident within Anne of the Ascension's writing, and in other Carmelite Lives. The Saint's works naturally had been widely distributed within the convents, and her *Book* was one of her first to be translated, including a 1611 version produced in Antwerp by William Malone, an Irish Jesuit (1976 ed., 48).

In addition, it is possible to trace to a lesser or greater extent the effect of other texts owned by the Antwerp Carmel during this period. Copies of books by Augustine Baker (1575–1641), for many years a spiritual teacher of the Cambrai Benedictines, were sent to the English Carmelites in the 1630s (McCann and Connolly, 1933, 139). Baker's method encouraged some degree of freedom for individuals to follow their own pious paths in contemplative exercises in which a nun 'rejects all mental pictures and representations of [God]. She transcends all operations of the imagination' towards the special end of an 'attainment of an habitual and almost uninterrupted union with

God in the summit of the spirit' (*Contemplative Prayer*, 1927 ed., 15, 18). Baker's ideas were controversial, and he was removed from spiritual direction at Cambrai in 1633 (Walker, 2003, 25). Whilst there may be traces of his thought in Anne of the Ascension's writing, she makes use of disciplinary systems, including mental imagining, that were more directly influenced by Francisco de Ribera (1537–91), a Jesuit and early biographer of Teresa de Jesus and, in particular, by Alfonso Rodríguez (1526–1616).

Rodríguez, in challenge to writers such as Baker, sought to develop and condense Ignatian practices for prayer, maintaining a restraining influence on ecstatic experiences that might otherwise allow the mystic unmediated control (see Walker, 2003, 162). Several of his texts have specific links to Anne of the Ascension. His *Practice of Perfection and Christian Virtues* was first published in Seville in 1609, and one English translation contained a dedication to the nun. The Antwerp and Lierre Carmels owned copies of his *Treatise on Mentall Prayer* (1627); these are still held in archives at St Helens and Darlington. The Antwerp copy is inscribed on the flyleaf 'For Mother Anne of the Ascension. Remember in your prayers, yours to command, John More' (Hardman, 1936, 75); and Rodríguez's *Short and Sure Way to Heaven* (1630) contains a dedicatory epistle addressed to 'To the Reverend and Religious Mother Anna of the Ascention, Prioress of the English Teresians in Antwerpe'.[1]

Clearly Anne of the Ascension drew upon ideas that were widespread within contemplative discourse, but there is some evidence of Rodríguez's specific influence in the nun's writing when she describes several paradoxes at the heart of contemplative discipline – a desire to minimize a sense of self through extreme personal awareness; a sense of the physicality of prayer from which one could acquire spiritual sustenance devoid of bodily association; and a concern to subsume prayer into the natural humours of the body.

In the first of these attempts – to reduce a sense of self – Rodríguez considers the benefits of mortification in which 'Iron is made softe, betweene the Anuile and the fire' (Rodríguez, *Treatise*, 95). In loose papers attributed to Anne of the Ascension, apparently drawn upon in the Antwerp annals Life, the nun writes of 'degrees of mortification' that are designed 'to haue so intier a victory ouer our selfes as easely to ouer come any inclynnation of feeling of natuer' (*L1.6.H*, 1).[2] Such successes are to be attained through an acute self-awareness that leads to forgetfulness. Anne of the Ascension's texts illustrate her progress in terms of Ignatian disciplines in which

---

[1]   This dedication is signed 'I.C.', and was previously identified as the Rouen printer, Jean Cousturier, considered to be the translator of the text. However, it is now clear this ascription is incorrect, and that the book was published by Boscard in St Omers (see A F Allison and DM Rogers, *The Contemporary Printed Literature of the English Counter-Reformation*, Aldershot and Burlington: Ashgate, 1994, item 900). (I am grateful to the editorial readers of my book for this information).

[2]   These papers are now in the Lierre archive at Darlington They include fragmentary pieces, some on the backs of letters quoted on p. 5 of this book.

'Prayer is to be the glasse of the religious man, and in this glasse are we to view and reuiew our selues daily' (Rodríguez, *Treatise*, 13). Her notes on mortification confirm the need for 'a continuall vigilance ouer our selues for without gret whachfulnes ouer our inclinations wee shall neuer obtaine this vertue … wee ar to speke out our spirituall deseares as ye fisisian doth dily gently examene the sicknes of his patient before he aplyes the remedy' (*L1.6.K*, 1). In the devotional passages she wrote for another nun (Appendix 3C), she draws specifically on 'a short and sure way to perfection' and writes of 'a continuall leauing and denying of our selves in all things which natuer desiereth …' (*L1.6*, 1; see p. 268).

Although Anne of the Ascension expresses doubt about her ability to achieve such ideals, posthumous tributes to her indicate otherwise. Again, these appear to draw upon metaphors, found in Rodríguez's work as well as more widely, in which the physical power of devotion is substituted for other kinds of nourishment; and prayer is compared to eating and drinking when a person 'wilbe so absorpt & inebrated (as it were) with a businesse that he remembers not himselfe' (*Treatise*, 21). Appreciations of the nun suggest '… she was so wholy forgettfull of her selfe' and

> … she was so transported in to God that wee war constraned to speck of other matars to deiract [distract] her Rd, parceueing that it ded her hourt in pont of heileth [harmed her health]. Sum times she for goet her ordenare sustenanc and so wold com in to our recreation with out remembaring that she had not bin in the rifictore [refectory] untill such tiem as her Rce was put in mind that of …. (*L1.5.D*, 1)

Rodríguez likens prayer to the 'naturall heate in a man's stomack' (*Treatise*, 14), the warmth of which would show upon a face; similarly, tributes to Anne of the Ascension indicate that 'her face would show the flames that burned in her hart' (*L1.5.C*, 1). Such effects were considered evidence of rapture or physical union, drawing upon the sexual imagery of the Song of Songs and other sources:

> That vocation of God, to draw the soule into his secret retiring-place, to treat so familiarly with it, and the bringing it into his Cellar of wyne, so to satisfy it, and inebriate it with his loue … her fellow Spouse took her by the hand, and drew her in. That raising of ones selfe to the kisse of his mouth, is not a thing which thou canst or oughtest pretend, unlesse he raise thee up …. (*Treatise*, 27)

Similar sorts of imagery were drawn upon by several Carmelites, sometimes including references to a heart pierced by a 'curious dart' (Bedingfield, 1884, 120) that recall the iconography of St Teresa herself, a relic of whose 'flaming heart' was donated to the Antwerp nuns by Tobie Matthew in September 1642 (Hardman, 1936, 76–7).

Though later tributes suggest that Anne of the Ascension was successful in her devotional endeavours, her own papers show how much she struggled. In her 'manifestation of conscience' (*c*.1632), she expresses concern that her negligence in prayer has resulted in distraction and 'unquiet'. Rodríguez's *Treatise* states that 'when Prayer is discomposed, the life groweth also into disorder': 'By not resorting to Praier all goes backward, and by and by comes tepidity'. The nun writes, 'My desires are so cold as tho I had neither soul or life' (*A1*, 28). Such language draws on familiar tropes used by Teresa de Jesus among others, as when Rodriguez writes of spiritual desolation:

> ... for one to go to prayer, and remaine there as if he were a stone with so great aridity and drinesse ... it seeming to him that God hath wholly withdrawne himselfe from him ... when euen heuen seemes to them to be made of Iron, and the earth of brasse ... this is that which we call properly spirituall desolation, aridity or drines .... (*Short and Sure Way*, 1630, 266)

Though Anne of the Ascension draws comfort in her 'aridity' from Teresian imagery concerning the 'waters' of prayer (*Book*, 78 ff),[3] she and others clearly believed that dryness and the temptation to neglect prayer were signs of 'deuils vexing them with that unquiet thought, that themselues alone are the cause of ...' (*Short and Sure Way*, 267), and it is no wonder that she found her situation so painful and bewildering.

Her personal notes, read in parallel to her Life and to the books that influenced her, indicate the mental processes in which she engaged. Whilst the nun herself expresses dismay at her imperfections, the appreciations written by other nuns suggest that after her death the convent collected testimonies about her blessedness. These include a statement which describes her illness and the apparently miraculous scent that surrounded her body:

> Wee could not detaine her Rce [Anne of the Ascension] from ueseting [visiting] sum of our religious sisters which war sick of the small poacx [smallpox] to the haseding [hazarding] of losing her lief, for hir Rce taking the inficktion [infection] thar of fill uery dangarusly sick. Of these my silf being oen ho tened [tended] her Rce and being agn out of the roem up on acation so that her Rce was aloen, Sister Teresa of Jesus [Anne of the Ascension's sister] cam to the doar to know how her Rce ded, for non war par met to entar the chambar but thos which had the sam deses. Sister Teresa ismelt a uery strong sweet smel: thinking it had ben sum raer parfuem which I had burnt in the roem, she saed it was not good for our Rd Mother to haue shuch swet odars ... She called othars of our sistar who finding it so conmforting a sweetnes that wee all thought it to be sum suparnaturall thing for thar was no such thing as parfuem in the chambar nor near thar abouts .... (*L1.5.D*, 1)

---

[3]   The nun develops similar metaphors, drawn from homiletic tradition, concerning the 'fruts of mortification': 'frist many of the holy fathers saye that mortification is licke a plowe which telleth the growend of our soule and maketh it fitte for the heuenly husbanmane to soowe his seedes of many vertues wherby it be cometh greene and florising. secondly it is as a knife which coteth of all the superfluus branches of the vine which makes our soules veri fruthfull' (*L1.6.G*, 1).

[*A1*, 1–77]

A short account of our first Dear Venerable Mother Ann of the Ascension (alias Worsley), Foundress of the English Teresians at Antwerp in ye year 1619 May ye 1st under protection of ye glorious St Joseph and St Ann, written by her self by ye orders of her Confessor

Rd Father to obey your Rev: I sett down what I can remember hath past in me

I find little till I was 14 or 15 years of age only that I was given … to desire such things as I then esteem'd: sometimes I thought of God, for I remember when I sayd my prayers at night I examm'd what I had done for God that day, when I found nothing I was ashamed and troubled. To avoyd this I was carefull to hear Mass and say some more prayers. When I was 15 or 16 years of age I began to take delight in ye world, and to be in company. I was troubled yt my parents could not maintain me as I desired; and that wee were in a strange countrey & had no friends nor kindred as I saw others had loosing thereby many occations of pleasures. Being troubl'd I thought the only way to come to some preferm[ent] was either to goe in to England, or to serve some Ladys … To goe in to England I durst not, fearing to lose my soul by heresy: the other I resolv'd upon.

Being one evening at my prayers, thinking to speake next day to my parents to give me leave to goe to ye Lady, I doe not know wether I was half asleep or not, but of a suddan a monstrous great head seem'd near unto me, gaping to devour me at wch I was much frighted, and call'd to our Blessed Lady promising to be Religious. From that instant I durst never think of any other course fearing to loose my soul. Soon after I heard in a sermon that only virgins might follow ye Lamb; and that once lost was never to be recovered: I made a firm resolution never to loose so precious a treasure, and from yt time I had great esteem of virginity, tho knew not wherein it consisted only not to be married.

My parents, perceiving I would be religious, begann to think how to help me in to Brussels monastery where according to nature I had most desire to be because they were English & in very good esteem, and I had some kindred whome I thought would be help to me by means of ye Infanta (because I had no portion) I hoped I might obtain to it. I thought sometimes of being a Poor Clare but it was much forced and did not enter far & my mother would not hear of that, that I should think of so hard an Order.

In this time my mother dyed, and the Order of our Blessed Mother came to Brussels, wch I heard was very strickt, but all were saints. Hearing this praise (that all were saints in yt Order), I could think of no other thought. It was made so hard to me, as though it would be above my strength to bear it, that I should not live two years, yt ye rudeness of Spanish natures was not fitt for me, and diverse such things were objected to me by many… I resolved to undertake it, with ye remembrance of ye Passion of our Blessed Saviour I was much strengthened. I apprehended I should never have content, and it would be like a Purgatory for my sins; I imagined I should not live long so it would soon be at an end, & I should goe to heaven soon. Many such gross intentions I had only to avoid hell and obtain heaven.

I had some difficulty to obtain a place because I had no meanes; yet after some time by ye charitable assistance of ye Infanta and a good holy priest who was then Superior, I was admitted for he layd out ye money necessary for me that I might not be delay'd till ye Infanta had payd. I enterd wth resolution to doe and suffer all, for I apprehended fearfull things yet felt joy & comfort. After I had been some time I lookt [wondered] when these hard things would come forth, for I found all very sweet & easy, only when I heard ye religious take ye disciplin [whip] I was much trouble[d] for yt was one of ye things I apprehended. But when I saw them after they had don look as well as before, I marveld very much for I thought they would be half dead; and seing ye contrary, ye apprehension past & I found great content in all & I was desireous to learn ye manner how to observe ye Constitution of our Order. This was my greatest care, for I was ignorant of all. I was carefull to minde [what] was told me & especially for meditation & had great care to observe in order all ye parts, tho I found some difficulty in it.

The Mistress of Novices was of a milde disposition: when she mortified us it was in a good manner, so I had little difficulty to leave or doe any thing she apointed. But one of ye novices was of a rude disposition, and she would speak harshly to us upon some occasions when wee were alone, and sometimes I felt passion against her, yet I grieved very much because ye convent would not keep her.[4] I have allways felt the grief of those I live with all. I remember no remarkable things to have happened during my noviceship.

It pleas'd God to give me feeling devotion towards ye time of my profession wch I made with great joy to see my self tyed to God. I made great purposes to serve his Divine Majesty wth more fervor and to be exact in all observances especially in prayer, and ye presence of God wch I took in an imaginary manner, wch so forced my head that I had continual pain. Sometimes I did not take it patiently, I did not know how to declare my self, therefore did things wth out advice & many pennances wch I thought I might doe, as to suffer cold, thirst, and such like things, in wch I immagined to doe great matter & when I did any humble work or act of humiliation I had pride & satisfaction so I had in all I did. In this manner I proceeded about two years after my profession when Mother Anne of St Bar[tholomew] came out of France to ye monastery where I was[5] for wch wee had all great satisfaction because wee heard so much of her sanctity. I purposed to marke her actions and to follow her as neer as I could.

After she had been there a week or two, as we all had leave to doe, because she was much esteem'd and was not to stay at ye monastery but to come to found one at Antwerp, I told her my manner of proceeding wch she misliked and sayd I hurt my health. [She] bid me not force my head nor press so much for ye presence of God, that I should make aspriations yt God did not exact any thing so much as our love ... I began to conceive it was not hard to please God for I took all she said as from his Divine Majesty. I had great comfort in ye assistance of this good Mother and was much afflicted that she was to goe from hence. One day she askt me if I would be contented to goe with her, I thinking she did jest saying it only for recreation because I was fitt for nothing & there were other fine religious, I putt it of[f], though after thought by my self, 'If God should sufer me to let me live wth a saint what I would doe to be gratefull', but I took it to be an impossible thing, though ye good Mother told me divers times she did intend to have me, which she shew'd when ye Provinciall came, asking to have me wch was granted. I knew not of it till ye night before wee parted. I was so joyfull to goe with her that I forgot ye grieff I had to part with those I left.

When wee came to Antwerp, in ye beginning of ye monastery [the 'Spanish Carmel'],

---

4   The religious presumably voted that she should leave the convent (see p.245).

5   At Mons, from which she later transferred with Anne of St Bartholomew to the 'Spanish Carmel' in Antwerp.

all had many exteriour emploments, in wch I was very much carest, & let my affections on exteriour things, and was very much distracted in prayers. I was earnest to have things according to my desire & sometimes shewing passion. Our good Mother told me of it in a very loving manner, as her custome was, but perceiving I continued, she told me in a sharp manner at wch I was much grieved. I saw she had great reason. I desired to mend but feard my self very much, because I was entangled in divers things that I knew not how to gett out. Our Mother promis'd to pray for me, & I found she did, for being in great desolation of minde, with fears that I should never attain to any perfection, one day hearing Mass I could doe nothing only say 'Lord what shall I doe, I have a great way to goe to come to you, and cannot stirr, nor move'. This being lively in me with great oppression, in one instant it seem'd to me I saw our Blessed Saviour standing some distance from me reaching out his hand to me, and sayd 'Follow me, I will be your way and strength'. I did not see with my eyes, for I was prostrate, as we used to be after ye Elevation of ye Mass, & I think my eyes were shutt. I think it was a lively representation wch suddainly passed away but made such alterations in me, that I was like a nother. My disposition was so altered, I found joy and confidence in God, plainly seeing I had no good in my self. After this I had more light in ye misteries wch ye holy church doe celebrate, and I did more comprehend ye good instructions of my Superiour from whome I did not reserve any thing. ... She was esteemed of us all and I loved her as tenderly as a natural mother. ...

... I had a desire for mortification and was carefull to mortify my senses, as not to hear or see out of curiosity and the like things. Almighty God gave me feeling devotion to void all wch facility. In these times came on an occasion of great suffering, and it was that the Fryers of [the] Order came to have all sign to a writing.[6] The Provincial sent to our Mother wth a command that she should procure by all meanes possible the consent of all her religious. Wee were but few profest, because it was the beginning of the Monastery. Our Revered Mother shewed us this writing and perswaded us to signe it. Wee, perceiving it was an thing whereby wee should foregoe ye priviledges wch our Blessed Mother St Teresa had left us, all found difficulty to doe it ... I durst not plainly deny our Mother, but prayd her with tears that she would not require such a thing of me. ... she saw wee were so much afflicted (as I was extreamly) ... so our Mother writt with all, that she her self found difficulty in it, and she advised him [the Provincial] to leave of yt business; but 1st he came himself to perswade us.

Wee had advice of learned men who tould us wee were not bound to obey in that case. So I tould him I would not signe to his paper, in more express terms then I could to my Prioress out of ye love I bore her. The Provincial, seeing he could doe no thing, was much displeasd, and give us hard words, but wee remain constant, and ye business was left, for he found ye same resistance at our convent at Brussels.

Soon after this ye same Provincial came to visit our convent. Each one had their part, but I was she who spoild all ye rest. At that time there was speack of the Lady Lovels founding for English,[7] wch I did apprehend very much out of ye fear I had of being removed from my Superiour, yet ye Provincial see I had a hand in it to perswade her not to doe it under ye goverment of ye Order, tho I had neither done the other or it, for it was

---

[6] I.e., the friars wished the female religious to agree to a change in their constitutions.
[7] In other words, there was rumour of a new foundation being made for English nuns, by Mary, Lady Lovel, in which endeavors she eventually succeeded in 1619.

like death to me hearing of it. The good Prior reproach'd me of divers things at wch I was ashamed being before ye whole Community, yet I found comfort in it, because I found my consience clear.

… In these times I had diverse other imperfections and great temptations that I should not be saved came upon me, and was so troubled wth scruples that I could find no satisfaction from any confessor, only in my Superiour, because I held her for a Saint, as it does now appear by ye many miracles God doth by her.[8] But when I had the least imagination that she was not so kinde to me, or once found her not so chearfull, I thought she saw yt God had not affected me: she would often answer me ye contrary, then I was quiet for a time. This did last 8 or 9 months, after wch I had more confidence in God …

I had a book of Father Robera[9] wch treated of ye presence of God, in wch I found great comfort, especially one thing he sayd, 'wee might be or where in God as a sponge in the water' in wch I found great joy because I saw more then before that I could nothing of my self. I had sometimes great desires of doing pennance & should have don indiscreet things if my Superiour had pemitted me …

… I feard only to be seperated from my Mother Prioress: for I did esteem ye being with her as a great a benefit as I could desire of God in this life, and to be seperated from her more grievious then any martyrdome I could think of. The esteem I had for her made me to observe all her actions and manner of proceedings in all occasions and to be very inquisitive to know her intentions; and I saw she had seen our Blessed Mother [St Teresa] to doe in such and such occasions. She, out of her goodness, was very kinde and free to me, wch did cause me much joy and comfort that I thought my self ye happiest in ye world in my state and place. But after 5 years that I had been with her, one day being much distracted, I set my self to prayer with intention to consider some vertue of our Blessed Mother for it was ye octave day of her feast.[10] I was no sooner settled but her great humility & obedience came to my minde and ye same instant it seemed our Bd Mother stood before me in ye religious habit with a cross in her hand, wch she offer'd me. I was stroken wth extream fear & seemed to refuse ye cross … I asked her if it was to yeild to ye fryers; she answerd 'no' … It seem'd to me yt she put her hand to ye side of my face in a kinde and loving way, saying she would help me and so vanisht … the greatest thing I apprehended was to loose my Superiour to wch I hardly resolved to resign my self.

I continued in this disposition two days when ye Provincial came for two religious of our house to begin a Monastery in Maclin,[11] our Subprioress for Prioress. I nor any of our convent had thought of my self; only ye same morning our dear Mother knew of it. At Noon, wch was ye time set for our departure, ye Provincial sent for me and bid me put on my mantle, and come to ye gate, yt ye coach was ready for us to goe to ye foundation. I told him he did that only to try me (for so I thought) and did not mean it. He answered me

---

8   Anne of St Bartholomew was declared Venerable in 1735 (*Catholic Encyclopaedia*).

9   Francisco de Ribera (1537–91).

10   I.e., the eighth day after the feast day of St Teresa (15 October) – the week (eight days) calculated by counting from and including the feast day itself.

11   A foundation at Mechelen was established in 1616.

yt he did intend it ... that he did command me in virtue of holy obedience to goe presently to ye gate, wch was harder to me then a sentence of death could have been ...

[I] went towards ye gate as he had commanded me. I met our dear Mother shewing more affliction then ever I had seen her to doe before: tell then I thought she and all ye convent had wept for ye departure of Mother Subprioress only. Being at ye gate to goe forth, I turnd back to see our dear Mother once more for ye last time. As I had my hand on ye vaile wch hung over her face (because there were people she was coverd), the Provincial call'd me to come without delay, so I left ye vaile with grief not to see her more, but thought I would obey till death, and how much more pleasing it would be to enter in to a fire where I should be consum[ed] then goe out of ye gate, if it were as pleasing to God. Being in extremity of grief as I went out, something did meat me that I doe not know what to compare it to; the nearest is some cloud or light mist in wch I perceived our Blessed Lady only shewing a chearful countinance saying that I should see my Mother again, yt my obedience was pleasing to God and that she would help me. This past me in an instant. I remaind much strengthen'd and comforted, and from that time I had more feeling and knowledge of God then ever I had before. Yet for ye present my nature was so fraile that I sounded [swooned] divers times that afternoon in ye way wth extremity of grief ... I cannot remember but that I was continually so resolved that if it had been in my power to goe back with a words speaking, yt I would not say that to enjoy the content I had before, if this was in ye least degree more pleasing to God: yet ye natural feeling caused me some sickness, and if two days past without receiving a line or express messenger from my Mother[12] I could not rest.

The Prioress I had at Macklen[13] did all she could possibly to comfort me. If she thought of any thing yt would be pleasing to me, or give me any recreation she would spare no cost nor diligence to procure it me. She knew what I felt, tho after 8 or 10 days I bore it wth out external shew ... yet I thought my grief well grounded because it was for being seperated from his [God's] true serv[an]t by whose meanes I hoped to be holpen to perfection ... I was so full of self love yt I did only seek my own satisfaction ...

... Being before ye Blessed Sacrament I made complaint, saying 'Lord will you reject me; you have taken me from my Mother' ... when presently came to minde, like if it had been said to me: 'It will be better for you to labour to be my servant you[r] self'. I answerd 'What shal I doe?' I was told 'Set your affections wholly on me and let all your care be to please me, and I will help you'. All this past in one instant, and I remaind comforted and wth great desires to please Almighty God. I did perceive so many defects in my self that I found nothing in me that could deserve any thing of God.

I continually saw my self like an empty vessel dry and negligent, and found such store of graces that somtimes it did hinder my health because I was naturaly vehement ...

After I had been about two years at Macklen,[14] Mother Ann of St Bar[tholomew] fell very dangerously ill, so far that I immagind yt she was dead but yt was kept from me. I continued in ye same desires to see her, and be wth her again, and being out of hope of

---

12   'Prioress I had lost' is crossed out here in the original text.
13   Eleanor of St Bernard.
14   *C.* 1618.

this, by the fear I had of her death, I was in extream affliction. One time after I had been a long space weeping and makeing my complaint in ye quire before ye Blessed Sacrament, being weary, I sat down in a corner half a sleep. There came like a bright cloud almost over my head, in wch I perceived our Blessed Saviour like of ye age of 10 or 12 years who I saw so beautiful yt ye content took away ye extream grief and heaviness of heart that I was in. He sayd to me 'What is there in my creature whome you love so much wch is not in me? If it be beauty you love in her, look on me; if it be wisdom or power, see if I have it not; if it be noble disposition, her meekness and love to you, consider mine to you and all yt is good in her is in me, and yt I am all good & fill all places'. So this pass and I remaind comforted both in soul and body tho then I did see my own folly and ingratitude to God more then ever I had done …

The Lady Lovell was to begin a monastery at Liege. I did mach apprehend to goe to it, so my Superiour got a consult of doctor[s][15] of Lovain yt I was not bound to goe out of ye country, whereupon I stood and refused to goe. The Lady Lovell used divers meanes to move me and so did ye Provincial, but I could not resolve. In ye mean while some difficulties came between Lady Lovell & ye Provinciall & ye business was defer'd[16] … I had so great an apprehension of going from my convent, and to leave my Superiour, being I was not to be wth Mother Ann, but to goe to a convent where I should have to doe with a foundress, and the fryers of ye Order were come to town … all wch I did apprehend extreamly … ye Provincial was displeased both at her [my Superior] and me, and sent us word yt he would not meddle wth me being we made such adoe, so took another in my place. …

When ye religious were at Antwerp I thought my self very secure. Mother Ann [of St Bartholomew] perswaded me to come and sayd I should be sometime with her and yt she would help me in all business, yet nothing could move me to goe … Father Provincial sent a coach with a command yt I should come the same hour, so I did to my great grief, and of all ye convent. At night I came to Mother Ann of St Bar[tholomew] wch would have been greater joy to me if I might have continued wth her, wch for a great favour was granted me for some days. She encouraged me & instructed me … she persuaded me to use all endeavours possible & that I should come to her after 3 years if I found as much difficulty as I apprehended. This was some comfort tho I thought 3 years long.

I came to this convent,[17] where 4 religious had been 8 or 10 days before. I was extreamly opprest & grieved: all things seemd strange to me, the very countinance of the religious I thought were not like others. I was so immortified that ye littleness of ye house did oppress me, and things seem'd so strange to me that I was glad when I could get into a chamber wth ye dore lockt upon me. The conversation of the religious, or any seculars without, was tedious to me, neither had I any interiour comfort. The religious shewed kindness to me. Some five weekes after they elected me for Prioress (till then there was a Dutch woman stayd till the election should be made).[18] When this was done my affliction

---

[15] This is one of several uses of this collective term within the papers. Here, Anne of the Ascension obtains, in effect, a doctor's note that she is unfit to move.
[16] This was one of many such difficulties between Lady Lovel and the ecclesiastical authorities.
[17] I.e., at Hopland in Antwerp, in 1619.
[18] She had acted as Vicaress until the election took place.

was redoubled; I thought there was no case of a religious in ye world so hard as mine. ... I had never seen the religious before only one, I was yong, the house was poor, & divers other difficulties I apprehended, as ye strange disposition of ye Lady Lovell, and to be in a place where the fryers of ye Order were. I feard (as it happened) I should not agree with them in matters of government ... I was 10 or 14 days in extream grief & could find no comfort: all our Mother Anne of St Bar[tholomew] could write, or others could say to me, did nothing to move me ... the words of St Augustine were of great comfort to me, where he says: 'Lord give what you command & command what you please', so I began to have some feeling of God wch I had not before ...

The Lady Lovell who had founded ye Monastery pretended [wished] to dispose of things according to her liking, & because wee could not observe such things as she desired (being not fitting for our Order), she was displeased and spoke hardly of us to seculars wch was a great grief to us. ... Sometimes wee were driven to such termes wth her that I desired her either to desist from such proceedings or to take her money & let us return to our convents wch I did heartily wish, but God would not permit the effect of my imperfect wishes. After some time when novices came yt wee had some money wch she knew not of, wee had more quiet because most disquiet proceeded out of an apprehension she had that wee spent to[o] largely. It was often grief to me to contradict her, because she had don so much for ye founding of the monastery.

Besides this trouble, I had divers wth ye fryers of ye Order, because they would have me begin divers new ceremonies and customs to wch I did continnally resist wch I could doe ye better because I was in esteem wth ye Provincial who was loath to grieve me because he knew I had many troubles ... If the religious had not been very confident with me, wee had been in confusion and disorder one wth the other ... and because I had lived a space with Mother Anne of St Bar[tholomew] who had all directly from our Blessed Mother St Teresa, ye least thing contrary to yt was only hard to me, but seemed impossible for me to resolve upon. So I stood resolutely against any new things those fryers did pretend. From ye beginning I followed the advices I could have ... of Mother Anne of St Bar[tholomew] being in ye same town[19] I had often ye comfort to hear from her.

After this convent had been allmost 3 years,[20] the Provinciall sent us new constitutions wth a command in virtue of holy obedience to burn all ye old wee had or did know of. I was in great perplexity. Before I spoke of it to ye religious I resolved to take advice, and if I was bound to doe it under venial sin I would, and advise the rest of the religious to doe the same; if wee were not, that I would stand to any suffering and not yeald ... All the religious [were] of ye same mind, to endeavour by all meanes possible to maintain our Blessed Mothers Constitution ... From ye beginning to ye end of ye business I had such sensible feeling yt according to nature I was inclined to yield, for to give content to the fryeres who sought by all meanes possible to gain me, tho out of a foolish nature I have I was mooved yet I never made ye least show of it, but stood hard against all they said or did ... I knew if the fryers did prevail I should suffer all my life for what I did ...

Soon after wee were settled under ye government of the Bishop. Some gentlewomen of ye country desired to enter among us and to have our assistance to begin a monastery of

---

[19] Within Antwerp the two convents are only a walking distance apart of some 10 to 20 minutes, but clearly movement between enclosures was strictly restricted.

[20] These events occurred in c.1622. The Provincial mentioned here is identified later in the

the true Institution as wee had, for wch they brought sufficient meanes. After they were in the fryers made great opposition, so that I knew not what to doe to keep them amongst us, for to keep them or send them in to ye world was hard ...[21]

... [She was] very dangerously sick of ye small pox wch was painfull to her by reason of her weakness, so yt the doctors did wonder she could live suffering so much. It happened, being ye time of evening song that there was only one religious with her[22] who must goe out of ye roome upon some occation & when she returned there was such a sweet smell as filled ye whole room. It was well perceived, for it continued near half an hour and there came divers of the religious in to ye roome and did smell it, and some sayd they would not believe but yt our Holy Mother was or had been there ... [Sister Anne of the Ascension herself] sayd that she did believe her Blessed Mother had been there, but she had not seen her, and that she did leave that sweet smell that the religious might take no hurt by the illness ... This strengthened her so much that what was so loathsome to her before did now give her interior comfort ...

That wch was strange that they who washed the linnen that came from ye sick have often affirmed that they smelt a sweet smell wch did comfort them when they prepared to wash it ...

Manifestation of conscience wch our dear venerable Mother Anne of the Ascension made from time to time to her Directors and Confessors, left in loose papers in her own hand writing[23]

In discourse I doe sometimes bring in things to my own advantage or praise especially thereby to cover things worthy of blame. I have failing[s] and am troubled in minde with a kinde of dejection when anything is to my humiliation, some times more then another. ...

... I have to[o] earnest desire of the spiritual and temporal good of this convent wch doth often disquiet my mind, especially when any thing does happen contrary. I find help by considering the convent belongs to God and yt he can provide for it as it is most for his honour ...

---

papers as Thomas à Jesu (1564–1627), a Discalced Carmelite who founded a series of convents – at Brussels (1610), Louvain (1611), Cologne and Douai (1613), among others. From 1617 he was Provincial of Flanders, and in 1621 was recalled to Rome, where he later died (*Catholic Encyclopaedia*).

[21] There are gaps left in the original manuscript here, and the writer resumes in the third person with the narrative becoming somewhat fragmentary, suggesting that she was copying sections from other papers and leaving space for further details to be added. The extracts that follow reflect this somewhat haphazard arrangement.

[22] It was common to assign usually two religious to sit with a sick sister, to watch over her and alert the community if death approached so that last rites could be administered.

[23] The subheadings appear in the original text.

… I have been this 3 or 4 months negligent in my prayers and the presence of God, allmost continually distracted by my own negligence …

… In ye octave of our Blessed Mother I set my self more to prayer and found my self to have a better esteem then before I had of her ordinations, with desire to observe them wth more exactness. I found great confusion to have been so negligent in divers points especially in omitting to make Chapter and the custome of some other mortifications or pennances wch are in religion, but after a peevish manner [I] seeme to be discontented when any thing is amiss or not according to my likeing.

… When I am not well I have a feafullness of being wors and if those who assist me forget any thing I feel a kind of discontent and think it simplicity or unhandiness in those who doe it …

a nother loose paper

I can easily acknowledge God present in all things, and I find in my self a submission in his presence wth acknowledgmt of my baseness …

… This two years I seldom use prayer because the doctors have found it hurtful to my disease to be more attentive to any thing. I doubt divers times I leave it out of tepidity when my health would permit. I have no settled manner of prayer, but only sit in the presence of God, acknowledging that I am and can doe nothing of my self. I represent some Mistery according to the time, or some words out of Holy Scripture, more conformable to ye disposition that I am in: I doe not use discourse, because God do so please to give me more light wth a sole remembrance then I can find from any discourse of my understanding …

… I have had more aridity within these 3 ycars then I can remember to have found in former times … I use no remedy only humble and rays[e] my self … Sometimes upon some words or inculatory prayers I am suddenly moved. I think these ariditys does most proceed after my own negligences, out of a temptation I have against faith. I seldome or ever read as much[24] as one leaf comes to because of the weakness of my head for wch I must often leave divine office. When I say it I must divert my self from ye sence of the words when I am not in arridity because I find so much yt it makes painful to goe forwards, I think that proceeds out of weakness: I have remarked yt I am soonest mooved to sensible devotion when I am weak.

… I am very negligent in examine of conscience, when I goe to Confession tis often with little sorrow … For Communion my only preparation is to acknowledge my unworthyness wth desire to write my self to God … The greatest hindrance I find is in dejection of mind or heaviness wch I cannot resist. In this disposition it seems to me that many things come cross and so am troubled upon small occasions wch at other times I should easily pass. In this disposition I am most distracted …[25]

---

[24] The words 'as much' are repeated in the original text, reflecting the natural errors of the copying process.

[25] The extract here omits around one page of the original text.

... I am naturally inclined to pride & sloth, and a sadness or fearfullness wth out grounds. I have been more subject to coller[26] then I am now ...

Another May
This month I have had more lively presence of God then in some former months, and more easily recollected in prayer ...

... the feast of ye Ascension and of ye Holy Ghost, being my cloathing and profession days, I found great joy in ye Misteries ...

Another June
I am often troubled in mind because I have not health to observe things according to my vocation.[27]

... I have been much given to sadness this month for the death of one of our Sisters and have yielded so much to this yt it has caused me to be much distracted. I find remedy in remembering it was God's voice to call her to himself.

July
... [I] have been inclined to murmur and shew my self pevish to ye religious ... My desires are so cold as tho I had neither soul or life, only in seasons find comfort, I have a God on whom I depend. ...[28]

Another January 1632[29]
I have found my self in continual aridity in wch I find peace of mind with ye remembrance that poverty of spirit wch I so much desire to obtain does not consist in self satisfaction.
    I have been very much harast upon some external business, so much yt for 3 or 4 days my mind was all ways upon it I did not perceive it, and after yt I did reflect that I was distracted being in ye same occasion I could not easily recollect my self ...[30]

... One morning the Provinciall came and calld for our dear Mother and the rest of the religious to the speak house[31] and gave them a sharp reprehension for their disobedience, telling them they were all excommunicated with many such like things. In the mean time, it rung the Conventuall Mass,[32] upon wch our d[ea]r Mo[the]r said to him, 'If your Revce

---

[26] Galenic theory claimed that a choleric temperament resulted from an excess of yellow bile and imbalance in bodily humours (comprising phlegm, yellow bile, black bile and blood) (see Aughterson, 1995, 41–66).

[27] The extract omits several lines from the original text.

[28] Around one page of text is omitted here.

[29] The compiler notes 'This ye only one that is dated' [with the year].

[30] The extract omits some 14 pages of text that continue in a similar vein, resuming with details in the third-person from the nun's later life.

[31] The speakhouse is the parlour area in which visitors are greeted by the religious who are within the enclosure and separated from the 'outsiders' by a metal grate.

[32] I.e., the bell rang to call the religious to Mass.

will have the goodness to say Mass & communicate the religious, we will come to yr Reve again', upon wch he did. And after Mass, meeting as appointed, our dear Mother said to the Provinciall very grauely, 'Good Father how comes it that yr Rev durst communicate excommunicated persons?' upon wch the Provinciall, tho dash'd, said smileing, 'O Mother, Mother, you are to[o] cunning for me', and indeed he said true for all the different methods they used to prevail upon her proued fruitless ...

... She had a singular gift of discerning spirits, and took particular care that those she received to be religious, should be such as our Holy Mother St Teresa in the book of her foundation[33] requires; and was very resolute in soon dismissing those she found unfitt for our Order but when she found persons that had some difficultys, but otherways very proper, she was wonderfully judicious in facilitateing their overcoming them, as the following example will show. A novice entering who had lived a long time in the world, very much according to her own will and satisfaction, found great difficulty in many little observances, amongst ye rest she said she could neuer be able to pull of[f] her own stockins. Our dear Mother made light of this, and told her the religious would most willingly do this for her, and according[ly] she orderd them to go every night to her in their turns, and the Novice lett them do it, till it came to the turn of our dear Mother and she going with great sweetness and unconcern, knelt down before her, offering this service, upon wch the Novice was so confounded that she threw herself at her feet ...
... [She was] naturally of a hott temper, yet had overcome herself so much, that she seem'd all meekness, and on this account the religious used to call her Moyses ...

... Upon great feasts when they made and sung spirituall songs or little spirituall actions, or extraordinary recreations, wch she much approued and seemd highly delighted with, yet she still used to add these words, 'Works, works, my dear children', endeavouring to turn all such occasions to the spirituall profit of herself and comunity ... Some days she would cause the religious to exchange meritts with one another, writeing for this end little billets which they drew by lot. This happened once to be between her Rece and our Venble Mother Mary Margaritt of the Angels[34] who recounted afterwards how carefull she was that day to avoid the least imperfection, for fear that our dear Mother Anne of the Ascension might be the looser. But tho she was free and easy in permitting innocent libertys, yet she was zealously exact as to the perfection of the vertues ...[35]

... Upon an occation, she was speaking to an English merchant who to try in what perfection she had languages he, without her perceiving it, passd from English to Dutch, French, Spanish and lastly to Latten, when after some discourse she was at a loss to answer readily, and so reflecting with herself said 'Why do you speak to me in Latten for I cannot speak it?' He answered 'I see you can Rd Mother, when you do not reflect it is so'.

... Our dear Mother was of a weak constitution, and exstreamly sickly, particularly the last 4 or 5 years of her life, the peace and tranquility with wch she bore it did evidently

---

33 This was written by Teresa de Jesus in around 1576 (see 1946 ed., *III*, xvii).
34 Margaret Wake: 1617–78 (Chapter 29).
35 Around five pages of the original text are omitted here.

shew her perfect conformity to the Divine will … Our Blessed Lord appeared to her with a heavey cross upon his shoulders, and told her that before she dyed she should feel something of wt he sufferd in that mistery. She made a painter draw a picture just in ye manner our Bd Lord had appeard to her, wch euer since we call our dear Mother's picture, and wch we still hold in great veneration …[36]

… Many other prodigies declare[d] to the community her approaching decease, as a full quire of voices, singing these words of the offices *Vide Surbam Magnum*, at other times instruments of musick … and at the instant of her happy death, one of the religious, being only absent[37] was awaked by a full quire of musick, and being very much afrighted, ran that moment to the Infirmary lamenting and saying 'Our dear Mother is dead, and you did not call me, as you promised', as in effect it was …[38]

Our illustrious Lord Bishop of Antwerp Gasper Neimus[39] to shew his singular affection and devotion to her, came and sung the solemn Mass, and preached her funerall sarmon, after which he interd her with his own hands, a favour he had neuer done to any before or after …

Their testimony appears wch you will find placed at the end of this brief account, brief I say for the misfortune of not having sooner recorded these things, but only in loose papers, and many of them losd and carryed to foundations, we are deprived of the knowledge and certainty of more important matters in order to this subject. In fine what is her[e] colected is but a little, she being a person universally admired by all, who had any knowledge of her; and the caracter those who had this happiness gave, was sufficient to make her memory venerated by al.

… After her death the religious had frequently recourse to her tomb in their necessitys, and by this means found great help and assistance, particularly in interior troubles.[40]

loose papers in our first Venble Mothers own hand

Reasons to shew that our Holy Mother made our Constitutions

Our Saint shews us in ye books wch she has writ that she has made Constitutions … The changes wch the Fathers of the Order introduced doe not tend to greaten perfection only to their greater authority over the religious as the thing in them selves doe shew. They write

---

36 Around five pages of the original text are omitted here.
37 I.e., she was the only Sister not there with the community around the deathbed.
38 The text informs us that she died on 23 December 1644, aged 56 years, 35 years professed.
39 Bishop of Antwerp 1634–51.
40 The extract omits around 20 pages of the original text, which mostly repeat details already given, and it resumes with claims that the friars falsified evidence in crucial Teresian manuscripts.

several things otherwise than they are, even the life and writings of our Holy Mother as appears for the books wch now are printed doe not accord with the old, and have blotted out some of our Holy Mothers own hand writing.

They have printed things in the life of Mother Anne of St Bartholomew wch I have often heard her to relate quite contrary.
Father Gratian the 1st Provinciall and who had been 10 years our Holy Mother's Confessor, they turn'd out of ye Order because he would not admit the changes[41] ...
Our Holy Mother makes no mention in any of her writings yt she did desire her monasteries should be under the Fathers ... The first article of the Constitutions, wch says that the religious are subject to ye Generall of ye Discaled, has been falsifyed in ye French translation as it appears by ye Spanish original.[42]

---

[41] This was Jerome of the Mother of God (Gratian: 1545–1614), spiritual director of Teresa de Jesus from 1571, who had faced a turbulent time in the face of these controversies. Although he was initially supported in his defence of Teresian reforms by the Papal Nuncio, when that office-holder changed in 1577, Gratian was censured. The 1580 Chapter General again granted canonical approbation to the Discalced, and Gratian became their Superior – but despite the support he received from John of the Cross (1542–91), amongst others, Gratian was admonished again in 1585, and charged with having introduced mitigations to the constitutions. The nuns vigorously resisted interference in their affairs, and obtained approval of Teresa de Jesus' constitutions from Rome. Again, the Nuncio protested, and excluded the nuns from the Order. It was said that Gratian's own exclusion in 1592 was based upon falsified evidence. He was commanded by papal authorities to join another Order, but found difficulty in being received, and his case was eventually re-examined by Clement VIII in 1596 who rescinded his sentence. To avoid further problems Gratian affiliated himself to the Calced Friars, and finally returned to Brussels where he died (*Catholic Encyclopaedia*). Teresa de Jesus recorded a vision of Jerome Gratian in 1575: '... a light appeared in the interior of my soul, and I beheld him coming along the road, happy and with a white countenance, it seems to me that so do all those who are in heaven. ... I heard: "Tell him to begin at once without fear, for his is the victory"'(*Spiritual Testimonies*, 1976 ed., 416).

[42] The Life ends with the inclusion of a copy of the letter from Teresa de Jesus concerning her constitutions; of a testament to the virtues of the convent by the General of the Order (Mathias of St Francis, 1621); of the letter from Thomas à Jesu demanding the burning of the constitutions (6 February 1622); of the Bulls of Sixtus V and Gregory XV confirming the nuns' rights (dated 5 June 1590, 17 March 1623); and of a declaration of John Materius, Bishop of Antwerp, to whom the religious gave obedience (13 September 1627).

Chapter 3

Teresa of Jesus Maria, Sister of Anne of the Ascension: Her Career and Remarkable Death

Since the Antwerp Lives are initially presented in order of profession, Elizabeth Worsley (1601–42), Anne of the Ascension's sister and her first novice at the convent, appears immediately after her in the annals (*A1*, 135–75). Their brother is also mentioned: '[He] was a religious of the Society of Jesus, and very zealous … particularly in the time of the plague at London converting many in that afflicting occasion … [He] was long confined in prison, and like to have sufferd martyrdom as many others did at that time in England' (*A1*, 30–31). He travelled to Italy at various times; and also attended Father Henry Morse at his execution (Hardman, 1937, 24), a relic from whose breviary was later brought to the Antwerp Carmel where it was much venerated and believed to effect cures, among them that of Margaret of Jesus (Margaret Mostyn: 1625–79; Chapter 31A). From the annals, it is possible, then, to gain a sense of the variety of religious experience available for members of one family within both active and contemplative arenas. This Life is included for that reason and because it gives some sense of the mobility of nuns between convents and how opinion of blessedness was spread.

The opening of Elizabeth Worsley's Life is typical of most of the accounts, giving basic family details. It is followed by a description of her religious career when she was sponsored for her entrance by the Infanta who sent women from court to attend the ceremony. Later, the nun moved between different Carmels, in 1624 from Antwerp to Bois-le-Duc, then again in 1629 from that town when it was under Protestant ('heretick') siege, eventually to Alost, founded in 1631.

Her death is described in some detail, and from its tone the account is probably transcribed from an obituary likely to have been circulated between convents in the Order. It uses the language of blessedness and of martyrdom – of St Lawrence and of Christ. After her death, Teresa of Jesus Maria was highly venerated and crowds gathered at the convent to view her body, which was, in line with general practice, exposed next to the grate so that it could be seen by members of the public from outside the enclosure, many of whom passed objects through to touch her corpse.

[*A1*, 133–75]

In the world Elizabeth Worsley, daughter to John Worsley Esq and Elenor Harve, native of the citty of Lovain in the Dukedom of Brabant, made her profession 18 June 1620, then 19 years old, and the first professed in this convent.

She was younger sister to our first dear Superior, Venble Mother Anne of the Ascension, in whose hands she made her profession ... about a month after our settling in this town, her mother dyed when she was very young ... [She was] brought up in a monastery where she improved her self in all good qualities fitt for a young lady, and when at fitt age was thence introduced to the Court of the Infanta, where she was for some time but her solid judgment and pious inclinations made her soon discover the vanity of all the grandeur of this world and the happiness and security of a religious life so that she resolved to follow ye example of her sister; which being made known to the Infanta she with much pleasure contributed to all that could make her enterance more solemn. She gave her a rich cloathing gown and was at ye expence of all that ceremony sending several ladys of her court to be present at her cloathing, ye chife of which lead her in, and we supose this Princes[s] added to her fortune.

... [She] may justly be term'd the 2nd pillar of this new edifice ...

... When the foundation of Bulduke [Bois-le-Duc] went out from hence she was chos by our Venble Mother to accompany Mother Ann of Jesus in this work, with the Dutch young ladys wch were admitted here[1] ... The town of Bulduke becoming heretick, they were oblig'd to remove the convent and, being a full community, could not be admitted all in one place they devided into tow branches – the one going to Cullen [Cologne] under the conduct of Mother Ann of Jesus, the other part, after great difficulties and opossition of the fathers of ye Order, our first Mother att last obtained of the Infanta leave for their settlement at Alost ... The religious unanimously elected for their first superior there Rd Mother Teresa of Jesus Maria ... & reelected her tell her happy death wch was on the 17 of November year 1642 ...[2]

... We most particularly perceived, when being in the greatest extreamity of pain, she lay for sometime quite like one without any sence, tho we perceived that some extraordinary things pass'd in her interior. She spoke a great deal butt it was so low and inward that no body could understand what it was, but comeing again to herself she spoke wth a clear voice these words: 'O what can man refuse to suffer?' ... and her torments was then

---

[1]   When she founded the Carmel in Antwerp, Mary Lovel had insisted that it was specifically for English women. In 1624, Dutch religious and some English nuns moved to a new convent as a result of her objections (Guilday, 1914, 365).

[2]   Around 40 pages of the original text are omitted here. These give an account of her virtues, learning, wisdom, etc. The extract resumes with details of her death, written as if from a witness account.

so vehement, as she declared herself, that her body found [seemed] to her as if it were striched out upon a glowing grid … She would say with great resignation 'It seems to me as if my breast was pearced with nails and all my flesh and internalls were pulld in peaces', which we found to be so in effect for she was consumed to nothing and her bones was only held toghether by the skin and sinnews …[3]

… It seemd in this nineth hour she went with our d[ea]r Lord into the garden, there to begin her approaching agony with a general courage inflamed like a seraphine, raysing herself up as lightly as if she would have flown to the combate, her countinance sweet & venerable and her face more beautiful then we had ever seen her before but particularly her eyes which even sparkled with brightness … wee kneeling round about her …

… The next day her body was brought into the quire and placed before the grate where it remaind tell Wednesday afternoon, and as her vertue and sanctity was held in great opinion in the town so it caused a great concern to people who flocked to the monastery, and it was wonderful to see the great devotion with which each one desired to have some thing that had tuch'd her body, so that there was things without number flung in at the grate and given in at the turn for this purpose, as beades, medalls reliquarys & c. … which lasted so long that when the body was put into the grave it was necessary to hold up the lid of the coffin that we might touch what was continuelly given …

---

3   Around one page of the original text is omitted here.

Chapter 4

Margaret of St Francis:
The Holy Simplicity of a Lay Sister at
Antwerp and Lierre

Margaret of St Francis (1594–1678) was 'in the world' Margaret Jonson, daughter to Jane (née Harrison) and William Jonson, of Bishopbrick in County Durham. She was the first lay sister to profess at Antwerp (on 31 December 1620) and she transferred to Lierre in 1648 when the new foundation began there. Accordingly, her Life appears in both sets of annals – at Antwerp in order of profession, and at Lierre in order of death – and there is interesting correlation between the accounts, though distinctive stylistic construction. Both texts compare the nun, more or less explicitly, to St Francis.

The Antwerp annals (*A1*, 425) also describe the manifestation after death of Anne of Jesus (recorded only as 'A Hollander of great note and quality', who professed in 1619), who appeared one morning to Sister Margaret on the steps of the convent crypt. That this vision occasioned little surprise, for either Sister Margaret or the nun who wrote the account, indicates how normalized such notions were within the convent. This event happened at Antwerp and must be dated, therefore, to the period between June 1646, when Sister Anne died, and 1648, when Sister Margaret transferred to Lierre.

A further Life (Chapter 19) provides details of the daily routine of a lay sister which we should assume was also the pattern followed by Margaret of St Francis.

───────────

[*A1*, 181–182]

… and tho' she could neither read not writ, yet [she] knew very well how to discover and contemplate God in his creatures. She had such a holy simplicity, that as she gatherd herbs in the garden, she would call the birds, and they would come to her hand. She was much devoted to the humble St Francis, and like one in an exstacy when she heard him spock of …

*

[*L13*.7, 30–31]

... Her parrence [parents] were honnest contrey people. She intered for a Lay Sister ...
She was on all occations repeating the storries of [St Francis'] life: on[e] could silldome
speake wth her but she would find somthing of this Saint's life ore practice to intermingel
in her discourses. Her mortification was most excempeler [exemplary] for she not only, in
her labours and worke, euer chouse the hardest part for herselfe, but in her deayett [diet]
she would ever take the scrapes and leavings for her portion ...

... Though her great years made her uncapable of much laboure, yet she was so faithfull
to God that she was never iddell ... and when she grew holy empotent that she could not
hear nor scarcs understand us when we spooke to her, [this] was on[e] of her greatest
mortifications, so much did she delight in the society of the sisters. If we pointed up to
heuen, she would be ouer ioyed ... It was her ussiall expretion, 'heuen, heuen' att the end
... When she did apprehend that she had commetted any emperfection, she would call her
selfe most contemptable names, and say 'This is I, fowle beast', and use to her selfe all
the terms of contempt emagenable ...

*

[*A1*, 425]

A while after [Sister Anne's] happy death, Sr Margaret of St Francis, a holy lay sister ...
rising in the morning to ring [the bell], this Rd Mother appeared to her comeing up the
dead cellar staires, as in her mantle and vail. This Sister said, without the least surprise
'Deare Ma Mere, are you there? What doe you want?' She answered 'Such and such
devotion for my deliverance out of Purgatory' and disappeared and was seen no more.

Chapter 5

Anne of St Bartholomew: Her Sight of the Infant Jesus Handing out Sugar-plums, and the Remarkable Discovery of Her Uncorrupted Body

This extract provides insight into early modern Carmelite mnemonic practice and discourses of the body. 'In the world', as the annals tell us (*A1*, 184), Ann Downs (1593–1674) was the daughter of Elizabeth Hongin and Robert Downs: she was born in Norfolk and professed at Antwerp on 14 April 1622. Her secular and religious life is marked by spiritual interventions – a voice calling her and, later, a vision of Christ in the convent dormitory.

In 1672, aged 79, at the celebration of the 50-year jubilee of her profession, she asked permission from her Superior 'to call to mind' events of her earlier, secular life. This request gives a sense of both her obedience and the habitual practice of self-forgetfulness within contemplative discipline. It also suggests the sort of recreation enjoyed in the convent: the Life includes a copy of a poem written for the celebration that shows the language used by the religious about their own profession, making analogies between the convent and a garden that recall the *hortus conclusus* in the Song of Songs as well as later sources, including Teresa de Jesus' own parables of the soul as a plant in need of water (*Book*, Chapters 14–19). Images of trees and birds, also familiar homiletic tropes, are found, too, in papers from 1769, commemorating the 150-year jubilee of the convent: 'when Fair Britannias fruitful island bore ... this the foundation of this happy day ... twice fifty years are past in times barren / since first Britannias doves took refuge here ...' (unclassified papers, now at St Helens). Such language was fairly commonplace: the Franciscan convent at Brussels, for example, is described as 'transplant[ed]' and the Prioress of the Poor Clares in Gravelines writes that 'we ... forsooke our Country, Parents and freindes ... [to] conjoine our selves unto those which labour in God's vineyard, namely in our afflicted Country of England' (see Walker, 2003, 118).

In *c*.1706, some 32 years after Sister Anne's death, her incorrupt body was discovered, along with others in the convent's dead-cellar. The way in which her corpse is described is highly informative. Posthumous preservation was seen to be a sign of potential blessedness, the discovery of which was likely to bring devotional as well as political advantage to the convent, attracting new professions and influential secular patrons. In her Life, Sister Anne's body is compared explicitly to that of

Margaret Wake (Chapter 29), who elsewhere was herself compared with Teresa de Jesus, thus setting up a chain of reverence. Statements from several witnesses are included in this Life, suggesting perhaps that the convent was laying the basis of claims towards veneration.

[*A1*, 184–192]

... When in the world, walking alone, she heard her self call'd [by a voice saying] 'amor, amor, amor' [love, love, love] ...

... Being in her cell, which she singularly loved, she saw the devine Infant Jesus going along the dormitary, from cell to cell, regaling his spouses who he found there, with sugar plumes [plums], which he seem'd to take out of his little apron, at which she could not forbear laughing aloud ...

In immetation of her glorious patron St Bartholomew she kneelt upon her knees a 100 times a day, and when grown so old and weak as to be led and carryed to Mass & c., she would use sweet intreates to be put upon her knees before every little picture or image which she pass'd, and after she was confined to her bed she would ask leave to pray upon her bare knees.

... At her jubely of 50 years she desired leave of ye Superiour to call to mind some passages of her former life to recreate the Community when they came to see her, for she was then confined in the Infirmary; and amongst ye rest she told the forementioned particulers of her vocation. I will add at ye end of this litle account the verses made upon the occasion of her jubely ...

She expired smiling on 30 May 1674 just after the octave of the Blessed Sacrament, above 80 years of age and more than 50 professed. About 32 years after her death several graves were opend to make space for others, and two religious were permitted to go down into the dead vault with the work men. Sister Margaret of St Ignatius[1] assured Sister Winifrede of St Teresa[2] that her body was perfectly whole, and her countenance so much her own that had she not seen her taken out of her grave, she could have been certain that it was she; and said should it not have been an intire body, but presently added 'Alass, it is now to[o] late', for the work men with great force broke her to peices, and flung her under a great heap of corrupted bones, where she lay 12 years ... after which time[3], again re-opening the vault, at this time we found the intire body of the Venble Mother Mary Margaret the fame of which was spread through the whole town ...

---

1 Margaret Andrew: 1641–1716 (see pp. 16, 22).
2 A lay sister, Elizabeth Lingen (1662–1740), who is central to much of the narration (see Chapter 19).
3 On the basis of this calculation the date would be *c.* 1718. The body was actually discovered in 1716.

[About two years after that] our present Rd Mother Mary Frances[4] gave leave that 3 or 4 of the religious[5] should rise very early in the morning and privately endeavour to find some peices of her, tho this leave she gave with great difficulty and apperhension, knowing ye many bodys that were put in that place … [They took out] a vast quantity of rotten moist bones & some not intirely consumed, but at last towards the bottom they discover'd a little hand & foot, which seemed to stick up in the further end of the place & takeing them out found them entire, wch incouraged them in their chearch [search]. And after some time they found the other hand and foot with the arm bones joyned to them, and all so the head, and tho they were all wett and slimy yet had not the least ill seint. Rd Mother, apperhensive for them, would let them goe no further, the whole place being so wett and slimy … It was not thought proper that the Community should then know it … They rejoyced that their labour had proved so successful: the aforesaid hands feet and head they put decently up in a cloath and lock them in a room, where they soon grew dry, & has an agreable smell like to that of our Venble Mother Mary Margaret [Margaret Wake], and ye same couler, but rather whiter … They are now kept locked up in a box made for that purpose, and has been shown to severall divines …

[On another occasion, the Reverend Mother Mary Frances, then Prioress, the present Reverend Mother Delphina of St Joseph, then Subprioress, and our deceased Sister Joseph Frances of the Blessed Trinity, and Sister Winefrid of St Teresa] went privately into the dead cellar and after a lot of labour and seeking drew out entire parts of the body of Mother Anne of St Bartholomew, ye rest being so mangled and so confounded with other bones and half corrupted body's that it was not possible to distinguish them from hers. In testimony of what is here said, we the underwritten have sign'd our names on the 27 of January 1721[6] Mary Frances of St Teresa and Winefrid of St Teresa. I [the] underwritten do attest that the Rd Mother Delphina above mentioned did design to set her name to this paper, but was prevented by death,[7] Percy Plowden, Society of Jesus, and Mary Frances of St Teresa

Poem for the jubilee of Anne of St Bartholomew, 1672

Full half a hunder'd years agoe
heavens husband man began to sow
in Carmells garden English seed
which doth the virgins dowry breed.
The first fair seed how it did grow
a nobler poets pen should show.

This seed most small in its own eye
to the world dead, did fructify

---

4   Mary Birkbeck (see Chapters 1, 15).
5   Delphina of St Joseph (Smyth/ Smith: Prioress 1720–21), Joseph Frances of the Blessed Trinity (Lucy Howard: 1681–1719) and Sister Winifred (see note 2).
6   Signed at this point.
7   Signed at this point.

... solid tree not founded on sand
can thunder stormes and winds withstand

Its vertues branches still increase
stably shadowed ore with peace
even uncorrupt it seems to be
the Lord of Hoasts dwells in this tree.
Thô death quite round about did hew
of no decay this tree, it knew

... an eagle and three nightingales did hither fly
with fervour singing soon they die

Sister Mary of Jesus, Sister Mary Francis Spensor, Sister Ursula of the Holy Ghost
Wakeman all dyed young[8]

... A silent dove ... the eagle ... there fellow nightingales are there...

Sister Mary of ye Angells,[9] Sister Anne of St Joseph Chamberlain,[10] a lay sister, both yn
living these 5 were her novices

---

[8]   These names were added in smaller writing to the text. I have identified the religious as
      Mary of Jesus (Mary Morgan), born 1627, professed 1651, only five years in religion (*A1*,
      468); Mary Francis (Mary Spencer), born 1626, professed 1652, died of smallpox (*A1*,
      470); Ursula of the Holy Ghost (first name not recorded; Wakeman), who also died of
      smallpox, in 1650, whilst still a novice.
[9]   Again the names have been added: Mary of the Angels (first name not recorded; Harcourt:
      1631–c.1687) professed in 1651 (*A1*, 466).
[10] Anne Chamberlain (c.1623–1709), who professed in 1652 (*A1*, 471).

Chapter 6

Catherine of the Blessed Sacrament: The Vocation of a 'Poor Imperfect Religious' who Relished Patched Clothing

According to the Lierre annals, Catherine Windoe (1608–66) was the daughter of Jane (née Keyn[e]s) and John Windoe, from 'Compin-halle, Summersettsheer neer wymouth'. She entered the convent when she was only about 13 years old, and professed 'when she was turn'd of 16 on ye 21 of October in ye year 1623'. This was an unusually early age for both entry and profession, special permission for which was granted because of her 'fervent desires': the Rule states that there should be no admission before the age of 17. Initially, like other Carmelite religious, she had considered joining the Poor Clares at Gravelines, where she had an aunt, but she was drawn to Antwerp by reading Teresa de Jesus' *Book* – a commonly-mentioned factor in inspiring vocations.

The Antwerp account combines first- and third-person narration, the somewhat remote tone of the latter no doubt reflecting the fact that the writer had no personal knowledge of this religious. In 1648 she was one of the group of nuns who transferred to Lierre, so an account of her life appears in the papers of both convents. She expressed special affection for Anne of the Ascension, and a letter from the latter, as well as a scapular prepared by her for Sister Catherine, is included here (Appendices 3B, 3C).

The Lierre Life is far more personal. It describes her terms of office as Sub-Prioress and Sacristan (duties of which are listed on p. 252), as well as her particular devotions and humility, a virtue commonly enough emphasised in the Lives, here with close descriptions of her personal characteristics that nicely illustrate the immediacy of this Life. The text, dated to *c*.1666 when Sister Catherine died, appears to be in the hand of Margaret of Jesus (Margaret Mostyn: 1625–79; Chapter 31A), Prioress at Lierre from 1655–79.

[*A1*, 195–200]

She has left her vocation writ in her own hand which is as followeth

My vocation to religion

I have had a desire to become religious ever since I had the use of reason … by ye good education my mother gave me … She spoek much in commendation of a religious life wch at that time she was moved to by ye many letters she received from a sister of hers who was newly become a religious. Her letters my mother would be often reading to me, wherein I conceived so very great delight that, allthô I was but a meer child, I gladly left all childrens sport to hear related …

[A priest] gave me notice of our Bd Mother's Order & gaue me pictures of her & her life to read … which inclined me so ardently to imbrace our holy institute … so that at the age of 12 I left my friends and country with such excess of content that all admired it, only at the instant of parting with my parents & some other dear friends whom I loved extreamly I felt great resentment … [Strengthened by God] I went my journey with unspeakable satisfaction …

I came to Graveline, where my aunt which I spock of in ye beginning was a religious woman of St Clares order, where I stay'd a fortnight or three weeks, tell such time that the gentlewoman, my companion, came there. I was entertained with so much love as if I had been ye sister of each one in ye monastery … but yet I could never be moved with any desire to stay there. Notwithstanding my mother told me when I parted from her that it would be as gratfull to her that I remained with my aunt … she left me to my own choise. I thought them very rediculous, that would sometimes be asking me why I would not remain there, I gave them such short answers that they troubled me not much with it … We went on our journey, and be ye way we mett with the superiour of our Order, who was so delighted to see one so young come with so great a resolution that he dispenced with my years and gave me leave to enter …[1]

… There was in the town at this time 2 English gentlewomen, acquaintances of my mother, who seeing me by chance and understanding ye cause of my comeing, came to visit me & used many powerfull perswations to with draw me from my resolution … [I] shew'd my self much displeased at their words & after that time could never be brought to see them, much less to speak to them tell I was within ye monastery …

… When I was cloath'd I beseech'd Allm God not to permitt ye remembrance of my friends to distract me … [and] never thought of any creature in the world no more then if I had never lived with others then those in the monastery …

The vocation of this happy innocent soul seems most wonderfull … She lived there about 30 years with a constant fervour and zeal of all regular observance, and then was sent out subprioress to the foundation of Leire where she died most happily.

---

[1] Around one page of the original text is omitted here.

*

[*L13*.7, 12–22]

... Her great and feruent desiers moued Superiours to dispence wth her yonge years, and contrarie to our ordinarie custume, addmitt'd her to Clothing ... and noth wth standing most of thess nouices were persons of ripe years [16 years old], and very great abillitis, they had soe high esteeme of her that they called her the Angelle of the Nouiship. She was soe constant and diligent in the Quier, and applied her selfe soe seriouslie to learne her Latine, and how to singe and say, that wth in some munths her mistries imployed her to teach the other Nouices ...

... She begane this couent [at Lierre] in the office of Subprioriss, wher she lieued [lived] 18 years and all most two months to the euident increase of her owne spirituall aduancment, and singular proffet to all her religious sisters and those that treated [conversed] wth her. She was alsoe in this new planttation imploy'd in the office of Sacristen and keepeing the religious cloths, both wch offices she executed wth much diligence & care. She beinge the oldest in proffestion in our monisterie att Lier, it belonged to her offten to proseed in the communitie,[2] wch office she performed very exactlie, beinge a person of soe much spiriet, that though her compleaction [complexion] and body was of the wicker [weaker] sort, yet till her very last sickness she was euer in the communitie first and last ...

... Upon those days she did not receaue sacramentallie, she was obserued to be more diligent in taking all occations to speake of Hollie Communion, and offten times to addore the Bd Sacrament, wch practice she had in such perfection, that she was indeed att all-times observed neuer to passe by the Quier wth out kneeling and addoring by kissing the ground ...

... She would singe and say in the Quier the clearest and loudest of us all, and if we did seeme so to admier how she could doe it, she would answear, 'I haue now noe time to thinke of my selfe; perhappes this may be my last feast'. Her modestie and affabiltie in her conversation, and her playne religious behauiour was singular; her countenence chierfull and pleaseing shewing her interiour peace, wch was of soe great eddification both wthin, and wthout, that all secular persons that euen knew little of spiriet, looked upon her for a saint ... She would offten wish, 'Oh that I were but handsome handid that I might be worthy to serue our Mother and the Sisters in any thinge' ...

... She would say, 'what a tender mother is holie religion. I haue bin a poore emperfect religious aboue this 40 years, and I haue neuer taken care for any thinge, nor haue neuer wanted any thinge. How many better then I haue not bread to eatt; and had thay bin in this place where I am, would haue serued God infinittly better then I haue don' ...

... She could not abbide to heer any one say pached cloths were trouble-some, for it was her ioy to haue any old thing wch anothere had used, saying 'I will striue to wear this

---

2   Details in other papers also suggest that the religious processed, and sometimes sat, in order of seniority, either of age or of profession.

as perfectlie as such a Sister hath done. Oh that I could loue God in this old habbitt, ore peticott & c, as such a person hath done', and the like religious expreessions she would make, to[o] longe to express heer ...

... When it was time of recreation she esteem'd it the most perfect to be there, for, as she would offten say, to be in Communitie is of more proffet & more perfect then all our privat devotions ... and what disspossion soe euer she was in, one might playnlie obserue she did her best to complie and recreatt the religious, and she would offten upon occasions tell her Superiour that in her opinnion thoss whoe loued not recreation, loued not mortification ...

I cannot omett one excample amongest many: att sertine times when it was the Priorisse feasts ore the lik[e], accordinge to our custum the religious makes for recreation some little actions, ore representation of deuotion.[3] Att those times, what part someuer [so ever] they gaue her, she was as serious to performe it well, and would take as much paynes to do it perfectlie as if there were att that time noe othere thinge to be done to gaine heauen ... and though she were the Antiontis [oldest] in the conuent and was forced to use thess occations offten spectacles, yet it was of great edification to see her euen more readdy then the yongest religious in the house ...

... I must not omet also her constant mortification in point of quriossetie [curiosity]: if she chanced but to marke ore cast up her eyes quriousslie [curiously] as she passed, she allways spocke her fault, and hath often tould her Superiour that when she had forgot her-selfe in marking any thinge as she passed about the house (nay euen though it were when she saw her Superiour pase) if she marked what she did ore sayd, she could not be recollected in prayer till she had spocke her fault and done some penance for it. This shews her great tenderness of contience, and the neere unione there was, between this pure soule and Allm God ...

... [If she] conceaued her Superiour was disspleased, she would presentlie come to exposse her-selfe to the reprehention and acknowledge her fault, whethere she were guiltie ore noe. And when some-times the othere religious would be saying to her, 'Str Catharine, why doe you goe to our Mother so soone? Can not you expect a whyle, it is but a babele [trifle], our Mother will haue for-goetten it'. She would reply 'Marrie, God-forbid, should I thinke our Mother displeassed and leaue to goe to her. I had rathere haue 10 Chappters then the paine of conceaueing my Superiour were liss pleased wth me. When my superiour is displeased, God is displeased' – and trulie this was soe constantlie her practice that she allways declared herselfe wth great candour and sinceritie of hart, and where she found most shame ore difficulltie there she was readiest. She neuer spoeke to any externe att the gratts [grates], be they siculars ore spirituall person, but she allways gaue a faithfull account to her superiour of euery word that she could remember had passed ...

... [She was] unwilling to treat with any stranger of spirituall matters, for she would allways say 'I haue a Confessarious and a Superiour suffisiant, if I follow them, to carrie my soule to heuen. It is time for me that grow old to doe much and talke little' ...

---

3   The performance of devotional plays or pageants for recreation is often mentioned in the papers, particularly for feast or profession days.

... She shewed in her last sickness how habituall this vertue [obedience] was to her, for when she was out of herselfe in the hight of a burning feuour [fever] [she sought] some little refrishment by casting out her armes. The religious present would onlie say 'Sister Catharine, our Mother desiers you will keep yr armes in', she would presentlie rever[s]e them againe ...

... Her Prioriss ... [initially] desiered her to obstaine [abstain] from drinking as much as she could. Affter-wards, her sickness growing to a continuall high feaure, she would neuer call for any refrishment, but when the religious would offer her bier, ore othere things for her solies [solace], she would aske, 'Would our Mother haue me drinke?' and when they answeared 'Yeas', and that the glass was att her mouth, she would pull it a way, saying 'Doe you thinke our Mother had rathere I should obstaine?' And till they assured her it was the will of her Superiour that she should refrishe her-selfe, she would not admitte of any thinge ...

[At 4 pm, 27 September 1666] ... she answearing the *Latina* (said by our Confessarious) to the last gaspe, gaue up her holie soule in to the hands of our deare Redemire wth soe sweet a continance (fixzed upon the Crussifix and upon a picture of our Bd Lady wth the Sacred Infant in her armes) that we could not perceaue by any growne [groan] when she departed. Her eye-strings[4] neuer brocke, but her corpes remained wth a most sweet smilling countinance, giueing us all a deepe since of the great puritie of her holie life ... God in his infiniet mercie grant we may immitat her vertus ... Amen.

---

[4] I.e., the sinews that raise the eyelids.

Chapter 7

Anne of St Teresa:
Her Career at Various Convents,
Her Terror about an Apparition and Her
Instructions for the Enclosure
of a Convent

Anne Leveson was born in 1607, the daughter of Thomas Leveson and Mary (née Comberford), of Staffordshire. She professed at Antwerp on 16 July 1627 and was chosen in 1643/44 to go to the new foundation at Dusseldorf, and afterwards to Newburgh. Among her papers copied into the annals is a description of the ceremonials associated with the enclosure of a convent, together with various other letters, including one in which she tells of her alarm at hearing of an apparition of a soul sent to Purgatory for failing to keep silence. It is possible to understand from this account how real the concern was for other religious who mention their fears in this respect: Mary of the Holy Ghost (Mary White: 1604–40), for example, 'some 3 days before she dyed, she was troubled because she had spoken after Compline tell she was told that it was not silence that night' (*A1*, 205).

This Life indicates the political conditions within which some new foundations were made: it mentions 'Prince Philip William Palsgrave' (Wittelsburg: 1615–90), Elector of the Palatinate from 1685 (see also p. 27), who used the period of his governance to make new Carmelite and other foundations. The text refers to the costs incurred by the new convent, which suggests that, despite the generosity of insistent secular patrons, the Order itself still met various expenses, sometimes when it could ill afford to do so.

[*A1*, 221–237]

She hath left her vocation to religion writ in her own hand as followeth:
  My father offerd me freely to Allmighty God to serve his divine majesty in a religious course before I was yet born, but I knew not this, nor even seriously thought of any such state. One day, hearing a certain person discourse of religious … it pleased our mercyfull

God to touch my heart ... that I could not find any rest or repose of mind tell I firmly resolved to imbrace a religious life ...

... A Father of the Society who was my Confessor ... gave me notice of our Blessed Mother's Order: from that instant I felt such a cordiall love in generall to it that I could not endure to think of any other place but our monastery, only, in case I might not be admitted here, I thought I would force my self to accept the place which was offered at Graveline [with the Poor Clares], but ye thought was often accompanyed with aboundance of tears ... I acquainted my parents with my resolution who seem'd to give deaf ear to my petition ... My father answered me that if I continued constant some years, he would then begin to think of giving his consent ... & so there pass'd more then tow years before I obtained leave to come over from my parents ... Upon St Barthomes day [24 August] in ye year 1625 [my Confessor] told me that ye convent was content to admitt me, but the unspeakable joy which this news caused me far exceedeth what I am able to express ...[1]

... The year 1643 or 1644 when she was chose [by Anne of the Ascension] for the great work of founding at Dusseldorp ... she was accompany'd by Reverend Mother Lucy of St Ignatius[2] ... [The community] was extreemly beloved & admired both by religious & seculars, particularly by Serenissime Prince Philip William Palsgrave ...[It was decided that] ye religious from this house should be ye first that introduced our holy monastery St Teresa's Order into Germany & increase it there ... The foremention'd Prince ... in ye year 1657, gave to Reverend Mother Anne of St Teresa a house at Munsterfelt for the increase of our holy Order, where, ye year following, she went with one quire nun, named Sister Mary of St Joseph (one of those that is now intire here) & one lay sister to take possession in order to found a monastery. In the year 1659 she returned to Dusselldorp ...

She desired they would free her from being their Prioress ... [and] being now more at liberty [she] sett herself with a new zeal to ye compleating of ye foundation of Munsterfelt, where she proceeded as Vicaress[3] ... She returned again this same year to Dusselldorp where, ye day before they were chose the religious for ys new monastery, the Duke & Duchess made her a most friendly kind visit & order'd their coaches and carts to carry ye religious & their bagage to Munsterfelt, so that upon ye 9th of June ye year 1659, at 9 a'clock in ye morning, Rd Mother Anne of St Teresa with 7 more religious parted from the convent, & was carry'd by ye orders of the Duke & Duchess to the place, where they kissd the hands of the aforesade Princes & their children ... The Duchess gave to each one of ye religious a picture, writ upon with her own hand ... Upon the 3d of August 1659 [they] shutt up their inclosure[4] ...

In this time the Duke was very impatient for ye design'd foundation of Newburgh, & he admireing & esteeming so highly the 3 English that had come from this monastery to Dusseldorp, desired [their] move from hence for ye foundation of Newburgh ... [So she] return'd here [to Antwerp] & carryd back with her 5 of our religious namely [Anne of the

---

1   Around one page of the original text is omitted here. The extract resumes in the third-person.
2   Catherine Bedingfield: 1614–50.
3   An office held in the interim, until a new Prioress was elected.
4   Presumably using the ceremonial that appears below.

Ascension,[5] Anne of Jesus,[6] Anastasia of Jesus,[7] Clare of the Annunciation,[8] Margaret of Joseph[9] ... so that in ye year 1661 these religious went to Newburgh with Mother Magdalene[10] & some others from Dusseldorp, to begin this convent founded by the Duke tho we find in our accounts that we were at about one 100 florence [florins] expence at ye time of their going out, besides a yearly pention of 240 florence for severall years ... [11]

A letter to Sr Augustine from Anne of St Teresa, concerning an apparition of a black sister[12]

... Now, my dear sister, give me leave to tell you what has happened not so far from hence, within 14 days: it is that a black sister [a Benedictine] hath apear'd to a certain person the very night after her death & said it was high time to pray for her, she being to remain in Purgatory a whole year for not having esteem'd silence.

... I confess this example struck a terrour into us all when we heard it, especially the party haveing been only a black sister whose Rule I conceive does oblige to little silence & ours to so much, that it makes me make many good purposes to be more exact hereafter & so much ye more as we know this wch I have related to be no fable or imaginary fantasy, but really to have happen'd to one most worthy to be credited ... [13]

Manner of making Publick Inclosure in ye first begining of a Monastery

A day or two before, the church and house, with the garden, must be hollow'd [hallowed] ... you will find the manner of blessing a house more punctuall if you can have a book call'd a Rituall: I beleive the Jesuitts will have such a book.

The religious usually adorn the church and alter the day before, & let the remonstrance[14] be brought into the cathedrall or principall church, that a consecrated Hoste may be placed in it.

---

5   Catherine Keyn[e]s: 1619–78.

6   Anne Barker: 1620–?

7   Dorothy Wakeman: 1619–*c*.1659.

8   Catherine Darcy: 1610–94.

9   Margaret Goodland: born 1632.

10   Magdalene of St Joseph (Magdalene Bedingfield: 1620–83): her uncorrupted body was also discovered at Newburgh (see p. 26).

11   Around two pages of the original text are omitted here.

12   The letter copied here, dated 25 October 1650, is addressed to 'Sister Augustine', presumably Augustine of St Anne (Ann Bedingfield, 1623–*c*. 1659: *A1*, 383).

13   Around six pages of the original text are omitted here. These include fragments of letters, including one dated 18 September 1660: '... I pray you writ to Rd Father Saddler, inquire how old my Dear Mother is, allso rightly how old I am for I only guess at my age' (the significance of which enquiry becomes clear in the details of a processional which follow). The extract resumes with a copy of a letter from 1661 that describes the enclosure ceremony.

14   I.e., the monstrance, the receptacle into which the consecrated host is placed.

Upon the day you intend to inclosure, all the religious with mantles and great vailes must be carry'd in coauches to the church where they place themselves in quire, the eldest next to the alter, then the wax candles (which must before have been brought to the church) must be lighted & by ye custor or other person, given to each religious. Then Mass is sung or said, wch being ended, the Prest or Prelate, the sacramental host being in the remonstrance, kneeleth down & beginneth *Veni Creator*,[15] wch must be followed by ye musick. This being ended, the Prelate giveth the benediction then all rise up and the Channons [canons] & other religious, if present, goe in procession before the Blessed Sacrament & as soon as ye Priest goeth from the alter, the Prioress alone & the other religious, tow and two in order (the eldest first), to the inclosure gate.

In time of this procession, the Priest & others sing *Pange lingua*,[16] *O Gloriosa Domina*[17] and such hymes of joy. The bells of the church wherein the procession was begun must allso ring tell you come to ye monastery, & such other demonstrations of joy and triumph, the more the better; and next yr religious followeth the Duke and Duchess & then other people. When the procession is near the monastery such as went before the Blesed Sacrament standeth in ye middle, so that you may pass of each side into the inclosure, & when you are all enter'd you kneel down & receive yr benediction of the Blessed Sacrament, wch ended you shutt your gate and the Priest goeth to the alter & begineth *Te Deum Laudamus*.[18] Then your great bell doth first ring, I doubt not but other churches will allso accommodate so happy a procession with ringing where you pass. *Te Deum* you sing in quire, wch being ended the Priest singeth the versicle & prayer of the Bd Trinity, then begineth the Mass. You are allso to have a sermon fitt for such a solemnity. In this Mass you are all to communicate that so your first sustenance in yr inclosure may be the food of eternall life.

When all is so far concluded, your Rce, with ye other religious, kisses the hand of the Duke & Duchess by way & with other expressions of gratitude for their many and noble favours.

Your Rce must apoint one to keep your church door shutt tell you come, otherwise you will have it so full of the vulgar sort & little place will remain for such as accompany you, & to open it & light the candles upon the alter in time and good order.

Your maid or lay sister, you must also leave within the monastery, that she may open the inclosure door when you are near at hand, & allso ring the great bell when *Te Deum* is sung.

The Duke, Duchess & other principle persons, are to have lighted candles in yr procession, the more the better and for your profitt.

Being the [Duke] is to remain with you some months as I hear, I suppose it will be tell your inclosure is made, wch if it is to be it will be best, & the honour belonging to him to carry the Blessed Sacrament and perform ye other principle ceremonys as your Superior and thereby a Prelate.

---

15 '*Veni Creator Spiritus*' ('Come, holy spirit, creator blest') the opening lines of an ancient Latin hymn.
16 'Sing my tongue ...', the opening line of a processional hymn.
17 'O glorious lady ...', another processional hymn.
18 'We praise you, O Lord ...', the opening lines of a hymn of praise.

After all ceremonys ended & you alone, you congratulate each other in our dear desired inclosure.

My dear Mother to obey your command I have writ these particulars …

I am very busy in the Ceremoniall and should be heartily glad it were better writt … neither so far as I understand the language hath it a good stile, but the sense is plain & clear to be understood, so I hope it will prove of comfort and service to your Rce, and your charity will excuse other defects and wants.

I believe and it is allso other's opinion, that sister A.M.[19] will hardly come to right again, since ye last brunt [of illness] I writ to your Rce of, we cannot absolutly know if it [is] an impostum [an abscess] she hath had. Sister Mary of St Joseph is allso very ill of a great catar wch allmost took her to ye other world, in the night she is hugely faint & weak.

… Munsterciffe ye 20 of June 1661 Anne of St Teresa

---

[19] The name appears thus in the text: this religious has not been identified.

Chapter 8

Agnes of St Albert:
Her Overwhelming Sense of Vocation
that Led Her to Break into the Convent

Agnes Divine Roosendaell (1615–42) was a native of Antwerp, the daughter of Theodorus Roosendaell and Agnes Martins. Though the religious at Hopland had undertaken in November 1623 only to admit English women (see Chapter 3, note 1), Agnes of St Albert was one of several Sisters from the Low Countries who had joined the convent, professing on 31 January 1632 after a remarkable struggle in which her family vehemently opposed her plans, and sought every means to stop her becoming a Carmelite. The extract describes her determination that led her to break into the convent, semi-clad in order to fit into the turn, to the surprise of the nuns who discovered her and to the extreme consternation of her family.

This incident sheds light on conceptions of enclosure: imprisoned at home by her brother, she considers that domestic walls will fall down, enabling her to pursue her wish to be freely contained. The text reveals the dialectic between inner/outer, and claustration/freedom, and indicates the dilemma of a woman who wished to pursue a vocation against the wishes of her family, presumably in this case for financial reasons.

[*A1*, 263–275]

A short account was writ of her soon after her happy death and is as followeth…

… Between 13 and 14 she was placed for education (both her father and mother being dead) in a certain monastery of religious women in Brabant, of an ancient & famous Order … The religious of this monastery where she was were not only desirous, but earnest, to continue her amonghest them, and no wonder, for she was a most amiable creature both in body and mind, as also her fortune was very advantagious …

… She heard a certain sermon … where a particular mention was made of [St Teresa] … and then she gott her Life and read it more than once …

She then came soon home to her brother (who had taken care of her in place of her father), and she was placed by him in a choice schoole for a further advantage in education, where persons of condition were brought up, for the learning of such qualityes and language as might be of use and honor to her in the world ...

... She understood by an interiour way, and as expressly as if it had been utter'd by words, that she should 'throng herself in the English Monastery without speaking any more of it to any creature'. Now when once her friends and kindred began to suspect by what way she meant to walk ... they resolved to use the harchest meanes, and shutt her up in her brother's house, in such sort as that she was not suffer'd so much as to stir once abroad in many days; and some who were acquainted with their proceedings affirm them to have been so extream, as that their threats might easyly have endanger'd her more ways then one ... They [her family] declared that such obstinacy could not proceed from her self, but that certainly she was directed by some ill spirit ... [She told them] she feared them no more then so many flyes, and that tho they should shutt her up into ten walls, she made no doubt at all, but that in Gods good time they would all be ready to fly open to make way for the execution of her good desires ...

... She was extraordinarily moved and inflamed whensoever she did but come in to the very sight of the House ... but now once, as it fell out to be the last time, she came to the monastery in a morning with a firm resolution [to enter] ... When she arrived they were all att Mass, so [she] fear'd there would be no possibility of speaking to them at that time ... She was in pain her friends should miss her if they observed her to be absent to[o] long. A thought cast it self into her mind, that her only way would be to convey herself into the turn, and by that means to wind herself into the monastery without the privity of any creature in the whole world ... that the Rd Mother and religious would be moved to take compassion of her when they saw what a shift she had made to get in. And now putting her self upon the exploit, and having laid her upper garments aside, [she] crowded herself into the turn, which yet she did with difficulty enough because the place is incommodious and straight, and tho she were but 16 years of age and farr from being of full growth att that time, yet she made a hard shift, and turned herself in.

As soon as ever she was in the monastery, she felt her whole heart full of joy. ... The Porteress being then, by accident, not verry far and hearing an extraordinary noise and busseling about the turn, went towards it, and seeing a young creature there in secular attire, half uncloathed, found the sight very surprising and ran presently to tell Mother Prioress of it, who, with other religious coming from the quire, hasten'd towards the place, and saw this young creature there upon her knees and begging with her hands held up to heaven that for Almighty Gods sake they would have compassion upon her, and receive her; and the self same diligence she used to everyone of the religious, who by this time was order'd to injoy their severall parts of this strange spectacle.

The first thing which the monastery of Antwerp did was instantly to acquaint the Lord Bishop of Antwerp ... with the strange unexpected accident ... [He] was greatly moved by it ... and by degrees came to give way that she might be received ... But her friends and relations on the other side gave themselves a very contrary part and grew into a great deal of passion, and even rage, and threatened ... they would gett her out by meanes of the Popes Internuncio [the Papal ambassador] ... The Reverend Mother, hearing here of, sent them word that they should not need to take so much pains, for if it pleas'd them to come to the gate of the monastery she would cause it to be sett wide open, and intreate the party [Sister Agnes] to come thither ...

Now with this they were extreamly well satisfyed, and disposed themselves to receive that great satisfaction; but on the other side, when Mother Prioress informed the party of what had passed ... and was now ready to open the gate and bring her to it, and there leave her in perfect liberty to doe what she liked, the poor creature fell into a great passion of weeping ... When afterwards she was brought but to the speak house (for her friends must be content with that when they found that she would in no case be brought to the gate without the unseemly violence of dragging an innocent and tender virgin thither by strong hand) ... her suspition of their opposition [was] even beyond reason ... even to be affraid of impossible things, as if for example they would and could have pull'd her out through the grate. And therefore, when she was brought to the speak house, she stood at one side of the iron grate ... and yet the poor creature was so apprehensive of their violence that she would not so much as come near the very grate ... [They] used deep conjurations with many fair promises, but all served for nothing ... & she gave them so impertinent answers to all their propositions ...

... She earnestly did persist to have her hair cutt of[f], which, since it could not be granted at that time by the Mother Prioress and the religious, she quickly found meanes to doe it her self ... She moved all the religious to tears, and so her request was att last granted. Her relations, finding then that there was no other remedy left, grew to be satisfyed, but in the mean time their disgust had been very great ... for her fortune and meanes was such as prevailed towards a desire to hope for it themselves ...

Chapter 9

Clare of the Annunciation and Delphina of St Joseph: Two Religious Linked by Marvellous Events

These two religious are associated by what were taken to be miraculous signs connected with the death of one and the profession of the other. Sister Delphina knew of Sister Clare only through her 'dead bill', the obituary notice circulated after the death of a nun. In a situation in which numbers at convents were limited by the constitutions, to ensure sufficient provision could be maintained, such a notice suggested that there may be a 'vacancy' – and this was the case for another religious (Chapter 16), who was also thus encouraged in pursuing her vocation.

Clare of the Annunciation (Catherine Darcy: 1610–94) was the daughter of Henry Darcy and Frances (daughter to Sir Edward Monninges), of Northamptonshire. She professed in January 1640 amid 'sweet odours of linen', and the papers give details of her funeral and her subsequent appearance, in a dream, to Mary Xaveria of the Angels (Chapter 28). Before her death in April 1694, Sister Clare had predicted the arrival of her replacement – Delphina of St Joseph (Cath[e]rine Smyth/ Smith of Durham: 1677–1721), who professed in July 1695.

These Lives illustrate, as in so many incidents, the close associations between the religious who occupied each other's lives and spaces, in dying and in dreaming. Sister Delphina, whose niece also joined the convent (Chapter 24), was a witness to other dramatic events at Antwerp as one of a group of religious who discovered the incorrupt bodies of Anne of St Bartholomew (Chapter 5) and Mary Margaret of the Angels (Chapter 29).

[*A1*, 335–377]

I shall putt down her funerall ceremonys as are noted down, 1694:

This year dyed our dear Sister Clare of the Annunciation. Being Good Friday, the pardon [bell] was rung for her next day. After ye community had wish'd the good feast in the recreation, between 4 and 5 in the afternoon, 5 priests came in to bury her. They sung the responces and performed all the usuall ceremonys of buryall, but no Requiem Mass nor office of the dead in the community.

On Wednesday in Easter week the funerals were kept. We had Requiem Masses from the half hour before 6 till near a 11; a hers [a canopy over the bier] was raised of white stuff with a satten cross and white lilly topp as they use. The sung Mass was rung with both the bells together, two peals, 4 candles on ye corners, but none knelt there as when ye body is exposed, 4 chantresses at Mass. When Vespers was done we sung the Office of the Dead. Att 4 a clock the Cannons came and sung the responses with the usual ceremonyes: the community stood within ye seats with lighted candles till all was ended and the priests gone out again. Upon Thursday we began the processions, which lasted 9 days.[1]

... What followeth is taken out of the writings of our Venble Mother Mary Xaverius of the Angells, concerning this holy religious ...

...I often beggd of her but most particularly (a month before her death) that when she came to heaven she would recommend me earnestly to St Xavier ... About six weeks after as I remember [mid-April–May 1694] she appeared to me in my sleep and I cannot doubt of it by what followed, otherwise I am not apt to beleive dreams. I think it was about one in the morning, that I thought this religious was represented before me in my cell. Att first I was afrighted, knowing she was a spirit, but att length I resolved to take so much courage as to speak to her. Then calling upon Sister Clare, so she was named, [I] asked if she were in Heaven ... [and] if she had been to Purgatory. She said she had been there some time ... she told me Purgatory was a sad place and that one of the greatest torments was the sight of the devils.

Its impossible to express the change I found in myself ... With that I thought I saw St Xavier there, as it were on high over me and protecting me ... I cannot express the excess of joy I felt in my soul att that time ... I awaked and found my self much depleated but in great deuotion, and methinks like one come out of another world ...

*

[*A1*, 547]

[Delphina of St Joseph] was a pentioner in the English Augustines at Bridges [Bruges] and accidently came to know of our Order and house by the dead bill of Sister Clare who, a little before her death, had fortold the comeing of a novice whose name was Cathrine. About the same time one of the religious there gave her a little book of our H[oly] Father St Joseph to whom she had allways a very singular devotion ... She found how our Holy Mother St Teresa had very much advanced the honour of this glorious saint ... and thus also became much devoted to our H[oly] Mother, and informing her self more particularly of her holy Order, was moved with it that she perferr'd it to where she was ... She had 2 sisters then living, both religious, one a Poor Clare, ye other a Dominicaness, who desired much to have her with them, but she earnestly beg'd admittance here and was the first that enter'd affter the death of the aforesaid Str Clare ...

---

[1] The extract omits around 30 pages from the original text that mention her devotions and humility, among other aspects of her piety.

Chapter 10

Anne of St Maria and Tecla of St Paul: Childhood Friends in Religion, One a Favourite of the King

These two religious were childhood friends who joined the convent at the same time, and their Lives appear one after the other in the annals.

Anne of St Maria was born Anne Harcourt (1624–78), daughter to Francis Harcourt and Dorothy (daughter to Sir Alexander Brett), of Staffordshire. Anne's birth was attributed to the miraculous intercession of St Winifred whose shrine at Holywell in Flintshire her parents visited in 1622, after which a son was born, dying in infancy. The family returned again the following year, when Anne herself was conceived (Seguin, 2003, 6). She professed as a Carmelite at Antwerp on 28 August 1641, and she was Prioress at Hoogstraeten from August to September 1678, having held that position at Hopland from 1659 to 1665.

Tecla of St Paul (Catherin Clifton: 1624–71) came from a background of similar status: she was the daughter of Cuthbert Clifton and Dorothy (daughter to Sir Francis Smith), of Lancashire. She should have professed, one of 'four brides' on the same day as Sister Anne, but she was held back by one month, to 29 September 1641. It is unclear from the text whether this delay was deliberate on the part of her family or because of some confusion about her actual age, uncertainty concerning which is mentioned elsewhere in relation to other nuns.

This extract describes the women's early piety, and it also shows how the convent had important political connections with Charles II (1630–85) and his brother, the Duke of York (1633–1701), later James II, both of whom had strong associations with various religious communities in the Spanish Netherlands. The Carmelite papers frequently express loyalty to the royalist cause, and 'When King Charles the second was in banishment in these countries, there was a regiment of his quartered in this town, all persons of good quality, that had neither money, nor bread to eat…', whom the convent at Lierre supplied with food and shelter (*L3.30.G*). There is also a later reference to James II:

> Often troubles arising yearly in England made charity not only grow very cold there, but hardly to be expected. Court plots from which fresh persecutions sprang up every day, but above all the late incredible revolutions in that unhappy kingdom, ruined the estates of many & drove hundreds of Catholic nobles and gentry following the fortune of their banished master, the best & holiest of all our English monarchs, King James the second of holy & blessed memory, to ask charity abroad - he who used plentifully to give it at home …' (*L3.30.F*)

[*A1*, 384–386]

... The following sister, Tecla Clifton, who she [Sister Anne] was much with when
children as being in religion, they spent most of their time in reading the lives of saints,
and imitateing them by severall kinds of little pennances and devotions, and when found
out and forbid, they soon invented others ... These two made, when about 8 or 9 years old,
a vow of chastity and when they were about 12 the priest of the family read a Saint's Life
who had made ye vow, upon which the younger of them said 'My cosen Nany [Ann] and
I have done that long agoe.' The priest, examining them, said it was a childish thing and
signified nothing ... Both came as soon as possible to be religious ...

*

[Tecla of St Paul] was, as we have said before, with Rd Mother Anne Maria who was her
companion, [and had a] vocation from infancy ... the little time she staid in the world
[she] spent it wholy in practicing little pennances.

She was so earnest in putting her good desires of being religious in execution, that she
obtained leave of her friends att 14 years of age to enter our monastery ... The time of her
profession drawing near, some days before she received a letter from her relations, that she
yet wanted one year to be of age to make her profession. This was so great and sensible
an affliction that there was no pacifying of her: she was to have made the 4 Bride on the
same day, and att the time she was deprived of this joy. She still lamented that she was not
born when her br[other] Cuthbert was born. In fine, she took it so extreamly to heart that
it occasioned ever after constant vomittings so that she could never communicate till 11 a
clock, her vomitting not ceasing before, tho this for many years hindered not her faithfull
observance, yet it was a constant sufferance to her, and shortened her life ...

... She had a most angellicall innocence, and an agreeable sweet temper, and her person
so lovely and beautiful that when King Charles the Second and his brother came in our
monastery, the Duke of York came to the King and told him, if he had a mind to see a pritty
woman he must go to the Infirmary which he did, where dear Sr Tecla was ...

Chapter 11

Anne of the Angels:
Her Grand Entrance and Clothing

This extract describes the arrival at Antwerp of Anne Somerset (1613–51), daughter of Henry Somerset, Earl and Marquis of Worcester, and his wife Ann (daughter to John, Lord Russell, heir of the Earl of Bedford). She professed on 8 October 1643, and the papers duly emphasize her status and connections, recording that several other women arrived with her, sponsored by her family, to become religious in various capacities (see Chapter 12). It was clearly important to the Carmel to attract such a high profile entrant in order to draw other well-placed women, and she was encouraged in her initial enquiries by being allowed to enter the enclosure, where another nun was sent to chat with her. The annals also record that she was later sent to Lierre temporarily, 'to give a lustre to that new beginning', presumably in the hope of attracting similar new novices to that foundation. Her commemoration after death, as well as fulfilling pious intentions, assumedly has a similar promotional purpose.

The account describes how she initially arrived at Antwerp by chance, en route to Sichem, an important site of pilgrimage during this period. Its shrine in an oak tree is mentioned by several nuns; indeed the shrine was of such fame that there were many thefts of parts of the tree so that in 1604 the authorities cut it down and produced wooden statues of Our Lady, one of which was presented to the Carmelites by Lady Lovel (Hardman, 1936, 10–11).

After this visit, Anne Somerset's travelling companions suspected that she was being attracted to the convent at Antwerp and ensured that they returned home by a different route: like several other nuns, Anne Somerset needed to overcome obstacles in order to pursue her vocation, and eventually succeeded in her wish to become a Teresian, receiving a grand clothing ceremony that was explicitly compared by her father to secular marriage.

―――――――――

[*A1*, 395–400]

This lady was the eldest daughter to the Earl of Worcester of the family of the Plantaginetts, formerly Kings of England, and tho so great according to the eyes of the world, having disccovered by the light of heaven what a meer nothing all earthly grandure are … did by the noblest of resolutions so intirely surrender her self to his adored spouse of her soul …

… With this design she most generously left her parents, friends and country & came into these parts and took up her habittation at the English monastery att Gaunt [Ghent]. But, being as yet fixed upon no perticular Order, she undertook a pilgrimage to our Bld Lady of Sickam, that she might know the divine will … [and] passed by chance this convent of wch some part was then building, so that she came within the inclosure gate and satt upon a little bench with Sister Helena Wigmore[1] and some others who were sent to entertain her, our dear Mo[the]r [Anne of the Ascension] being then in the Infirmary. In this visitt, of about an hour, she found her self wonderfully moved … However, she persued her journey and they that were with her, suspecting somewhat of this her inclination, permitted her not to return again, but carried her back to Gaunt where after a little time she made know[n] her desire of undertakeing our holy institute.

… Att last she prevailed and accomplished her desire, entering into our monastery with great splendor & ceremony, cloathed in black velvett almost covered with pearl … The Marquiss, her father, seeing her perseverant resolution was so charmed with her … that he most generously declared that he would give her no less, who had espoused the King of Heaven, then he did to his other children who married according to the … world, which he effectually did.[2]

… Her death was, and still is, most sensibly lamented by the community. Our first venerable Mother, hearing of her having a vocation, promised our Blessed Lady a chapell in case she should settle here, which chapell was afterwards built in the garden.

---

[1]   Helen of the Holy Cross: 1599–1672 (*A1*, 238).

[2]   Around two pages of the original text are omitted here, including the detail that the nun died of fever on 19 September 1651, aged 38.

Chapter 12

Paula of St Joseph and Alexia of St Winefrid, Two of Anne Somerset's Entourage: A Sudden Death whilst Whitewashing and the Life of a Little Mouse

These Lives offer pictures of a religious career very different from that of Anne Somerset (Chapter 11) 'upon the fortune' of whom the two women entered. Although Sister Paula held various choir offices, Alexia of St Winefrid was a lay sister, and both women had much more humble beginnings than their sponsor.

Sister Paula was born Elizabeth Poulter (1613–72), daughter to Edward Poulter and Ann Hayter, of Oxfordshire: she professed in October 1643, and is described as being a convert and good singer. Her death was sudden, and quite dramatic within the domestic life of the community.

Alexia of St Winefrid (Catherine Powell: 1622–84), has a relatively short entry in the Antwerp annals (*A1*, 402): she was the daughter of Henry Powell and Jane Renals, of Monmouthshire, entering on 5 May 1644 and moving to Lierre in 1648. The Lierre papers (*L13.7*, 145–8) provide much more detail, and show that she had been taken on as a wash maid by the Somerset family after the death of her father in an accident on their estate, and that, as a lay sister in the convent, she served as cook. The daily duties of a lay member are described in Chapter 19, and it can be assumed that Sister Alexia's work, though focussed on the kitchen, included similar routines. Her humility was said to be marked by her frugality with food, abstention from which is frequently cited in the papers as a means of pious self-expression.

[*A1*, 400]

[Sister Paula] came upon the fortune of Sister Anne of the Angels and was a convert ... She was chose Subprioress in the year 1653 and severall times Discreet [treasurer]. She was struck with a fitt of palsey [a stroke] as she was with a brush in her hand, whiteing the walls near the Reffectory dore, and one of the religious passing that way, seeing her hand shake, asked her what ailed her. She answered 'I am struck, it is my death, but God's will be done', and never spoke one word more...

*

[*A1*, 402]

[Sister Alexia] was a lay sister, and came upon the fortune of Sister Anne of the Angels, and the last that had the happiness of makeing her profession in the hands of our first Venble Mother Anne of the Ascension.

She was a most holy and good religious and so extream silent that on this account the religious used to call her the Mouse, having all things in such readiness in the kitchen that, when any came thither on whatsoever account, she presently gave them what they wanted without speaking a word. After she had been here 4 or 5 years she was sent to the foundation of Lier where she lived a long time, and dyed there most happily.

*

[*L13*.7, 145]

Our dearlie beloued sister, Allexia of Saint Wenefrid, called in ye world Chatrine Harres,[1] natiue of Wales, borne of honnest parence, in Momorhsheere. Her father was a poor labering man, and belonged to ye Marquis of Wosestor [Anne Somerset's father], who once haueing desinged some work to be don about his caselle, this good man, her father, was unfortunatly killed by ye fall of ye walle upon him as hee was diging, one wch acount my Lord prouided for ye weedow, and her poor children. Amungst wch this our deare sister fell to my Lady Anne Somersets lott, to take care of [and] bring her up a good Catholicke wch she did, and taught her to read, and gaue her meny pious instructions, haueing her allway about her. She was her wash mayd, and my Lady brought her ouer wth her, to our monastary att Anwarp, to be religous there, in ye quality of a lay sister, upon her portione. She toke the holy habbet there, 6 munths affte my Lady Anne was clothed ...

She was but weeke, and not fitt for heard and laborious worke, yet she was very handdy about ye sicke, and saruisable to ye comunity, being of a quiet peaceble youmor [humour],[2] and extradinary neet a bout her work, and neuer idle ...

... [To Lierre] she came wth ye rest from Anwarp to this beginning [in 1648], wher she liued 34 yeares, in wch time she did not spare her selfe in doeing ye laborious work of ye house. She was constantly in ye kichen, and dressed all ye mett [meat] for ye community.

---

1   Her surname is given as Powell in the Antwerp annals, where she professed, but she is clearly the same religious. The mistake in the Lierre annals may be explained by the proximity in the sequence of another religious called Harris. There is also some discrepancy between the two sources on her exact dates.

2   This seems to contradict the assessment made by Margaret of Jesus (Margaret Mostyn: 1625–79) who wrote 'Sr Alexia is naturally very melancholy and as apt to fall into discontent as any in the whole house' (*L3.31*, 70; see Hallett, 2007).

One would wonder how she did compas so great a charg for aboue 20 yeares togeather, wth out euer repining att it ...

We allso ubsarued in her meny other virtues, but perticulerly ye practis of true meditation, for tho she was coke [cook] so long together, and had ye liberty to take yt for her selfe wch she licked best, haueing but a weeke stomake, and allways eatt but lettle, yet neuer was seene to cherish her selfe, but made choyes of ye worst, and fasted constantly most rigourusly, till she grew ould and decriped [decrepit], not able to work more, but must be tended ... and if ye Sisters did chance to forgett to giue her meatt, or any other nessicareys, she would neuer complaine, nor aske for anything, but simplie take what was giuen her, so yt those yt loked to her must be upon there gard not to forgett her ...

... Wee firmly beliue this good soule was one of those yt steles heauen from ye wise of ys world, for she was a most innocent life ... Not long before her death, she was trubled wth a disenes [dizzyness] in her head, and a great weeknes in her limes [limbs], yt she could not helpe her self, nor walke a bout, wch after wards ye doctor sayd was a speacy [kind] of ye palley [palsy]. It being Saint Barnabe Apostles day [11 June] att night, she was as wee thought beter then visall [usual], as she was gouing to bead a fitt take her in wch she lost her speech, but not her understanding ... and remained in that maner ... tell 22 of June, in ye yeare of our Lord 1684, about nine a clock att night, she rendered her hapy soule in to ye hands of her deare redimar [redeemer], being 78 yares of age, and 58 of her profession. Sweet Jesus make us pertakers of her meritts for ye Glory of his name. Amen.

Chapter 13

Anne of St Bartholomew and Mary Teresa of Jesus: Their Entries at an Advanced Age

When Catherine of the Blessed Sacrament (Chapter 6) was given permission to enter at an unusually young age, she was allowed to do so because of her 'fervent desires'. Two other religious who professed at Antwerp within four years of each other were at the other end of the scale: both were in their 50s, and both also required particular dispensation from the Bishop.

Anne of St Bartholomew (Anne Nettleton: 1621–93), daughter to Jane (née Boroughs) and Robert Nettleton of Berkshire, professed in March 1677, having persuaded the religious to let her enter after many years as companion to a Lady whom she had struggled to convince to release her from service. Similarly, Mary Teresa of Jesus (Cathrine van Tilen: born c.1631), a native of Antwerp, appears to have been a woman of independent means for many years. She had lived as a 'fille devote', in a semi-religious 'open' situation, and after she entered the Carmel she did not actually take her final vows until on her deathbed, being allowed to live the life of a 'full' religious meanwhile.

_____

[_A1_, 523–524]

[Anne of St Bartholomew] had a great desire to be religious from her youth, but the Lady Elizabeth Pirepoint, who was her relation and who took a perticular affection to her, would not consent to part with her, but took her with her to Rome and in all her other travels. Her vocation continuing, this Lady proposed her to our Monastery when she was about 35 years of age, but was not accepted on account of being to[o] old, upon which she continued with this Lady as before, conforming her life as much as possible to that of religious and never omitted one day to say the long littany of the saints … And 20 years after this, the Lady finding her desires daily increase, ventured to propose her again, and the community was moved to receive her …

The Confessorius who was sent to procure leave of the Bishop for her enterance mistook her age and told him she was 35 years of age, to wch he made great difficulty, saying she was too old for his nuns … [but] att last gave his consent. The Confessorius, coeming back, told the Superior how much difficulty the Bishop made on the account of her being

35, to wch Superior answered in surprise 'Lord, Father she is 55', to which he replyed 'For God sake, Reverend Mother, take her presently in, for if the Bishop knows it he will not admitt this'. His advice was followed for she imediately entered privatly and began as if she had been her whole life inured to all observance, and so plyable in the hands of all as if she had no will of her own ...

*

[*A1*, 528]

[Mary Teresa of Jesus was] a fille devote many years, and highly esteemed by all for her great vertue and devotion, in so much that she had leave to comunicate every day. She came casually to be acquanted with this comunity and was a very considerable benefactress before she enter'd, in building the alter of the church, adorning it with images & c, which was only tell then like a chamber. And being upon this more conversant with the religious, gott a vocation and, tho so advanc'd in years, couragiously enter'd amongst them, and at the end of her noviceship was solemnely vailed by the very Rd Lord Bishop Ferdinand van Bergen, on the 16 of October 1681 being about 50 years of age ...

... It is to be noted that Str Mary Teresa of Jesus van Tilen was not profess'd at the end of her noviship as it was suposed by the world and by all her relations who never knew the contrary, so had the black vail publickly given her by the Bishop himself. The reason was that she haveing lived so long in the world after her own way and tyed to her little conveniences & c. that she herself as well as the religious very much apprehended her perfectly complying with the vow of poverty, so that it was not thought proper, both for her and on their own account, poverty being so nice a point ... She and the community prudently judg'd it much better not to run the risk of it, tho on the account she had a great desire of remaining amongst us, and had been a very advantagious benefactoress, she was expected of to live as a religious and make her profession at her death, which she did some time before her last lingering sickness ...

Chapter 14

Francisca of the Blessed Sacrament: Her Near Abduction as a Child and Her Later Seduction by Witchcraft

This Life contains details of two remarkable events concerning Elizabeth Osmund (1674–1720), who professed on 26 December 1698. She was born in Berkshire, the daughter of Thomas Osmund ('always a good Catholic'), and his converted wife, Margaret (the daughter of Ralph Pierpont). As an only child, she was doted on by 'her Uncles and Aunts who wer Protestants except one Uncle'. During her childhood, whilst living in London she was almost abducted 'for the plantations'. Later, when she lived in France with her uncle in exile, she became friends with a woman 'who call'd her self a Countess' who was said to have beguiled her by witchcraft, gaining power by asking the young woman secretly to keep a paper on which she had added her name. This is similar to other accounts of bewitchment through writing – for example, Martin del Rio's text, compiled in Antwerp in 1595, includes an incident in which a youth signed a paper at the instruction of the devil, a document which his confessor afterwards told him to retrieve and destroy (del Rio, 2000, 267).

[*A1*, 569–74]

… God shewing from her infancy a speciall providence over her, amongst the rest the following passage is very remarkable: being very young and standing one day at the dore in London, a man passing by snachd her up under his cloack, and putt his thumb in her mouth to pervent her crying out. She, not easily daunted, strugled so hard and bit him so violently that he was forced to drop her a good street distant, where a gentleman, knowing her, carried her back to her frinds. His [her abductor's] design was certanly as usually practised by such kind of people, to sell her for the plantations.

When she was about 15, her mother carried her to St Germans in France where her Catholick Uncle then was with King James ye 2d. But her mother some time after, having gott a cancer in her breast, went to Dijon to a famous phistion [physician] where she dyed, and left this young creature alone, whose gay and vain temper ingaged her in company and the vanitys of the world. Amongst the reast, there came to visit her one who call'd her self a Countess, which she believed to be so … This Lady ingaged her with all the indearments imaginable, assuring her that she shuld be as happy as her self, makeing her large promisses of honours, riches and pleasures, only desiring her to keep a paper she gave her. She, thinking nothing of the matter, took it. Whether this Lady desired her to sign it, or if she did sign it, we are uncertain, but to secure it [she] put it within the lineings of a trunk with promis never to let it be seen. Soon after her Uncle sent for her back to St Germans where the same Lady came to visit her, continuing her marks of affection and kindness, and this she did in all company apearing to her to be allways one of the cheif of them …

[God] gave her a strong vocation to religion, and to pit[c]h upon this house. Haveing made this known to her Uncle, who was a very pious good man and the only Catholick frind she had in the world, he extreamly incouraged her, knowing the dangers her vain temper ingaged her in, and also that of her Protestant relations. This forementioned Lady, who was certainly the Divell, diswaded her from this undertaking, telling her she would be the most miserable creature in the world if she made her self religious … yet God gave her grace to remain firm, and with great resolution [she] came to the monastery where, haveing taken the habit, [she] was immediately after called to the speak house to some Father & c. where the same Lady apear'd with out the grate, with all her attendance, making signs to intice her to come out, but did not speak.

She suffer'd violent temptations in her noviceship, and her relations, who were rich, made her great proffers to whome she knew she would be very wellcome in England, but [she] overcome them all and happily made her profession. But when she took the black vail, she see again the Lady amongest the crowd of people, threathening her with signs of indignation, all of which things she then kept to herself. Soon after her profession, she fell into unusiall strang distempers and fitts wch continued allmost 2 years and was continually thought to be a dyeing. In ys time of her sickness, she made all this known, her eyes being then open'd to the great dangers she had pass'd and was yett in, performing what ever was required of her, and caus'd the paper to be burnt which the Lady had given her, and she had left at St Germans in the linengs of the trunck, which her Uncle, according to her desire and derections, faithfully cast into the fire all together.

She then suddenly and perfectly recovered, and never more fell into the same distempers, allways blessing All: God for delivering her, and most gratfull to those that incessantly prayed for her at this time, particularly Rd Mother Mary Xaveria of the Angels [Catherine Burton] who Allmighty God was pleased to inlighten in these matters … Being now recouer'd, she resum'd her dutys with great fervour and love of observance wch she was very faithfull to her whole life …

… [She] perfectly understood how to carry her self to all sorts of people and did the comunity much honour in occations when persons of quality came to the monastery of other nations, speaking French as well as English …

… [She] had a long and strong agony, and tho … sometime speachless before her death, made signs for absolution and dyed most peaceably and holyly as fortold by Mother Mary Xaveria of the Angels, thus happily triumphing over all the malicious designs of the enemy who used such stratigiems to ruin her, on the 27 Aprill 1720, aged 46 of her holy profession 25.

Mary Frances of St Teresa: The Instigator of the Antwerp Lives, a Treasure of the Community, Drawn to Her Vocation by Reading

Mary Birkbeck (1674–1733) was the prime mover behind the compilation of the Antwerp Lives (see p. 35 and Chapter 1), and her own Life appears at the beginning of the second volume of the annals. Her parents were Thomas Birkbeck and Mary, daughter to John Caterick, of Westmoreland, and, like some other nuns, she came into religion after reading a book by St Francis de Sales (see p. 19) and Teresa de Jesus' *Book*. Her Life gives details of her profession and her time as Prioress, during which the incorrupt body of Margaret Wake was discovered.

[*A2*, 1–15]

… She had the happiness of having very vertuous parents, but had the misfortune to be born at a time when there was a great persecution raised in England against our holy religion, in so much that many priests were obliged to abscond and those who remained were much indanger'd by performing any function – which made her baptisme to be offer'd between 14 days and three weeks, but [she] at last received this happiness upon the feast of the Annunciation of Our Blessed Lady, and on that account had the name of Mary given her, to the great consolation of her pious parents who both dyed very holyly wn she was yet very young and left this only daughter and four brothers who were all religious but one.

She was ever very tractable and of a most sweet amiable temper and disposition, and a prevented soul from her childhood, having a great innocency, sincerity and natural prudence … allways very pious and faithfull to God … yet never a thought of becoming religious on the contrary seem'd on occasions quite averss to it, till reading St Francis Sales *Introduction to a Devote Life* …

She thought it allmost impossible for her to save her soul if engaged in the world and, being allways a great lover of reading and looking into all books she met with, was once in ye chamber of a priest, tumbling over his little liberary and he, perceiving it, chid her for disordering his books, but bid her chuse any one and he would lend it her most willingly. Upon which she was put to a stand, and viewing them all she fix'd upon one that was placed very high wch had a guilt back, without knowing what it was. The priest told her she had made an excellent choice, for it was the life of the great St Teresa, upon which they had some discourse of the wonderfull saint and Holy Order & c. She read it severall times over, and every time was more and more delighted with it, till at last she was so effectually confirm'd in ye thoughts of ye dangers of the world and the security of a religious life, and so inspired with a desire of being of her Holy Order that she immediately beged the same Father to procure her admittance here, which he did, but on account of her affairs [she] was after this detained two or three years in England to her great mortification and sufferance ... [She was] transported with joy when she arrived here ... It was easily perceived from the very first what a treasure the community possess'd ... which made her singularly beloved by all, particularly by Reverend Mother Mary Xaveria of the Angels [Catherine Burton] whose novice she was ... Her humility, obedience, charity ... all other vertues shined brightly in her very beginings ... a hidden saint ...[1]

... Notwithstanding her great weakness and infirmityes, her fervour and love of observance was such as made her follow the community till 6 months before her death, all which time she was mostly confined to the Infirmary in ye day, but having a particular difficulty in leaving her cell, slept in it upon her straw bed and woollen sheets, assuring us it was much easyer then any thing we could make in ye Infirmary ... Yet, during these 6 months, her painfull and suffering distempers dayly augmented with an intermitting fever and great opression upon her breast, which made all this time a lingering kind of maryrdom ...

... She often expressed a great joy for the happiness wch she esteem'd it to dye in the same room which Rd Mother Mary Xaveria of the Angels had sanctified by her holy death ... When Rd Mother told her she was to communicate, tho very much inclined to be heavey and sleepy, she immediately brisked up her self and thanked her, using a forceable violence to prepare herself for that happiness, beging others to assist her and keep her awake ... The two last days and nights she was obliged to sit in a chair, not being able to ly down for the great oppression which she suffered, remaining the whole time perfectly sensible and present to herself even to ye last moments with a short warning and struggle with death in the same chair gave up her dear soul into the hands of her divine spouse [on Tuesday 5 May 1733] ...

... It pleased his divine goodness to discover in her time [as Prioress] the hidden treasure of the incorrupt body of our Venble Mother Mary Margarett of the Angels [Margaret Wake] in the year 1716, and allso the remainder of that of Sister Anne of St Bartholme[2] the year 1718, as it is related in what is said of her. She also procured ye writing the lifes of Mother Mary Xaveria and Mother Mary Margarett, the first by Rd Father Thomas Hunter, the 2d by the Rd Father Percy Plowden[3] ... she took the pains her self to transcribe all the memoires for this, as she allso did when they were finish'd by the aforesaid authours.

In her time we procured the inlarging of our garden ... and this cost her no small trouble and concern, but her invincible patience, courage and continued devotions overcame all

---

[1] Around four pages of the original text, listing her various signs of pious virtue, are omitted.

[2] Chapter 5.

[3] Chapters 28, 29.

the difficultyes and the many seculars which oppossed themselves to this design. The night before the house and garden was to be sold, she went with the community in procession round our garden with a little Image of St Joseph ... and at the end of it order'd one of the religious with a ladder and cord to put the little image over the other side of the wall, desiring the Bd Saint to take possession of that peice of ground for us, which ye Saint did so effeicaciously that contrary to all expectation we accomplished it ...

In the time of her Superiority, we solemnized the hunder'd year of the foundation of our house, ye 17 of May 1719; and in the year 1722, the hounder'd year of the cannonization of our glorious Mother St Teresa; in the year 1727, the cannonization of Saint John of the Cross[4] ...

Monsr Veickmans left us a legacy of £300 sterling without the least acquaintance, only once accidently speaking to this Rd Mother on occasion of seeing the entire body of Mother Mary Margaret, allso Monsieur and Madam du Bois settled a yearly musick Mass and anthem ... the first that ever were founded since the beginning of the house by any seculars. Allso ye church was paved with marble, wenscotted, painted & C, by different English benefactores, with many other reparations and convenient improvments in our convent, remaining proofs of her great power with heaven and our great obligations to her.

---

[4]   St John of the Cross (1542–91) was a Carmelite associate and spiritual director of Teresa de Jesus.

Chapter 16

Teresa Joseph of the Sacred Heart of Jesus: Her Father, Like a Jealous Lover, Resists her Teresian Vocation

The Life of Mary Charlotte Bond (1690–1735) provides many insights into family relationships: like several of the other religious before they joined the convent, she acted as mistress of her father's house, in this case following the early death of her mother, Mary, the daughter of Lord Jermyn. She clearly had a very close relationship with her father, Thomas Bond. For many years he resisted her desire to join a convent and, when eventually he did agree, he wished her to profess at Bruges where he was then living. Like another nun (Chapter 9), Sister Teresa became aware through seeing a death notice of a place made available at Antwerp. Once he was reconciled to his daughter's vocation, Thomas Bond became a generous benefactor to the Antwerp convent (see Chapter 29, notes 4, 16): it was he who paid for the enlargement of the dead-cellar in 1716 during which the uncorrupted body of Margaret Wake was discovered, after which he is said to have witnessed miracles associated with that nun.

[*A2*, 24–34]

[She was called when aged 14] but she could not resolve to quit the world and these first pious thoughts were soon banished by the conversation of her relations and friends, of which many were Protestants and most of them of quality who lived in greatness, and all sorts of devertions agreable to her inclinations, so that til about 20 years of age she comply'd with the form of the world according to her birth and fortune, tho allways very faithfull in her duty to God in so much that she very sensibly found her obligation of serving Almighty God could not consist with that of pleasing the world and thought it impossible to save her soul if she remained in it …

  She resolved to break thro all difficultys and save her soul in the happy haven of religion, but for this she was to expect great conterdictions particularly from the part of her father who loved her tenderly, nay even to fondness, she being his eldest daughter living, and the mistress of his house (her mother dy'd when she was but very young) … The affairs of her father [obliged] him to come over about [that] time ... Thus the family left England and settled at Bridges [Bruges] where she was again mistress of his house, and lived a considerable time there before she durst declare her intentions ... Her first thoughts were of being religious of the order of St Augustine amongest the English at Bridges ... but, coming acidentily to this town to see her brother who study'd here and [had] fallen ill of the small pox, she could not well avoid the seeing this monastery tho her father, who came with her, took his precations and beg'd as a favour that if his daughter should happen to goe to ye monastery, that none of the religious would say one word of her being a nun ...

... She came [to visit the convent] much againest her father's inclinations, and he with her as guard, but at a time when we were building and the inclosure [was] open which, when she saw, said 'I know I may enter the monastery' upon wch her Father ... enter'd with her. But all the religious kept faithfully ye orders which had been given them, for very few words pass'd on any side ... her father watching her the whole time. Dear Mother Mary Xaveria [Catherine Burton] gave her a pecture of our holy Mother and a little book of the 10 Fridays devotions of St Francis Xaverus[1] ... but [she] could not obtain leave to come any more, tho she remained some time in town ...

[Eventually, her father gave] leave to her making a tryall amongest the Augustines at Bridges ... because he was then fixed [there] and could often have the consolation of seeing his dear daughter. Infine, after more difficultys and sufferings then can be express'd from her father (and from those he had engaged in his interests) who acted in all not only like to a passionate father but even like to a jelous lover, [she obtained his consent though] she was obliged to return into England to settle her affairs ... and returned immediately to take the schollers habit [at the Augustinian monastery] tho still continued to have an ardent desire to be a Carmelite if in her power ...

She did not find her vocation satisfyed in the habit she had taken ... but was councell'd ... to enter upon her noviceship, upon which she was cloathed but still found a great reluctance to it [convinced her vocation] was in a particular manner to our Order and house ... Every body was against her, as judging our Order to[o] hard for her constitution ... She allso had heard that our numbers were compleat ... and rejoiced extreamly when she see the dead bill of Sr Mary of the Holy Martiers[2] who died ye Aprill before she enter'd...

[Mother Mary Xaveria] propheisd her coming to be religious here[3] ...One night when the Blysed Sacrement had been exposed, after shutting the reposoire [which contained it, she] said to Mother Teresa Joseph, then novice, 'Dear child, I never locked this dore since I first saw you without locking up your heart here' ... She [Teresa Joseph] answered that she believed it to be so, for tho she was distant in body, she was allways with us in desire ... [Her father] brought her himself to the Monastery and lead her to the gate for her cloathing.[4]

---

[1]   A devotion to which Mary Xaveria attributed her own cure (see Chapter 28).
[2]   Mary Gifford (born 1639) died 23 April 1713 (*A1*, 528).
[3]   Around one page of the original text is omitted here.
[4]   Around two pages of the original text are omitted here.

... [She was elected Prioress in 1730, and] justly meritted the respect esteem and affections of the community ... [being] so great a lover of neatness and cleanliness that it was her greatest pleasure to be so her self, and to see the convent offices & c neat and in right order, which she left us a most perfect example in her office of Prioress, every letter paper & C being dated and marked what they concern'd, and every little thing in the nicest order and easy to be found with out loss of time ...

Clare Joseph of Jesus Maria: Her Dreams and Spiritual Favours; and Her Appearance to Another Religious in a Vision

Clare Gerard (1694–1730) was one of 11 children born to Thomas Gerard and his wife Mary Wright, of Lancashire, of whom two died before they reached the age of 20; eight of the remaining nine became religious. Two of her brothers were Jesuit missionaries to Maryland, and another was confessor to the English Augustinians at Bruges; one of her sisters became a Poor Clare at Gravelines, two were Carmelites at Lierre, and two others were 'in our convent, of which dear Sister Clare was ye youngest' (see pp. 13, 17, 231 and Chapter 38).

This Life gives details of her dreams and visions; and of her appearance to another religious sometime before that nun's own death.

———————

[*A2*, 46–55]

[She was allowed] even at a tender age to frequent the Sacraments, often very extraordinary in a heretick country … she suck'd in by reading in her lisping years a tender devotion to our Bd Lady …

… About these years [when she was around seven years old] she was frequenly troubled with very frightfull dreames, in which she allways found herself assisted by Saint Apolinarius, waking her self by calling upon him by his name, and by this meanes was quite freed from them, retaining ever after a singular devotion to the saint … Hearing accidently of our monastery … she found in herself great resolutions for the quitting her country …[1]

Two or three days before her death she told us her dream in which she was wishing that the infirmary was larger, to the end she might see all the religious together without being opress'd by to many in ye room, and looking up she saw it inlarged according to her

———————

[1]   Around one page of the original text is omitted here.

desire, our Bd Lord, our Bd Lady, with many saints and angels attending them, and all ye religious in the room standing about …[2]

Some months before [her own death] a vertuous holy religious[3] and one to be credited, was wak'd one night out of her sleep by a great light in her cell, and being frighted that she was call'd to some one a dying was going to rise, but harkening, and not hearing any thing stir, look'd about her to find from whence the light could come, and perceived the little wooden cross on which is painted a Christ invision'd with a bright glory like to the sun at midday and which continued so long that her eyes was weaken'd with the sight tho most delightfull. And, shutting them to relieve them and looking again, she see the same as before, and allso a religious in her habit like in a sort of cloud standing before the Crucifix in deep contemplation … She could not see her face, nor know who the person was, and all this remain'd so long a time that she was even spent with looking, sitting up all the time in her bed. And shutting her eyes a second time, and when she look'd again all was vanish'd, leaving her in admiration and devotion, suposing that what she had seen signify'd the death of some one, but fearing to put the Superiour into aprehension did not speak to her of it tell after the death of dear Sister Clare, but informed her Confessor at the time that this happened to her.

---

2   Around one page of the original text is omitted here.
3   'Sister Hellen' is written in the margin here: this is presumably Helen of the Cross (Helen Eddisford: 1672–1755) (*A2*, 233).

Mary Margaret of the Angels: Her Conversion from Protestantism by Reading Books of Controversy; and Her Death from Gangrene

The Life of Penelope Chapman (1693–1739), daughter of Elizabeth (née Louth) and John Chapman of Dorset, describes her conversion from Protestantism, one in which 'books of controversy' played a key role. It ends with an account of her death which, as ever, provides insight into the bodily rituals undertaken by the religious.

[*A2*, 62–72]

This dear Sister does not only show the great goodness of God … but allso to that of our holy faith, being a Protestant till less then a year before she came over, and I may say was favoured with both these happy calls at once, as a writing which she has left in her own hand, clearly shews the chief particulars of which are as follows:

I was converted to the true faith by reading books of controversy which one of my brothers (who was then upon his conversion tho unknown to me) took care to put in my way. I was now about 19 years of age, and reading was all my delight. I used often to reflect on ye shortness of this life and consider'd what if I should live 60 years, 20 would would be intirely gone in sleep, and what provission out of the other 40 I had or should lay up to secure a happy eternity. These thoughts were continually in my mind … When I came home late at night from such occassions [in company], my heart used to be extream heavy … With reading I began to have great doubts that I was not in ye true religion …

… Returning home [from church one Christmas] I found a new book on a table, placed there by my brother, which I immediately open'd at this point: 'Parsons, not being true priests, has no power to consecrate, so that you might as well eat a piece of bread and drink a glass of wine at home, it being just the same'. This put me into the greatest affliction in the world, not knowing who to apply my self to, all my friends being Protestants … Then I immagin'd my self all alone, without any relation, poor and destitute, forsaken of all, but God alone, and then asked my self the question 'Were it truely so, what religion would I wish to be of?' Then, when immediately Allmighty God infused into me so lively a faith as took away all further doubts … *Here she relates the many difficultys and opposition*

she found from her friends in regard to her being religious at least so soon ... [she] was
prevailed upon as ye most prudent to stay the winter.

... The chief motives to my coming here were first to see the intire body,[1] [a]nother was
that no religious had any thing in perticular at their own disposall ... [and] that they
did not eat meat unless for sickness, and lastly that our holy founderess St Teresa was a
woman and had practiced her self all that she has left us to observe.

On the 8th day of July the year 1716, on a Saterday, I made my happy abjuration of
herisy and was received as a member of the Holy Catholick church, and admitted to Holy
Communion the day after in parish chaple at Chidock. On the 8th day of Augst the same
year I received the Holy Sacrament of Confession.

On ye 28 of June 1718 I was admitted to the holy habitt, on the 16 of July 1719, I made
my happy profession in this holy community ...

... Some years before her last illness she had a swelling in her hip wch she thought she
found somthing of from very young, but now it increased and was very painfull between
times and which caused a constant sufferance and in all probability was the cause of
distemper of which she dyed ... [She] kept her self up in ye community as long as she
could, and even to the performance of her office of Portress which must needs have been
very painfull and troublesome ... I believe she found our abstinance and fasts very hard,
but never let it appear, and was very constant to them. Thus being quite overcome she
was obliged to yeald and goe to the Infirmary where her illness, and others added to it, as
dropsey, fever, great heat in the breast, and shivering fitts ...

She was near three months for the most part confined to her bed, and so intirely corrupted
within that great peices of flesh came from her ... [She had 40 hours of agony] ... I have
often thought since that we who see her had not much less to suffer, for I think I never had
a greater comfort then when they told me she was expired, being in a kind of agony for her
and had not the courage to look upon her towards the last, having found the greatest tryall
and sufferance in religion to be the seperation which death causes, she dyed at about 8 at
night, upon the eve of All Saints [Saturday 31 October 1739] ...

... When the religious lay her out, they see more plainly what she must have suffer'd, her
whole body being quite over gangreen, and being very much swell'd, [they] fear'd great
difficulty in dressing of her & c. but did it with so much ease that they were all surprised,
saying she seem'd light in their hands and that they had never laid a dead out with less
difficulty. She remained that night in the Infirmary and coming next morning to put her
into her coffen, thought with the same ease to have done it, but found their mistake. 4 of
ye nuns not being able to stir the board upon which she lay, so was forced to have men to
help to do it.

---

[1] Presumably that of Margaret Wake, discovered in 1716. The families of other nuns also
     visited Antwerp for this purpose (see Chapter 26).

Chapter 19

Winifred of St Teresa: Her Miraculous Recovery as a Child; Her Life and Death as a Lay Sister

Elizabeth Lingen (1662–1740), the daughter of Ralph and Elizabeth Lingen of Hertfordshire, played a pivotal role in the compilation of the Antwerp papers (see pp. 10, 160, 163; Hallett, forthcoming). Her Life contains anecdotes that were presumably repeated by the nun in her lifetime and were later affectionately embodied into the narrative by her contemporaries. The text tells how she fell ill as a child and was saved by the ministrations of an old woman. Although invited to enter the Carmel as a choir nun, Sister Winifred professed in 1679 as a lay sister. A detailed account of her duties is appended to this Life.

_____

[*A2*, 81–146]

She was an only daughter of a most pious worthy family, both by father and mother ... of a solid judgment quick witt, apt in learning, knowing and understanding ... When she was about 3 or 4 months old she was subject to violent convoltions, and in one fitt she was looked upon as dead and as such laid out upon a table in order to be buryed. When, after many hours lying thus, there came in an old woman who loved her extreamly and lamenting over the child said 'Give her to me and I will doe my best to bring her to life again'. She took ye child before the fire, rub'd it with spirits & c. till in effect the child began to stir, and after some time was as well as before, to the great joy of the parents and whole family. This she used to tell us with great resentment, that the old woman had then hinder'd her from going to heaven.

When she was about 7 years old she had many companions to play with her that were Protestants, but her mother very carefull[y] kept her to constant times for her prayers, after which she gave her all liberty. But one day they came sooner then ordinary and she, hearing them, was very much tempted and impatient to be done, and so turn'd over to the concluding prayer and went to them. And they, knowing it was not the usuall time, [said] 'What, miss, have you done so soon?' which words struck her extreamly, but she quickly answered by way of excuse, 'You must know that we Papists have one prayer that serves for all the rest' ... but from yt moment found a great uneasyness ... esteeming this her first fall and lamenting it to her dying day ...

... She resolved to be religious tho she thought she should not be able to live above one year, having strange notions of a religious life, beleiving that when she enter'd the monastery she should never more see the sun and such like...

... Being only about 15 years of age, she enter'd some weeks after her arrivall, and according to our custome for those in the station of lay sister, for the first tryall wore her secular cloaths; and the community, seeing her in all respects so well qualifyed, that they had many thoughts of cloathing her for a quire nun ... but her humility was such that she allways declined these offers.

... She was of a tender complextion but very healthy and strong, baring great sickness as violent fevers, small pox & c. so laborious that it was surprising to see wt she could dispatch ...[1]

... [She had] a particular devotion to assist the sick and to releive them in what ever she could, and by her constant attention to the doctors perscriptions which with long practice and experiance aquired a great deal of skill, as she allso had in apothecary things ... When any one was in danger, or on sudden accidents, she was one of the first that was called to their assistance, and she told me that for a great many years she was seldome a night wherein she was not call'd to some one or other ... [She] had a very particular devotion to prolong the life of those that were in their agonys, giving them from time to time proper cordialls tho only with a feather[2] ...

... By her continuall labours and great fatigues [she] had so strain'd and weaken'd her back that she went allmost quite double many years before her death, but wt was the most sensible of all was the loss of her eyes so as not to be able to read or write, nor scarce find out her way about ye house, tho some ladys of ye town, who had a great veneration and love for her, were at the expences of having one of them conack'd[3] by a famous master 12 years before her death, which operation she indur'd couragiously and her sight [was] much better for some years, but then return'd to be much the same as before ...

... Upon St Anns day [26 July], she heard the first Mass and communicated, after which I sent her to the kitchen to take something, which she did ... and after fell asleep by the fire side very quietly. But, observing she did not stir when a Mass [bell] tole'd the sisters said to one another 'It is a sign yt Sister Winifride is very fast indeed that she does not goe to Mass, being allways upon the watch for that'. Others said 'Doe not wake her, perhaps she has had a bad night'. Infine, the double bells rung for the musick Mass and she minded them not, which frighted us, and we calld her and shaked her, but she still remain'd as in a profound sleep and quite insenseble. So we sent for ye Confessor, doctor and surgeon. We placed her upon a quilt on the ground where she received the Holy Oyles, and afterwards was blooded, but still she did not come to her self. Towards night we carryed her to the

---

[1]   Around one page of the original text is omitted here.
[2]   This detail occurs several times in the papers, and suggests a means of administering liquid, or medicine, to the sick. (Around two pages of the original text are omitted here.)
[3]   Presumably similar to a cataract operation.

recreation room, not knowing how to get her above stairs, and after remedys used, about 10 a clock, she return'd from that kind of lethargy, but not quite present to her self till the next morning when she received her Holy Viaticum[4] with great devotion, answering and joyning in all the prayers. But afterwards, tho she knew us all and answer'd to many things very reasonably, was between times not so sensible. She remain'd thus about three weeks ... till she fell into her agony which began the night before ... and gave up her dear soul to her mercyfull creator about half an hour after nine in the morning, on a Tuesday, the 17 of August, in the octive of the Asumption of our Blessed Lady [1740].

An exact distribution of time for the lay sisters and the dutys that belongs[5]

Those out of ye kitchen are to open the reffectory windows, sweep it, empty snuffers,[6] fill the salts[7] and put them in ye refectory with the spoon, put away the candle sticks, leave the pots in water;

Stir the meal flower [flour] and brans, in hot weather dayly boult [sift] ye batch;

A little before ye half hour, cary out the hens pot and bucket, doe ye bread and bear [beer], cut bread for offering about, provide sups [soaps], dishclouts and water to wrinck [rinse] the dishes;

After ye Reffectory, ring the pardon [bell],[8] furnish the dish washer with warm water, wash the pots and trumperys, wipe and put them in there places, put ye dishes in the grate and the tubs to ayre. If not belated, sweep ye house, pump ye furnace, wipe ye reffectorys tables, carry the leavings of bear to the celler. All this is to be done again at night, except on fasting days of the church, when the help in ye kitchen washes ye dishes at night;

The bells to Vespers, Mattens and prayer are to be rung, and in winter fires made and fuel provided;

After ye boulting is done, and the boulter [room] and garret sweept, which commonly done by Wedendays, if no holy day or hinderance happens or that ye boulting is behindhand, or to be advanced against a feast, or ye tubs, chest and boulter to plack or smoak. The tubs of flower are to be carried down to the celler, the bread chest swept and ayrd with fire;

At ye half hour, ye candle sticks are to be sett and the bread, laid if not in danger of freesing;

Thursday mornings: time must be found to rid up the two courts by the kitchen and to cobwebb and sweep ym when needfull. The dish tubs must be scrubed once a week, the dust tub emty'd;

Friday: the cesterns and gutters within dores clean washed, as allso the shelves, the house cobwebb'd and the ground taken up, the candle ends and clouts [cloths] carryed to the celler and brought up to the wash, dryed in the garett or oven, and put in the basketts;

Friday afternoons: the bear taps must be wiped and the undervats emty'd twice a week

---

4   The Eucharist and accompanying rites given to people believed to be approaching death.

5   This is written in a different, somewhat cruder, hand from previous sections of this Life.

6   Dishes or trays for candle snuffs.

7   I.e., salt cellars.

8   I.e., a bell signalling a prayer in honour of the Annunciation, opening with the words *'Angelus Domini nuntiavit Mariae'* ['An angel of the Lord declared unto Mary ...'].

and washed once, that and the turf and fagot cellers sweept and cobwebb'd, the bucketts and broomes look'd after, and new knockt on when necessary, the mops and the uppening ducks washed and repared, wisps and gopelett ready;[9]

The refectory to be cobwebed throwly [thoroughly] upon Saterdays, and sweept, the spots taken up and clean sand, the knives to be whetted [sharpenend] and salts renewed againest [in preparation for] Sundays;

Friday nights: the pots, porrengers [bowls], beir cans and tubs is also to be washed once a week in hot water, and ye candle sticks scoured, the box provided with pounded salt. Also, those out of the cichen are to provide bromes for scouring the house, weeding the causes, and after to put them in there places;

Besides this, time must be found for every ones sweeping office and cell, humble office and quire candle sticks, when they come to their lott and for doing what is their perticular care, as the cleaning, setting and taking away the recreation candle sticks, tending the hens, the dressing, lighting and putting out the lamps;

The mingling the flower, laying the leaven [yeasted dough], and providing water for the baking;

The renewing the brine for the butter, scraping and washing out the stones as soon as empty, scalding them twice ere they are fitted again, the butter stampers and covers brought down and scalded againest [for when] ye provision comes in, and scalded and carryed up when done withall;

The 6 fish tubs are to be brought down and scalded against Lent, and twice scalded and carry'd up when done with;

The recreation turf basketts plack'd and carry'd up when done with all.

---

[9]	The *Oxford English Dictionary* gives 'wisps' as a bundle of straw, while 'gope' is defined as 'splash' in a dialect dictionary for Westmoreland, suggesting perhaps brooms and splashy (i.e., wet) mops. (I am grateful to Sarah Hamshere and Barbara Hawley for this suggestion).

Chapter 20

Anne Maria Joseph of St Xaveria: The Widowed Sister of Catherine Burton

Ann Woolmer (1662–1740) was a sister of Catherine Burton (1668–1714: Chapter 28). She married Francis Woolmer 'and did not degenerate even tho' settled in the world', becoming a 'desolate widdow' within a few years, with a son and daughter. At this stage she wished to become a religious, but needed to care for her children. Having settled her worldly affairs, she eventually professed at Antwerp where, despite her 'good solid understanding', she had problems learning Latin and so she was relieved of some of her duties as a choir nun.

A letter from the Antwerp archive (now at St Helens) dated 30 June 1727 and addressed to the Prioress, 'Madame Birkbeck aux Angloises en Hopland at Antwerp' from 'D Gage', mentions that 'Mr Thimel payd me Mrs Woolmers Lady day rent: and by the last post, I returned 10th in part of it by Antwerp. I would have done it a week agoe, but could gett no bill.' Assuming this is the same 'Mrs Woolmer', this note suggests that she continued to own property from which revenue provided support.

———————

[*A2*, 153–60]

... Behold what she has left writ of her self in relation to her coming to religion.

Some time after I was a widdow, I prayed to our Lord that I might live so long as to see my two children bread up and after that to be able to enter into a religious state, to prepare my self for a happy death ... These my two children both lived to the age of 21, but then both dyed in a short period ... [so I] writ to my dear sister at Antwerp, Rd Mor Mary Xaveria of the Angels, to pray to God for me and if it was his holy will that I should be a nun [then he would dispose my affairs accordingly]... I had much business then to finish before I could leave the world and besides this I was very sickly and had been so for many years and was then about 48 years of age ...

[My sister prayed for me] she heard a voice say, 'Her son shall not have the full injoyment of the glory of God till she is cloathed and prostrate before the Blysed Sacrement' – by wch she understood that my sons soul was then in glory, but not that full glory wch his soul should have after I was cloathed. My sister did allso tell me that my daughter, some little time after her death, came to her and said 'Pray Aunt, pray for me' in the same voyce she had when she was alive, and she did assure me that her soul was in heaven soon after. My sister did not tell me these things till I had been about six months in the novicship ... [She also told me, when praying to St Teresa] she heard a voice say 'I have enroled her in the number of my children'...

... There is severall other things that she relates wch Rd Mother Mary Xaveria told her but as I think they are all mentioned in ye book of her life I will omitt them here.

As soon as this dear sister received a favourable answer from ye community she made all possible hast to settle her affairs, and tho she had but just recovered an ague came immediately over and took ye holy habit on the Eve of the Nativity of Our Blessed Lady [in 1711] and found her self full of joy and content of mind ...

... In the time of her noviceship she shew'd a solid good understanding, great simplicity of obedience, humility, fervour and constancy in her good resolutions ... edifyed and pleased the community exceedingly, seeing a person that had lived so many years in the world after their own way and inclinations, I believe as much as any could doe, to conform themselves to the manner and customes of religion, so that both partys being intirely satisfyed she made her holy profession at the right time the 8th of September the year 1712 in ye hands of her own dear sister ... and [to] the whole communitys great joy and satisfaction.

She had not the obligation of reading the divine office on account that she was not able to learn Latin, but said the lay sisters office, tho allways assisted at great feasts in the quire ... [She came to] Vespers and Complain [Compline] which she could say pritty well, joyning with ye quire. She was a true lover of her cell and of solitude, very cheerful and recreative at proper times, and applying her self to her companion in ye times of recreation, most asidious in whatever she had to doe, performing the office of Sacrestain very compleately ... [and worked in the infirmary for around 20 years].

... She was naturally of a hott hasty temper, but by her constant endeavours and continuall victorys over her self was all sweetness and mildness ... [Even when she was ill] she prayed so heartily that one might see she was wholly intent upon what she was doing ...

[She had a special devotion to Our Lady, St Joseph, St Ann] allso all ye widdow saints that she could not hide it particularly upon their feasts wch she celebrated with tears of joy and devotion ... We have reason to believe she had favours of St Francis Xavier[1] ...

... About an hour after her departure [on Monday 21 November 1740], I was reflecting of her not having lived in religion it suddenly came to my mind yt it was 33 years to that very day since the death of her son, at which time she resolved to dedicate her self to the service of God in a religious state, so that we doubted no longer wt was intimated to her of 33 years beleiving she had the merit of her good desires of being religious from that time.

---

[1]   Francis Xavier (1506–52) was her name-saint, and also that of her sister Catherine Burton who thought herself to have been miraculously cured by him (Chapter 28). A Spanish missionary, canonized only in 1622, the same year as Teresa de Jesus, he was a popular figure of devotion with the Carmelites of this period.

Chapter 21

Mary Joseph of St Teresa:
The Life and Death of the First Compiler, who Knew Her Vocation at a Country Dance and who Left Loving Instructions for her Sisters

Mary Howard (1688–1756) was one of several religious from her family, all daughters of Jane and William Howard. Joseph Frances of the Blessed Trinity (pp. 16, 65) and Teresa of Jesus (Chapter 22) were her sisters. She was the first compiler of the Antwerp annals, continuing in this role until shortly before her death, and she is at once a shadowy and central figure: shy, 'backwards in speaking', self-effacing and anonymous until this point in the narrative, she is also a self-conscious compiler who sets out her editorial manifesto (Chapter 1). She was Prioress from 1735 to 1750 and left behind her own statement for posterity which was included by the next compiler in Mary Joseph's own Life. Throughout the papers, her affection for the community and her evident emotion at various events give a human touch to the tone of the convent chronicle.

———————

[*A2*, 241–76]

This Reverend Mother ... was the person who collected these lives our d[ea]r deceased from the first foundation till ye year 1750, and left at her death an account of her own, to which she added most profitable instructions to the religious which I insert as follows:

Jesus Maria Joseph

I have been a long time deliberating with my self if I'd leave the following lines or no, many reasons presenting on both sides, but, as I confide in God, my intentions are good ... & only to be seen by my dearest sisters & beloved children. I resolved upon it, asuring my self yt I shall have their more frequent & earnest prayers when in no capacity of helping my self; and that it will allso make you praise God & be more faithfull to his graces & preventing mercys of goodness than I have been ...
    [From my childhood, I sensed the shortness of life] I sufferd a kind of martirdom,

keeping all my uneasiness to my self, and found such a mixture of good & bad yt I am not able to express it. I had allways an inclination to be a nun but never woud say so ... In ye midst of a country dance [I] truly experienced wt St Augustine says, that God created our hearts for himself alone & they would ever remain restless and unquiet till they reposed in him. Thus I went on till Allty God was pleased, by the death of my eldest brother whom I loved most tenderly, [to give me] such a disgust to any thing of the world that all was now quite disagreable ...

Note she so entirely renounced all vanitys that novice young, she never wore any thing but quite plain clothes & a night cap wth out a border to it, like our infirmary caps.

I now was more desirous of being religious, and had many thoughts of this holy Order from hearing it spoke of by a Father of the Society & reading our Bd Mothers Life wch accidently came to my hands; and that I might come over at the same time my sister did, was the intention I made in our pilgrimage to Holy Well [in Wales] ... My exceeding backwards in speaking made all pass in silence till just upon the point of her coming away, I then got so much courage as to make my desires known ...

... It was also in time of war, when the English were on ye side so yt [my brother Howard, who opposed my plan] thought I might be in more occasions of danger than at home. In fine, as I was to accompany my sister & a priest ... we were upon our journey from June till ye middle of August, being obliged to stay at London on account of the difficulty of getting a pass as I have often related ...[1]

... My very shy & silent disposition made every thing I had to do on such an occasion very uneasy & mortifying to me ... I found a strange strife in my own heart which effected me so ... [I did not give this away to my sister and brother at my clothing] only appeard a very serious thoughtfull bride. But I had no sooner set my foot within the monastery ... but I found my self quite changed: all ye anxiety & melancholy left me wth my secular clothes, finding my heart in peace & joy ...[2]

... What I found the hardest was wearing woolen, & a great pride & bashfulness wch made wt ever I did in com[muni]ty a very hard task, particularly quire dutys & reading in ye refectory, on account of a great imperfection in my speech wch made these things a torment to me ...

[I promised St Joseph that if he would help me, I would say his litany every day for a year] & before it was ended I found my self quite another thing in speaking & reading, but to this day have not lost ye difficulty in performing many exteriour dutys ...

...[I was] allways sloathfull, tepid & negligent in ye dutys belonging to my state [and the death of my friends affected my health so, after 7 years I] fell into an illness wch lasted my years. [I was] often obliged to use all my courage to go about the house ... I fear it was want of courage & self love ...[3]

---

[1]   Around one page of the original text is omitted here.
[2]   Around one page of the original text is omitted here.
[3]   Around 10 pages of the original text are omitted here, discussing what she perceives to be her own shortcomings. The extract resumes with a copy of her statement left for the other nuns.

... I must own, dearest sisters, it would have been much more proper for me to have given you a rehearsal & inlarged upon my great sins ... than to have sum'd up all the little things that could make you have more favourable sentiments of me ... for did we truly endeavour to know God & to know our selves it will soon damp our pride & self complacence. Besides, you have been eye witnesses of my irregular life & seen how I have neglected my greatest obligations, and ye sad effects of my pride, sloth & self-love, & want of true courage in every occasion, a truth wch far outbalances any thing I could say & wch cannot fail moving you to assist me more particularly wth your fervent prayers ...

... If any thing in ys moves yu towards a good thought, give ye glory to God, wch I confide is my motive in writing. It the same in those papers wch I undertook by obedience to collect of the deceased religious, wch as much as I know of my self I did in simplicity of heart to comply wth obedience, and for the comfort of ye community, to animate them in ye way of perfection, & as an incouragement to follow the steps traced of so many prevented souls that have so long traced ye way for us. Do not read them for curiosity, to be more knowing, & still worse to find fault & draw consequences: this will raise disputes & even cause defects in charity, quite contrary to ye intention of Superiors who orderd it & those who wrote it. Take wt is edification & profit to your selves & leave ye rest as it is ...

[I feared others would] say things of me that I no ways merited, so resolved to leave ys simple account of my self, but to concern my design yu must not be angary if I add a few things more wch indeed gives me a real confusion – but as yu have allways taken in good part what my duty in ye office I am now in obliged me to remind you of from time to time, so my tender love for all & each of you prompts me to say wt follows.

My most dearest sisters, constantly bear in mind ye grace of your vocation, remember you tread upon holy ground ... dayly sanctified by the fervent acts, vertues & suffering lives and deaths, of so many happy, generous spouses of Christ, the hunderd fold to them and a paradise upon earth.[4] Can you be too gratefull to God? ... no, no, in all you think say or do, tho may make your selves slaves to every one, beleive me you can never shew enough ... Never excuse your selves by complaining of those who taught & instructed you ... [blame yourself] for there is none so deaf as those that will not hear, so there is none so stupid as those that will not learn ...

... We are not to look on each other as servants, but as sisters & spouses of Jesus Christ, and treat each other as such with civility respect & affection ... Don't meddle, nor trouble yr heads wth ye affairs or concerns of others, neither publick nor private ... when ever you find yr heart disturbed & agitated in this manner distrust yr selves ...

---

[4] Teresa de Jesus used this same phrase 'a paradise upon earth' in a letter to her nuns, a copy of which Sister Mary Joseph transcribed in her Life of Anne of the Ascension: 'It hath pleased God to call and assemble such persons together in this monastery of ours as makes me even amazed ... [God pleased] to give them such alacrity and joy as to make it usual and familiar to them, that they seem to be in a kind of paradise upon earth' (*A1*, 78).

[5] Around three pages of the original text, largely in repetitive mode, are omitted here.

[6] The narrative returns to the third person at this point, for an account of her final years'

... A great help to all this will be a guard of the heart, endeavouring sweetly by degrees to draw your self within your self & beg succour from your divine spouse ... which a little book intitled a *Method of Conversing with God* teaches in a pritty sweet way ...

... What are we good for when we are hurried & disturbed in mind? Neither to converse with God nor our sisters[5] ... You know, dearest sisters, I have often said to you, 'Love one another' & now I say it again: 'Love one another' & that yu may never forget it I leave it to you in writing, 'Love one another' ... not only in words, but in reality, in truth & effect, that none may doubt it ... faithful spouses, go on, go on dearest sisters & love one another, comfort, rejoice and recreate one another ...

... But I forget my self & make this much longer than I at first designd it, but my sincere & tender love for all & every one of you is the cause ... Pardon me, dearest sisters, for presuming to say so much, but when occasion serves for the love of God, remember it and pray for me.

[During the last 3 years of her government, she suffered a][6] slight stroke of a palsy or appoplexy wch changed her very much & left a dimness in her sight ... a few months after she was struck wth a palsey which deprived her of the use of one side ... but, by ye violent remedys which were applyd, she recoverd so far as to be able to walk with a crutch & ye assistance of one person ...

... She suffered much interiourly & had a violent apprehension of death ... She had a violent fever for wch she was again administerd, & had not quite recovered it when she was seised wth a 2d fit of the palsey, much more violent than the first. Every one thought her in her agony ... In this fitt she quite lost her speach, wch she never perfectly recover'd, and from that time till her death above four years after [she] was intirely confined to her bed & chair, unable to help her self but as she was moved by others, never coud drink a draught & was often in danger of choaking when she eat, by the contraction in her throat.

About a year & a half after this stroke, she had an inflamation in her leg wch was in danger of turning to a gangrene, joind to a strong fever ... It seemd incredible that a person worn out wth distempers should get through so many dangerous ones, yet not long after she had a kind of a lethargie wch she likewise recovered ... continuing to act in ye same manner to ye last, tho her head was much weakened by so many reiterated stroaks ... She was watch'd wth every night for above 5 years, & for ye most part by two [religious] ... [during which period] I scarce ever knew them enjoy better health, nor [be] free from colds & other little disorders. In fine, a cold wch at first we did not much apprehend, terminated in a few days her many years sufferings. On the 16th of March as they were taking her up she fainted away[7] ...

---

illness and death.
[7]   She died on 18 March 1756, at 7:15, after 'a violent agony of about 5 hours'.

Chapter 22

Teresa de Jesus and Ann Joseph of the Ascension: Two Lives of Mutual Care

These two nuns were mutually supportive over many years. Teresa de Jesus (1694–1764) was born Bridget Howard, sister to Mary Joseph (Chapter 21). She professed on 26 April 1711, having previously spent time at both the Benedictine convent at Cambrai and with the Ursulines at Antwerp. When she was Mistress of Novices the first under her instruction was Ann Joseph of the Ascension (Ann Holm: 1716–64), who afterwards succeeded her as Subprioress and Prioress, and who later nursed her for many years. The two women died within a few months of each other, and their Lives, which follow directly one after the other in the annals, supply moving testimony to the comforts of community care, not least in the poignant last words of one of them, written as she died.

_____

[*A2*, 291–2]

… During the last three years of her [Teresa de Jesus'] government [as Prioress] she was struck with a palsey wch deprived her of ye use of one side & renderd her quite helpless the remainder of her life, but no ways affected her senses wch she retaind to the last. She suffered much for above three years, not only by this distemper but by the stones of rheum. Yet her courage and resignation made her bear up with great chearfullness & patience in the midst of so many corporal infirmitys, to wch was added troubles of mind on occasion of some mortifying affairs related to the change of Confessors.

When the election came she gave up her office[1] & the Bishop accepted her renounciation before we gave votes. Rd Mother Ann was chose to succeed her, who till then had been the chief person to help & assist her …

[They were deprived] of this mutual consolation for Mother Ann Joseph's cancer in her breast, which she had before conceald, put her out of a capacity of doing it any longer, & no one could do it with the same dexterity. I beleive none but God knew what she sufferd in this last year, her strength dayly diminishing & being never able to change her posture neither night or day, but as she was moved by others. Tho reduced to this condition she was continually employd, either in praying, reading or working bobin to trim beads with one

_____

[1]   In 1750 (she had been Prioress since 1735), at which point Ann Joseph of the Ascension, the subject of the other Life in this extract, succeeded her.

hand, which was the only limb she had the perfect use of. Some months before her death her speech grew very unintelligble & [she] had so intirely lost her appetite that she scarse eat enough to sustain life. Notwithstanding this long series of sufferings, Allty God was pleased to send her another severe tryal ...

She fell very ill but none suspected what her illness was. The doctor orderd her the last sacraments at his 2d visit wch she received ... but did not seem to think her self in imediat danger tho she appeard to us allmost agonising ... At last the fatal distemper shewd itself & proved the small pox & of ye worst sort. As several had never had it, the community was obligd to be seperated & she deprived of the assistance of some of those she was accustomed to ... who had attended her during the whole time of her illness ... This was indeed a severe tryal to all ...

The last night of her life, those who were about her were pierced to the heart to see the torments she endured without being able to give her any relief or even daring to remove her, tho she earnestly desired it. She was so perfectly sensible yt, not long before she dyed, she made a sign for a pen & ink, & wrote down something she wanted & which she could not make them understand by speaking.[2] Between 5 & 6 in ye morning she fell into her agony which was peacefull, tho strong, & lasted about an hour. The community was call'd up & assembled in the *Deprofundis*[3] where we recited the prayers for the agonising. A little before 9 in the morning she gave up her soul to God on Monday the 20th of February 1764 aged 70, in religion 54. She was the 17th Superiour of this convent.

*

[*A2*, 296–8]

During the last 3 years of being Subprioress [Ann Joseph of the Ascension] got a cancer in her breast but not knowing what it was, and not caring to complain of it for fear she shou'd be hinderd from assisting & lifting Rd Dr Mor Teresa who was become quite helpless by a palsey, she conceal'd it, till it was too late. In all probability she got it by some hurt in assisting Rd Mother Teresa, wch made her more unwilling to speak of it. When she perceived it was broke, she own'd afterwards, she was a little shock'd but went to the quire & made an offering of herself to Alm God ...

She never enjoy'd a day of health after she was chose Superiour, and within less than a month was allmost reduced to extremeity by a violent cholick of wch she had three bad fits in less than a month. The cancer eat into a wound ... but what she suffer'd in mind far exceeded all ... in the death of Dr Mother Teresa of Jesus who was the person in ye world for whom she had the greatest affection and regard ... [tending her] with tenderness and asiduity ...

The cancer, wch for some time was so much better as to give hopes of a cure, began again to make most raped progress & eat into a deep wound, shocking to all who saw it,

---

2   Amazingly, movingly, the small slip of paper on which she wrote has survived, tucked within the pages of the book at this point. It has spidery, barely legible writing on one side, which appears to be a request for a 'candle'; on the reverse it reads, 'This was wrote by Dr Mother 3 or 4 hours before she dyd'.

3   Literally, 'out of the depths': the opening words of Psalm 130, used in prayers for the dead and dying.

herself excepted, who view'd it with as much pleasure as a worldly lady wou'd look on her richest jewels. She also suffer'd violent pains in her limbs and often told me that, her hands excepted, she had not one part of her body free from pain, nor had one moment of ease from the day she took the infirmary, ye 9th of March, till that of her happy death 26 of October [1764] ...

In June she received the last sacraments, and was not only confined to her bed but unable to move in it or even to lean her head back against ye pellows, but allways in a sitting posture even when she slept & her head bent forward. For about three months she took no sustenance but liquids wch was her greatest comfort & consolation, not being able to swallow a small particle wth out danger of vomiting, but that did not last much above a fortnight ... The violence of ye pains she sufferd can scarcely be express'd, one leg was contracted to such a degree that it was near a quarter of a yard shorter than the other, and her thigh bone seem'd quite out of its place. Tho we moved her with the greatest care, & only lifted her upon a mattress from one bed to another, yet we often put her to ye greatest torment ...

Chapter 23

Mary Magdalen of St Joseph: Her Dramatic Journey from Maryland, Her Teresian Vocation, and Her Cure from Rheumatism

Following the arrival of Jesuit missionaries in Maryland, several women came to northern Europe to join convents, including this religious and her travelling-companion as well as another religious who settled at Lierre (Chapters 27, 40). This nun was born Margarite Pye (1724–77), daughter to Margarite Tant and Walter Pye, whose family had Essex connections. The Life gives some sense of her domestic conditions in Maryland, of the perilous journey she undertook, and of her time within a community far from her place of birth. In common with those of some other nuns, her father was a slave-owner: Mary Xaveria of the Sacred Heart of Jesus (from 'Prince George county', Maryland) who professed at Lierre in 1751, similarly '… spent [her youth] in charitable offices of visiting & serving sick and infirm slaves, procuring them all necessary helps, both spiritual and temporal & zealously endevouring for the baptizem of their children' (*L13.7*, 314). Teresa Joseph of the Annunciation (Eleanor Wharton: 1723–93), also of Maryland, broke away from her family, and 'being entirely her own mistress, kept house and had her negros at command …' (*L13.8*, 15).

———

[*A2*, 312–15]

[Her father kept his children] out of dangerous company: he was very humane and tender to his slaves, carefull as well of their souls as of their bodys, to this end he obliged his children to teach them their prayers, and instruct them in the Christian doctrine. To this charitable occupation Str Mary Margaret gave a considerable part of her time, and also in working for them. In her younger days she was much given to pleasure, company and dress, but ye watchfull care of her father kept so great a restraint upon her inclinations that there was no excess …

... She got herself inrolled in the sodallity of Our Bd Lady[1] & in the Confraternity of the Bonne Mort ... She was first drawn to embrace a religious state by reading the life of Lady Warner.[2]

... After having settled things with her friends [who opposed her being a religious], they began to contrive for her journey ... Mr Hunter, who was her Confessor, conducted her with another young lady[3] to the sea side, who was comming over also to take ye habitt in our convent, of whom I shall speak in its proper place. After some days spent near the water side expecting the ships sailing, Mr Hunter ... gave them his blessing ... and, after having recommended them to ye captains care in the strongest terms, bad them adue. They sett sail with much courage & a fair wind, but in the cours of their navigation a most violent storm arising in the darkness of the night & [from] which the ship and passengers were in eminent danger. In this distress Str M[ary] Mag[dalen]: began to pray with all her might, and to make the strongest promises and resolutions concerning her future conduit, to our Lord if he would vouchsafe to deliver them from the danger.

After some hours the tempest began to asswage, & after many adventers, & a six weeks navigations, they arrived safe to London where, after some stay to recover their fatigue, [they] sett of[f] for Brabant. And being arrived as far as Gant [Ghent], a deep snow falling, were there containd for a month. At length the happie moment arrived wch conducted them to Antwerp: but here Str Magdalen found a new source of affliction for, having been accepted at the Benedictine Dames of Brussels before she left Maryland, and coming here with her companion, [she] found so strong an atract for this hous[e] that the thought of leaving it was like death to her. Infin, the day of her departure arriving, she prepared herself to go with Mr Mulleneux who had been missioner in Maryland[4] ... but a moment before she sett of, beg'd to speak to our Superiour in private in which interview she disclosed to her the secrets of her heart, most humbly intreating she might be admitted here, in case she should not be content at Brussels ... Consoled [to be told yes] she went with Mr Mulleneux for Brussels ...

At her arrival [there] she was received by the community with great marks of affection. She was very tall of stature, [with] a good complexion... & had an exceeding good voice, with which that comty [community] was much pleasd for their quire wanted such a one ... [But] nothing could content her [and she] was ashamed to own her inclinations were quite for the Teresian Order ...

She took our habit with much satisfaction ... but after a short time, our Lord was pleasd to make her pass through the fyre tryal of interior afflictions, scruples, aridities and darkness, which continued for the greater part of her noviship ... Our Lord was pleased to disipate these clouds & place her again in the land of peace, tho she was always rather inclined to anxiety ...

---

1   A lay fellowship, of which Mary Joseph of St Teresa (Chapter 21) was also a member before she became a Carmelite.

2   *The Life of Lady Warner*, published in St Omer in 1691, was written by Edward Scarisbrick (1639–1708/09), who also used the alias 'Neville' during penal times.

3   Mary Margaret of the Angels (Chapter 29).

4   From 1634, a number of Jesuits (generally four per year) served in Maryland as missionaries. Several members of the Molyneux family were Jesuits in this period (*Catholic Encyclopaedia*).

… Silent, patient & resignd in suffering, the greatest pains of which [she] had her share, drawn by the rhumatism till her legs almost touchd her back, and used to creep upon her hands & knees … All human remedies proving ineffectual, I left her one night to go to the reffectory, sitting before the table [beginning her devotions] & taking the multiplyd flower,[5] but when I returned to my great surprise she mett me at the dore and cryd out 'I am quite cured and can walk as well as ever I could in my life'. And thus she continued, and never after had so severe an attack …

5   Presumably a medicinal remedy made from diluted flower essences.

Chapter 24

Mary Xaveria of the Angels: Her Mental Affliction in which She Fancied Herself to be a Priest and Excommunicated the Bells

The annals contain Lives of several women who suffered from mental illness. In this account, Margarite Smith/ Smyth (1697–1777) of Durham, niece of Delphina of St Joseph (Prioress from 1720–21; Chapters 5, 9, 29), became ill in middle age and was confined thereafter to the Infirmary for some 27 years, cared for by the religious. This extract focuses, as the Life itself does, on an incident in which the Bishop intervenes to persuade her to eat.

———————

[*A2*, 316–18]

… At 15 years of age she made a vow of chastity, her parents dying, & her two sisters were sent abroad, one of them became a Poor Clair at Gravline, the other a nun of the same Order in Portugal … [She was] sent pensioner to the Apostulines in Antwerp, where she learnd the Flemish tongue … Her aunt being then actually Superiour in our convent, she often came to visite and reicive instructions from her, and by this means became aquainted with the religious …

… She had often, in a transport of joy, kist the convent gate, as the happie [cause] of shutting out the world from her, & inclosing her in this holy house … [Always of an ardent temper], about the turn of life[1] she began to be somwhat disordrd which, increasing even to extravagences, we were obliged to confine her to the Infirmary where she remaind for the last 27 years of her life. She fancyd herself a priest & therefore dayly, in her way, said Mass, made holy water for her own use, and blessed her habit & c, sometimes excommunicated persons and things, as for example the bells.

———————

[1]   The same phrase is also used of Beatrix Xaveria of Jesus (Beatrix Chantrell: 1704–82), who 'did great service for 20 years, but at the turn of life she quite losst her reason, and was never more capable of any thing, and generally very furious' (*A2*, 324).

... She once took a fitt of fasting so that we feard she would starve herself as it was impossible for us to make her eat. We sent to my Lord Bishop Dominick de Genentis to inform him of it, and to tell him of her great atatchment to his Lordsp & all Ecclesiasticks, hoping an order from his Lordsp might engage her to eat. In fine, my Lord had the goodness to come himself, in person with his secretary, to try what he could do. At first she would not believe him to be the Bishop ... till she accidentaly espyd his white stockings from under his habit wch was also white, being a Dominiccan, then she was convinced. And his Lordship was so good as to call for a poringer [bowl] of broth, held it in his own hands and, at length, after many preambles, prevail'd on her to take it, indeed she was most ridiculous & so clever that none [could] help smiling. At length his Lordship got her to promise to take whatsoever the Infirmarian gave her, which afterwards she did, but always took care to say, before she toucht it, 'In obedience to my Lord Bishop'.

In fine, the last 2 years of her life she became more reasonable, and pritty often permitted to communion ... She was so agreable & recreative in these last years that the religious had great pleasure in visiting her, to hear her little innocent storys and deverting immaginations, all which herself belived to be true ...

Chapter 25

Mary of St Barbara: The Life of an Oblate from the Coffee-house

Mary of St Barbara (née Leymons: 1701–77) of Deist in Brabant, joined the convent in *c*.1729, having previously worked in an Antwerp coffee-house. Her brief Life is included here to show the varieties of religious experience available within the Order. She joined as an oblate, wore the habit and shared in the exercises of the convent, but without taking vows beyond promising obedience to her Superior.

[*A2*, 319–320]

… Born of creditable parents by whom she was brought up to piety and labour, according to their circumstances, [she] was sent out to service as soon as capable of it, & gave great content in the places where she served. She had lived for some time in a coffe hous in Antwerp, & it was from thence we took her, we being in want of a servant: a worthy ecclesiastick, who for many years had said our dayly Mass, and being very well aquainted with her merits, recommended her …

… [She] had not been long in our service before she conceived a longing desire of becomming a lay sister … [We] opposed against such a choice seing in perticular the much greater service she could render the community in the station of an oblate …

… She was very capable and clever in the management of all that concern'd the out-quarter, civil and obliging to all … very laborious, keeping herself always employ'd; when at home at her [spinning] wheel, when [she went] to answer a bell she immediately took up her knitting, not to lose a moment of her time, a constant goer to market … the weather be good or bad, being always at the washes [laundry], to keep ye washers to their duty … indeed a treasure to us.

In her last sickness we took her in to the convent, that in case she dyed there might be no objection made to her being buryed in the convent. A cold & fever joined a surbutick[1] humour, to the latter she been long subject to, and at length falling into her legs, terminating in a gangreen terminated her vertuous life …

---

[1] Presumably from 'surbate', suggesting she was prone to foot-sore bruising or lameness.

Chapter 26

Angela Maria of St Joseph: Her Early Life in which She Almost Dies of Malnutrition; and Her Seduction to Become a Carmelite after which She Once Drank her Own Urine in an Act of Misplaced Obedience

This extract provides insight into the practice of wet-nursing during which, as an infant, Catharine Kingsley (1707–84) was ill-treated and almost died. Subsequently, she travelled with her mother to northern continental Europe, and professed at Antwerp in 1725 as a result of her brother's careful persuasion. As well as giving insight into family relationships, this Life refers to Sister Angela's obedience: as in the cases of other nuns (pp. 21, 48), the incident described here suggests how deeply embodied was this concept, which Mary Joseph of St Teresa, the first compiler of the annals, had described in St Teresa's words as the 'first touchstone of virtues' (*A2*, 263).

[*A2*, 325–328]

This dear sister was a twin. The other who was born with her dying, all possible care was taken to bring this up, who was put out to one [who] was thought to be a very good and proper nurse, for the tender infant. But she proved of a quite contrary caracter, and so unnatural that she so neglected the child it was very near dying with hunger. As soon as Mrs Kingsley got informations of what a miserable creature she was to whom she had committed the care of the child, [she] sent immediately for her home, and by degrees revived the poor infant whom she found reduced to a shadow …

… As soon as she was of a proper age for a convent, her mother brought her over, & placed her at the Separcharins at Liege, where she had her other daughter. And, after having stayd some days there to see her child settled, in her return to England took Antwerp in her way, [and] had leave to enter the inclosier and to see the intier body of our Venble Mor

M: M: of the Angels[1] ... saying she had a good little girle whom she wisht might be so happy as to be a nun here. She dyed soon after her arrival in England, to the bitter grief and affliction of her dear child at Liege, who was then committed to the care of her elder brother, then studiant at the Coledge at Liege, together with her 3 other brothers, who all became Jesuites ...

She soon got an inclination of being religious, and to fix at Liege ... [However, her brother] had a great inclination in case Allm: God should favour her with a call to have her a Carmilite, yet [he] never disclosed his sentiments to her, but to bring his designs about went to her to perswade [her] to leave Liege for a time & go to Antwerp, there to pension at the Ursulines, thus underhand to bring her to an aquaintance with our community, to wch she expressd a very great dislike & repugnance. She utterd many reasons against going to another convent, but at length, by his unwearied endeavours & frequent solicitations, he gaind her consent & conducted her himself to the Ursulines, promising her if she was not satisfied he would come again and take her back to her former convent. With this assurance she remaind very well content. After she had been a few days at ye Ursulines, our religious sent for her to come and pass an afternoon at the great [grate] to recreat her; but the thoughts of Liege so occupied her mind that this first visite pass'd dry enough. The 2d things grew better ... and by degrees she gave Antwerp the preference to all other places ...

[She was excellent] in obedience and submission to her Superiours, as dosel [docile] as an infant ... When in her noviship she compland [complained] of the beer being flat & not good, upon which her [Novice] Mrs sharply reprehended this small want of mortification, saying 'Drink your own water'. This humble and truly obedient soul, without reply or making any reflections upon the matter, went to execute what she thought the intention of her Mrs and performed it with all simplicity...

... At the desolution of the monastery she burnt all her papers, so that we have nothing of her interior discours or communications with our dear Lord write here for the edification [of] our the reader ...

---

[1] Margaret Wake, whose incorrupt body had been discovered in 1716. Several nuns, as well as influential visitors, arrived at the convent for this reason (see Chapter 18).

Chapter 27

Mary Margaret of the Angels: Her Journey from Maryland in which She Almost Falls in Love with a Young Gentleman; Her Burial as the Convent is Threatened by Imperial Edict

The Life of Mary Brent (born 1731, professed 1752) is the final entry in the Antwerp annals from this period, written with a sense of impending change imposed on the convent by 'Emperial Edict' and in the face of advancing French Revolutionary forces. Like Mary Magdalen of St Joseph (Chapter 23), with whom she travelled, and Sister Mary Rose (Chapter 40), this religious was born in Maryland, the favourite of three children of Mary (née Wharton) and Robert Brent. Her arrival to the safe haven of the convent, after a hazardous journey, contrasts with her burial in the convent garden, described with a sense of the prevailing new circumstances that were soon to dramatically affect the nuns.

———————

[*A2*, 340–344]

… She never had the least fear in all the 6 weeks navigation, tho once the ship was in eminent danger. In her joirney from America to England the enimie [devil], envious of her approaching happiness, laid snares in her way to hinder her pious designes, putting into the heart of a young gentleman who was embarked in the same vessell, to try her constancy, by presents preventions & c., and who gaind her esteem & affection that she at length told him that, in case she did not succeed in her holy pretentions, he should have the prefferance in her regard to any other …[1]

[She] was buried on Thursday afternoon. We were obliged to shut up the coffin in time of ye dierge, she being very corpulant & her whole body mortified. Her Revce was buried in the garden, at the foot of ye Calvary by her own desire, as ye Emperial Edict

———————

[1]   Around two pages are here omitted from the original text, which describe her lengthy period as Prioress and her death.

was about that time promulgated concerning buryals, and thought ourselves since she might not be caryed to our dead celler, that were permitted to keep her in the inclosier, after having used all our care to obtain permission. Mr Neal, our Confessor, blessed ye ground for her interment. We went as usual the procession 8 days round the cloisters & for 9 days after her buryal[2] to the ---[3] & there said the *De profundis* for the repose of her soul. Rd Mother gave a musick Mass & hung the lessoners in the same manner as if she had dyed Superiour … She, with Str Mary Magdalene of S: Joseph[4] received ye sacrament of confession before their profession in our quire from the hands of my Ld Bishop Dominick de Gentis.

---

[2] See also the account of the funeral of Clare of the Annunciation in 1694 (Chapter 9).
[3] There is a gap here in the original text.
[4] See Chapter 23.

Chapter 28

Mary Xaveria of the Angels: Her Illness, Miraculous Cure and Her Spiritual Favours Before and After Death

This book-length Life of Catherine Burton (1668–1714) was compiled by Thomas Hunter.[1] It was commissioned in 1723/24 by Mary Frances (Mary Birkbeck: Chapters 1, 15) during her second period as Prioress at Antwerp (1721–30)[2] and must have been completed by 1725 when Hunter died. A summary of Mary Xaveria's Life also appears in the Antwerp annals (*A1*, 539–47); it mentions that details of her supernatural favours 'would fill a whole Book as it now does being writ on order to be printed' (*A1*, 541). If this refers is to Hunter's text, since the annals appear to have been started in around 1731–33 (see p. 36) after Hunter's death, the reference is presumably retrospective, transcribed without correction from an earlier source (a common feature of the composite Lives). However, Hunter does mention in Mary Xaveria's Life his hope that 'a more able pen … in time will publish these things' (p. 138), and while this may simply be a formulaic statement, it is possible that a further text was indeed prepared.

Hunter based his text on accounts written by Mary Xaveria herself and by her contemporary religious, knitting the various narratives together within a framework that was designed to defend the nun from ongoing suspicion of female mysticism. His opening preface anticipates scepticism about the nature of Mary Xaveria's experiences; throughout the Life he therefore takes great care to present material in a manner that diffuses doubt. It is important, then, to read this Life rather differently from those contained in the annals: it appears to have been intended to be at least a semi-public document, for dissemination beyond the convent, potentially perhaps to be presented to ecclesiastical authorities in the light of claims for Mary Xaveria's blessedness. As such it is designed to stand up to scrutiny and lays bare its compositional methods in

---

[1]   Thomas Hunter (1666–1725) studied at the English College at St Omers and became a Jesuit in 1684. He acted as spiritual advisor to Catherine Burton for several years (Coleridge, 1876, viii).

[2]   Her first period was 1714–20, immediately following Mary Xaveria as Prioress. Hunter himself mentions Mary Frances' commissioning letter – see note 7.

a spirit of empiricism that underlies such imperatives (see Hallett, 2002a).

Hunter gives details of Burton's secular and religious experience. She was born in Suffolk, where she lived for the first 25 years of her life with her father and siblings. Hunter names her parents as Mary (née Suttler) and Thomas Burton, of Bayton, near Bury St Edmunds. 'Her mother left nine children behind her, 4 sons and 5 daughters, she dyed of her tenth child in the five and thirtith year of her age' (*A3*, 315). By the time that Hunter was writing, one of Burton's brothers was a Jesuit priest, her oldest sister was an Augustinian nun at Bruges, her youngest sister (with whom she travelled to Antwerp) was Superior at Hoogstraeten, and another, widowed, sister also professed at Hopland (see Chapter 20).

Following a lengthy debilitating illness (she credited her cure to St Francis Xavier) Catherine Burton eventually arrived at Antwerp in December 1693. Her account, begun when she was around 30 years old, describes in fascinating detail her early life, her illness and medical care. Hunter incorporated this material into his biography of the nun, adding details of her spiritual favours and providing his own commentary (which he indicates by quotation marks in the text). Because this Life is so rich and occupies a whole book that is no longer fully available in print,[3] this extract is longer than others contained here. It opens with Hunter's preface, and then continues with Mary Xaveria's own account of how she was commanded to write her Life amidst conflicting instructions from her confessor and Saint that reveal much about ideas of obedience and authorship within a contemplative female tradition. The narrative then flashes back to her childhood, her illness, cure, arrival and life in Antwerp. Throughout, Hunter supplements the nun's own statements with witness testimony designed to authenticate the narrative.

[*A3*, i–457]

Jesus Maria Joseph Teresa Xa[vier]

The Preface

I present the Publick with a Book which will be differently received according to the different dispositions of those into whose hands it will chance to fall: the mentioneing of visions, revelations and supernatural favours will raise the curiosity of some and prove a jest to others, and in all probability with relish with very few, in an age so little inclined to belive any thing of this nature. However since I am perswaded that those who are piously disposed will reap advantage by it, I see no reason why it should not be published, for their sakes, notwithstanding whatever less favourable reception it may meet with from others.

----

[3]   An edition of Hunter's Life was published by Coleridge (1876) and Hardman (1939); a limited extract appears in Booy, 2002, 285–90.

I am very willing to give so far into ye sentiments of those who declare against the publishing any thing which apears singular, as to agree, that nothing in this kind should be made publick wch is not grounded upon sufficient testimonies to secure the Reader from being imposed upon; tho' this caution is always necessary, yet more particular regard must be had to it when we treat any thing of this nature with relation to weamen, there are not wanting those and in great number, who exaggerate so much in them the weakness of nature, and the force of imagination and fancy that they value themselves upon discrediting every thing in this kind; and they seem perswaded that the only way not to be imposed upon is to belive nothing ...[4]

... if we reflect besides on ye artifices of ye enemy who as ye Apostle says, 2: Cor: 11.14 *transfigures himself into an Angell of light* to seduce unwary souls, we shall still find greater danger of delusion in these uncommon paths; hence it is yt all those who have either experienced these effects in themselves, or who pretend to treat as Masters of this Mistical Science in ye direction of souls, lay this down as a certain maxime, that all these visions, whither exteriour or interiour, imaginary or intellectual, are allwayes to be suspected as dangerous; never to be desired or sought for, and not easily to be relyed on, unless accompanyed with certain effects & signs wch may secure a Director of souls yt they are ye operations of ye Divine Spirit. What happened to St Teresa in this kind is very notorious; we know this Blessed St was left for severall years in great uncertainty and all ye help she could get from the most learned & experienced men of her age was thought little enough to secure her, yt the favours she received proceeded from ye spirit of Alm: God.[5]

... She foretold to several of her directors things yt were to happen and ye event proved always ye truth of her predictions: in particular above ten years before ye treasure was discouer'd of ye incourrupt body of ye Venble Mother Margaret Wake, she positively told her Director yt God had revealed to her yt there was an incorrupt body in ye dead celler of ye English monastery at Antwerp ... and she opend her self several graves ... I might add several favours obtained by her intercession and prayers, both in her life time and since her death, I refer as before all these particulars to ye different parts of her writen life ...

... ye reader will be more satisfyed in reading these extrordinary visions and revelations, when he is informed that they were not taken by hear-say, but penn'd down by her self[6] ... It would be a thing very much out of ye way to put every one upon pening down to posterity whats most commendable in his life and actions, yet there are circumstances in wch this method is not unprecedented; St Paul thought it was for ye glory of God yt he should declare to ye world those wonderfull extasyes and rapts with which God had favoured him ... This seemed a sufficient warrant for vertuous and learned men to put St Teresa and other saints upon this methode of declareing what God has wrought in them

---

4   Around four pages of the original text are omitted here, citing scriptural and other authority for both spiritual favours and doubt about them.

5   Hunter here cites various sources, such as St Augustine, St Bonaventure and St John of the Cross, counselling against 'gieveing too easily credit to supernatural favours'. Around 10 pages of the original text are omitted here.

6   Around one page of the original text is omitted here.

... the Reader, I hope, will be satisfyed with ye directors who put this holy wom[a]n upon ye same methode[7]...

... I realy judge that this piece, as it lyes, is very imperfect and faulty, but I hope it may serve as memoirs to a more able pen wch I hope in time will publish these things, to the greater honour and glory of God, and to ye memory of his faithfull servant, ye Venerable Mother Mary Xaveria of ye Angels.

N.B. these ["] virgulas in ye margent denote some short remarks made upon her writeings by one who had sometime been her Director, but ye reader may intirely omit them without interrupting ye course of her Life.

1st part: Contaneing an account of what happend to her before she was religious

The Life of Mrs Catherine Burton, alias Mother Mary Xaveria of ye Angels written by her self in obedience to the orders she received from her Directors[8]

... at ye end of these ten Fridays [I made in honour of St Xavier] ye sick [sister] recovered to ye admiration of all, and St Xaverius appeared to me, as I was in our cell at work, and bid me write my life ... I cannot express ye peace and joy I found in my soul; I remained an hour in a rapt; yet I found great repugnance in doeing wt the Saint required of me, haveing no talent in writing, nor time for it (I was then in ye office of Subprioress, and had care of ye Novices) so yt considering ye little time I had, I was concerned I must be years about it ... I proposed to the Saint ye example I had heard of a vertous women who being bid by our Saviour to write her life differ'd [deferred] it for ten years, I desired to do ye same, but ye Saint gave me a gentle reperhension for this, and asked me how I knew I should live so long ... I found great difficulty resigning to this, thinking it would take up all my thoughts. Ye Saint told me he would help me, that he would indite it for me, and yt there should be nothing in it but what was true – I was in fear, haveing a bad memory, yt I should write some things not so exactly as I could wish – upon this I submitted and resolud to acquaint my Director with wt had happen'd ...

He answer'd, if the Saint helped me ... all would go well, otherwise knowing what a writer I was, he thought it could not be done. However, he bid me begin, at wch I was much troubled. After this I fell into temptations and was in great affliction, & anxiety about it ... I apprehended it would disturb my head, and entirely take away my peace of mind, because I found my self strangely distracted when I went to consider any thing of

---

7   Hunter concludes his preface with a standard protestation in obedience to Urban VIII's decree of 13 March 1625, that the account is grounded only on 'human authority', and that his use of any titles (such as 'Venerable') is not meant to imply that he has any power to ascribe a beatified or canonised status on his subject. He also cites his authority to compile the text, a letter of 9 February 1723/24 from Mary Frances Birkbeck. Around two pages of the original text are omitted here.

8   This section opens with Catherine Burton's own account of the cure of a sick religious for whom she had used the Ten Fridays devotions to St Francis Xavier, an observance that she believed had cured her when she had been ill herself (as described later in her narrative): it is after this that she is told by her earthly and holy directors to write her Life.

my life past. I beleived I should never put any thing in order; and often thought, that if I writ any thing, I should repent it ...

After this he appointed me a day to begin, and bid me write down my first years sickness wch I did without alleadging any farther difficulty. I found still repugnance enough, not knowing what to say, yett as soon as I had set pen to paper, I found no more dificulity then if it had been all writen before me & yt I had transcribed it ...

... Then I told him what I had done ... I shewed him my papers, and I was commanded to begin from my childhood ... I had now continued writeing as far as my cure by St Xaverius, when I received a letter from my Director who order'd me, without delay, to burn all ye papers I had by me. At ye same time he let me know that ye reason why he permitted me to continue writeing so long was only to try my obedience, adding that if every nun were to write her fancyes we should have pleasant volumes. He allso put some very slight expressions in regard of ye papers I had given him to transcribe. This letter gave me great comfort; I burnt immediately all ye papers I had, without haveing a thought to the contrary, or ye least repugnance in doeing it, but rejoyced to think I had thus imployed my self for Alm: God. Two or three days after, when I had told him yt according to his orders I had burnt ye papers, he bid me again from my childhood, as if I had writen nothing. Upon this I felt some repugnance at first, yet began as soon as I could find an opportunity, and thanked God to see my self thus imployed in writeing the same thing over again.

I had writ half a sheet of paper when St Xaverius appeared to me, and said I should write no more ye same thing over again, and that I had fullfilled my obedience ... He orderd me to tell my Director to go on transcribeing without scruple. I remained for above half an hour in rapt, without being able to stir my right hand or make a letter; tho I endeavour'd never so much ...

... I never asked to be dispensed from any of my spiritual dutys on account of writing, only twice from half an hour of reading; neither did I exempt my self from any act of community, nor from ye hour allotted for recreation, because I thought ye Saint would not have this done, but I took such by-times as I could steal to my self in our cell. I am even amazed to see yt I have writ in four months time, wt I thought would have cost me some years; and when I read over what I have write, it seems as if I had not done it but as if some other had done it for me ... If it should be thought fitt after my death, to expose wt I have writ down, I beg ye reader to pray for my soul, for I shall have a much heavier purgatery then if I had dyed in my sickness, before I came to religion[9] ...

... "She was neer thirty years of age before she put pen to paper and considering ye multiplicity of favours she had received before that time, as appears in her writings, what a confusion it naturally breed to think of bringing all these into there order with all their circumstances. And yet I have several times, on set purpose, put her upon recounting some particular passage wch had happened many years before and allways found her as exactly precise to every minute circumstance, as if she had seen it then translaited before her eyes, a convinceing proof to me yt it was not a fiction of her own head, made at random by ye force of imagination and fancy: this would have alter'd sometimes, and

---

9   Around two pages of the original text are omitted here.

by this have discouer'd it self. She was so farr disingaged from any tye to her self or her own performance yt she was perfectly indifferent whether her writings were kept or burnt, liked or not liked. It was this perfect disingagement from her self wch drew Alm: God and her Saint (as she called St Xaverius) so near unto her when she was imployed by her Directors in this work. At those times she seem'd as recollected[10] as when actually imployed in prayer … She received all these orders [to burn her papers] wh ye same sedate calmness of mind, as unconcernd as if it had nothing belonged to her … She had great difficulty in mentioning favours from God and more particularly to think of pening them down" …

Chapter 2d: Of her infancy

… God did me ye favour to let me be born of vertuous and pious parents. My mother dyed when I was 8 years of age; she left eight children behind her;[11] I was ye youngest but three … [My Father] encourage[d] us [and] promised money to those who learnt best their catechisme[12] …

[I had a] sensible devotion in my vocal prayers, yet I loved my play … When being at my prayers I heard my play-fellows were come, yet God moved me forceably to stay and put an end to them … I was then about seven years of age. I was counted wild and higher spirited then my brothers & sisters, yet when alone I had very serious thoughts. My greatest difficulty tel I was ten or eleaven years old was to be obliged to go early to bed with ye others. I used to keep them awake, sometimes by making them say prayers with me, sometimes by telling storyes … in place of it [I] would relate some passage of ye passion, saying it was a true story. I remember I was cheifly moved with the whipping at ye pillar, and changing of his garments, wch I used to explicate by some familiar comparisons …

From 10 or 11 til 16 I lived a more sensual life, following too much ye bent of my own passions. Tow or three times, on occasion of some words of humiliation said to me by servants, I found my blood to rise and my self tremble with passion, tho it was not my nature to be angry long …I loved to be esteemed handsome, tho' I had a scruple to spend much time in dressing my self … I did much harm by converseing with a young gentlewoman of my own age, and commited several faults without knowing them … I was not inclined to talk of good things as in my tender yeares …[13]

I remember I was one day in a chamber where the chapel was set up, neither praying, reading, nor thinking of God as I know of. On a suddain I had a light of some things of my life past wch I had never confessed: I thought our Bd Lord stood on my right side in mean apparel, like one wearyed out with seeking me. I found great remorse of conscience, and

---

10 See p. 40 for a discussion of recollection.
11 The number of children is different from that given elsewhere by Hunter, *A3*, 315; see p. 136.
12 After the Council of Trent (1545–63), a large number of catechisms was produced, in Latin and in the vernacular, in a campaign to improve devotional knowledge. These emphasized the importance of learning the Pater Noster, Ave, general confession, Apostles' Creed, Ten Commandments and Seven Sacraments, the catechism as a whole ideally being rehearsed by an adult with children and servants (see Bireley, 1999, 102).
13 Around one page of the original text is omitted here.

an alteration over my whole body ... and from that time began to change my life ...

I took delight to read once a week the advices of our Holy Mother St Teresa wch were commonly found in ye manuals ... I endeavour'd to follow her advice as near as I could, yet I thought it very hard at first not to eat nor drink, but at ye ordinary hours of dinner and supper, and to forbear fruit wch was a great mortification. It often came into my mind how Adam was overcome by eating an appell, so I thought I was inspired by Alm: God to mortify my appetite in these things ...

... I would sometimes rise in ye night as soon as I was awake, and kneel down by my bed side without putting on my cloaths thô ye weather were very cold. At other times I would go in ye evening when it began to grow dark into an orchard and field nigh [near] ye house. There I would make stations,[14] walking them ... sometimes without my shoes ... tho ye weather were very cold and ye ground all covered with snow, this did not stop me when I thought my self moved by God ...

My greatest dificulty was from ye apprehension I had of being in ye dark, and there was talk of the appearance of some evill spirit nigh one of ye places I frequented ... and once I thought I saw a light in ye place before me, yett I went on with confidence in God and a resolution to overcome my self ... I took delight this year in reading ye life of Saint Catherine of Siena;[15] tho I read no where these practices I made use of, I used in imitation of her when I went up and down staires to say Ave Maryes and kiss ye ground, I belive fifty times a day, without ever knowing that religious persons or any others did this ...

What I had practiced in ye world made all things in religion easy to me ... As I was once kneeling down in an allay to make my adorations, I thought yt some of ye house were watching to see what I did; I was much confounded to think wt they would say of me ... I wonderd many times that I was not ye talk of town and country, yet I never knew any body speak of it except a Protestant neighbour. He had seen me as I walked, often kneeling down and kiss ye ground, lifting up my hands and eyes to heaven ...

... I had more liberty in [visiting people who were sick] than ordinary because my eldest sister (who since our mother's death had kept my father's house, and taken great care of us who were younger), was for ye most abroard, at which time my father left us all to me, as being ye eldest at home. Before this year I should have been glad to play ye Mistress but now I employed my self in ye meanest offices ... I would sometimes dress my self in a contemptable manner to be laught att ... Many times when I dressed my self as my other sisters did I would lace my self so straight, that my stayes were more painful then any chain I have wore since I came to religion[16] ...

---

[14]   I.e., Stations of the Cross: a series of tableaux or pictures representing scenes in the Passion of Christ, arranged at intervals to allow contemplation of the chief moments of suffering and death. They are said to have originated within Franciscan affective devotion, coming into more common practice only towards the end of the seventeenth century (*Catholic Encyclopaedia*).

[15]   Catherine of Siena (1347–80). Her Life was relatively widely known in England, having been introduced during the fifteenth century and printed by Wynkyn de Worde in 1519; it was a highly influential text, recommended by Teresa de Jesus, for whose *Book* it was a formative model (see Ahlgren, 2000).

[16]   Several nuns mention wearing a chain around their waist for mortification: see also p. 201.

... After I had practised these mortifications about a year, for want of a Director I fell into anxiety ... fancying it was a sin ... I found after some time my head much disturbed and almost half-turned. This did not continue long tel notice was taken of it ... My father ... sweetly told me I must do nothing of mortification without leave of my Confessor ... [He told me I should] conforme my self in my dress to my other sisters ...[17]

Chapter 3d: Her first years sickness and violent convulsions ...

... In ye 19th year of my age I was taken with a violent sickness wch held me in all seven yeares wanting two months ... I was taken first suddainly with a giddiness in my head, & violent pains in my stomack. My aunt, an experienced woman who took a tender care of us, put me presently to bed and gave me something to drive ye sickness from my head. Upon this my face and body broke out into red spotts wch they took to be ye meazells. A nurs was sent for who used to tend those in that distemper ... I was put to bed again and had several cordials given to drive out ye spotts, but all in vain, excepting only that four or five would by fitts appear upon my hands. I continued so fourteen days in a high feaver, very sick and faint, shut up in a separate roome with a nurs least ye distemper should communicate it self to my other brothers and sisters.

[The nurse] her own house being in ye same town, she would go secretly away, and leave me whole hours alone ... When she saw I did not mend [she] gave me remedyes wch struck ye distemper that had laid before in my blood into ye nerves as ye doctors said afterwards, and this was ye begining of all my sickness ...

... ye doctor begun with bitter portions, sweats, vomits, bleeding and spanish flyes[18] applied to my neck arms and leggs. I fell into violent convulsions which continued yt whole year in great extreamity, and was become so weak as not to be able to go, stand, or even sit up in my bed. sometimes I shooke in so violent a manner yt I did not only make ye bed and roome shake, but even ye glass windows rattle ... att other times my joynts would turn out of there places and snap so loud yt ye noise was heard all over ye room and in my father's closet at ye further end of it ... he would say he would not go [to bed] tel my bones had done snapping, thus I used to continue for hours togeather, sometimes ye spade bones of my shoulders would turn out of their place, and rise upon my breast ... there was scarce any bone in my body remaining in its place. When these fitts were over they used to swathe my wrists and anckles with fillets, for I found my self so weak as not to be able to lift a spoon to my mouth, sometimes I was streched out as violently as if somebody had stood at ye feet of my bed and endeavoured to pull me limb from limb, this pain was extream and would make me cry aloud ...

" ... her Confessorius who treated with her at Antwerp when she writ this, took ye pains to draw out of her writeings an abstract of what she mentions here of her sufferings dureing these seven years of her sickness, and sent it to England to ye place where she had lived ...

---

[17]   Around two pages of the original text are omitted here.

[18]   A preparation of cantharides made from the dried bodies of the Spanish fly or blister-beetle, used to produce blisters (or, in other cases, to be used as an aphrodisiac).

[it] was attested by several both Catholicks and Protestants who had been eye wittnesses of all that happened. Ye paper signed by them in confirmation of it is still in ye monastery of Antwerp"

… they had recours again to my first doctor. He, by ye advice of another, began to bleed and blister me a new: but now no plasters would take place on my feet or leggs, but put me to a great deal of pain, tore of[f] the skin and burnt up ye flesh without drawing any blisters. They often took them of[f], renewed them, & rub'd ye places with vinegar, wch put me in mind of something ye martyrs suffer'd. When they could fasten them no where els, they order'd the top of my head to be shaved, and a strong blister to be laid there, to draw out what the chymist had drawn into my head. After some hours, this putt me to intolerable pain; I did not ask to have it taken of[f], but my aunt and others, seeing ye torture I was, in removed it. I endeavour'd to bear it with all the patience I could, and to think of ye Crown of Thorns.[19]

… sometimes I sunk after these violent shakeings, and lay for three hours or so, yt they could find no life in me by puls, breath, or any other sign. They often said I was dead, and it was reported so in the town, but I remember very well I heard them talk and pray about me, I seemed to my self to be closely united to God, and lay in prayer and contemplation. I found no pain, only my hands lying upon my breast oppressed me, but I could not remove them nor stir a finger … … The prayers of ye church were often said over me, and witch water[20] was used, but it pleased God that nothing should do me good.

Chapter 4th: Her pains are augmented by new remedyes … she lyes for a month speechless …

… After I had lain 9 months [my father] was advised of a French doctriss lately come into England and who was famous for many great cures … My father immediately sent for her. When she saw me, she said I was very weak yet she doubted not but she should doe me good. My father took her into ye house for a fortnight or three weeks … Her very looks at first affrighted me … she put me into a course of physick as if I had never taken any thing. She gave strong vomits and after that endeavoured to keep me in continuall sweats, ye windows shut, a fire in ye roome and many cloaths heaped up on me, and this in very hot and faint weather in ye month of May. When my convulsions came upon me and I began to shake, she chid me for haveing catch'd cold, upon this she would pin ye bed-cloaths to my pillow as high as my head; if my aunt and sister had not releived me I think I should have been stifled.

… One morning she gave me something as she said to make me spitt, for ye doctors thought I was too weak for vomitts. But after two hours I was so sick yt I beleive I shall not feel more in ye agony of death then I felt that day with vomitting. Some call'd out to me to pardon ye woman, for they thought she had killed me … no body knew what to do with me because they knew not what she had given me, as soon as I had taken it she went into ye fields and appeared no more til she heard I was a little revived … She was

---

[19] Around five pages of the original text are omitted here.
[20] I.e., to dispel the effects of potential witchcraft.

in a great passion and chid me for complaining so much and makeing people beleive she had killed me … She was found after this to be a cheat, who went about the country and understood nothing of physick …

…. A while after this woman left me I lay a month and some dayes speechless, without being able to speak one word, or swallow anything but only once in four and twenty hours. After midnight I used to fall into a gentle slumber, for less than a quarter of an hour … I had power to swallow for about half a quarter of an hour, what I commonly took was either beer or ale or silly-bubb … once I think I tried to take part of a candle … When I came out of these fitts, I found my self very much defeated but in great peace and tranquility of mind, some said I was bewitched … The convulsions were now inward, with trembling, rattling in my throat, fainting, beating of my heart, they say I used to ly severall dayes without so much as opening my eyes so that they thought my eye-strings were broke, those who came to visit me (many came because of ye novelty) would say certainly she is dead … and I became the talk of ye town …[21]

Chapter 5th: She passes ye 4 years following in a languishing condition … she is seized again with a violent sickness, what she suffer'd by dangerous impostumes for three months …

… Once in particular, when I found my self at ease, I was taken out of my bed to have it made … but before I got to bed such violent pain seased me, as if one of my teath were tore out of my head, and from thence the humor gathering raged so violently ye whole night yt I took no delight in my soft bed … They said that if ye impostumes [abscesses] broke inwardly it would immediately kill me and it did little less, for it broke before morning and ye blood and corruption fell in such quantity into my throat that all thought it would choake me, but yet a greater quantity discharged it self by my eares …[22]

… I dreamt I thought about that time yt I was in ye churchyard looking about to find a place where I should ly … I lay after this manner two or three dayes, like one drawing towards an end .. in ye morning [my Confessor] said Mass in ye chamber after which I fell into a strong agony, I could not draw my breath without excessive pain & that short, with rattleing in my throat … My ghostly Father gave me several times absolution … soon after this, I lost my speech, my hands grew stif and cold, and quite without feeling …
[I heard it said that I was dead] and found it true, wch gave me new courage and joy in my soul, me thought I was desirous to look death in the face and would willingly have looked upon my hands to have seen them turned to clay, but I had not force to stir my eyes, thus my soul seem'd forced out of my body by a strong agony and they say my senses failed me: I cannot express in what light all things of this world appeared at that time, how contemptible in themselves …

… I thought I saw our Bd Saviour stand like one considering whether he should take my soul out of my body then or no, or like one who design'd a thing but was held back by importunities of others, and after some consideration thought best to lett yt alone which he

---

[21]   Around three pages of the original text are omitted here.
[22]   Around one page of the original text is omitted here.

had design'd. This disapeared and I return'd to my self again to the admiration of all that saw me, and to my own great affliction: I had much adoe to resign my self when I thought all would have been concluded and finished, and to see my self return again to the prison of my body with its miseryes seemed a sad thing ...

... I am amazed now I am writteing this to think that I am still ye same creature ...

Chapter 6th: Her former convulsions return ... she is comforted again by an angel ...

... so in this dying condition I lay for a month ... I saw an angel in ye very place over my bed towards ye feet, where I saw our Bd Saviour when I thought he came to receive my soul. This angel looked very beautiful and sweet, his countnance divine. He seem'd about ye bigness of a child of 4 or 5 yeares old ... giving me to understand by a way very interiour yt it was my crown [he held] ...

... "Those who have not a sensible feeling of ye goodness of God ... may be apt to treat several of these things as fictions of ye imagination in a person piously inclined who may seem to take her own fancy for visions ... particularly seeing she tells us she never saw any thing exteriorly" ...[23]

... What I said concerning my seeing these angels is not meant to be meant yt I saw them with eyes of my body, for I never saw any thing of this kind in that manner, but with ye eyes of my soul, and it appeareth now much more clear to me tho these things happen'd many yeares ago then any thing I have seen with ye eyes of my body. I had never read nor heard yt there was any other way of seeing things (if I may speak so) then with our corporeal eyes til I came to religion and heard our Blessed Mother St Teresa speak of it ... yet I remained as certain before yt I had seen them ... I thought he [my Director] would not understand me when I should say I had seen things other ways then with my eyes...[24]

Chapter 7th: The Divel appears to disquiet her, but her peace of mind soon returns ... she is struck with a palsy, first in her arm and after some days in all her left side ...

... ye divel stept in as it were, seeking to disquiet me. He seem'd to stand at my beds feet, not raised up on high as ye angel was but low upon ye ground like one much troubled. He put these following thoughts of disquiet into my mind that I had by doing my own will in fasting and pennances before my sickness without leave brought my sickness upon me ...[25]

---

23 Around three pages of the original text are omitted. The narrative that follows gives a sense of a dialogue operating between Mary Xaveria and Hunter, one in which his comments affect her thinking and subsequent rewriting.

24 Around one page of the original text is omitted here.

25 Around two pages of the original text are omitted here.

... Mass was said every day in my roome when ye priest was at home. ... for about ye time of ye elevation, as I could guess, I was suddenly recollected and transported as it were. ... me thought I saw heaven gate open with a great noise and mighty force ... I seem'd to see also, into ye heavenly country, some little glimps but I cannot express how it was, only that many angels were there. This is as present to me as if it had lately happen'd and I cannot write it without being moved extreamly ...[26]

Chapter 8th: ...she is perswaded to make ye 10 Frydays devotion in honour of St Francis Xaverius ... she finds ease at ye end of ye devotion, but soon relapses into her former paines in body and mind and continues in them six months

I am now come to relate my last yeares sickness ... I seem'd deep in consumption, many times I spit blood with almost a continual feaver, palsy, jaundice, ye impostumes ... convulsions with other infirmities. The doctor ordered me asses milk cordial drinks and what els I could take ...

In the mean while ye supernatural favours were withdrawn, I lay for ye most part of ye time in great disolation ... The April following, Mr Collins[27] one of the Society, came to my father's house. Tho he was a stranger he had heard of me ... He was mighty earnest I should begin a devotion of the ten Fridays of St Xaverius ...[28]

... At the end of these ten Fridays I unexpectedly found ye help of ye Bd Saint, perceiveing some life or agility in my lame side and so much strength as to be able to make a step or two in ye chambre with help ... Soon after I relapsed again into my former distempers, only some little strength and agility was left in my lame side. I found no releif in my arm in this first devotion: it continued wither'd, ye sinews being drawn up into knotts, my fingers shrunk so that the nails were like to grow into my hands and so stif that there was no possibility of opening them without breaking ye joynts. I ended my first devotion in August, and relapsing immediately, lay in a dying condition tel ye February following ...

Chapter 9th: She is perswaded to begin again ye ten Fridays devotion ...

Father Louis Sabran[29] of ye Society was lately arrived in England, and being in our neighbourhood my father, out of civility, went to meet him and invited him to our house. He heard of my long sickness and desired to see me ... He advised my Confessor to make me begin [the ten Fridays devotion] anew.[30]

---

[26] Around two pages of the original text are omitted here.

[27] William Collins, who entered the Society of Jesus in 1699, worked in Suffolk from *c.* 1690–98 and died in 1704 (Hardman, 1939, 16).

[28] Around three pages of the original text are omitted here, describing her devotions.

[29] Born in London in 1652, Sabran was the son of the French ambassador in England. He entered the Society of Jesus in 1672, becoming a chaplain of James II, after whose fall in 1688 he fled to the Continent. He visited England in 1691 (which gives us a date for these events), and was then for 10 years President of the episcopal seminary at Liege, then Provincial of the English Jesuits, Rector of St Omers, and finally was at the English College in Rome, where he died in 1732 (Hardman, 1939, 17).

[30] Around one page of the original text is omitted here.

... I had laid thus [in some despair] a long while, ye curtains being drawn [around the bed] and those that tended me retired ... A little child of six or seaven yeares old, a neice of mine[31] who was left in the roome ... came runing to my bed side and opening ye curtains jumped upon ye bed, saying to me in an earnest and devote way, 'Aunt God Alm: loves you and will take care of you' ...[32]

... [I] used to dream that I was religious and beyond seas conversing with nuns. Whether these were only dreames or particular favours from Alm God I know not, but as soon as I came afterwards to this place ... I told my Confessor yt accompanyed me that this was the church I saw in my dreams and I find within the monastery those places which were represented to me and in wch I seem'd conversing with the religious ...

Chapter 10th: ... she is cured suddainly after Communion ... her cure is divulged in the neighbourhood ... she has hopes of being received among ye nuns of Gravelinnes[33]

... I had great confidence our Bd Saviour would doe as much or more for me [as curing the bed-ridden man, and others] haveing him realy present in my breast in ye Bd Sacrament. This I experienced this last Friday after Communion, so great a joy seazed my soul that it diffused it self all over my body, finding my self as if new life and blood were inffused into me and such an alteration all over me as gave me extraordinary agility ... [my joints] became on a suddain plyable ...

... I was amazed to find this suddain change and my self so well, I knew not what to think of it, whether it would continue or whether, perhaps, it were not some suddain transport wch wrought on my imagination ... [My 'sister widow'[34] saw the change in me] ... I told her being pressed, that it seemed as if new life and blood were infused into me ... When my aunt came back she met me walking about ye roome to her great surprise ... They made me keep my chamber 3 or 4 days for fear of catching cold, for tho this happen'd ye 12 of May, the weather was very sharp ...

... In a short time I was stronger then ever in my life before, and in journeys, in walking and riding or the like, I tired out the strongest of my company ...
    The noise of my suddain recovery being spread abroad, few would beleive it but those that saw and conversed with me. Hence I was advised by my Confessor to return the many visits wch had been made me in my sickness, both to the rich and poor. The first time I came into ye aire I found no alteration nor giddiness in my head, and I refused to be lead by ye hand by my sister ... As we walked we said *Te Deum* and other prayers in thanksgiveing ...[35]

---

[31] Daughter to Ann Woolmer (Chapter 20).
[32] Around four pages of the original text are omitted here.
[33] Around six pages of the original text are omitted here.
[34] Ann Woolmer (Chapter 20).
[35] Around one page of the original text is omitted here.

... Goeing out one day to seek some solitary walk, I was followed by one of my sisters children. I found my self moved to goe with her and visit one of our neighbours, who had been lately in my sickness to visit me ...ye woman herself was ye first who appeared when I knockt at ye dore but she was so amazed to see me yt she could not recouer herself ye time I stay'd, but said if I was ye same person, calling me by my name, it was ye greatest miracle that ever ye Lord wrought ... This was not ye only person thus surprised, but its to[o] long to relate all. They used to follow me and invite me to there houses. I went to see a lady of quality about a mile of[f], she was so frighten'd yt she was obliged to call for cordials to recover herself ...[36]

Chapter 11th: She puts her hip out of joynt ... begins ten days devotion in honour of St Xaverius ... is instantly cured ... a small contraction left in her hand ... was looked on as a mark left to remind her of the favour[37]

On the Assumption of Our Lady, I made ye 2d or 3d pilgrimage to the well [of Our Lady, two miles away], in company of my father and several others. In our return in ye evening, the way being wett and slippery, I was like to fall into a ditch by ye path side. I saved my self from falling but with ye violence of ye motion put my hip-bone out of joynt. I did not think then I had hurt my self so much ... I desired my brother to give me his hand ... pretending it began to grow dark. I was in great pain all the night, and in the morning found I was not able to walk ... [My Father] immediately sent for a woman very expert in surgery. As soon as she had examined it she said it would be a hard cure and made me keep my bed for ten days applying all sorts of remedies but without any effect ... She bid me apply my self to my doctor yt had cured me before, meaning St Xaverius ... tho she were a rigid Protestant ...[38]

... The last day being come, it happen'd to be a Friday and ye feast of the Nativity of Our Bd Lady ... I confessed and heard Mass sitting up on my bed ... I durst not venture to kneel, finding my self too weak for that. As soon as I had received I found my self entirely cured and ye bone set fast ...[39]

Chapter 12: Her designs of passing ye seas that winter is diversely cross'd ... she persists in following God's call and at last emberques; a tempest arises ... she is obliged by accident to pass thro' Antwerp, several things determine her to settle there, she quites ye thoughts of accompanying her sister to Bruges and immediately takes ye habit[40]

---

[36] Around one page of the original text is omitted here.
[37] This mark is often referred to in her later life, when various people ask her to touch them with this hand.
[38] Around three pages of the original text are omitted here; in them she undertakes the devotion, but reduces the 10 weeks to 10 days with her Confessor's permission.
[39] Around three pages of the original text are omitted here.
[40] Around three pages of the original text are omitted here.

... My frinds ... would have perswaded me to lay aside all such thoughts that winter, that in ye spring my father and aunt would accompany me. They both design'd to be religious ... besides my youngest sister desired to go along with me ...

... My youngest sister came over with me, to be a nun of ye order of St Teresa, and I came with design to be a Poor Clare at Graveline. I was very glad when I gott into ye choach and out of ye town where I lived all my life excepting three months ...

My father and brothers accompanyed us to the sea port town ... but here I found no less difficultes then I had met with before. My sister fell sick of a feaver and was obleged to keep her bed ... My father and Confessor [Father Ireland[41]] ... resolved we should not go til spring but return as soon as my sister was able ... I told him I would make a devotion to St Xaverius to cure my sister and said I hoped she would be well enough to undertake ye journey by ye time ye packett boat arrived ... Her feaver left her ye next morning. I gott her up and tho she was so weak (she was scarce able to walk alone), yet I perswaded my father and F Ireland to lett us embarque that morning ...

We set to sea in ye worst of seasons, ye 23 of November, F Ireland accompanying us ... We were only 24 hours at sea. A tempest arose about midnight ... I apprehended nothing, seeing St Xaverius standing by me in a black cassock and protecting me. I thought he had not cured me to lett me be drown'd then and seeing he was call'd by ye infidels God of ye sea ...

... F Ireland resolved to make ye best of our way for Graveline. In order to [do] this, he sought out for some convenience to carry us directly to Bruges without passing through Antwerp, at which I was much concerned, for tho I had no mind to be a nun here, yet I had a desire to see these nuns. ... [I] was glad to hear after all inquiry made that he could light of no other convenience ... but was obliged to pass through Antwerp. We arrived at Hooghstraet on ye Eve of St Xaverius [2 December] ... At our first appearing at ye grate ye Rd Mother bid my sister welcome ... and told me I should be wellcom att Antwerp. I answerd I had no such design but was goeing to Graveline, upon which she was surprised and said I had been expected there ... it seems all was effected by a Protestant gentleman liveing in England, a stranger who had a daughter at Hooghstraet ...

... I was very loath to change my resolution of being a Poor Clare. Tho my inclinations carryed me to be a Teresian, I thought ye other Order was harder and chose it on yt account ... [Father Ireland] told me ... I was not always to strive against ye stream and chuse ye hardest things ... [I] took my resolutions of staying here just before I came into ye gates of the town.

We arrived here late in ye evening ye day after ye Feast of St Xaverius. The Rd Mother and Subprioress bid me wellcome at ye speakhouse-grate. They told me afterwards I looked very sad and pensive: ye truth is I was in concern, doubting whether this was ye place [for me] ... ye Church was perfectly lik what I had seen in my dream ... I had an excessive joy when I embraced ye religious that [Saturday] night at ye gate ...

---

[41] Francis Ireland, born in 1656, had entered the Society of Jesus in 1675. In 1689 he was captured by pursuivants and imprisoned in Ipswich; after his release, from 1701–04, he worked at St Ignatius College, London (Hardman, 1939, 13).

They desired I should enter ye Tuesday following, being the Conception of Our Lady, but I was not sufficiently disengaged from my self. I designd first to go to see my sister at Bruges and my sister that was to be religious at Hooghstraet was come so far with me on the same design. ... [After a devotion to St Xavier] I presently laid aside all thoughts of my joureny to Bruges ... My sister took it ill of me ...

I took ye habit without further delay on Our Lady's Conception, and found no difficulty then to part with my sister. I passed my Noviship with great alacrity ... The first year I had few visions or supernatural favours ... once in my Noviship St Xaverius told me I should be Superiour wch I told my director with teares in my eyes, because I desir'd nothing so much as to live privately and unknown ...

To my confusion I was chose Subprioress soon after I came out of my noviship, and now as I had done so much of this relation, ye heavy cross of Superiour has faln upon me, very early, haveing been but six yeares and a half in religion. I have pass'd my time since I came hither in perfect health and have gon through all ye rigours of ye order without dispensation, and am able to do much more then my order requires. All Glory be to God and St Xaverius in whose name I began this relation and end it.

2d Part: Giveing an account of what happen'd to her during the first six yeares of a religious life

Chapter 1st: She takes ye habit ... sees one of ye deceased religious learns several things from her ... St Xaverius appears to her ... she makes her vowes with great devotion[42]

... The Rd Mother told me yt when I prostrated at cloathing as is our custom, I should obtain whatever I asked ... I begg'd of Alm: God ye conversion of that Protestant gentleman who unknown to me had procured me this place, as also ye woman I have mentioned who was so surprised at my cure: not long after this I heard that they were both converted ... My greatest trouble was to learn my Breviary haveing never learnt Latin ...[43]

... About four months after my admittance one of ye ancientest religious dyed[44] ... About six weeks after this, as I remember, she appeared to me in my sleep and I cannot doubt of it by what follow'd otherwayes I am not apt to beleive dreames. I think it was about one in the morning yt I thought this religious was represented before me in my cell. At first I was affrighted knowing she was a spirit ... then calling upon her, 'Sister Clare' (so she was named), I asked her if she were in heaven. She then seem'd to come nigher me and appear'd extreamly beautifull and answered 'Yes' ... She told me Purgatory was a sad place, and yt one of ye greatest torments was ye sight of ye divels ...

... I asked her how St Xaverius looked in heaven ... and with that I thought I saw St Xaverius there as it were on high over me and protecting me, he looked very amiable beautifull and sweet beyond wt I am able to express ...[45]

42　Around four pages of the original text are omitted here.
43　Around three pages of the original text are omitted here.
44　Clare of the Annunciation (Catherine Darcy: 1610–94; see Chapter 9).
45　Around two pages of the original text are omitted here.

... When I took ye habit ye Rd Mother understood ye day before my enterance yt I had an aversion from eggs, and upon demand I told her I had not eat one in seaven yeares ... She thought it impossible for me to comply with our constant rule of abstience from flesh, egges being ye cheif part of our diet ... She told me afterwards some of ye community wondered she durst venture to admitt me, seeing I looked pale and thin and could not eat eggs ... I was order'd [by my Saint] to try to eat an egg at dinner ye day before I entered. I took one into my hand, but my stomack immediately turn'd to yt degree yt my Confessor ... made me lay it down ... Ye first day I came to dinner with ye community my stomack was so much alter'd yt I longed tel they gave me some eggs, wch they did that day and I eat ym heartily: ye Rd Mother was transported with joy saying St Xaverius had done this for me ... I continued after this constantly to eat them with as good an appetite as ever I did any thing in my life. My Mistress asked me how I liked ye other fair as sallets [salads] & c: I could not but own I had never been accustomed to eat them, but I thought all that came to the refectory savoured to me like manna yt fell from heaven ... and when I had been here three or four months I grew so fatt, yt those of ye house and others who saw me enter, were amazed at it my very cloaths wch were too big in ye begining grew too straite for me.[46]

Chapter 3d: St Xaverius frequently appears and instructs her; in imitation of him, she gets to suck a loathsome ulcer ... she falls into a rapt before her mistress, but procures she should keep it secret

... A while after this ye Bd Saint appeared to me again in ye same place as I was sitting solitary at my work upon seeing him I found inward sentiments of respect and reverence and as I remember I fell down on my knees before him like one surprised ...

... I had been, one morning in ye noviship, with ye rest of my companions learning my Breviary. My Mistress chid me very much for being so dull and reading my Latin so fals. As I went thence to ye vestry to sort ye foul linnen ... whilst I was in this desolation and anxiety, ye Bd Saint appeared to me saying in a sweet way 'Child you shall have yr Latin as perfect as any of them'...[47]

... I found in particular a great want of that perfect disengagement, my affections being still tyed to my relations and my self passionately fond of my Mistress who taught me. She often chid me for speaking so affectionately of my father, and expressing so longing a desire to see him. He was dayly expected to take ye habit of ye Society in there noviship att Watten[48] ... I used to argue with my Mistress in this point ... I have seen clearly since yt I should have had too much of natural satisfaction in seeing him. The first newes I heard of him after this was yt he was dead and from this time our Lord began to send me crosses to disengage me from all sensible things ...[49]

---

[46] Around 27 pages of the original text, describing her early religious life, are omitted here.
[47] Around one page of the original text is omitted here.
[48] A Jesuit college established *c*.1570.
[49] Around two pages of the original text are omitted here.

... it has never cost me any trouble to consider what I am to say, and has not cost me so much paines in writeing, as if I had transcribed a paper put before me, because there I must have lost time in looking on it.[50]

Chapter 4th: ... she receives ye newes of her father's death and practices wt St Xaverius taught her to do on ye like occasions ...

... A little after my noviship I dreamt I saw my father in his agony. I was much afflicted and it was as sensible to me as if I had been present at his death ... I told my Superiour and others what I had dreamt, and the first letters from England after this brought newes of his death. I had heard nothing of his being sick ... I was willing to look upon it only as a dream ... [but] by computing [I] found it to have happened ye very night as I think on wch he dyed, I was apt to look upon it as more then dream ... My Superiour kept ye newes private for some time ... to waite some favourable occasion of breaking it to me. But she began at last to have some scruple of depriveing his soul so long of prayers, hence one morning she call'd me to her cell before Mass ... She knelt down and kist [my picture of St Xaverius] asking me if [he] was not my physitian and frind, and if he would not also be my father. Att these words I was struck, and ask'd her if she had heard my father was dead ... After a little she shew'd me my sisters letter wch gave me ye newes of it ...

At ye first newes of his death I did not shed a tear but disguised ye greif I felt for some time ... But as soon as I had done [with my Superior] I retired into our own cell and, shutting ye dore, my heart was afflicted more then I ever remember'd it to have been in my whole life. In this distress I immediately cast my self upon my knees, and took my Crucifix in my hand ...

... I was extremely afflicted day and night & could not forbear shewing it sometimes by teares, sometimes by sadness in my countenance, for which my Superiour would often chide me ...[51]

... Tho I had great feeling at my father's death, yet my sentiments were very much changed from what they were when I first left ye world ... [Father Ireland had told my sister and me] we should have as great a greif to part with those we were to live with in religion, but we did not then conceive how farr a spiritual love surpassed a natural one, but now I knew it by experience, finding I should have a much greater concern to loose my present Superiour then I had for ye death of my father ...[52]

Chapter 5th: ... our Blessed Lady appears to her, ye effects of this vision ... her Superior's death ... Alm: God makes use of this cross to disengage her entirely from all creatures

... The great cross Alm: God made use of to disengage me thoroughly from all things in this world was ye death of ye person who was Superiour, ye first year after my noviship ...

---

[50] Around five pages of the original text are omitted here.
[51] Around one page of the original text is omitted here.
[52] Around eight pages of the original text are omitted here.

She foretold it me pritty clear about fourteen dayes before it happen'd ... [saying] that she should drop down on a suddain even when she went about ye house ... She order'd me, as soon as she was dead, to close her eyes with my hand wch St Xaverius had cured ...

[The] very day the community were assembled in ye quire for ye reception of [a] novice, she haveing ended her speech to ye religious, was reciteing ye usual prayers which are allwayes said before we give our votes, and having just finished yt of St Xaverius, she was suddainly struck with a palsy, and all apperhended she would have dyed upon ye spott ... I immediately prostrated upon ye ground ... [asking St Xaverius] yt at least she might live to have all ye rites of ye church. After this I went to ye other end of the quire where she was. I found her a little revived, but one side quite dead ... [She] gave me a picture of St Xaverius, with some papers she had about her ... After her Confession her palsy seized her toungue. She was then removed out of ye quire to a lower roome: I help'd to carry her, and tho' we did it as gently as possible, yet by moveing she lost her senses ... The nine days she continued alive, she was for ye most part sensible[53] ... I knelt by her in her agony wch lasted three or four hours ... I looked upon her and begg'd strength to perform my last obedience, wch was to close her eyes ... hence I went to ye Bd Sacrament, begging our Lord to possess my heart so yt I might never more be tyed to any creature ...[54]

Chapter 6th: She continues writing after a long interruption ... is chosen Subprioress and soon after Mistress of Novices ... Her deceased Superiour appears to her ...

Its now about a year and a half since I left of[f] writing, and ye troublesome charge of Superiour being again faln upon me for three years longer; I think I shall have little leisure to write, yet in compliance with obedience, I begin again: I hope this may draw ye Saint nearer me, for if I go on writeing he must be by me, and dictate to me as he has already done; as to myself I remember little or nothing when I take my pen ... I have none of my former papers by me, but as I think I had there finished my first year after ye noviship.[55]

... My first four months in this office [of Subprioress] were putt in great desolation, particularly on account of ye death of my dear Superiour. I saw my self placed in ye same station she was in ye two years of my noviship: I had her cell, her place in ye quire, refectory and ye noviship ... I see since it was a great goodness of God to take her from me, thus to disengage me from all creatures; for tho my love to her seem'd altogeather spiritual, yet I often found when I was deprived of her company, or when she was sick, I was much troubled and disquieted ... [Now] I repose much more in God ...

... I found great oppressions and desolation these four months ... my Superiour appointed me a gallary to walk in, at those hours in wch, according to ye distribution of time, we were to say our beades. On ye second or third day being in this place, I saw on a suddain my deceased Superiour ... She appeared to me in no form, but like a white cloud ... I was no longer able to continue my vocal prayers, nor even to walk, being to my thinking almost disjoynted. I fell down upon my knees before her, and asked her interiorly if she was in heaven ... She said, in an interior way, she had been [in Purgatory] for ten dayes,

---

53 Around one page of the original text is omitted here.
54 Around one page of the original text is omitted here.
55 Around one page of the original text is omitted here.

and that St Xaverius had then obtained her release; that she went to heaven ye same day yt I was putt into this office of Subprioress ... She let me know yt one reason [she spent time in Purgatory] was the following of her own will even in things which seem'd to tend to devotion ... I believe this was manifested to me for my own direction ...[56]

... She disappeared and I strove to get to my cell which was not farr of[f] ... [This event] took away all ye greif I had felt so sensibly at her death ... tho this apparation gave me a singular comfort, yet at the same time it struck me with fear beyond what ever I had felt before ... to see one I knew so well here come now to me as a spirit from ye other world. When I pass'd afterwards thro' this place in ye dark I found my self seized with great apprehension, but at ye same time with great respect ... I cannot but blame myself for being so much affraid of a soul which I undoubtedly beleive to be in heaven ... I understand now I am writeing this, it's a gift of God ... otherwise it could never have moved me so much to ye love of God ...[57]

Chapter 8th: One of ye religious is helpt in an extraordinary way by her prayers ... her mortification on account of ye illness of one of them, and her behaviour in all this troublesome affair

... Alm: God was pleased to help one of ye religious by my prayers, wch I think fitt to mention here. She was a very vertuous soul, but troubled with scruples to yt degree that her Confessarius was affraid she would loose her senses. He told me as much to move me to pray for her. She had leave to have recourse to me when ever she pleased, and I spent a great deal of time in comforting her and animating her to obey and follow ye advice of her Confessor. I was affected to see this poor innocent soul suffer so much.

Her Confessor, being obliged to absent himself for ten days to give the spiritual exercise to an other monastery, called for her before he went, and ... order'd her before me to communicate in his absence with ye rest of ye religious at ye dayes appointed, and bid me put her in mind of his orders ... [At Mass] I offerd my self to suffer some of her troubles, if it pleased God, in exchange to bestow on her some of those favours he had designed for me in Holy Communion ... She was like a soul in purgatory, in continual anguish and pain as she told me afterwards ... [At the elevation] then, on a suddain like one awakeing out of a slumber, she found an unusual peace of mind, all her troubles being at once removed. Upon this she came to me (haveing leave to do so) and asked me, 'Did ye Father bid me communicate today?' I answered, 'Yes, he did'. Then she said with a quiet calm voice, 'I will' ...

[At Mass] I thought I saw our Bd Saviour seated in ye middle of my heart, speaking most amorously to me, as if he designed me some great favour, but on a suddain he seemed to ask my consent to go and caress this Sister in place of me. I consented to it, but on a suddain wonder'd to see my self in anguish, desolation and dryness, thinking of ye sins of my life past, fearing I had not confessed ym well and several of ye same scruples she used

---

[56] Around one page of the original text is omitted here.

[57] Around 22 pages of the original text are omitted here; they describe her fears and the means she used to overcome them. The events in the Chapter that follows are those included in the annals' version of Mary Xaveria's Life (*A1*, 539–47), incidents which were, as she says herself, 'ye heaviest Cross I ever felt'.

to have. But all this while I did not reflect of ye bargain I had made, and that I had offer'd my self to change communions, til a little before dinner she came to me chearfully in an unusual way, and asked how I did. She added yt she fear'd I was in great desolation, but for her part, that she had got well by ye change, that she had never felt such consolation in all her life, as she had done that day after Communion. This calm and peace continued, as she told me her self, for ten days after, in wch time she desired to communicate oftener than we were generally allowed, and this most earnestly. I was amazed at ye change, and thought it ye work of God. As to my self, I was all this time in ye greatest darkness ...

... "The Confessarius who directed both these souls at this time, and who is mentioned in this passege, always looked upon this as something more then natural, which he thinks cannot be otherways, unless we suppose the whole thing to have been a colusion between these two religious on purpose to deceive him, and he is truly satisfyed that this neither was nor could be done by any agreement between themselves "...[58]

One of my novices under my care was very young. She seemed to be a soul in a particular manner prevented by Alm: God, but I have found in her afflictions one of those black crosses wch heaven designed for santifaction of my soul. I loved her very much for her pious inclinations ... I was often moved to devotion in speaking to her of heavenly things and have sometimes been in a rapt before her, but I charged her, when I came to my self, never to speak of it, and I am confident she never did. She often put me upon those discourses; I once found my self very dry and therefore willing to yeald to her importunity, but in speaking I was so moved yt I could say no more. She kneelt before me and, seeing what passed, imbraced me, and with a great deal of innocency said, 'Mistress, I have made you love God tho I cannot love him my self'. This novice gave me great confusion to see how she advanced in all vertues, and I used often to wonder what this child would come to; but ye designs of God are secret and always adorable ...

... About a year after her profession she fell ill of a soar throat and a feaver, which kept her from sleeping some nights, but she concealed it, for she never complained of any indisposition til it appeard. We consulted ye doctor as soon as we perceived her indisposition, but he did not much apprehend it, til on a suddain she fell out of her self. I first perceived a great change in her, but it was not then so visible to ye rest of ye community, however I acquainted my Superior and Director; within a day or two she fell raveing mad.

... This afforded many tryalls of patience both to me and ye rest of ye religious. She was heard not only in our house but by ye neighbours. At first she spoke of nothing but spirituall things, but afterwards ye enemy seem'd to make use of her tounge to distract and vex ye whole community. I have several times gon from her in ye middle of ye night to prostrate before the Bd Sacrament, bathed in teares and oppress'd with greif; but our Lord was pleased in this great affliction to leave me in desolation and darkness without any answer to my prayers. Many difficulties were raised both from within and without, that is from my own thoughts and from other persons. I feared, as to my own particular, that I had been wanting on my side, and indiscreetly permitted her to apply too much in prayer. Others spoke with mistrust of me, imageining I must have seen some tendency to

---

[58] Around two pages of the original text are omitted here.

this before her profession, which they had reason to suspect I had concealed from them, but God knows I never mistrusted any such thing ...

... I do beleive and allways shall yt this soul was and is highly pleaseing in [God's] sight, yt he first advanced her in a short time, and afterwards permitted her to fall into this condition ...

... About six months after she first fell ill, in time of a devotion wch was made to St Xaverius for her, I promised if she came to her self so as to be capable of ye Sacraments, that I would take upon me again ye care of ye novices ... After this she presently came to her self, and continued perfectly well for three months ... yet after three months more she relapsed again, and continues stil in ye same condition. We perceived nothing of it when she went to bed. About midnight I heard some body come into my cell and, being awaked, asked who it was. She answered in a trembleing voice, wch made me speak very kindly to her. She told me she was loath to awake me, but yt her head was so troubled yt she was sure she should go mad again, and never more return to her self, this she said God had given her light of. I did all I could to make her put of[f] these thoughts, tho' I see she was farr gone ... She imbraced me, and beged me not to trouble my self for her, but leave her in ye hands of God. After this she went quite out of her self.

I was at that time in ye office of Prioress, being chosen a month after she first fell ill, and I have had much to suffer on her account, particularly one time when she broke out from us: I was ready to sink down when I first heard it, fearing it might bring come scandal upon ye house among those who did not perfectly know her condition, yet God gave me so much moderation as not to loose my interior peace of mind, and I was moved to mortify my self and say nothing at that time to those who should have taken more care of her, but I sweetly admonished them of it afterwards to make them more careful for the future. I called the community to the quire where, after some short prayers, I went where she could see and hear me, and she immediately return'd again of her self. She was only seen by two or three honest neighbours who soon perceived her condition and pittyed her and our misfortune.[59]

... Chapter 9th: Her different visions of Purgatory, Hell and Heaven ...

Whilst I was in this office of Subprioress, as I was makeing ye mediatation of Hell in ye spiritual exercise, I was deeply recollected and I seem'd to see my self transported into ye sad region and placed near some of yt horrid crew, where I was to be racked and tormented by them. I seemed laid upon a huge planck in ye middle of a place of fire under ground, above me all was dark and black, below me fire ... ye Divells came round to torment me in all parts with red-hot irons, giving me to understand at ye same time with a kind of envious spite and malice what ye faults were (wch I had committed dureing ye two months I was absent from my father's house & c. ...) [I understand now] that this place was Purgatory, and that I was to have remained there for many yeares if I had died of the small pox which I had aboue two yeares before my great sickness ...[60]

---

[59] Around four pages of the original text are omitted here.
[60] Around 10 pages of the original text are omitted here.

... As I have been transported into Purgatory and Hell, so I have allso seemed to be in a place of Paradise of pleasures and delights. I know not how to express what this place was like, but I think I may say with ye spouse in ye Canticles, I have found him whom my soul loveth ... This place seemed something like a delightful spring as to the exterior composition of it, a place of great solitude ... In this place there's no speaking for ye soul ... she has not time to speak one word ... she sees her spouse knows all her wants ... without noise of *words*, by this I do not mean only vocall prayers, but even mentall, for here ye soul languishes with love. She is, as it were, wholy overcome and can doe nothing but enjoy ...

I do not say [some experience of this] shall be granted to all who read these papers, yet I think ye Saint promised me yt none shall read them without benefit of their own souls; I have some mortification in writing this, because it seems as if I invited others to read what I write ... I fancyed I should never be able to look any body in ye face who had read it, but God has taken yt so intirely from me ...[61]

... I am obliged to take spare moments to write and have interrupted my writeing for months and sometimes for yeares; hence not haveing any of my papers by me. When I take pen in hand I often know not what is to come next, but I think ye St dictates to me ...[62]

... Chapter 10th: The lights she had in ye spirituall exercise whilst she was yet Subprioress

The second day, being in my cell a little before Mass in great recollection, I was much distracted and troubled by ye apparition of ye Divell, who enter'd my cell like a filthy ugly monster creeping on all four[s]. He disturbed me with impure thoughts and representations wch, by ye grace of God, I rejected with disdain and horror ... The Divell seeing as I hope yt he could gain nothing, soon quitted me and when, after this, I came to ye quire, my thoughts were perfectly quieted; but I saw him go in ye same filthy manner to ye next cell of a vertuous young religious. In effect I suppose he disquieted and disturbed her so much that our Director thought fit next day to make her break of ye exercise for fear she should do her self harm ... I neither told ye Director nor her what I had seen, but understood afterwards from her self how much she had been disquieted ...

This day after communion I found great devotion and union with God, and I thought I saw my cell in spirit (for I was now in ye quire), surrounded with virgins cloathed in white. I had some disgust of ye place before, by reason of ye bad companion I had seen there in ye morning ... [After communion] I then immediately went, opend ye dore of my cell and knelt down with great devotion ... for above an hour, in wch time yt Bd company was very busy about me, putting a crown upon my head ... and I think they put a lilly into my hand. Who those virgins were I know not: St Catherine of Sienna was one, I had a tender devotion to her from my childhood ... and I am apt to beleive St Teresa among

---

[61]   Around six pages of the original text are omitted here.

[62]   Around 10 pages of the original text are omitted here. The extract resumes with an account of incidents that occurred over several days when the community was following the meditations of St Ignatius.

them tho disguised … They neither touched ye ground nor any other part of ye cell with their feet, thô they had ye shape of mortall bodyes …

… The Third Part of the Life … The Preface[63]

… Least ye great treasure of her vertues should be entirely lost to us, ye Superior of ye monastery in wch she lived was desired, some years after her death, to order all her religious who had been her cotemporaries to mark down wt they have observed in her, and that this might be performed with great sincerity, each one was order'd to write apart, without consulting each other, and to send what they had writt to ye person who was transcribeing her writeings. Several were then dead who had been most intimate with her, by wch it's more then probable yt a great deal is lost wch would have served to give us a fuller account of her vertues …[64]

The present Superior of ye community at Antwerp who was not only an eye-witness, but had also some part in ye following passages, assures me yt in Mother Xaveria's life time ye community was sensible of ye many favours God did them …

" … In ye year 1709 when all things were so excessive dear by reason of ye hard frost, yt a quarter of wheat, sold at other times for 7 or 8 shillings, was then sold for above 30, and so proportionately of other things … I had care of buying in provisions, and told my Superior Rd Mother Mary Xaveria yt we were almost out of beer, and wanted money to buy malt. She bid me nevertheless bespeak it … [and] as I was seeing it weighed, a gentleman came to ye grate, desired to speak to ye Superior, and told her he brought her an alms. He gave about ten pound wch was more or less ye summe we wanted to pay ye malt …

… An other time she was obliged on a fixed day to pay a summe of money wch she endeavour'd, but in vain, to borrow against yt time. The day came, she waited for ye person who was to call for it. She told me she was to pay it in two hours, and tho' she had not a farthing she confided still God would find some meanes to help her … Mass was not quite ended when a gentleman, a stranger and one of another town, called for her. He told her he was travelling farther and found he had more money then he wanted for his journey, and therefore desired she would take £30 sterling and give him a note for it payable on demand. This was exactly ye summe she was to pay that morning; she had time enough to procure the money again, it was not called for til almost half a year after" …

… " I have often seen (says one of the religious) and felt ye efficacy of her prayers … I had a mortification in my jaw wch ye surgeon judge[s] incurable. He proposed indeed razing of ye flish and applying fire to ye bone, as ye only remedy … The excess of pain was followed by a violent feaver [I asked Mother Mary Xaveria] to strock my face with her hand in wch St Xaverius had left ye mark of his cure, and presently it grew much better, ye wound soon healed up without leaveing any scarr" …[65]

---

63 Around 15 pages of the original text are omitted here.
64 Around 65 pages of the original text are omitted here; they give an account of the nun's blessedness. The extract resumes with testimonies from different witnesses.
65 Around 16 pages of the original text including similar accounts are omitted here.

... [Another says] "I saw her feet raised off the ground ... she seem'd to hold her self down by the seats ..."

This passage is solemnly attested under ye hand of ye religious woman to whom it happened, tho' it did not come to light til after Mother Xaveria's death. "I was retir'd says she on Sunday ye 17th April of 1712, [and was ordered by her] to write a French letter in her name to a person of very great distinction ... I leaned back in my chair to compose my self a little, it was a time in the afternoon allowed for repose ... But I was suddainly roused by a melodious harmony of heavenly musick, and putting my head out of ye window wch looked towards the infirmary where our Venble Mother Xaveria was, I distinctly perceived great numbers of voices and instruments combined as it were in ye aire ... It seemd to me an evident sign she was hastening to her heavenly country ..."[66]

Chapter 10th: of her last sickness and death

... On ye 17 of January 1714 she fell ill of a violent feaver, and was confined to ye Infirmary ... Within a few days ye doctor press'd her to tell where she felt her greatest pain. She answer'd in her back, he order'd it to be rubbed with an oyle which he prescribed ... By thus, says ye religious sister, the person who was imployed in it, I came to discover a wound greivously inflamed, already mortifyed; and ye inflamation was spread over great part of her side ... [She] said she hoped I loved her too much to occasion its being exposed to a surgeon, a mortification a thousand times greater then death to her ... [She] could not oblige me in this case, and I ... presently acquainted Rd Mother Prioress ... I desired her (continues ye same religious) to tell me what she had suffer'd before this was discover'd, she said (I think) 'Tounge cannot express it' ...

... I was once present (says one of her religious to me in a letter dated 9br [September] ye 7th 1722) when ye surgeon was dressing her wound in presence of ye doctor. Haveing made a very deep incision with his lance, she did not make ye least sign or shew yt she had any feeling of it, so yt ye doctor supposed ye flesh so much mortifyed yt she had not felt it, wch made him order ye surgeon to cutt in deeper til she came to have some feeling. She, hearing this, replyed calmly, he need not do so, for that she had felt ye same very sensibly ...

... ye surgeon ... has given to ye monastery an authentick attestation of what happen'd, wch I shall here set down for ye edification of ye Reader:

I underwritten, surgeon of ye Citty of Antwerp ... came twice a day to dress it [a mortification on her side] tell her death ... To prolong her life I found it necessary to make dayly deep scarifications into ye live flesh, whence issued forth great quantity of blood, with great pain to ye patient; notwithstanding I never heard her complaine of her pain ... Rd Mother made me procure a medall which after her death I applied to her body wch I still keep with great respect and esteem in my house in testimony of ye truth of this I sign my name att Antwerp August ye 9th 1722 John Gobel

---

[66] Around 22 pages of the original text, listing similar incidents, are omitted here. The extract resumes with an account of the nun's final illness.

... The same pastilentious humour which caused a gangreen in her back, spread it self (as ye surgeon said) all over her body even to her hands and feet ... but she never made ye least shew of suffering ... tho' for ye most part allways confined to ye same posture ...[67]

... Whilst she lay exposed in ye quire, dress'd up in her habit ... one of the religious, putting her hand to her side, thought she perceived a perceptable warmth ... and tho' no body could reasonably doubt but yt she was certainly dead, yet to satisfy ye desire of ye religious, ye surgeon who attended her was sent for to view ye body[68] ... She was found certainly dead but her countenance ... was now become so sweet and breathd such an aire of sanctity yt one present cryed out it was a pitty they had not taken her picture. Upon this proposal a painter was sent for, who took her features craion, and afterwards drew her picture. Notwithstanding she had been so often moved, and as she had said her self began to corrupt before she was dead, yet there was not ye least offensive smell when her coffin was thus opened. Her features being taken and ye religious haveing satisfyed their devotion in kissing her feet, and touching her body with their beads, pictures & c: ye coffin was nailed up and deposited again in ye vault.

Chapter 11th: of what happen'd after her death ...

On ye same day that ye Mother Mary Xaveria dyed, a lady at Antwerp ... found herself in an unusual peace and calm ... Ye night following, being in bed, she saw suddainly ye Venerable Mother Mary Xaveria standing before her at her bed's feet in her habit, but with her face partly shaded, she saw on one side a resplendent starr which dazelled her eyes ... This lady has ever since had a great deal of confidence in her intercession ...

... Some few dayes after Mother Xaveria dyed, Mrs Barnevil went to ye Jesuits church to pray for her brother who was dangerously ill and dispared of by ye doctors. She found at her entrance a dead billet by wch Mother Xaveria was recommended to ye payers of ye faithfull ... She was moved to have recourse to her [for her brother's health] ... At her return home, she found him so much better yt when ye doctor came to visit him he cryed out 'A miracle, a miracle' ...

... A preist ... whilst he was in ye church with others singing ye dierg for ye repose of her soul, saw her body environed with glory ...[69]

... I shall conclude this short account with a prediction of hers [Mother Xaveria] ... God gave her to understand yt there was in ye vault where dead bodyes of religious are deposited an incorrupt body ... It did not please God to discouer to her in particular whose body it was, yet she open'd several of the graves or vaults in ye dead cellar, and calling to her one of the religious[70] who had about 40 yeares agoe been a novice under ye Rd Mother Mary

---

[67]   She died on 9 February 1714; the extract resumes after a gap of two pages.
[68]   Around two pages of the original text are omitted here.
[69]   Around nine pages of the original text are omitted here.
[70]   Winifred of St Teresa (Elizabeth Lingen: 1662–1740), a lay sister central to much of the life-writing at Antwerp (see pp. 10, 163; Hallett, forthcoming).

Margaret of the Angels[71] who dyed in ye repute of sanctity, she asked her several things concerning [her] … Ye party, who is yet liveing … remembered that blood flowed out of ye vault after she had been buryed, wch its supposed made her [Catherine Burton] belive that this was not ye incorrupt body, and upon wch she desisted from opening ye grave. Yet this was ye very person in whom ye prophecy of Mother Xaveria was verifyed as will more appear in ye following Appendix.[72]

---

[71] Margaret Wake, whose incorrupt body it indeed turned out to be.

[72] This is included in the Life of Margaret Wake to whom it relates (Chapter 29).

Mary Margaret of the Angels: The Discovery of her Incorrupt Body and the Writing of her Life

There are three accounts of Margaret Wake (1617–78). One, by Thomas Hunter,[1] is contained in the appendix to his Life of Catherine Burton (*A3*, 488–90: and see Chapter 28); another is a discrete, book-length Life of Margaret Wake herself (*A4*), written by Percy Plowden;[2] and the third is in the Antwerp annals which notes that details of the nun's

> singular vocation, eminent vertues and most saintly death are writ in a book apart ... We must still lament our misfortune that the particular relations which has been left writ of many of our religious are lost and taken away by those that went to severall foundations etc which deprives us of many more great examples of vertu and sanctity of this Venble Mother ... (*A1*, 298–9).

This last statement underlines the concern to restore lost records that was the strategic and devotional impetus behind the compilation of the Antwerp Lives as a whole.

Plowden drew his material from personal knowledge (as spiritual director to the religious) and from the testimony of contemporary nuns, particularly two of Mary Margaret's novices, Mary Electa Howard (who had later transferred to Hoogstraeten and who died just before Plowden completed his book) and Winifred of St Teresa[3] who, as Plowden says, 'remained allways at Antwerp where she still lives, ready to attest the truth of all I have written in the following life ...'. Indeed, Plowden's chief process is to gather witness statements, to authenticate details of the discovery and its miraculousness. Like Hunter in Catherine Burton's Life, he is concerned to head off scepticism, and he appears to be establishing evidence for potential claims of blessedness.

Plowden's account accordingly adopts a 'reverse narrative': he opens with details of the discovery of Mary Margaret's intact body, then records her ancestry and early life, when her family had 'in the reign of King James the first retired out of England to settle in the Low Countries'. Plowden gives her mother's name as née Thorny of

---

1   See Chapter 28, note 1.
2   See Chapter 1, note 1.
3   Elizabeth Lingen (1662–1740): see Chapters 1; 19; and 28, note 70.

Essex and her father's as Lyonel Wake, the latter from a large family whose father 'could give him but a younger sons fortune to set him up a marchand, & Antwerp being at that time one of the most flourishing towns for trade in all Europe, he went over thither...'. Both parents 'by the misfortune of the times were both brought up in the Protestant religion which at that time had gained an upper hand in England'; but Lyonel's 'curiosity led him to see the Catholic church' where, after being handed a lighted torch to carry during the octave of Corpus Christi, 'he was so struck with reverential awe [that] he resolved to become a Catholick...'. Margaret Wake's mother converted rather later, during an illness. One of their sons became a priest in Spain, two daughters became religious in Brussels, and a third chose 'a meddle state between secular and religious ... without the tye of perpetuall vows ... call'd in Flanders spirituall children or devotes'. Their fourth daughter was Margaret Wake, who professed at Hopland on 11 June 1634.

Plowden is not alone in this narrative approach: all of Margaret Wake's Lives focus on her posthumous fame and begin their accounts at the end, as it were, retrospectively seeking signs in her life that led to a later state of blessedness. She is clearly spiritually and symbolically central to the historic narrative the Carmel wishes to record, and, naturally enough, other Lives are associated with hers, sometimes through linked favours – for example, Catherine Burton's own spiritual gifts are partially endorsed by her prediction of the discovery of an incorrupt body, even though in her own life-time she did not find out whose it was.

The opening section here is from Thomas Hunter's account (*A3*), followed by an extract from Percy Plowden's Life (*A4*), cross-referenced to other documents that both correspond and deviate in certain details and concluding with Plowden's own testimony, bolstered by other independent witnesses.

In the process of examining Mary Margaret's intact body, medical and theological experts clearly worked closely, each having different interpretative authority about physical and spiritual matters. Eventually, after the nuns had fled the Low Countries at the approach of the French Revolutionary forces (leaving Antwerp on 29 June 1794, travelling via Rotterdam and arriving in London on 12 July), the incorrupt body was interred in the cathedral in Antwerp. Once they had settled in their new convent at Lanherne in Cornwall, the religious sought to transfer the body to England, but the Antwerp ecclesiastical authorities resisted this.

[*A3*, 488–90]

An Appendix to the Life of Mother Mary Xaveria
An incorrupt body is found in a dead vault of ye Monastery of Antwerp as she had foretold

About two years after ye death of Mother Mary Xaveria, ye religious found it necessary to enlarge their burying place and being for this end supply'd with mony by Mr Bond[4] who has a daughter in yt monastery ... They set to work ... [They found several bodies that were corrupted, including one of only 10 weeks] ... When they came to [Mary Margaret of the Angels'] grave ... that coffin was open in ye presence of 3 or 4 of ye religious. They perceived when the top of ye coffin was removed something spread and drawn over ye coffin and fasten'd to the edges, through wch they discerned perfectly ye body from head to foot, what cover'd it was like a thin tiffany or gauze. They immediately gave notice of this to ye rest of ye religious, in the interim one of those present being too eager to touch ye body broke through yt wch cover'd it.

The community was much surprised to find ye body perfectly entire, fleshly and firm. This they perceived more distinctly when they had brushed of[f] ye habit in wch she had been buryed wch was all rotten, consumed and moist; (by pulling of ye head dress with too much eagerness one of ye sisters plucked out one of ye eyes[5]). The religious, not knowing how far this incorruption of her body might be attributed to natural causes, thought best to consult Monsr Trahy an experienced doctor who served ye convent,[6] and for yt end sent to him, but he being informed of ye reason for which he was call'd, brought with him Myn-heer Vrylings one of ye best doctors of ye town. They both examined ye

---

4   Thomas Bond, the father of Teresa Joseph (Mary Charlotte Bond: 1690–1735), whose entry at Antwerp Mary Xaveria had predicted (see Chapter 16), became a generous benefactor to the convent: as well as paying for building work in the crypt, for example, Sister Teresa 'was much pleased when she heard a little before her death yt Mr Bond her father had given our Order when at Bridges [Bruges] a very rich banner of the confraternity of our glorious Father St Joseph' (*A2*, 38). Thomas Bond later witnessed miracles associated with Margaret Wake (see note 16).

5   The Lierre archive has a statement about this, on a single sheet in a box of documents that also contains a picture of Margaret Wake's effigy, inscribed 'This picture had touched ye entire body'. The statement reads: 'you desire to know how the eyes of our Venerable Mother Mary Marguerite of the Angels came to be taken out: it was not done with design, a lay sister who had been her novice [presumably Sister Winifred] and who was then living when the holy body was found incorrupt ... in a transport of joy eagerly took of[f] the linen that had been put on her face when she was going to be buried, to which the eyes stuck and were thus pulld out. There is no one living who knows who got possession of them, it might probably be the Bishop who had a great veneration for her ...' (*L4.41*).

6   The Lierre annals mention an Irish physician in Antwerp, uncle to Joseph Teresa of the Purification, a lay sister at Lierre, whose mother was born Trohy (see Chapter 39). Presumably this is the same doctor, mentioned again below (note 14) as a witness to the incorruption of the body.

body, and were strangely surprised to find it so sound flexible & c. Being asked what they thought of it, they then refused to give their oppinion, but ye religious could not hinder their publishing what they had seen.

An other doctor was call'd in afterwards who had seen in his travells ye body of St Catherine of Bolognia[7] & c. When he had view'd and examined this body he congratulated with ye religious for ye treasure they possess'd. He declared his opinion yt it was ye body of a saint ... and offer'd himself as messenger to carry this agreeable newes [to the Bishop] ...

The Prelate with his secretary came within an hour to ye convent ... He was mett by ye Confessor, three doctors and a surgeon. Ye body was removed out of ye dead-vault which was dark, moist and wett, into an adjoyneing celler yt it might be examined more conveniently ... Then his Lordship and ye doctors went with ye workmen into ye vault to examine ye grave ... allso ye other coffins ... and found those yt were last buryed corrupted, ye other quite consumed. Being returned, he order'd ye surgeon to make an incision in ye pit of ye stomach, through wch they discouer'd ye diaphragma perfectly sound. The Prelate put his hand into ye wound ... and perceived a balsamick[8] smell proceeding from ye body wch his fingers retained two or three days tho' he washed them several times. Upon this strict examination ye doctors and surgeon declared that a corruption had never enter'd that body. The Bishop would not let it then be removed out of ye coffin, neither would he permit them to remove ye rotten and consumed habit wch lay very thick and moist under ye body ...

After ten days his Lordship order'd an other consult of 4 doctors and a surgeon to examine ye body again. The celler in wch it had been kept these ten days was so moist that every thing in it used to turn moldy in a night or two, yet ye body received no prejudice from this place ... [They] open'd ye diaphragma by wch they found ye heart, liver, lungs and all ye inward parts perfectly intire with all ye mussells & c. ... [They declared] it must be supernatural, leaving it to ye divines to determine whether it was to be tirmed miraculous ...

Supplying ye want of ye habit, wch was rotten and fallen of[f], least any indecency should appear to the eyes of ye beholders, ye religious after this had leave to remove ye body to a little hermitage or oratory within ye inclosure, where the religious dressed it up in a habit of silk, which a devout lady was inspired to give ... It appears of a brownish complexion, but full of flesh, which like a liveing body yeilds to any impression made upon it, and rises again of it self wn it is press'd: ye joynts flexible, you find a little moisture when you touch ye flesh ... and this very frequently breaths out an odoriferous balsamick sent ... [which] has sometimes filled ye whole roome[9] ...

... They all took notice yt both ye sides and lid of ye coffin seem'd all to have been tinged with blood.[10] It is now kept in a decent case made for that purpose, with two locks, one

---

7   Catherine of Bologna, 1413–63, who was canonized in 1712.

8   Though the text asserts that Margaret Wake's body was not embalmed, balsam (commonly used medicinally for its healing properties) is also used to preserve corpses.

9   Similar details were recorded by Francisco de Ribera (1588/1671) in his account of the incorrupt body of Teresa de Jesus.

10 This detail is supported by Sister Winifred's testimony that she had previously seen blood flowing down a wall.

key in the hands of my Lord Bishop, ye other in the monastery ... At present [it] is found as incorrupt and plyable as ever, retaineing still ye same agreable balsamick scent.

This discovery ... was immediately published all over ye town by physitians and others who had been eye-witnesses of it. This drew vast numbers of people about ye monastery who, once or twice at ye opening of ye gate upon some necessary occasions, surprised ye religious and rushed in, in great numbers, insomuch that they were several times obliged to call soldiers from ye cittadell to guard ye inclosure ...

... The next day [the Governor-Prince] sent ye Princess his spouse ... In token of her respect she took the ring off her own finger and desired ye director of ye monastery to put it on ye finger of ye holy body, where it yet remaines: it has a ruby in ye middle, set round with daimands. The concurse of ye people who came even from ye neighbouring towns was so great yt the nuns could not for some days upon any account open their gate. They cry'd out in ye streets yt God had not given ye Saint for ye monastery alone, but for them all ... When they saw they could not find access they sent in such numbers of beades, meddals, pictures & c. to be touched yt it was sufficient imployment for one or two of the religious for some dayes to comply with their request in touching ye body and bringing them back. They have great numbers of testimonyes signed by ye parties concerned where they declare ye great benefits received by her intercession. I shall say nothing more of these till Superiors think fit to have them published authentically: several have own'd yt ye sight of ye body has proved their conversion to a better life ...

... The body is kept in a little roome joyning ye quire of ye nuns, and not in ye quire itself, because they would not do any thing wch may seem to have ye show of publick veneration till ye Superiors of ye church allow of it, yet as they tel me, if ye voice of ye people may be said to be the voice of God, she has long since been canonized.

... ye Reader may easily satisfy his own curiosity or devotion by becomeing an eye wittness of it when he pleases[11] ...

... If we want courage and resolution to imitate, we may at least admire ye power of divine grace triumphing thus gloriously over all the sentiments of flesh and blood in this client of St Xaverius, and great servant of Jesus Christ, the Venerable Mother Mary Xaveria of the Angels.[12]

*

[*A4*, 256–93]

The Body itself ... is generally accompanied with a very odoriferous agreable smell proceeding from it, sometimes more and sometimes less ... One Mr Price, an English priest, comeing in with other company to see the body & putting his hand into ye incision

---

[11]   The reader is thus invited to take part in the authentication process. Indeed many visitors did visit the convent to view the body, and this led to increased revenues and, in some cases, a desire to join the community (see Chapters 18 and 26).

[12]   This marks the end of the text and of this volume.

made in ye stomach, the whole room was suddenly so filled with ye spicy perfume wch
came forth from the incision, that several of ye religious, as well as seculars (for the place
was full of people) cryed out that they never in all their lives smelt any thing so delicious
… I can assure my Reader yt I have often percieved something coming from yt body very
agreable.

In a word, several people of ye town of Antwerp have assured ye religious that after they
had touched ye holy body thô they often washed their hands, yet the sweetness continued
in them for 2 or 3 days and yet … ye body was never embalmed, never purfumd, and never
had any sweet thing about it from ye day the Reverend Mother dyed to the day that her
body was found uncorrupt: and from yt time to this present, all possible care hath been
taken that no sweet thing, no perfume, or even natural flowers should even come near it,
in so much yt once when one of the religious brought some linnen wch had lain amongst
sweets to the Prioress to be touched to ye holy body, in order to given them away to others
who were desirous of it for their devotion, the Prioress very prudently refused to touch ye
body with it till it had been washed.

Finally, after the body had been exposed almost 2 years, without any alteration, only …
it was a little drier, and after yt ye religious had long oportuned ye Bishop to know wt was
to be done with it, whether it was to be buried again or to continue exposed, or in fine to
be locked up and kept privately above ground … [The Bishop] sent his secretary to lock
up the body in a decent new chest made for that purpose, and to place it in a room or rather
an open passage joyning to the nuns quire; where it now rests without any exterior marks
of veneration: and to take away all suspition of publick worship, a crucifix is placed upon
ye chest for those to pray before …

… Amongst the several doctors and surgeons, who were called at different times to inspect
the body & to give their opinions of it, Ignatius Vandendyck is ye only one who has given
in writing a distinct account of the state and condition he found it in before ye incision was
made … wherefore for ye Reader's satisfaction I shall give Dr Vandendyck's attestation
translated into English from ye Latin original:

> I underwritten do attest that on ye 17th of August 1716, I was called to the monastery …
> and that I found the same body lying in its coffin … naturally intire, dried up, covered
> all over with flesh, the arms flexible, the back very moist without the least ill smell, but
> rather a very sweet one.
>
> … My wonder still increased when I understood yt ys religious during her life, and
> to her very dying day, was of a gross replete body, full of ill humours, and that she dyed
> of an empyema,[13] all of which ought to have consumed the body in a very short time
> … they shewed me in ye dead vault, a little sort of oven, wch I found to be very moist.
> I ordered the masons to open some other ovens round about it … and finding not only
> the bodies, but also ye coffins of them all intirely corrupted and consumed, I was seized
> with greater astonishment than before.

---

13 Literally, a collection of pus in any cavity, especially the pleura. Plowden records that
    'when she was a young religious [she] had contracted an illness in one of her breasts, wch
    was very painfull and troublesome to her ever after & at length was ye cause of her death
    … it caused a hardness in ye pitt of her stomach yt for eight months before she dyed she
    was forced to take ye Infirmary. The doctors … attributed yt hardness in her stomach of
    wch she dyed to no other cause but ye want of sufficient nourishment & moisture …' (*A4*,
    84).

... And what is still more wonderful is that this body for ye space of several months had been kept first in a little moist celler afterwards in ye nuns' quire for the people who came in great throngs to see it, and in fine always exposed to the open air, without suffering any change or alteration ...

I affirm to be true, Ignatius Vandendyck, sworn doctor of ye city & hospital of Antwerp[14]

... Sister Winefrid of St Teresa Linghen being yet a young religious and going upon some occasion with a light into the dead cellar, knelt down before ye place where her dear Superiour [Margaret Wake] had been lately buried ... about 5 or 6 weeks after ye Rd Mors death, to ye best of Sister Winefrid's memory as she has often assured me, whilst she was praying & looking fixly upon ye place, she saw a little streake of blood upon ye wall, just in that where the Rd Mor lay ... She clearly perceived it was fresh blood, and saw it sensibly runing down, thô not very fast: she wiped it off with her finger, and still found by the staining of her finger, and ye wall, that it was truly blood ... Fearing perhaps she should be chid or laughed at in ye community ... she never made ye least mention of it, or even thought of it more till many years after when yt Superiour [Catherine Burton] [investigated] to whom God was pleased to reveal that there was an incorrupt body in the cellar ... Sister Winefrid interposed and said 'No dear Mother, do not open that grave for I am sure ye body ... cannot be ye uncorrupted body you seek ... I saw fresh blood coming out of her grave ...'[15]

... A boy in England was instantly cured of sore eyes by applying some of ye linnen that had touched the body ... and other Protestant boys were ready to pull his eyes out for it, because they said he was cured by a ray of Popery ...

... Whoever is acquainted with the stile & method of ye Roman Rota in examining and approving of miracles when ye question is to canonise a saint, will easily be convinced yt it is not upon slight grounds or flying reports that Catholicks believe such miracles[16] ...

---

[14] This testimony was also signed by Mary Frances of St Teresa [Birkbeck], Prioress; Delphina of St Joseph [Smith], Subprioress; Mary of St John the Evangelist, Depositary; Joseph Francis of ye Blessed Trinity, Depositary; and five doctors, including Edmunys de Trohy (see note 6) and John Gobel[s]; see p. 159. The extract here omits around seven pages from the original text.

[15] Around 10 pages from the original text, giving various accounts of miraculous events associated with Margaret Wake, are omitted here.

[16] There follow numerous examples of cures related to touching the body – for example, Joanna Catherina Truyts, on 18 February 1717, with a broken leg, found herself afterwards able to walk without crutches; Antony Vanderberch, witnessed by Thomas Bond (see note 4) and Charles le Brun, recovered from a fever when dust taken from the coffin was mixed with wine and drunk; Charles Quise, a soldier at Antwerp castle, recovered from malignant ulcers on his legs when touched by linen that had touched the body; Elizabeth Vandegraef, a beguine of Antwerp, who had suffered with crippling rheumatism for many years that visits to Aix-la-Chapelle and other places could not cure, touched the body and 'now could carry a pitcher of water with yt very hand with wch before she could not so much as stick a pin or hold a glass of bear'.

Chapter 30

Margaret of St Teresa, the First Prioress at Lierre: Her Early Sense of Vocation and Progress towards a Religious Life; Her Skill in Resolving Conflicts; Her Devotion to Anne of the Ascension and her Death in which She is No Longer Wrinkled or Crooked

Margaret Downs was the first Prioress of the new convent at Lierre. She travelled there from Antwerp in 1648 with a group of other nuns, their numbers and 'quality' all in accordance with the Rule (see Appendix 1). The group included 11 professed religious: Sister Margaret herself, initially Vicaress until her election as Prioress the following year (which office she held until 1655); Catherine of the Blessed Sacrament (Chapter 6) as Subprioress; Anne of Jesus [Foster]; Elizabeth of the Visitation [Emery]; Eugenia of Jesus [Leuesson]; Margaret of Jesus [Mostyn] and Ursula of All Saints [Mostyn] (Chapter 31); Hironnima of St Michael [Susanna Wintour]; two lay sisters, Margaret of St Francis (Chapter 4); Alexia of St Winefrid (Chapter 12); and a quire novice, Mary of St Joseph [Vaughan] (*L4.39*).

Margaret Downs (1600/03–1682) is described in the Antwerp annals (*A1*) as the daughter of Thomas Downs and Mary Bedingfield of Suffolk, but she is identified at Lierre as the daughter of John Bedingfeld of 'Readinfield' (presumably Redlingfield). There is some contradiction, too, about her dates: the Lierre papers state that she died in 1682, aged 82, whereas the Antwerp annals suggest she was born in 1603. Her own autobiographical text mentions that she was 23 when she became inclined to join a religious community, and she is said to have taken the habit at Antwerp in (around) 1621, 'upon ye Sunday in corpos christie octiue', and to have professed on 'St Alousas day' in (around) 1622. When she died in Lierre on 13 April 1682 she had been professed, on whatever computation (and in general the convent at which a nun professes is most likely to have the correct details at entry) for some 59 or so years. One of her nieces joined the convent at Lierre after she had seen a vision of her mother (Sister Margaret's sister) on her way to heaven (see Chapter 35).

The Antwerp annals gives Margaret Downs only a one paragraph entry, recording her re-election to various offices, including her nine years from 1636 as a Subprioress at that convent, 'wch showed that she was a woman of parts & esteemed by ye community' (*A1*, 208). The main information about her life is derived, therefore, from the Lierre archives, where there is a first-person autobiographical paper as well as an entry in the annals.

The first extract that appears here is Sister Margaret's own account (*L4.39*), written, as convention – or rhetoric of it – dictated, at the command of her confessor. As in so many of the Lives there is an attempt to pinpoint early signs of her vocation. The narrative describes the stirrings of her wish to join a Carmelite convent and subsequent doubts that were not resolved until one Palm Sunday when she was only able to swallow the host once she had decided to follow her vocation. She did this eventually, along with two of her sisters, in the face of opposition from their father, from whom they obtained permission to travel, telling him their real intention only when they were well on their way to Antwerp.

The Lierre annals (*L13.7*) describe her life in various convents as well as illustrate some of the early difficulties experienced by the nuns in their new foundations in the face of opposition from the friars, a *leitmotif* of the Lives. To illustrate her credentials and stress the legitimacy of the new foundation, the papers stress Sister Margaret's close association with Anne of the Ascension, spiritual founder at Antwerp in a direct line from Teresa de Jesus through Anne of St Bartholomew. Among other incidents, Sister Margaret was also witness to the miraculous recovery in January 1680 of Anna Maria of St Joseph (Chapter 39), attributed to the intercession of Margaret of Jesus (Margaret Mostyn: 1625–79), lately deceased (Chapter 31A).

[*L4.39*, 1–9]

Written by Herself

As I remember, a bout the age of 4 or 5 yeares, God ded of his goodnes giue me som thoughts of the presence that all ware scene to hem, and I was somtimes afrad when I ded omit to say such prayers as I was taught, yet mani times I was cared away with childers play and omittered them.

Whin I was 5 or 6 yerres ould ther cam a nould man [an old man] to ore houes which ded teach me to rede, and he spack much of God and the end wherefor we were created and of heuene and hele …

… About 8 yeares of age I was to goe to confesion: as I remember [I] was so full of joy that I begane to tele my great sins until he bed me say nothing I had done untill I cam to the Sacrament. I delighted much in reding and I toke St Charene of Sene [Catherine of Sienna] for my pattern and desired much to imitate her, and out of simplicitie I did think it wold be no hard thing to be a St …

I wold get in to som corner and wold som times doe penances, but I was quickly warie and as a child anconstant in all ... I considred that St was a religious and for that I done not remember I did so much desier as that I might sarue God in verginitie ...

... I can not remember any grat euel I was in clined to other wass [otherwise] then childes sportes ...

[Aged 12 or 13, I spoke to a Father of the Society of Jesus] I tould him that I desired to sarue God and he understod I wold be religus. I answered I was a frad of it but I durest not holy deni it for fere of linging [lying], but I remember I was not glad he understod me so ...

... I doe perticulely remember, and this I am veri sarttan of, the first tim I commucaded I was so full of joy in my soul that I did not know how to contine my self so I procured most of that day to be alone...

... Be twin 13 and 14, by resone of som companie, I neleged thos tim[es] of pray and reding, only conting [contenting] my self to say som few pray[ers] in the morning and iueng [evening] and then my thought wer on others thinges, not of any euell but things of recration ...

... Whin I was about 14 and we had a fa[ther] to liue with us[1] who was veri carfull of my good ...

...I had mani time a grat fieling and desie to plese God, and whin I went to the Sacrament I thought many tim, if there war no other testimen of the Catholic church, the conten and pes of mind it brough it war sufficien to proue the truth ther of. I had extrem compasion of errictes [heretics] and such as liued out of the church, and I though[t] what I migh doe for ther conuersion ... I though[t] if I could conuer[t] on[e] soul I could be conten to be relilious, and as I rember that was the first motiue. I did not know what meditation was but I found a grat dele of content to think of the passion ...

... I toke so much content in this and reding ...[and spent so much time alone, my family sent me to talk to the priest] ... He excamend me so [and] though I had no mind [to do so] I was forcsed to tell him how I spent my tim. He then gaue me som instrotion for meditation which, though I indeoued [endeavoured] all I could to obseru that, I had extrem difficulti becaus I was so acostomed to keep no order but follow that which I was moued to ...

... I often considre[d] what a religis life might be ... yet I found extrime difficutie to leue my mother for none ded loue any more thin I did and I kneu I was as dere to her. This things ded take so one me as I feles [fell] in a siknes [from] which they ded think I wold haue ded [died] ...

... [My parents] say thay wold not hinder me, but I was yet young and so it was stil defared from spring to faul [fall] for 2 yeare. I was moued to this Order by reding our B[lessed] Mo[ther's] life ...[2]

---

[1] Several of the Lives mention that a spiritual director or priest lived with the nuns' families in their extended household.

[2] Around one page of the original text is omitted here. In this Sister Margaret describes the form that her devotion took, namely half an hour to an hour of meditation each morning,

... The deuotion I used was, in the morning, half anouer and most comly anore of meditation, the ofes of our B Lady and a pare of bed for reding nand othe deuotions (thay war longer and shorter ac cording as occation and my deuotion sarued) ...[3]

My vocation

Att ye age 23 I began to haue a desir of a religious life ... Ther was noe meanes for me to attaine perfection unless I were a Teresan. I continued many weekes striuing against this good inspiration wch caused me much trouble & unquitines of mind; in ye end I remember I sayed 'O Lord, you know what hinders me' ... then I retoured againe to diuert my self. But that very night I began to be so much amended in point of halth yt I scarse knew my self & within three dayes I was wholy cured of that wch had most hindered me ...

... I procured a [travel] pase,[4] but as priuitly as I could from the knowlige of all my nerest frindes from whom I intended to dissemble my intentions ye better to affect my desirs, but it happned, as I and one of sisters were upon ye point as we thought of taking ship, our dissines [designs] were crost, so yt we were to retorun unto my fathers house againe. I began to think that perhapes Allm: God had permitted this to happen because I had taken but one of my sisters, and I knew the other one had ye same desirs. I found noe remedy but that I was to stay another yeare to expect my opportunity of taking both my sisters with me.

Now I grewe to mak some delayes, under a pertence of seeing wherther my cure would continue. Yett was I not mindfull of my vocation, nor would haue wholy nelicted it for ye whole world. But going to communicate upon Palme Sonnday, I found that I could not by any meanes swallow the sacred host although I procured to doe it for ye space of three misereres[5] ... I first made my examin[6] and begann to think that, peraduenture, my delayes might offend Almightie God. I purpossed to ineruour [endeavour] wth all my fources to accomplish my vocation [and] att yt very instant I did find the sacred host to remoue and I swallowed it very easily, all my feare left me ... I write a little note of what hapened and gaue it to the prists ... I did not long after [leave] taking both my sisters with me, my father not mistrusting any thing of the busines we had then in hand but expected our retourne ... He had giuen us leaue to be from home for some lettle time, but then I wret him word that we ware in the way to Antwarp entending to become religious where soone wee ariued.[7]

---

the office of the Virgin, a pair of rosary beads and other devotions, according to time and the occasion. She goes on to tell how her entry to the Order was delayed because she heard of the 'differences of the friars' – that controversy concerning the constitutions that had so involved Anne of the Ascension (Chapter 2).

3 Around three pages of the original text are omitted here.

4 Other religious mention their difficulty in obtaining permission to travel during the period of civil war.

5 I.e., a Misere, a prayer setting of Psalm 50 of the Vulgate, from its opening word, '*Misere mei, Deus, secundum magnam misericordiam tuam*': ['Have mercy upon me, O God ...'].

6 A private examination of her mind and soul (as opposed to verbal confession).

7 The account ends at this point.

*

[*L13.7*, 122–30]

Her life at Antwerp, Aalst, Cologne and Lier

... She was the right hand of our most venarable Mother Anne of the Assincion, ye first Priourße and Superiour of our English Tearesan Carmellats, a parson of emenent saintytie ... one wch account she left ye gourment [government] of the Carmellet Friers, and suffered much to mantaine, our holy constitution; besids ye noyes of these great dificultys wth ye friers and ye cha[n]ge thay pretended made much discurce in ye world, and was a maine hinderence to ye increse and advantag of yt new foundation ...

... Att ye age of 5 or 6 yeares her puer, innosent soule had ye giuest [gift] of prayer, and would spend some houers in ye day contemplating heuenly things, wch custome grew to so great a hight yt in her riper yeares, [aged] 12 or 13, often times [she] had ye giuest [gift] of teares ... [She liked] to read good bookes ... and [was] a parfect emitator of St Chatrine of Sieane [Catherine of Siena], whom she had taken for her pattronese, from her infancy ...[8]

... ye comon enemy of peace raysed a storme in our conuent att Collen [Cologne], so yt superiours thought it nessecary to send our deare mother Margaret of St Teresa to stope yt streme of disorder, wch she allso braught to happy conclution, reformed some relaxations, and made them in all comformable to ye rest, under ye ordinary [Rule], wch uniformety established them in parfect peace wth one another; so yt before that ware in a maner one ye point to be quit ruinated, and ye couent come to nothing by permeting seculare parsuns to intermedle wth there affares, lost there reputation, so yt non would enter amungst them, wch detained our Mother Margaret there, more then a yeare ... yt this couent from yt time hath florished to this day. Haueing ended there, it was nessicary to call her back, for ye aduantag of her owne house, wch was very lettle and inconvenient and nessisary to be inlarged, tho there was lettle wher wth all [wherewithal] to doe it. This charg was layd upon her, wch she parformed wth great prudance and care, contriuing and plotting, day and night, to haue it conuenient, and don to ye profitt of ye house. She payed ye workmen herself, and baught all ye materialls for ye bilding, and was euer first and last obsaruing ye workmen, [so] yt she had scars time to take any refreshment, and in all this troublesome busnes, she neuer lost her peace of mind, or disquieted her selfe ...

... [She] purely saught ye honner of God, and the parfect accomplishment of ye will of her Superiour [Anne of the Ascension] wch was ye guid of her thoughts and actions, for she reuerenceed her as a saint, and loued her aboue all ye wemen in the world: in fine, thay ware one hart, there could not be a greator simpathy in nature then ye spirituall unione of there soules and spirit, yt it simed thay could neuer be seperated and suruiue.

---

[8] Around three pages of the original text are omitted here; they record that she spent some time at Alost, where she clothed three new novices, then returned to Antwerp as Mistress of Novices before she was sent to Cologne.

But our Bd Lord designed other ways: not long affter his Deuine Maigesty called our Venarable Mother Anne of ye Assincion to injoye his glory affter a long sicknes [in 1644], ye greatest crosse yt could befall our good Mother Margaret – tho she bore it wth an admirable corrige and resignation to ye will of God, as yt she did not shead so much as one teare but dispached all the busnes of ye house wth ye same peace and equality of mind as if she had not bine att all consarned, tho there was nothing in ye world [that] could trouble her more then to part wth so worthy a superiour and deare a Mother …

… In ye yeare 1648, ye foundation of Lier was made and, as she was ye most experinced, [she] was comanded to take ye charg of managing this great affare, haueing wth her 12 religous wth a small alowance in a heired house, and poore, in want of all nessicaris amungst strangers; but her corrig [courage], and confidence in God, was so great yt she feared nothing … yt in ye [space] of 6 yeares she baught a house, made it conuenient, and so settled affares yt wee ware able to liue wthout much solissitud [solicitude], upon ye nouisses portions [dowries], wch our Bd Lord, in a perticluar maner, inspired to come to this new plantation … but finding her selfe declining, and subigct [subject] to meny infirmetyes, she could not beare ye heauey burthen of Superiour, being allways under ye doctours hands, and forst also to keep ye Infirmary; ye couent made choyse of our most deare uenarable Mother Margaret of Jesus,[9] who was her right hand, in erecting this new begining …

… [She] would often shead meny teares att ye feett of her Confessarious, bewaileing her sinns, aprehending ye last houer of death, who comforted her and would often say, to her and others, yt it was very strang yt a woman of so inocent a life, and so highly fauored of God, should haue such deepe aprehentions exceapt it ware to purify her soule, and keepe her in humility. She allso had ye heauey cross to haue him dey [that he died] before her, wch she bore wth ye same equality of mind, as uisall. It was obsarued affter his death, her fiears and aprehentions declined …

… Tho she was of so great age, [she] neuer omitted to say ye deuine offi[c]es, wth attintion, tell some few days before her death, tho she was very infirme, and weake sighted … She would not easily lett passe imperfections in ye com[m]unity wth out taking notis of it when she prosseeded, and was zealous of ubsaruance [observance], and yt each one should doe there duty wth out any human respect, being a great enimy of idlenes, and hatted all yt sauored of vanity, of selfe consayet. Her discurce was religous and not superfluous, but sollaed [solid], plaine, and to ye purposse … and tho she was but of a low statued [stature], and wth age growne very croked, yet her presence had so much of wisdome in her countinance yt all ye relgious stood in awe of her, she haueing, in her way of proseeding, ye markes of superioritie … euen to ye end of her life, wch now draws nere, being taken of a sooden wth a catter [catarrh] yt so violently [had an effect] upon her noble parts, yt ye doctur found her in great danger in a short time, and ordained her ye last sacraments[10] …

---

9   Margaret Mostyn (Chapter 31A), who was Prioress from 1655–79.
10 The physician was responsible under the Rule for calling the confessor, and this marked a transition between physical and spiritual authority. Sister Margaret died on 13 April 1682.

... Her dead corpes, when it was braught doune and expossed in quiere, did testifey to all yt saw it ye angelicall purity of her soule, remaining wth out any ill sauour but looked wth a siearene and saintlie cuntinance, so yt all yt came to our outward church[11] to see ye corpes could not beliue she was more then 50 yeares ould, nather could one desarne [discern] one rinckle in her face, of wch she had meny persepttable ones when she was liueing, and she was allso strayt and full chested, where as she was from her youth much arey [awry] and, wth ould age and meny infirmeteys, went in a maner doble, and was forst meny yeares to walk about ye house with a staffe. Now it simed there was nothing wanting in her parsone yt was not gracefull and pleasing ...

---

[11] The dead religious were exposed in the choir, visible to members of the public in the outer chapel through the grate.

Chapter 31

The Lives of the Mostyn Family

Several members of the Mostyn family were members of the Carmelite Order; some still are. Most prominent among them in the early modern period was Margaret of Jesus (Margaret Mostyn: 1625–79), who professed at Antwerp and then transferred to Lierre in 1648 along with her sister, Ursula of All Saints (Elizabeth Mostyn: 1626–1700). The Antwerp annals contain brief details of Sister Margaret's early career: '… she has writ an account of her own Life and great favours att large, so that it is not necessary to add any more here' (*A1*, 403). Indeed, the Lierre archive contains many papers relating to Margaret Mostyn, including several versions of full-length Lives, providing rich and vivid detail of the two sisters, not least an account of their possession by some 300 devils and their exorcism in 1651 (see Hallett, 2007).

The extracts here are drawn from the Lierre annals, subdivided by the names of the Mostyn religious who were at the convent, either together or in succession, and presented in order of birth date. As well as Sisters Margaret and Ursula, the Mostyn nuns include their nieces, Lucy of the Holy Ghost (Elizabeth Mostyn: 1654–1707), Margaret Teresa of the Immaculate Conception (Margaret Mostyn: 1659–1743), Mary Anne of St Winefrid (Anne Mostyn: 1663–1715); and their great-niece, Francis Xaveria of the Immaculate Conception (Frances Poole: 1697–1763). Mention is made elsewhere in this book of Frances Poole's sister, Teresa of Jesus Maria Joseph (Mary Poole: 1696–1793; see p. 14); and a further Mostyn relation is recalled at the beginning of the second volume of the Lierre annals: Teresa Clare of the Annunciation (Elizabeth Poole: 1726–79) was 'very good and quick at her needle'. She was 'carryd off rather suddenly and unexpectedly in I may say the flower of her age' (*L13.8*, 2).

The Mostyn family were prominent Catholics from Talacre in Wales. Their fortunes were similar to those of many other Catholic families after the English Reformation and during the Civil War. Margaret and Elizabeth were two of eight children of John Mostyn and Anne Foxe (daughter of Henry Foxe of Lehurst in Shropshire, where Margaret spent her early childhood). Their brother Edward, married first to Elizabeth Downes, was created a baronet by Charles II in April 1670 (*Burke's Peerage*): his daughters Elizabeth, Anne and Margaret (when a widow) became religious at Lierre, and his son, Andrew, is mentioned in the Carmelite papers as a confessor. Edward Mostyn himself also features in the Lives, accompanying his sisters and daughters to the Continent and frequently visiting his family after they had settled in Lierre. Frances Xaveria of the Immaculate Conception was the granddaughter of another of Edward Mostyn's sisters, Mary (who had married into the Poole family).

In 1626 there are records of what appears to have been a secret religious school at Greenfield Abbey, the Mostyn family home (see note 27), a school that was closed the following year. On the feast day of St Winifred in 1629 around 1400 people, including 150 priests, gathered at St Winifred's well near Greenfield, these sheer numbers indicating that there was a degree of religious tolerance of Catholic activities by the Protestant authorities. In 1640, Anne Mostyn and her second husband, George Petre, built an inn at Holywell (Seguin, 2003, 10; 13).

Although some limited parts of the Mostyn Lives have previously been published (Bedingfield, 1884; Hardman, 1937), these texts are long since out of print, so a longer selection is included here, richly illustrating the varieties of religious and secular experience within one family. Each entry as it appears below has a separate note introducing the nun at the start of her individual Life. The length of entries varies, of course, in the original documents.

A Margaret of Jesus[1]: her early life in which she governs her grandmother's household; her perilous journey to Antwerp and her transfer to Lierre where she is set upon by an evil spirit who causes a great storm; her spiritual favours before and after death

[*L13.7*, 40–99]

... I shall indeuer [endeavour] to sett downe some lettle of yt much wch might be sayd of this most deare Mother of ours; and we will begine wth her childhood ... She being about 6 yeares of age was ubsarued [observed] to haue a great deuotion to a pictur of our Bd Lady wth lettle Jesus in her armes, spending much time in adorning it wth her brasletes, and what other lettle curiossities she had, and was so searious att this imploy yt once she lost [forgot] her diner ... She was also deuoted to her good angell who she visiblely saw, and hee would often cary her downe staryes, and conduct her thorowe darcke entres when she was sent of avents about, being naturally very fearfull of going in ye darcke.

And euen att these tender years, she began to haue a venaration, and knowlidg of ye most Bd Sacrament. One Mande Tharsday [Maundy Thursday] it chanced she was left for

---

[1] Margaret Mostyn: 1625–79. Her Life was most probably compiled by Sister Ursula, who succeeded her as Prioress at Lierre. It records that she was clothed at Antwerp on 'St Larrance day', 10 August 1644, and professed on St Clare's day, 12 August 1645, 'it being nessicary for seuerall reasons she should expect a day more, then ye profixt time, wch simed to our deare Mother an age, so vemently she thursted to be a profest spoues of Christ'. The Life describes her secular experience governing her grandmother's extended family household from the age of 12, then gives details of the sisters' perilous journey to Antwerp, their encounters with witchcraft, Sister Margaret's friendship with Edmund Bedingfield (Chapter 32A), her death and subsequent spiritual favours.

some lettle time alone in ye chapell, and some of ye house returning found her climing one a high chere [chair], reaching at ye challis, att wch being much surprised, [they] toke her downe and asked her what she ment by doing so. 'Only' sayd she, 'I would faine see my lettle Jesus yt is there', wch she did visiblely behould att her first Communion, and then was inspiered to a religious course of life ...

... She also would often tell her granmother yt sartanly she must be a religious woman. 'Why?' sayd her granmother. She replyed 'Because I can neuer goe to my pray[er]s but I think of it', att wch her granmother would be highly displeased, saying thay ware childdish fancis, and comanded her neuer to think or speake of such a thing, if she expected any loue from her. She was allso much delighted in reading ye saincts liues, and other pious bookes, often spending whole howers in reading to ye saruants, by wch she conuerted too [two] soules yt ware protistance [Protestants]; in fine she gaue light and instruction both to ould and young in ye house.

Att 12 yeares of her age [she] was found capable of gouerning ye house and famelie, [since] her grandmother, tho a wise and virtues woman, was not able to doe it herself by reasone of a lamenes in all her ioyents, and could not moue a finger nor stor out of her chamber in meny yeares. It is almost in credible, not to be exprest, ye care and paines, this deare grandchild of hers toke in tending and sarueing her, constantly dresing, feeding, and rissing up out of her beed four or five times in a night, to turne her in her beed. ...

... Her great discression in maneging ye house was [to] ye admeration of ye whole cuntrie. [She did it] wth so much order and prudince yt she gaue a genarall sattisfaction to all, tho it consisted of 2 or 3 seuerall famelys, difernt in youmers [humours] ... Besides her naturall goodnes of youmore, sweetnes and vertue, she was indued wth an extreodinary beauty, comliness, behauiour, and sharpnes of witt, besides ye good education her piouse grandmother gaue her, wch alltogether rendered her one of ye most acomplished parsone of her time.

After this good grandmothers deceasce [death], she returned to her mother, wth a resolution to settle in ye world ... tell one day as she was walking in ye garding alone, very pencif [pensive], striueing against these good thoughts, our Bd Lady and our holy mother St Teresa apieared to her. Our Bd Lady bid her put her first good desiers in excecustion if she would be happy, and St Teresa would assist her. She presently thought wth in her self, how it could be posscible for her to leaue her sister Elizabeth, thay being all one hart [had] promised each other neuer to part. Our Bd Lady replyed 'She shall goe wth you, for a religious cource of life is allso proper for her' – as it fell out soone affter. Her sister declared her good desiers to her, wch confirmed her in ye beliue yt was ye will of God to haue them both religious, tho [it was] not in her powere to put it as yet in excution, there being great obstikles in ye way ...

... She ariued [at Antwerp] affter meny difficultis, part[ing] from her frinds who ware all oppositt [opposed] to her desinge [design], and also past a most perolleus loing and teadious jurny [perilous, long and tedious journey], abue 6 munths. In wch time there fell out diuers strang accidence yt did clearily show ye perticular prouidence of God, it being dangours for any to leve England, the times was so seuere, espessally to be religious was a great crime, not pardonable. Arrueing then at Waymouth,[2] a seeport toune, to take

---

2   Weymouth, a port in Dorset, England, was then embroiled in struggles between royalists and parliamentarians for control. During the Civil War (1642–48) it was dangerous for members

shiping for Flanders, ye toune was (whilest she & her company expected, a fauerable wind) besieged by ye parlement armie and their fliet of shipes lay allso att ye mouth of ye hauen [harbour], [so] yt there was no pashach [passage] to esscape ye danger by sees, and land. It twas propossed by my Lord Wardor to goe wth him to Exittor, hee haveing a party of horsse to conduct him there, and to gard ye Queene. This her Confessare and 2 or 3 Fathers more of ye Society, found most conuenient and secourest, [considering that] her eldest brother was wth her, [that] it would hasard [endanger] him and ye losse of his estate to be taken, wch afflicted her aboue messure, to find all things fall out so crosse ... there being nothing but confuission and great danger on all sides.

'Lett us' sayd she, 'say our Bd Ladys Lettines, and doe what she shall please to inspier'. Affter wch she, wth an undanted corrige [undaunted courage], [she] resouled to goe by seae in a frogot [frigate] yt was forst to goe wth letters of great consarn to ye king for Holand, and was wiling, if she and her company would venter ye hassard, to take her along wth him. [They] being 10 in nomber, and forst [to go] when it was pich darke, and the whole toune in ye hight of confussion, stoping all yt past, so yt thay ware in danger of death by ye insolency of ye rable. It tis most wonderfull yt in 2 houers walking from ye ien [inn] to ye batt [boat] thout ye opene streets, na one did once guest [guess] on who thay ware or whether thay ware going – tho diuers others yt went before and followed affter war stopet by ye gardes, theire trunks and goods throne about ye streats, and wonded yt thay lay for dead, wher as it simed this good company went invisible.

[Then] ariueing to ye watersid, and being all in ye bott to take shiping, ye sintinell [sentinel] who had order to shout [shoot] who some euer should dare to passe ye water, lifting up theire musckes [muskets] ment to shout att them, but could not make them take fier or goe of. Att [this] nouelty thay war astonished and bid them 'Goe one in ye name of God, for hee is wth you or you had perished'. As soone as she and ye rest was shipt, thay fell all to prayer, confiding our Bd Lady would assist them to pas thorow ye parlament shipts, wch as strangly succeeded, wth out being perceued, till thay ware some leages of[f] them. But towards ye breake of day thay, perceauing ye escape, sent 2 swift frigots affter them, wch followed them hard, and ye captin perseuing it was much perplext, saying hee must fight and [would] rather be sunke then taken. [This] alaromed ye company wth great dread, & [this] lasted ye whole day till, [at] 7 a clock at night, ye frigott got strangly in to ye hauen att Hauerde Grace [Le Havre], and cast anker [anchor], wher by good fortune ye Frinch navie lay, so yt thay ware out of danger, other ways those 2 parlement shipes would haue forst ye frigat out of ye hauen wth ye passingers, as thay had don formerly to others. This made our deare spouse of Christ put on a resolution, neuer more to goe to see, and made choys rather to suffer ye inconuenience of a loing troublesome jurney thorow France, in wch there ware many accidence yt did show she was deuinly protected.

One was so remarcable yt I cannot lett it passe: being all in ye coach, in ye greatest heats of the day, her brother had a mind to walk, but could not gett ye choch to stope so loing. He leaped out of the choch and, falling doune, ye hinder [back] wheles rune ouer him so that all gaue him for dead; wher as hee got up, wth out ye least harme, but a rent in his stooking on ye shin bone, not so much as rayse ye skine, or leaft any marke in his body. Our Bd Lord & his Sacraed Mother must be euer praysed for this, and meny other signall fauours, wch we leue to recount, for breueties sake.

She being ariued att Anwarp, ye couent receaued her wth singular joy, and my Lord Bishop was pleased to examine and cloth her wth his owne hands, tho a thing not uissall wth him. Ye ould Countis of Arandall [Countess of arundel], liueing then att Anwarp, and ye Lady Chatrine Houord [Catherine Howard] dressed and adorned ye brydes, wth her

rich & pressious jewelles, of wch her honner had great plenty, and allso out of her great
bounty gaue all things to ye conuent for ye marige feast, and was ye parsone yt lead her in
to ye monastary, and assisted ye Priourse to put on ye habit ...[3]

... ye forssable and violent remedyes, wch [the doctors] has uised before had so martered
her boody, and cast her into so great weeknes yt she neuer could recouer her parfect health
againe. [She] bacome subict to all sorts of infirmetys and paines. Her stomak was growne
so weeke yt she could not digest ye quantytie to one ege in a day, but liued meny munths
wth only ... piles of orringes ...

... [She] was allso made Infirmarine wch was then a great labour, being then a boue 40
religous, and constantly a considrable number of them in ye infermary. Amungst [them]
was one [who was] blind, in a deipe cunfousition [confusion], allways vometing and
spitting most lothsome filty matter and stouf, and [she] smelt so strong of ye corruption yt
came from her yt non of ye religous could beare to be neere her, only this deare sister. She
cherished and tended her wth all ye loue, care and charity imaginable, empting her poots,
washing those nasty foule cloths & continnually performing those disgustfull things about
her wth so much joye and allacrit as if she had no disgust in it[4] ...

... [She was deputed as one of group to go to Lierre] ... a sett plant, to giue this new
garden life and vegore in its begining ... Lier was the theater, aloted by her spouse, to
spend ye rest of her days ...[5]

... She was surprised, and violentlie sett upon, by an euelle sperit yt hanted ye house,
being confind there by wichcrafft, who afflicted and tormented the poor religous most
sadlie. But it seemed his greates spitt [spite] was against Str Margaret of Jesus, often
apiering to her in fierfull horred shapes of hidioues monsters wth fierey eyes, ready to
devoure her; some times licke a furious wild horse, runing so fersslie [fiercely] to and
froe as if hee would rune ouer her, and did so sometimes, leuing ye print of his feet in
her boody. Other times, [the spirit would] left her up in to ye ayer, threating to let her

---

of Catholic families, in particular, to travel. Weymouth at this point was surrounded by
Cromwellian forces, and the Mostyn entourage joined a group, led by Lord Arundel of
Wardour, escorting Queen Henrietta Maria to Exeter.

[3] Around two pages of the original text omitted here, give details of her illness and cure by
use of a relic of Father Henry Morse (p. 58).

[4] The Antwerp annals record: 'This Reverend Mother Margarett was here Infirmarian in the
time of the sickness of Sister Dorothy [Sara Hickx: c.1613–48] and thought it a slavery
to be confined to doe some things about her, in which she had great difficulty and disgust,
when behold she presently perceived her good angel perform them ... About 3 years after
the death of Sr Dorothy this Rd Mother Margaret was praying before an image of our Bd
Lady, the sacred virgin appear'd to her, with our Venble Mother Anne of the Ascension.
"Our Blessed Lady asked me if there were any other friend I desired to see, and presently
I thought upon Sister Dorothy, she indeed sayd our Blessed Lady is great in glory" ...'
(*A1*, 293).

[5] Around one page of the original text is omitted here; it gives details of the illness that
afflicted her soon after her arrival at Lierre, when the religious at Antwerp petitioned for

fall, or carrey her a way; and if it chanced she was alone, all ye dores would be made fast [locked] one a sudan, and ye place filled wth a black cloud, wch did cause so great fiere and alteration in her yt she could not so much as moue a finger, or make ye singe of ye crosse. Then would this weecked sperit trayle her about tell she was out of breath and not able to pronounce ye nam of Jesus, and meny times [it would] throw her downe stayers and brus [bruise] her all ouer, but had not power to doe her or others any other harme; but to tempt them in ye interriour, her in perticuler wth all sorts of malencolie fancies, and seuerall temptations, so yt she could take no rest, night nor day, yt she confest to some of ye religous, and often tould her superours, yt some times she was euen ready to disspare ...[6]

... It was thought fitt for this reason to remoue from yt house, to this our couent. It being his last farwell, it semed hee called all Hell to helpe him – for, tho it was a faire sonshine day, there arose one ye sodan [suddenly] so great a storme of wind, thunder and lighting, as if ye day of judgment had bine att hand, wth such a horred stinck of gunpouder and brimston yt all thought thay should haue bine choked, and a wherlwind wch raysed such a dust, [so] yt one could [s]carce see ther way ...

[The Confessor arrived from Antwerp, and read aloud from St John's Gospel] ... whilest one of ye sisters,[7] coming downe stayers wth ye image in her hands, her fott slipeing, it simed to her yt ye image was snached from her and cast againes ye payment [pavement], wher it most neds haue bin broken in peacies, tho there was not ye least harme don to it, nor ye crowne and septer [sceptre] defast [broken off] wch was tender and couriouslie cout ...

... [The Confessor] kneelling doune began to resitt [recite] our Bd Ladys Leattines [litanies] wch, no sooner ended, but ye storme ceased, and ye ayre became calme as if nothing had bine of yt nature. Str Margaret afirmed yt during ye tempest she saw ye Diuele in a great clape of thunder, raging yt hee was forst to tell her this was his last farwell, and ye worst hee could doe ...

... Tho our Bd Lord had bine most liberall to her, both of his crosses and fauours, now was ye time hee viseted her in a more marvielus and extradenary maner, as you may read att large in a faithfull relation of her Confessarious who had ye most part of it out of her owne papers.[8] As those visiones and revelationes hapened to her, our Bd Lady commanding her to writ them downe and giue them to him, wch was a great torment and affliction ... and

---

her return, 'alleaging what ill accomadation, and also ye meny inconuences of a new foundation being poore' had caused. However, she could not be persuaded to return, and 'crept about' after a long and tedious illness, at which point she was 'set upon' by an evil spirit.

6   Around one page of the original text is omitted here; it details how the novices, of whom Sister Margaret was then Mistress, were also affected, the spirit 'tempting them to wauer in theire good resolutions'.

7   Another account names Sister Ursula as the religious involved in this incident.

8   Her Confessor, Edmund Bedingfield, wrote several Lives of Sister Margaret (see Hallett, 2007). His own Life appears in Chapter 32A.

had she out liued our dear Father Mr Bedingfield of holy memory,[9] she had wth out dout burent her writinges and so depriue ye world and us of so great a treasur, and heauenlie instructions ... This worthy and holy man, infirme and euen att deaths doere, [lived] tell hee had finished ye writing of her life,[10] wth in ye compass of one yeares time affter her decese ... falling sicke un her aniuersarie day ...

After her death hee neuer inioyed [enjoyed] him self but simed to wast[e] away, dispossing him self for heuen; and when hee was writing her life hee would be all bathed in teares, [so] yt those present must take him from it by forse, and devert him a while. But alas it twas ye same, when hee came to writ againe, wch mad him so long about it, wheras our deare mother was lettle more then a munth about writing ye account she gaue him of her self[11] ... but noe wonder if we reflect one the helpe she had: ye Holy Ghost was seen, some times ouer her head, and our Bd Lady by her elboe, dictating and explaining to her those highe and sublime matters in so easie and familiar a stile, wch deuines and lerned men are forsed to couch in strang and hard words ...

... But this sweetnes had also itts betternes ... ye comone enimie of manking [mankind] would often transforme him selfe into an angelle of light,[12] [and] by yt menes to create in her meny fears and aprehentions yt all was elusions [illusions] and cheits [tricks] of ye Diuele. [This] gaue her excessue greif and affliction, for according to her owne nature she was very tememerous and fearfull ...[13]

... Friday nights she spent wholy in prayere, or att least 3 or 4 houres upon her knees, in meditation one our Bd Sauours sacraed pasione, and other nights [she] compossed her bead [bed] so as to take but lettle rest, obliging her selfe to wake euery time ye clock stroke, to doe some deuotion. Some times she lay wth a bo[a]rd under her, att other times to ley ye whole night in one posstour [posture], wthout once turning; and [she] had a great deuotion, when she was att her prayers, to kneele in an uneasy poustour, for 4 or 5 howers together, hoping by that, to sattisfy for her many distractions. Her Rce had so great contrary [aversion] in wearing of wollen [clothing] yt euen ye only touching of it wth her hand would alter her all ouer, yet for all yt wore it constantly wth out euer letting her superiours know ye dificultie she had in it. Ye two first winters affter her entering

---

9   Edmund Bedingfield died in 1680, the year after Margaret of Jesus.
10 This is the second of his main Lives (contained in *L3.27*).
11 Sister Margaret's speed of writing is often commented upon in the accounts that the religious wrote of her. In this they echo the Lives of both Catherine of Siena and Teresa de Jesus: the latter wrote '*The Interior Castle*, a work of two hundred and sixty printed pages, or about the length of the average novel, in four weeks' (Sackville-West, 1943, 47). She 'used to dictate those letters of hers with such rapidity, without the slightest pause to take thought, that one would have fancied she was reading out her words from a book lying open before her', whereas 'When [Catherine of Siena] wrote it was with great speed and with such great beauty in her face that it caused this witness to admire her' (see Ahlgren, 2000, 64).
12 See II Corinthians 11:26: 'even Satan fashioneth himself into an angel of light'.
13 Around three pages of the original text are omitted here; they give details of her devotions.

in to religion she neuer aproched ye fier [fire], but only for forme, to sattisfy others, exposing her selfe night and day to ye extremetys of heat and coulds, as much as she could, wth out apiering singular. Her dyett was allmost contineuall, eatting so very lettle, euer making choyce of yt wch she had ye greates contrarie in & mortifying in what she loued, perswaiding ye religous yt she could not eat flesh when as yt was ye only thing yt pleased her appetiet, and agried wth her bad stomak ...[14]

... She was gided by ye inspirations of ye Holy Ghost: yt deuine sperit did her meny signall fauours, amungst wch, upon ye Feast of Penticost, all ye religious being in ye quiere, prepared to sing Teres [Terce], it being our costome to lett fly a wite doue att ye time of '*vene creatur speritus*'.[15] Ye doue toke its flight to an image of our Bd Lady in ye quier, and from there to her Rce head, wher it contineued wthout storing from Tieres till ye Agnos Day [Agnus Dei], it being a soung Masse, and her Rce one of ye chantreses ... Ye doue neuer altred it postur but remained, as wee haue sine [seen] painted one ye heads of saincts, and was so mouing yt it simed to ye sisters ye whole quiere was filled wth the sperit of God ... She reallie saw and felt yt deuine sperit, in ye same forme, as hee came upon ye Apostles, wth a sweet gaile of wind, which filled her soule ...[16]

... It hapened when ye king of England was in banishment in these cuntres, there was a regement of his quartered in this towne, all parsones of good quallity, but poore distress[ed] cauelleirs [cavaliers] yt had not nathere mony, nor bread to eatt, and most of them sicke, and euen ready to drope doune as thay walked in ye streets for want. [Their] missarable condistion moued our Rd Mother ... she comanded ye Portrese not to deney relife to any yt came. And about 20 wch was more in want than ye rest, some of them being Catholicks, eat and drunk in ye speeckhous [speakhouse] and lower rome euery day, wher they had also fiere to warme them, for seaurall munths: besids [this] wee prouided medisines [medicines] for ye sick, and payd there docturs, and gaue them firing and candell, it being a very sharpe winter; and yt wch was strang[e], our prouistion [provisions] of corne, wood, butter and beere held out as well as othere yeares ...[17]

[We expected the flood would have resulted in]... an unsauery smaell [unsavoury smell], and cause much filth; but on ye contrary, when it was opened, it rather smealt sweet and wholsome, and not ye least corruption in it ... [Her coffin was dry] ... this seuearall parsons of quality ware an eye wittnes of, for ye inclosure allso att yt time hapened to be opened, her owne brother Sr Edward Mostyn was one ...

---

14   Around three pages of the original text are omitted here. The incident that follows, the one with the dove, is not told anywhere else in the papers; it draws, with mention of the wind, on Pentecostal imagery. Cecilia Ferrazzi, in sixteenth-century Italy, tells of something similar happening to her during her own devotions (Schutte, 1996, 43).

15   '*Veni Creator Spiritus*' ['Come Holy Spirit, creator blest'] from the opening of the ancient Latin hymn.

16   Around two pages of the original text are omitted here; they give details about similar signs of her many virtues. The extract resumes with an account of incidents that relate to the period of Charles II's exile, during the time when Margaret of Jesus was Prioress (1655–79); the events can be thus dated to between 1655 and 1660.

17   Around 15 pages of the original text (giving details of similar signs of her blessedness) are omitted here. The extract resumes with events two and a half years after her death, when the dead cellar which had been flooded the previous year, was opened.

... [He had heard a noise in his chamber the night she died] but rising in ye morning hee found ye picture [of Sister Margaret] taken doune, and sett ye other side of ye rome, ouer againes ye dore, yt all wch came must see it; and to his thinking it semed to cast a more resplendent sweetnes then ordinary, att wch hee was much amased, and called seuerall in ye house who obsarued ye same change in ye picture, saying it loked heauenly, but [they] could not tell what judgment to make of it, not dreaming of her death, this being in England thay had not so much as heard of her being sick ...

... Innumerable secular parsons [people] beggs [begged] for peeses of her habitt or anything yt belonged to her Rce, wch thay estime [esteem] as rellickes, and in troubles and afflictions comes to recomend theire nessicities to her and begge her interssestion, and braught wackx light to burne att her toumbe ...

... [On first profession day after her death] St Clars day ye 12 of August in ye yeare 1680 [at] ye begining of the first Vesperis [Vespers] there came out of ye dead cellar, wch is all ways massen'd up [bricked up], a strong and pleasing perfume, wch not only filled ye whole cellar but [also] ye quiere ... and so contincoued [continued] tell ye seond Vesparis was sayd. And it was smelt by ye whole comunity, who ware all transported wth joye, and found them selfs a perticular deuotion, not visall haueing neuer experienced ye licke – it being much diffarent from yt wch some times wee are acustomed to smell, wch wee call our Bd Mothers St Teresa smell, or yt of liles and roses wch when our deare mother was a liue would very often be about her parsone, perticularly in ye chapter, or att prayer, and most comanly, when she treated of heauenly matters, wch gaue a great adiscion [addition] and power to her words and made them haue so great, an influence ouer our harts yt sometimes, thay would euen melt wth deuotion. But this kind of sweet[nes]s ware neuer before smelt by all ingenarall [in general], only 2 or 3 sisters att a time, or but one and yt for a short time, whereas this lasted so long, and all ye house ware pertackars [partakers] of it, & it semed to be somthing lick a hott burning perfume. And allso wee fancied there came, as it war, a smoke out of ye chincks of the dore, perticularly from yt side wher our deare mothers body lyes. It was so strong and sweet yt it euen remined us and comfort all yt war present, and wee was all lick filled wth it, wth in us, tho not ungratfull as other parfumes are wn in excesse. Wee injoyed ye same fauour one her Anaversary day, and very offten, and in in seuerall places, some of them not very sweet of themselves, as ye kichin, wash house and other placese, but it continews not so long, and most times all doth not smelel it, but those yt doth it moues to great devotion wch makes us hope yt our dear Mother according to her promese, remaines wth us, and will assist and helpe her poore chillderne in this banishment tell she bring us to injoye Eternall Glory wth her, wch our Lord Jesus Christ of her mercie grant us. Amen.

B Ursula of All Saints[18]: her particular friendship, spiritual favours and cures; the cuttings and slashings of the surgeons

[*L13.7*, 192–201]

... There was in the monasterry a certain religiouse woman, of good parts and edefeing [edifying] cariage, but other wayes occasion'd from interiour perplexities she was giuen to melancholly and uneasyness. With this person Sister Ursula had a sort of particular friendship, speaking more friely to her, and she again to Sister Ursula, then was proper or convenient for 'em. Their mutaull discource did but heighten one anothers meloncholly and, instead of easinge, increased their difficulties and scruples.

Sister Ursula, being very much afflicted, she meets with this same religiouse woman, & both speaking their mindes freely to one another, but as Sister Ursula was presently afterwards passinge [through a corridor] ... she heard herself called in a shrill voyce and, turning to see who it was that called, she saw our Blessed Lady, who reprehended her for what she had done, and told her the Divell was very busy, and that she should goe and tell her Confessarious all her condition, and hold no more discources with that person, which she neuer did as long as she remained at Antwerp ...

... They were no sooner arrived at Lier, or scarce settled, when Sister Ursula's first tryall was to see her deare Sister Margaret fall most dangerously ill, and confined to her bed, with a continuel hott feiuor for many weekes ... She was hardly able to walk about after so tediouse sickeness, but she was surprized and violently set upon by an evel spirit which haunted the house by witchcraft, who afflicted and tormented the religiouses but his greatest malice and spite extended not only against Sister Margaret, but also with much violence and fury against Sister Ursula, by great tryalls and suffrances of mind and body, who being of a tender delicate constitution, was in much danger ...

...[19] Upon another time (says she) as I was hearinge Mass, a little before the Ghospel, that usiall presentation of Christ Crucified was present with me and asked me how I durst presume to communicate, your Reverence haveinge commanded me no such thinge ... but I know not what inspired me and assisted me to obey your Reverene in making the signe of the cross, which I did five times together, with much contradiction, for when I saw it remaine, I was possess'd with a deep apprehension it was really God ...

---

18 The Life of Sister Ursula (Elizabeth Mostyn: 1626–1700), who professed on 12 August 1645, appears to be in the hand of her niece, Margaret Teresa of the Immaculate Conception (Fettiplace), who became Prioress after Sister Ursula's death, from 1700–15 (and later periods) and whose own Life is included in this chapter. The extract begins with an account of Sister Ursula's particular friendship and the warning she receives to abandon it, conveyed in terms similar to those of Teresa de Jesus (see p. 12) and Anne of the Ascension (see p. 48) in the same situations.

19 The text shifts from third to first person here, and is addressed to her confessor (Edmund Bedingfield), presumably being drawn from papers she had written for him as a form of spiritual testimony.

... She spent a great part of her life time in finne workes and embroideris [embroideries] for the church, which are remaining still for our best ornaments as a memory of her infatigable piety[20] ...

... [Her favours were] never known to any till after her death, when the seal of there liues written by their Confessours own hand was broken oppen,[21] out of wch we have only drawne here the beginning of Mother Ursulas life, from her infancy to her first arriual at Lier. She was naturally of a very secret temper ... thus did she hide from humane eyes, as much as possibly she could, the knowledge of euer having been favoured ...

... [The first time she was miraculously cured was on the octave day of the Feast of St Teresa]. When those that tended her returnd, they found the room full of stronge perfume like a smoake and, coming to her bed side, the bed was also full of the same odour, and her face like – inflamed and chearfull, whereupon the religious said, 'Ma mere, our holy Mother has surely been hear'. Upon which she said 'Praise be to my holy father, St Joseph. Pray tell Father Confessour I wou'd speake with him', who was immediately call'd, and when he had been with her some time, cominge from her, he told the comunity that they should render thanks to the glorious St Joseph, for he had cured their dear Superioure, who from that time was perfectly recouered ...

... [Her second cure was five or six years years before her jubilee, in 1695]. All human art was dispaired of working her recouery; when the afflicted community preuailed to haue the great miraculous image of our Blessed Lady of the Sluce.[22] This they passionately desired, to which the very Reverend Fathers of the holy order of St Domminique (who have possession of this sacred treasure) condescended. The image being very heavy, two men had difficulty to bring it to her Infirmary where all the community made most ardent prayer before it, all the whole night, which she her self passed in sillint prayer. The morning being come, between 4 or 5 a clock, the good lay Brother Johen, (who was a great seruante of our Blessed Ladys & who had the particular care of the image) came for it, and the sisters thought to helpe him downe staires to the gate. But he coming to the image, took it up in his armes, as light as if it had been made of wicker or basket, with no smale surprize to himself and others. Whereupon he broke out into these very words:

---

20 A separate document, attributed to Sister Ursula, gives details of 'the maner how to gume silke for flowers', including instructions to use a 'braud English knife, and keepe it for yt purpous uis it for nothing ells' (*L4.40*). It is possible such decorations were sold for commercial purposes: in 1712, John Leake, an English tourist bought 'pictures, flowers and purses' from the Carmel in Antwerp (see van Strien, 1991, 505; Walker, 2003, 97). (Around three pages of the original text are omitted here.)

21 This reference suggests that Edmund Bedingfield's Lives of Sisters Margaret and Ursula had been sealed until after Sister Ursula died. It is possible that their contents had been thought especially delicate since they contained details of Bedingfield's exorcism of the sisters at a time when such matters had become controversial (see Hallett, 2007).

22 This word is variously spelled in the papers ('Sleuse', 'Cluse', 'Clusa'); it refers to a particularly venerated image in the care of the local Dominican community. It is also mentioned elsewhere in the papers (see Chapter 35).

'When I brought my Lady', says he, speakinge of the image, 'she was so heavey that I could scarce bringe or bear her, and now she is light that I scarce seem to have any weight in my hands'. Turning about he said, 'Grace is gone forth of Maria and your Superioure will very cartainly recover', and added 'Maria has left grace behind her'. [Then he] rune downe staires with her, and without any difficulty caried her to the Sluce, which at other times was more then two persones cou'd performe. And, from the very instant in which the image was caried out of the Infirmary where our sicke Mother lay, all the signes of a speedy and perfect recoverie imediately appeared to all present ...

... [Around five years later, there appeared a] rose in her left legge [and she was given the last rites]. Neither doctour nor surgeon could not give her hopes of her life, but added to her torments, made an incission in her legge, of full a quarter of an elle long ... also a mortification the most terible in the smale of her back, which she lay upon, not beinge able to moue the least for the torment of her legge, whien all the skill of doctours and surgions ioyned to their most terible cuttinges and slashinges of her wounds could not giue her afferwards aney relief ...[23]

C Lucy of the Holy Ghost[24]: her childhood convulsions, fear of the dark and her visit from the Infant Jesus

[*L13.7*, 230–34]

... in her infancy she was very tender and sickly, and very frequently subiect to conuulsion fitts ...

... She used to fling her self every morning on her litle knees ... and then would she frequently beg (inspired by the Holy Ghost to ask what at that age she could not possibly understand) that they would please to giue her leaue to cross the seas, and go and make her self a nun in the house where her three Aunts were at Lier ...[25]

... [She was] little in stature but great in vertue. Sister Anne of the Angells[26] with whom she willingly conversed as often as the Rde Mother gave them leave to be together, their whole discourse was nothing but pietty and goodness, no other talk but of God ...

... She made known to her Mistriss, who taught her Latin, how litle Jesus had been pleased

---

23 She died on Friday 19 March 1700, the feast of St Joseph, 'between 12 and 1 at noon', aged 74.

24 Elizabeth Mostyn: 1654–1707. She was the daughter of Edward Mostyn (brother to Sisters Margaret and Ursula) and his wife, Elizabeth Downes, daughter of Edward Downes of Norfolk. She is said in the annals to be their second child, and the first who had lived. This Life appears to have been written by her sister, Margaret Mostyn-Fettiplace, who was Prioress at the time of Sister Lucy's death, having succeeded Sister Ursula.

25 Around one page of the original text is omitted here; it records that she had the care of the vestry for many years.

26 Anne Bedingfield: 1651–1700 (see Chapter 32C).

to giue her a visit and was so kind as to let her take him into her armes, permitting her to embrace him, and he embracing her with a mutual kindness, endeavouring to express how sure she seem'd to be of the reality of his appearance. She said his litle prity hands were so soft, so very soft, that she never felt any thing so pleasing and agreable to her feeling in all her life. But these fauour she only discouerd att this occasion, if any other she might perhaps haue receiued at any other time she kept closs to her self shut in the priuate closset of her own heart …

… She was from her infancy of a strangely timorous and fearfull nature, so afraid of being alone that her parents seldome dared to let her be out of their sight or some seruants eye, for fear she should fall into convolsion fitts. For this very reason, when Sr Edward sent her ouer, he writt most earnestly to his sister the Prioresse [Margaret of Jesus] intreating her to take all imaginable care she should neuer be left alone, but always have some one of the religious in her company, and never be permited to sleep without a lamp or candle, burning all night in her chamber … But it lasted not long, at least with any excess; after her entrance into the monastery one feare quickly droue away another … She would go all alone to the top of the house, at any hour of the night, without candle or lanthern in her hand, to shut the garret windows … to fetch what [her neighbour] wanted from the most solitary and remotest part of all the house …

D Margaret Teresa of the Immaculate Conception[27]: her problems in building the church in which she is helped by the Duke of Marlborough

[*L13.7*, 282–4]

… [This building work] never wou'd have been compass'd had not his grace the Duke of Malborow, who was then att Bruxsells, zealously espouse[d] ye cause; & allso she had much

---

27 Margaret Mostyn: 1657/59–1745). Although this Life appears in the annals (which are ordered by date of death) later than that of her sister Anne Mostyn (1663–1715), it is included here before that account since it reflects their birth sequence and makes sense of some details in Anne's Life. Sister Margaret Teresa was born at Greenfield, 'formerly the abbey of Basingwark, inhabited by the monks of St Benedict, in Flint, in the province of England call'd Wales, near St Winefreds well'. She was educated in Paris 'suitable to her birth and fortune' and visited Lierre on her way home. When she married Bartholomew Fettiplace [or Fettyplace] of Swyncombe, 'a widdower gentleman of Oxon', Margaret of Jesus, her aunt, wrote to her, congratulating her and predicting that she would one day return to the convent. The Life records that Margaret Fettiplace read this letter to husband, to their amusement. They lived several years together, with no children. When he died in 1686 she found in a book the words 'Do as you think & you'll do well', so resolved to join the Poor Clares at Rouen. She remained there 'till by going barefoot she lost her hearing' and was obliged to leave. Having recovered from her deafness, she was advised to choose an easier Order, so she went to the Benedictines at Dunkirk, still determined not to return to Lierre because of what her aunt had 'prognosticated'. There, while she was in heavy spirits, her aunt's views at last prevailed, and she travelled to Lierre, where

difficulty in bying so many different houses of wch our monestry is composed.[28] Indeed the best of them, wth ye gardin, was purchas'd by our worthy Confessor Mr Benefeild [Bedingfield] for his own use & left by him to ye community at his death.

This was a vast undertaking ... the expences was unavoidably great, but exceedingly augmented by the ingineer or head architecter's unbeadiness of mind: ye workmen's imploy of one week he wou'd order to be pul'd down ye next, to be built up again in some other form ... & tho she procured amongst friends in England a considerable sum towards ye discharging ye expences, yet it put her & ye comunity to great straites, notwithstanding her joynter [inheritance] was so great a help ...

... She procured that ye great miraculas image of our Bd Lady be longing to ye Cluse should be brought, in whose stand she tyed ye stone yt was to be ye foundation; the religious going in mantles & vails with lighted candles in their hands in procession, singing Our Ladys litanys. When they came to ye place, the image being sett down, Lady Winber took ye stone & placed it where it was to be, whilst ye string remain at ye head of ye image. She was extremely devoted to ye Immaculate Conception of our Blessed Lady & caused ye Church to be dedicated in honour of her & St Joseph ... & had it with great solemnity consecrated by his Lordship Peter Joseph, Bishop of Antwerp,[29] procuring a foundation to be made for musick on the feast of ye Immaculate Conception ...

... Mother Margaret Teresa was perticularly devoted to ye little image of ye rosary beloging to ye Cluse, which she prouided & made ye close [clothes] for, allways dressing it her self ... She was a great client of St Gammars[30] ...

... [She was preparing for her 50-year profession jubilee] when it pleased God to visit her with ye then reigning cold, attended with a fever which a great many of the community was ill of. Ye first 3 days ye doctor assured there was not ye least danger, but on ye 4th she fell into a lethargy, tho she came so farr to her self as to receaue ye rites of Our Holy Mother ye church with great presence of mind, after which ye lethargy returning. She had got such a habitt of praying yt tho we supposed her in a sleep, yet her lips moved in prayer ... till by degrees yt ceas'd & she grew gradually weaker ...

---

she recovered her peace of mind. She was elected Prioress after the death of her other aunt, Sister Ursula. The extract describes her trouble in building 'our present church', eventually obtaining permission to do this from the Court. Bartholomew Fettiplace had left financial provision for his widow, and this legacy had caught the attention of the Protestant authorities, who followed her to Flanders after a visit to England in 1715, concerned she might be giving financial aid to the Jacobites (Hadland, 1992). The Duke of Marlborough, then at Brussels, used his influence to support her in the building work, and, as the annals indicate, in obtaining other provision for the convent.

28 The convent at Lierre occupied a range of attached houses, first on one side, then the other, of Kerkstraat.

29 Peter Joseph Francken-de-Sierstorff, Bishop 1711–27 (Hardman, 1939, 148).

30 St Gummarus (*c*.717–*c*.774), who is sometimes represented carrying a pilgrim's staff covered in ivy – the origin of the town's name (*lierre* being French for ivy). The church of St Gummarus, where Edmund Bedingfield was a canon, is at the top of the road on which the convent was located.

E Mary Anne of St Wenefrid[31]: her mother's death, her education in Paris; Titus Oates and the 'Popish Plot'

[*L13.7*, 256–8]

... She was but about five munths old when her mother died, to the exceeding grief of Sr Edward and the whole family.

The young infant by her death lost the best of mothers, but had the good fortune to find another in the truly motherly care of her grandmother, Mrs Petre, who was also her Godmother, and took her immediately into her own house, and brought her up till she was about seuen years of age as if she had been her only child. Then the Lady Mostyn, her Mother in Law [step-mother], took her home, tho' the grandmother could not part with the child without a most sensible affliction, nor the child be separated from her without a deluge of tears ...

... The grandmother dying within a year or two afterwards, and Sr Edward designing to send her elder sister, Margaret to Paris for education. My Lady was so tenderly fond of her as to resolue not only to accompany her to London but also from thence to Calais, and not to leave her till she had seen her on the other side of the seas and put her into Doctor Gages hands, who had affairs at Calais, and promised to conduct her bake with him to Paris and to take particular care of her their.

In order to the journey, Sr Edward himself came as farr as Chester, and took his daughter Anne with him, intending to return back with her alone. But when the moment of parting came, and that his daughter Margaret was taking her leaue and blessing from him, the child clung fast to her sister, and would not, by any perswasions, promises, or enticements, be separated from her; crying most bitterly and in a most mouing manner begging of Sr Edward to lett her go with her sister to Paris. Sr Edward did what he could to diswade the child, so did my Lady, and all that were present, telling her what great things should be done for her if she would stay at home, and that she really was too young and tender to undertake so long a journey ...

At last, [they were] so moued by the constancy and tears of the child that they granted her request, and let her go with her sister. She remained at the monastery of the English Austins [Augustinians] seueral years, till such time as the pretended plot of Oates and Bedlow against Roman Cathollques broke out. Then was Sr Edward and his Lady forced to go ouer to Paris, as many others did to decline the cruel persecution that raged all ouer England ... They took her from the Austins, and placed her among the French Ursulins to perfect her self in the French tongue, and afterwards remouing her to them, made her remain with them till their return into England.

---

31 Anne Mostyn: 1663–1715. She was the youngest daughter of Edward Mostyn and his wife Elizabeth (Downes). The annals tell us that she, too, was born at Talacre, though, following the death of her mother, she lived for some years with her grandmother before going to Paris, where she was later joined by her parents following the 'Popish Plot' in 1678. This was a fictitious 'plot' instigated by Titus Oates (1649–1705), supposedly directed at the life of Charles II, the aftermath of which created a wave of anti-Catholic activity in England.

32 On St Matthew the Apostle's day, 21 September 1682, after which the Mostyn parents remained in Lierre for several months. The Life records that this religious held various

The storm being something blown ouer, Sr Edward and my Lady thought it necessary to leaue Paris and return to London, determining to take her along with them. As soon as she was acquainted with their design, she discouered the ardent desires she had cherished for seueral years of embracing a religious state of life, in her aunt's monastery at Lier, in Flanders …

… Sr Edward and his Lady and family were present at the solemnity of her clothing,[32] defraying generously all the charges of within and without …

… Some years before she dyed she was frequently subiect to the stopping and retaining in her urin[e] which often caused dangerous consequences, which were born with as great patience as they were attended with pain and torments. Her last sickness was the same most violent and mortal infirmity. Nine days she underwent the cruel torture, nor could any remedy be found to afford her any ease or relief in all her sufferings … in her full sences with her perfect memory and understanding … continuing to moue her tongue (euen when wee thought her dead) …[33]

F Francis Xaveria of the Immaculate Conception:[34] she visits the baths in pursuit of treatment for her dislocated hip

[*L13.7*, 303–6]

… In ye 2d year after her profession by an accedent [she] was confind to ye Infirmary by disjoynting of her hipe; ye joynt not skillfully replaced, together with ye hurts attending it, occasion'd her pains to be excessive, tho nothing was left untry'd to give her ease & promote a cure for 10 years in which time she frequently kept her bed for months together & had nothing else to expect but to endure yt misery all her life.

[This] caused Lord Bishop of Antwerp, our Superiour, to oblige her to be transported to Aix la Chapelle where she suffer'd like a martyr & like them was in a constant combate, the surgeons without cease tormenting her with ye most violent applications … tho she had crutches she was not able to make much use of them but was obliged to be carry'd in to the baths. Wn ye season was over she return'd with some little amendment; by which it was judged proper she shou'd goe there ye following year, in hopes that ye 2d & third time would finish wt the first had begun.

---

offices, including that of Sacristan, and had special devotion to Our Lady, the rosary and St Gummarus. 'She was entirely mistriss of her needle …'

33   She died between 7 and 8 pm on 26 June 1715, having been communicated by, and confessed to, Father Roper, SJ.

34   The annals provide her genealogy and introduce her as Frances Poole (1697–1763), who took the habit at 15 years and professed the following year in Lierre, on 14 October 1713. She was the daughter of William Poole (whose mother was Mary Mostyn, sister to Edward Mostyn and to Margaret of Jesus and Ursula of All Saints), and was born at Burchley, in Wigan, Lancashire, her father being the only brother to Sir William Poole in 'Worral', near Chester. Her mother was Mary Estcourt, daughter to Sir Thomas Estcourt of Wiltshire. The Life describes her infirmities and treatment in spa towns.

35   The entry concludes with details of her election as Subprioress in October 1730; her acquisition of relics of Our Lady and of St Joseph; her design of a garden wall to protect

With vast pain she arived there & persued her remedys, till she was able to walk with her crutches into ye bath. At ye end of the season she came back with her cure far advanc'd … & walked wth ye help of a stick…[35]

---

the community from being overlooked from the river and 'ye rabble from ye boats', as well as other aspects of building work in the convent. Her final illness was a 'distemper' which the doctors tried to abate by bleeding her and applying plasters to her head. She died on 10 April 1763.

Chapter 32

The Lives of the Bedingfield Family

Like the Mostyns (Chapter 31), various members of the Bedingfield family were associated with the Carmelite Order during the early modern period, and subsequently. Of these, Edmund Bedingfield (1615–80) was confessor at the Lierre Carmel from its foundation in 1648 until his death. His close spiritual relationship with Margaret of Jesus (Margaret Mostyn: 1625–79) is at the heart of many of her personal papers, and he personally wrote several Lives of Sisters Margaret and Ursula, including that which he completed just before his death, one year after that of Margaret of Jesus. In the annals of this period, his is the only male Life; and appropriately enough it appears immediately after that of Sister Margaret because he was the next of the convent to die.

Other family Lives included in this chapter are those of Edmund Bedingfield's nieces, Margaret and Anne Bedingfield, daughters of his brother Henry and Margaret (née Paston); of Anne and Mary Cobbes, the daughters of his sister Elizabeth and her husband William; and of his great-nieces Martha and Catherine Eyre (granddaughters to Henry Bedingfield). These Lives are of interest not least because of their account of extended family life and of what appear to be shared genetic propensities to reduced growth. Each person is separately introduced in a note at the beginning of their Life.

A **Edmund Bedingfield:[1] his childhood and education; his perilous journey in which his ship is attacked; his early career and great devotion to the convent**

[*L13.7*, 99–122]

All tho it is not our costome to writ ye liues of our Confessars, yet wee cannot forbeare to take notis heere of a parson so highly desaruing in all respects as this our most Rd deare Father, Mr Edmond Bedingfield, Cannon of St Gomares church in ye Citty of Lire. [He] was ye first Confessurious and only parson to home [whom] this couent of English

---

1 Edmund Bedingfield (1615–80) was son of Elizabeth Houghton, the second wife of Henry Bedingfield, an active royalist imprisoned in the Tower of London during the Civil War, dying on 22 November 1657 soon after his release. *Burke's Peerage* states incorrectly that he was survived by only one son, Henry (1614–84), who married Margaret, the daughter

Carmelets must owne (next to ye deuine prouidence) hee was our only suport, both in ye sperituall and temprall, liberally bestowing his fortune and continuall labours to establish this new bigining, in all perfection. And [he] had so many years assisted our dearest Mother Margaret of Jesus in ye hapy gouerment of ye monastary, and was also the geayd [guide] of her soule, and helped her att her death; and tho hee was of so exallant a temper, as neuer to be transported wth joyes or sorowes ... yet hee not ye lesse sincible of our losse, in so holy and deare a Mother, wch hee did venarat and esteme as a derect sainct ... yt simed to us hee only liued to expose what hee did know of her life, falling sicke one her aniuarsary day, ye yeare following ...

... Our most dere and worthy Confessarious, called Edmond Bedingfield, natiue of England, was born at Oxbouer in ye county of Norfolk, one ye 13 of August in ye yeare 1615, sonne to Henry Bedingfild knight, and of his wife Elizabeth Hautin,[2] who, when she was wth child of him, would often say she should haue more comfort of yt she bore in her waame [womb] then of all ye rest of her other children, tho it pleased God to blesse them w[ith] meny more, for hee was ye second sonne.

It was remarcable yt as she was walking in ye garding wth a Father of ye Socittie & spaking of ye comfortable thoughts she had of this child, there flew a robin redbrest upon her great belye, and remained there all ye time wthout offaring to stor, wch was a considerable time, tell goeing to her chamber it flew to ye windoe and remained still by her, as her companion many days ... [This was said by the Father to be] a emblne of his singular purity and inosent life, wch began to apiere before hee head ye vise of reason – for att 4 or 5 yeares ould his father and mother, seeing him so modist, would for sport, and to trey him, not only by promises, of all ye fine toys imaginable, but also by threats, forse him to pull of his lettle short beford them, wch thay could never obtaine, or make him doe it ...

... When he was a young man, in ye flower of his age, hee liued both in Spaine and Itally meny yeares. It was obsarued by seuerall yt conuersed wth him daylie yt hee neuer looked any woman in ye face, nor would hee euer conuerce wth them, when hee could auoyd it ... Hee was a great enemye of all such idle talke, and would blosh and leue place, so great was his auerting from any thing of yt nature ... Afferwards ... wee had ye curiosity to quston him about some Ladys yt hee had sene. Hee could giue you no account, inienusly [ingeniously] confessing not haue taken notis whether thay ware hansome, or had fine cloths one, or any such thinge ... And one his death bead, allso, hee made a confession of

---

of Edward Paston. (These were the parents of Edmund Bedingfield's nieces who were afterwards at Lierre.) On 2 January 1660/61, Henry was created a baronet by Charles II in lieu of a debt the King owed the family for losses whilst in his service. This Life describes Edmund Bedingfield's childhood and education, and tells us that, after he decided to become a priest, he was for some time estranged from his father. The account of Bedingfield's journey from England, and of speculation about his possible amatory interests, raises interesting issues about male representation within the early modern period (see p. 25). In 1651, whilst he was confessor at the convent in Lierre, Edmund Bedingfield exorcised the Mostyn sisters (see Hallett, 2007). This Life was most probably written by Sister Ursula, who was at that time Prioress.

2   *Burke's Peerage* gives this as 'Houghton'.

his whole life, and ye prist yt hard it tould us yt hee did not thinke it possiable for a man of his age, knowlidge and judgment could be so pure and chast, and euen ignorant, of any thing to ye contrary, and sayd it was aboue human frailty, therefore must be a perticular gifft, and singular grace ...

Not wthstanding his singular modist[y], and ye strick gard hee euer had of his scencis, hee was not scruplelous nor pind up, but would discurse farmilerly, wth wemen in time and place, for his Rce was very genorous, and of a plesant mery youmar, full of wity consayts, and loued a iest [jest] dearely, being allways of a constant peaceable, contented cherfull nature, and a gracefull parson, well bread, proper and hansome ... an example, both to ould and young, for his pieety and deuotion ...

... [From College at St Omers] hee went to Leige, for his philoscify, making ye same improuiment in all virtue and lerning ... His intention was, from his infancy, to be a priest, before hee did know what it ment, therfore hee went ye more willingly for England to uptaine [obtain] wth more felicity his parantes leaue to accomplish his desiere. Thay, being not willing, thought to deuert him from his resolution wth seuerall indearements, sports and recarations; and his father toke him euery day a long wth him to hauck and hunt, a pastime his father loued aboue all other recarations [recreations], and demanded of him once how hee licked this fine sport, but hee, not relishing any thing of yt nature, plainlie tould his father hee did not see what pleasure or content there could be in kelling of innocent beasts. Att [this] his father was a lettle startled, and tould him hee might then freely goe and take his owne cource, for hee saw now hee was good for nothing but his prayers and book.

Hee then departed, affter haueing bine only 3 munths in England, to goe for Siuell [Seville] in Spaine, to take holy orders, affter hee had past his deuenity wth great uplaws [applause] and dedicated his defentions in deuenity to ye Qeene of Angelles, and soule mistris of his hart. But in his jornny there hee strangly escaped two great dangers, ye first was by a tempest, of thunder and lightning, wch splet [split] a great part of ye maine mast and made one of ye greatest cannons goe of[f], wch killed and wonded all yt ware aboue deck. Ye ship was no suner got into order againe, but thay war sett upon by 2 tuckesh men of ware [Turkish ships: men of war]. Thay faught 4 houres hotly, and tho so much weaker then there enimes, by ye helpe of God and our Bd Ladys protection, thay ouer came them, sincking one of the Turckes ships, and put ye other to flite, killing 79 of there men, ye captene wounded & lost his arme, and seuerall, or most of ye men sadly wonded, wher as wee lost only 3 men and some 5 wounded, and ye shipe not much battered. All ye time of ye fight our Rd deare father assisted ye capten, wth boullets to shout and, being in ye captens cabine, ye enime plased all theire battry there, so yt ye boullets past, in great nomber, round about him, but did him no harme ...

... After hauing spent 4 yeares in Spaine, in wch time hee toke holy orders, and was made Deacken [deacon] upon St Thomas ye Apostle day [21 December], and receaued ye dignity of pristhod St Stiuens day [26 December], and say his first Masse, one St Thomas of Canterberys day [29 December] ... In a short time after, hee went to Rome, wher hee remained as long as there might haue had great perferments ... [He] shunned all honnors and hatted a court life, therefore hee left Rome, and came doune in to these cuntres, and liued a yeare att Leige, wth great edification and piety. From thence [he] came to Brussells, and setled there for a time, but coming to Anwarp in ye yeare 1648, this foundatione of Lier was to be sent out and, being destitued of a pastour, our Rd Lord

Bishop intreated the fauour of Mr Bedinfeld, to come a long wth ye religious tell hee
could prouid them of a nother. [This] hee did ye more willingly, because wee war poore
English ... yet did not intend to stay wth them aboue 8 or 10 days ye longest, but our Bd
Lord had desinged other ways, and yt Lier was to be ye place ... to ye end of his life ...
for there could be nothing, of human respects in it, for a young man indued wth so meny
exalant parts nobly borne, well qualified and lerned ... to make choyse of so mene and
trouble some imploy, in a corner of ye world, a poore place, where hee could nather haue
pleasure, nor profiet, noe so much, as a conuenient loging amungst strangers yt scarce
knew comane seuelity [common civility]; and wee being new beginares, had lettle wear
wth all to maintaine our selfs ...

And [he] settled him selfe wth ye pastor of ye toune upon his owne charge [expense],
not would hee euer take any present from us, not so much as a lettle linen, but hee would
pay for it, tho att yt time hee had but a small alowence out of England, ye times being
troublesome, and his father much perciuted for ye kings cause. But, affter his [father's]
death, hee injoyed his anuity intier [entire annuity], wch was very considerable, tho hee
liued as sparing as before, imploying him selfe and substance in pious workes, wheras hee
might haue liued acording to his qualitie, showing by this that what hee did was purely
for ye loue of God ... saruing [serving] ye monastary 39 yeares for nothing, wher as wee
could not haue kept a chaplen [for] under 45 pound a yeare, wch would haue amonted to
a considarable some, in all these yeares. [However it] pleased God so to prouid [provide],
as to rayes us such frinds as to helpe us to a cannory [cannery[3]], wch hee would neuer
haue exceapted but for our sakes, to benefett ye monastary in all hee could, haueing a reall
scripule [scruple] to spend of ye reuenew [revenue] of ye canory ...

... Truly may hee be justly called, a carfull pastor and a genarall Father to all his charge,
each one of ye sisters was alick to him in his affection ... if hee seemed parshall [partial]
to any, it was to those yt ware most shiftlesse and least estemed[4] ... ... [He] spared nather
his purs[e] nor labors to defend his lettle flocke, and obpose [oppose] who some euer
predended ye least changs in our way of gouerment, acording our Bd Mothers practis,
haueing a great regard and estime, of euery lettle thing of our obsaruance, nor was his
sufference lesse from some parsones yt enuied our peace and hapynes in so worthy a
Father ... where upon raysed meny scandellous reports, aleging yt his age and discresstion
was not att all feet [fit] for such a charg, and did there best to make him out wth our
Superour, our Rd Lord Bishop, but [his] Lordship knew full well his worth ... allso was
very intimat wth him ... Ye same was it wth ye paster and otheres where hee liued: thay
admiered his lerning, and singular vertues, and all doted upon him yt did know or conuers
wth him. Nor would the pastor, who was one of the lernest men in ye cuntry, conclud or
doe any busnes wthout his aduice: so great was his estime of him yt, att his death, hee
trusted him wth ye dispossall of all his goods, to be giuen to good & pious uises, and could
neuer part wth him all ye time hee liued, and would be all in teares wth deuotion when hee
spoke of him saying he was a iust man, and an angelle in human flish ...

---

3   Presumably, the revenue for the cannery supported Bedingfield.
4   This statement appears to defend Bedingfield from claims that he showed partiality towards
    any particular religious (such as Sister Margaret, perhaps); and this may be linked to the
    following reference about 'scandalous' reports about him, which are also mentioned in
    Sister Ursula's other Life of Margaret of Jesus (*L3.29*, 81).

... [He preferred] his sweet sollitued before all other fauours or pastimes, saying hee neuer found more content then when hee was alone. All time simed short to him, att prayer or stoody [study] ... being allways most punctall to his hours, fallowing a distrebution of time wch hee had sett for him selfe, according to our hours. And wee may well say hee liued ye life of a Carmellet – [he] lay one a poore straw bead, and made 2 hours of mentall prayer dayly, stooding latt and rising early a morneings, for meny yeares ... [He] subdued all sence and delicacy by a strick mortification of him selfe, both inteaorour and exteriour, contenting him selfe wth ye grosse fare of these parts, in such a places wher hee neuer could haue his meat drest to his apittet, wch was a great mortifigation to him, tho hee neur complained or seemed to dislicke what someuer came to ye table for aboue 20 yeares.[5] ... In all yt time [he] scarce drunck a coupe of beare between mieles, all tho' hee had ye fridome to comemand what hee pleased in ye house, conforming him selfe in all to the customes of ye place not to be singular from ye rest.

Other ways hee was abtt [apt] to be very rigoures [rigorous] to him self, in point of fasting and riged pennancie, wch hee priuetly impossed upon him selfe, continually wearing of heire [hair] cloth, and a haire gerdle full of knots, yt would some times eat in to his flesh, att other times a chaine, & dissiplines of Iorne wch hee did frequently uise.[6] And [he] would find out strang[e] ways to ponish and torment his body, so great was his feruer and loue to sufferrence; and [he] uised great diligence in preparing him selfe for Masse, and all great feasts, espeasially those of our Bd Lady, fasting [on] her eues and keeping her octiues, spending much time in his deuotions in ye churches ... Aboue all the Rosarry was his most beloued and constant prayer ... and [on his death-bed] thay allso found about his medle a courd full of knots teyed so strayt yt thay ware forst to cut it, yt hee might haue some ease ...

... Our Bd Lord had allso indeued [imbued] him wth ye giuest [gift] of deserning ye good sperit from ye bad, and finding out ye trickes and desayts of ye Diuell to whome hee was a mortall enimie, and all ways perciculed [persecuted] yt infernall beast, for hee could not wth stand his firme faith & singuler humelity, haueing occation to deale wth seuerall parsones yt war molested wth meny greious temptationes, caused by wi[t]ch craft, ware both posest, and obsest, wch hee released out of yt slauery, by his prayers, continuall labours, fasting and pennance, tell hee had expelled ye wicked enimie of man out of them to his confussion.[7]

---

5   The papers frequently mention that the English Carmelites found local food to be unpalatable. Edmund Bedingfield's servant and some of the lay sisters evidently sought to respond to this, learning to cook in the 'English manner' (Chapter 39).

6   Such bodily mortifications were not uncommon within religious and lay devout circles: Margaret of Jesus (Mostyn) also wore such chains, and when Cecilia Ferrazzi of Venice (1609–84) was ill in bed she recorded that her confessor noticed 'I had on a chain as thick as a finger and a half with links the length of half a finger attached in the back and fastened with a padlock'; this was too painful to remove 'for it had grown into the skin. I called on the Glorious Virgin Mary, went into a trance, and three days later found myself with the chain detached from my flesh without any pain at all' (Schutte, 1996, 69).

7   This reference to 'several persons' suggests that Edmund Bedingfield may have exorcised others besides the Mostyn sisters (see Hallett, 2007). The pastor and others are subsequently mentioned as witnesses to Edmund Bedingfield's talents.

... Wee haue reasone to thinke his great zeasle in helpeing such poore soules did much impare his health, for hee would not spare him selfe when it consarned ye good of his naighbour, attribirting this grace and power ouer ye wicked sperits was only by ye fauour of our Bd Lady, hee being but ye instrement by which she would show her powere from yt malishous tierant [malicious tyrant] and fine of heall. [The devil] had so much great a horrour of this, her chamption, yt if hee chanced to come into ye churches or other place wher there was possest parsons [possessed people], ye Diuelle would show him selfe and gett out of his way, houling and tormenting the poore creaturs, so yt the pastor wth whome hee liued, and others, would greatly admiere, who had seene it often, and would say yt ye diuelle could not beare ye puerity of his soule and holy life ...

... [He] spent no more upon him self affter hee was made cannon, and had allso 100 pound a yeare of his owne, then when his Father was a liue, yt hee had but 40 pounds a yeare to maintaine him selfe wth all, payed yearly, 25 pound out of it for his deyett. Nor did hee adorne his chamber or beg fine thinges, as othere cannons and priests did, but liued frugally, and gaue largly to ye poore, and most comanly priuetlie [privately], yt his allms deeds might not be knowen ... and others hee alowed so much a munth to each one ... was neare 6000ss pound hee gaue to ye Monastary att his death, wth his house and movables, and left not a farthine to any of his relations ... (besides what hee lefft for his soule) & layd noe other obligation one ye comunity but only to song a Masse of Requime one his Anauersary day, perpetially euery yeare, as long as ye couent stands ...

... There came a religous wth us from Anwarp, to trye if ye chang of ayre could recouer her, being fare gon in a consumcion [consumption] caused by this sad desease of ye mind: othere ways [she was] a strong, yong, fine woman, and full of wit, but so strangly weaded [wedded] to her one opinione yt seuerall parsones, both lerned and sperituall, had for 3 or 4 years in deuered to sattisfy her, but in vaine. She rather grew worse and wasted a way yt she was nothing but skin and bone, just licke mier shadow, not able to rest, day or night, wth ye perplectity [perplexity] of her thoughts and disquiet mind. Our deare Father perceaueing [this], out of compation [compassion] began to treat wth her; and in a short time she was wholy read [rid] of her crupeles [scruples], and would laffe [laugh] att her owne follie, and she returned back to Anwarp ...

... [He was] wth this comunity for 30 years together, [and] neuer mised a day to selebrat holy mass, and other functions, tell his declining yeares, a lettle before his death, being subiect to a pallcicall youmor [palsical humour] and swiming in his head, hee was forsed to leaue Masse ...

... His dissease war ye grauell, stone and stranguenun[8] ... his Rce had all his life, injoyed a constant health, haueing nothing to suffare in yt kind before, being of a strong and wholsome constetution ...[9]

---

8   Presumably stranguary, described by Joannes Groenvelt, a Dutch doctor, in his 1670 treatise on bladder stones as a condition in which 'urine comes in drops only, accompanied by a constant inclination to make water' (Cook, 1994, 83).

9   Around one page of the original text describing his ailments is omitted here.

... Upon a Thursday, one the 29 of August, in ye yeare of our Lord 1680, affter haueing celebrated our Venarable deare mother Margaret of Jesus anauersary wth great deuotion, hee found him selfe not well, and about 3 and 4 a clock in affter none called for our Mother as hee youst to doe ... She, perseuing [perceiving] a chang in [his] face, found by his pules there was a distemper upon him and ... [she] sent immediately for ye doctour, and parswaided him to sweat, wch ye doctor found nessicary, for hee fered it would proue a ague [fever]. So wee perswaded him to goe to bead, and gaue him my Lady Kempts powder,[10] and hee sweat very much and was well affter it, so yt ye doctur found him wth out ague, but would haue him take phisecke [medicine], saying hee douted not but it wold passe. But, alas, this purgation was ill aduised, as ye other docturs sayd, for it drew ye feuer more inward, so yt wee neuer saw this deare Father of ours more.

His Rce remained for 2 or 3 days much ye same, tell Monday then the doctors found him much worse, and it proued a violent hott feauour and thay tould him hee was not wth out dangere, wher upon, as one hightly pleased wth ye newes, hee ernestly desired to haue ye last sacraments, and hee ordered how meny candles there should be to acompany ye Bd Sacrament, and apointed how ye allter in his chamber should be desently plased and adorned ...

Affter his Rce was armed wth ye holy rights of ye church, hee toke leue wth much cherfullness and sweetnes of his fellow canons and other prists of ye cathedrall church, who war all presant in ye rome lamenting theire losse ... saying hee had ye sattisfaction to leue them in perfect peace, and concourd, unitted wth one a nother ... 'I will pray for them, as I am sure, thay will be mindfull of me': these ware his last words, turning him selfe to prayer, and ye company all gone. But thos yt tended him, in hopes hee would take a lettle rest, but alas it was not long affter but his Rce was taken wth a fitt of ye pallcy [a stroke] yt robed him of his speach, in wch hee lay wth out giueing any singe more – only ye religous of the ospitall yt tended him sayd yt hee was ye whole time praying, for his mouth went constantly and his hands was euer found upon his beads. And once thay remoued him, for to giue him some refrishment & to mend his bead, and by chance shifting of him layd his beads a side, wch hee missed and was so restlesse, sarching about his beed and his necke, wch one of ye saruants reflecting it was his beads hee wanted, thay put them about his necke, att wch hee was well peased and heald them fast wth his hands, tell ye moment hee rendered up his hapy soule in to ye hands of his creatour ...

... His body was beured [buried], acording to his will, in St Gomarch Church, in our Bd Ladys Chapell, wth out any pompe, for his great humelity did order it so in express teremes [terms], least our affection and respects might exceed in yt point. [However] our Rd Mother placed a marble stone ouer his graue, yt it may be knowne from others, and against ye pillor is allso seatt our glorious mothers image wth ye searaphen percing her hart,[11] and his cott of armes att her feet, cout out in stoone, for a perpeatuall memory to all yt shall visit his tombe. [They] may see & know by yt how much hee had don for her honner & the saruies [service] of this couient, in assisting her poore chilldren so meny

---

[10] An early modern remedy, to induce sweat: like bleeding, sweating was believed to draw out impurities.

[11] This is part of the iconography of St Teresa. The Antwerp religious were given a relic of this event by Tobie Mathew in 1642 (Hardman, 1936, 76; and see p. 42).

yeares; and therefore wee place heere this short relation, and not the hundered part of what might be sayd of this raer virtues, and exsampler [exemplary] life, so yt those which come affter us may understand some lettle of ye great obligation this house hath to this Bd man, and deare Father of ours. Sweet Jesus make us partissipant wth him in Glory. Amen.

B Anne of the Ascension:[12] her fortuitous arrival, with her sister, because their uncle purchased the wrong stagecoach ticket

[*L13.7*, 168–9]

... this religous was, from ye age of 8 or 9 yeares old, piously brought up in a English monastary in France [and] when she came to ye age of discression, [she] had a desiere to be a religous there, & in order to it was clothed, & went on with much corrige & satisfaction. But affterwards [she] was disgusted wth some indiscressions [indiscretions] yt fell out upon ye occation of conuersing wth seiglars [seculars], wch was permetted there – but ye maine resone was the uery much singing & museck yt ... she could not beare, tho she had a very good voyce, strong & loud, very proper for there quier. [She] was no louer of musicke, so she leaft yt place & went for England to her parentes.

She had not bine [there] for scarce halfe a yeare, but it hapened yt our Rd Father Confessar, who was her owne unkell [uncle: Edmund Bedingfield], had some bussnes yt called him into Ingland &, meeting at London wth his nerest relations & those frind he had to treat wth, resouled not to goe into Norfolk, but to make a iurny [journey] into Walles, to performe his deuotions at St Wenefreds well – but, by mistake, [he] hire'd a place in Chichetcher coch in steed of Chester. This simed an acident of fortune, but was decried by ye Deuine Prouidence for ye good & saluation of this deare str of ours, for he, being thus disapointed of his pretended [thwarted] jurny into Walles, went doune in to Norfoke to her fathers house & braught ouer wth him, she & her sister, upon pretence of a jorney of pleasure, to see these countreys – for all thaughts of being religious was then wholy vanished and out of her mind, haueing bine so long in a monastary & now att liberty, she was lick [like] a bired [bird] flowne out of the cage & carred a way wth ye vanities & fooleres of ye world ...

... [Her uncle] gott leaue of our Right Rd Lord Bishop to lett them be in ye monasstary in secular for some time, tell he ware at leassure [had the time] to carre them to other placese [places]. But she had not bine long wthin our inclossure, but ye good example she saw amunght us, & ye Holy Ghost working wth it, her former good desiers returned againe wth so much viguer yt in a shourt time she most humblely beged our holy habbet ...

---

[12]   Anne Cobbes: *c.*1650–92. She was one of Edmund Bedingfield's nieces, the daughter of Elizabeth (daughter to Sir Henry Bedingfield) and William Cobbes. She professed on 2 February 1671, having arrived at the convent by chance. Her sister Mary (born in 1651) professed as Mary of the Incarnation on the same day.

C Anne of the Angels:[13] her childhood suffering from measles and rickets after which she wears iron boots and a bodice

[*L13.7*, 212–16]

... She was very lettle of stattar [stature], having in her infancie bene very infermie [infirm], being borne full of ye mealles [measles] of wch her mother had like to haue dyed. Then, at halfe a yeare old, [she] fell into violent convoltions which lastd a long time; then [she] had ye rictrets [rickets] in so sad a maner yt she was 7 years old before she was able to goe ore put one foot befoer any other. Had it not bene for those accedents it was thought she would haue bine a tall strong women, but she offten gaue God Allmt thanks she was not and [said] that leg wch was bent like a bow would be straight in heauen ...

[In later life] her limbes waer stife & could not sture one joynt about her – for sometimes thay remained whole weeks together so lame you might sooner break then bend them. Yet would she at the same time saye 'Tho I can't sture hand nor feet, thay are not nailid to a Cruxefes [crucifix] as my Sauouers was'... She recouerd of this sicknis but not of the rickets, seury [scurvy][14] & seuerall other impedements which cost her parents some hunders of pounds trying all sort of remides [remedies], both from God and Man, to make her capable of a state ...

She got great desiers of being religious & [was] wonderfully devoted to St Teresa and had her pituer [picture] hung at her beds head. ... She would lye a wake houers, prayen & making assperations [promises] to this pictuer, offten setting right up in her bed to kisc it. Looking upon it as a childist fancie, I[15] put the pictuer into my closet, but yt night she slecpt not one winke but lay lamenting that God Allmt was angery with her & our Bd Mother had forsaken her, so wee put it ther againe & as long as she stayd in ye house [she] uesed ye same devotion ...

She sufferd much with waering [wearing], night & day, ieron bootes and bodys [bodice] for meny yeares together. [She] came hether in them but left them all of[f] affter her cloathing, only kept her lambe [lame] leg (wch was bent like a bow so that one would think it would break & yt the bone would come throw ye skine) always swaded [sueded]. She being thos weak and infierme, her mother and other relations ded ther best to put all thoughts of being relegous out of her head, thinking her not fett, at least for some years,

13 Anne Bedingfield: 1650–1700. She was the daughter of Sir Henry Bedingfield (Edmund Bedingfield's brother) and his wife, Margaret (née Paston), professing on 16 July 1670. Her sister's Life is also in this chapter; observations are made about their short stature, a condition shared by other members of their family (pp. 206, 208). This presumably reflects a family genetic condition and/or nutritional deficiencies that caused her also to develop rickets, creating softness of the bones, attributed by modern medicine to a lack of vitamin D. The measles she contracted at birth from her mother is also blamed. She wore for many years iron boots and a bodice for support. Sister Anne is described as being friendly with Lucy of the Holy Ghost (Mostyn) who was also 'little in stature' (see Chapter 31C).

14 Presumably scurvy (referred to as 'scurry' later in the text) – a disease marked by bleeding and sponginess of the gums, due to lack of vitamin C.

15 Presumably the Prioress writing this Life.

to be from her tender mother. But her unkell [uncle], our Confessorus Mr Bedingfeld, goen into England, ye child was so very earnist & impertune with him ... Our Rd Mother and all ye relegoues out of respect of her good unkell waer pasinet [passionately] fond of her ... She grewe in a short time healthfull & strong, tho never with out much to suffer ye youmour of ye rickets and scurry, allways remaining in her with a continouell paine in her back, perticular when in bed yt it was a torment to her to think of goen into it and most allways lye upon her back ... for ye paine would kepe her whole nights a wake. Wee haue reason to beleiue it was an impostume [abscess] for, ye night she dyed, ther cam away in her stoole matter like yt of a sorre when it breaks and as soone as she was dead her whole back turnd as black as our vayle.

At her profesion she was dispencd with ye chiefest rigouer & hardship of ye order, ore any strick oblegation to the devine office by reason of a lettins [hesitancy] in her speeck & could not pronoune some words right ... [She] parformd ye weeckly offices, as ringen ye bell, candellsticks, ser[v]ing the table etc: [and] would stand whole days foulding [folding] of linnen ... looking to ye Refictory for 5 or 6 and twenty years together, kepen it as clene and neat as a pearle & in all that time never any sister wanted knife, fork, nor spoune ...

D Margaret of Jesus:[16] her proposals of marriage, despite her low stature

[*L13.7*, 251–3]

... She was very handsome, but of a low stature, which thing, notwithstanding all her virtue, did very often not a little trouble and deject her. But [her mother] would be continually encouraging her, saying [that] the queens of France and England, and many other great and noble women, were as low and lesser then her self, that her littleness of stature would not be any hindrance to her settlement; and that she designed to procure her a match which would render her as happy in euery respect as her heart could wish.

The proposal of mariage was very disagreable to the young lady, as having fixt her resolutions (tho' unknown to her mother) to dedicate her youth and beauty to the spouse and louer of virgins. This made her decline several aduantagious [advantagious] matches my Lady proposed to her: one she could not fancy, the others humour did not suit hers, a third was of a morose temper – and, in fine [in short], euery one had some thing or other

[16] Margaret Bedingfield (1646–1714), 'the most beloved of her mother's children', was sister to Anne of the Angels (above). She was one of the witnesses to the miraculous recovery of Anna Maria of St Joseph (Chapter 39). Sister Margaret's mother had tried to dissuade her from following a religious career, setting up various marriage proposals all of which her daughter rejected. Eventually, she overcame the reluctance of her mother, who then tried to persuade her to go to Lierre, where she had family, but the young woman preferred instead to join the English Benedictines in Paris because she was already familiar with them from her education among the Ursulines there. She therefore left for Paris 'to the unspeakable affliction of her disconsolate mother', but was delayed, changed her mind, and went instead to Lierre, where she received her habit on the Eve of the Feast of Thomas the Apostle, 1670.

particular displeasing. At last my Lady found out and proposed a match against which her daughter could bring no plausible excuse, and therefore only pleaded the present aversion or unwillingness she had to tie herself to a state of life, which would make both parties unhappy.

This answer did not satisfie my Lady, as being (as she told her) both groundless and capricious, wherefore with the authority of a mother she commanded her to admit of the courtship of that person she had prouided for her, who had all the good qualities to make a woman happy in him. This resolute proceeding forced her to recurre [turn] to the the friendship of Sr Henry, her eldest brother. To him she discouered [revealed] the resolutions she had taken of being a religious woman, and with tears besought him to take her part, and declare to her mother the vocation which heaven and the holy spirit inspired her to embrace. To this end she asked, and obtain leave, to go somewhere from home, to make a visit to some of her nearest relations or friends who passionately desired to have her company. In her absence, Sr Henry took an occasion to discouer to his mother the pious and immoueable intentions of his deare sister. At which my Lady was so surprized, that not being able to master her first passions, she was quite ouerwhelm'd with grief, fell sick, took her bed; nothing could recouer her but the presence of her dearest child.

[On her daughter's return, she sought to change her mind with all her powers of persuasion] … when these failed, she tryed what company and journeys to London would do, under pretence indeed of diverting her own melancholy disposition; but the true reason was to put her daughter in those occasions which might by degrees inure her to take a pleasure and satisfaction in those vanities the world delights in, and so insensibly extinguish the ardour of those desires she had so long cherished of embracing a religious state of life …

E Mary Martha of Jesus:[17] an impressionable soul removed by her mother to a nursery of piety

[*L13.7*, 224–228]

… She was only nine years of age when her pious mother brought her out of England, accompanied with her two younger sisters … The eldest son was latley maried to a young Catholique lady of birth and fortune. His inclinations at that time suiting with a country life, his Lady also was easily perswaded to embrace the offer Mr Eyre and his Lady had made them, of liueing all together (at least for some time) at Eastwell … But this satisfaction (as generally all ye sweets of this world are) was attended with a notable inconuenience: they must bring their seruants along with them, friends, and much gentry of all thos parts must nessarily pay their visits to the young bride and her spous. Neither one nor the other could happen without some distractions in the family, which Mrs Eyre's prudence must so prouide against, as not to let them take any impressions in the tender soules of her three

---

17 Martha Eyre (1672–1706), was born at Eastwell, Leicestershire, the daughter of Thomas Eyre and his second wife, Mary, the daughter of Sir Henry Bedingfield, 'both of very ancient and honourable Catholicke familys'. The Life shows some of the tensions of extended family living; following the marriage of their eldest son, the younger daughters were removed abroad for education. The Life of her sister, Catherine, follows in this chapter.

youngest daughters ... No thing was to be done in their sight, nor a word spoken within their hearing, but what should relish of pietie, Godliness and deuotion: the whole course of their future liues did much depend upon those first impressions of good and euill which in those tender years they receaued from exteriour sensations entering into their minds, by the litle gates of their curious eyes and eares. When once got in, they were not easily to be remoued from thence, but were usualy layd up in their memories, and from whence readily brought out as often as any occasion of good or euill presented it self during the whole course of their succeeding liues ...

[So their mother] resolued to remoue them to a nursery of piety abroad, where they should neither see, nor hear, any thing but what should be good or perfect ... Not trusting to the care or conduct of any friend or seruants, ... and exposing her owne person to the trouble of a tedieus journy, [she] brings them ouer along with her into Flanders, to our monastery ...

... Mrs Martha was the eldest of the three, her father's fauourite and endowed with a ripeness of witt and judgment aboue her years, being then only nine years of age ... she perfectly acted the part of a litle mother towards her two younger sisters ...[18]

... [She was] cropt of the very flower of her age, to be transplanted into the paradise of divine pleasures, the glorious garden of her heauenly spouse: some heates broke out upon her which at first seemed no other then what she was frequently used to haue, but in a short time they degenerated into the measells and were soon attended with a violent mallignant feiver[19] ...

F Mary Catherin of the Blessed Sacrament:[20] short of stature, she grew as a novice

[*L13.7*, 271–3]

... [She was] subiect, from a child, to tormenting paines from graualle stopages, and to be consumptive ... and groth beinge no biger then a child of 12 yeares old ...[21]

---

[18] Around one page of the original text is omitted here.
[19] She died on 26 June 1706, aged just 33 years.
[20] Catherin Eyre (1674–*c*.1729), sister to Mary Martha of Jesus (above), was eight years old when her mother brought her to Lierre. Like others in her family she was 'short of stature'. She also suffered from 'gravel stoppages' (stony accretions in her kidneys or bladder), the passing of which could be extremely painful. This was a common early modern ailment, mentioned frequently in the papers, considered by modern medicine to relate often to dietary insufficiencies. If her height was also related to nutritional problems, this may explain why she grew when her diet changed after she joined the convent. Out of compassion, despite her physical ailments and size, she was admitted on trial and later professed on 30 April 1691.
[21] Around one page of the original text is omitted here.

... [She was] neuer sicke her whole year of nouiship, grew so vastly as to have a new mantle made for her profession, much longer then what she clothed in. She not only became one of the tallest of the community, but likewise a seruisable member of what euer obedience appointed ...

Chapter 33

Mary Gertrude of the Annunciation: An Impediment in Her Head, Her Early Vocation and Subsequent Afflictions

Gertrude Aston (1637–82) was from a well-known Catholic family from Tixel in Staffordshire, and the annals record her illustrious birth as the daughter of Lord and Mary Aston, whose father was Lord Weston, Earl of Portland and Chancellor of England. Clearly such an entrant was a feather in the cap of the early foundation at Lierre, so her profession in 1671 was cause of celebration by the chronicler, much as Anne Somerset's entry was joyously recorded at Antwerp in 1643 (Chapter 11).

This extract provides details of her various 'impediments', exacerbated by a fall from a horse and the ministrations of the surgeons. She came to Lierre almost by chance after short periods in other convents, and she worked for many years making the 'spargatts', the sandals worn by the religious, before she was once more afflicted by a series of physical and mental disorders.

[*L13.7*, 134–45]

… Her vocation to our holy Order was singuler, haueing had a desier from her infancy to a religious course; tho, when she came to ye yeares of discression, she did not know where to pick, but by ye advice of her ghostly Father, and other frinds, she made choyse of ye monastary of our English Sepulcrance att Lieg[e], being as thay thought most sutable to her youmore [humour] & weaknes – she haueing had an inpeaddiment in her head wch was, by ill surgence [surgery] in ye cure, unfortunatly poysened, so yt it was a mericale she did recouer of it. Besids she had affter yt the misfortun, by a fall of a horse, to put her shouloder out of gient [joint], and broke her knie [knee], by wch acceedence [accidents] she suffered much to her deying day – tho, other wys, she was strong and healthfull.

For these reasons, she made tryall there [at Liege], but could not injoy her health, nor haue any sattisfaction there, but all simed disgustfull unto her, and she was so very doull that she could not, for her life, learne to readd Latten. This, and diuers other reasons, made her leaue ye place … resolueing to retourn [to England]. But her aunt, ye Lady Mary Weston, being then a petitionary att ye English monastary att Louine [Louvain] … ye religious procured, by her aunt's menes, to haue her come to liue wth her, in hopes thay might succeed better wth her. She pentioned [there] about a yeare, and thay uised all there indeauors to giue her content, but it did not take any effect: she simed, rather, to be wholy avers from yt course of life, and resouled for the world, and was more vayne then euer, so yt her father called her back into England … where it pleased God to visiet her wth meny afflictiones and great crosses, [and] by yt menes to bring her to him selfe … and made her euen uncapable of converse or comfort, tell she mett wth a Carmellet Father of our Order, who had ye reput[ation] of a virtus holy man. By [his] menes she attained not only true peace of mind, but allso light to know ye will of God and what was most advantagious to her spirituall profitt, and eternall hapynes.

Hee taught her to praye mentally and advised her to read good bookes, perticularlie our Bd Mothers workes, wch did store [stir] her up to a great desiere of saruing [serving] God in a more parfect maner, and by degres awakned her first desiers in her of becoming a religious, with houlding of ye world and all its vanitys in great contempt … [She resolved] to be a treasion carmellet [Teresian Carmelite] and as soone as she had, wth much a doe, procured her fathers leaue by a desing and promis she had made, to viset our Lady of Sickome,[1] before she could resule one any c[o]urse …

Forsaking her fathers house, and all her deare frinds, wth out sheeding one teare, nor making any stay, but one day att Gaunt [Ghent] … to trey if she would take a licking [liking] to ye Du[t]ch Teresions [Teresians] there. But she could not fancy them, haueing no languige, nor capasitey to learne it, and thought Anwarp was ye place, not reflecting there was a nother house of our nation … By chance, ye Priouress of Gant [Ghent] spoke of our house att Lire [Lierre], desiering to be remembered to some of ye religous there as she passed, wch ioyed her hart, to heere there was another conent of English Carmellets. But [she] would resoule nothing tell she had bine att Sickome, and performed her promis to our Bd Lady; one wch accunt she would not be known to any of our English monastarys in her jurney, not Louine [Louvain] wher she had meny relations in ye monastary, and her oune unkle [uncle], ye Earle of Portland was allso there, but she would not see any of them, but lay privetly in ye towne yt night. Next day she ariued [at] Sickome, and stayed there 3 days, and resouled to liue and dey a child of our Bd [Mother], in her Order.[2]

… As soone as she ariued att Lire [Lierre], ye wagen passed by our couent … She, looking out of yt wagien, cast her eys first one ye imag of Our Lady ouer ye gate, wch filled her wth unspeakable ioye, saying 'This is ye place wher Our Bd Lady will haue [me] remaine' … yt she could not be perswaided to see any other place, nor was any rigour able to dant [daunt] her currige [courage], tho she was in ye world very delicat … She was able to passe wth only bread and water, tho she allways had a good stomake, and was ussed to dainty fare, very diffarent from what she could expect in religon …[3]

… She was imployed to mend and make ye sisters spargats [sandals], wch she applyed her self so seriously to learne how to doe them yt in a short time, she did them better then any other … She would neuer goe to ye grat[e] wth out her basket, or spargat worke, and was more prowed of her paches [patches] and rags then Ladys are of rich iuelles [jewels] …

1 Anne Somerset also went on a pilgrimage to this shrine (see Chapter 11).
2 Around one page of the original text is omitted here.
3 Around two pages of the original text are omitted here.

... She spared noe paines in her indeuers to lerne, espessally her Lattan for ye quier. [This] was hard to her, haueing a lettence [hindrance] in her speech, yet it tis incredable ye paines and diligence she yoused to attaine ye perfection of it, tho she was very bashfull and aprehenciue [apprehensive] ...[4]

... Her deuine spouse was pleased to vised our beloued Sister wth a lingering sicknes wch ye doctor, nor any other, did well understand, being more inward then it apered exteriourly – wch proued in ye end to be an imposton [abscess] in her head. [She had] a lettle distemper, wch was constant but not so great as to keepe her bead, tho it caused a great lothing in her meatt, and what some euer she toke it gaue her no norishmen, but turned to a better soubstance [bitter substance], wch she spett [spit] up a gaine wth a violent paine in her wch tormented her very much, and made her restles a nights, not able to sleepe, nor to take lettle or no norishment, haueing euer a good apitett [appetite] att other times. [All this] made us fear ye worst, and she, from ye very first moment she sickened, was fully perswaided she was to dey, tho she was up and walked about ye rome euery day, and loked as fresh and well as vissall [usual], only her discurce [speech] was much disordered and very difarent from her owne way by ye disorder of her head. Haueing in some weekes taken lettle or no rest, other ways she continewed much ye same, tell ye day before she deyed: her feuere grow strong, and she was seased [seized] all ouer her wth great paines, yt wee saw it was nedfull to give her, ye Last Sacraments, and in less then half an houer affter, she rendered her angelicall, pure soule into ye hands of her Creator ...

---

4   Around one page of the original text is omitted here.

Chapter 34

Mary Magdalen of Jesus and Agnes Maria of St Joseph: Their Double Deaths and Burial

These two religious appear one after the other in the annals, having died on the same day, 18 January 1692. Magdalen Leves[t]on, the daughter of Anne (née Cooles) and Sir Walter Leves[t]on of Staffordshire, professed on 26 August 1657; and Mary Basson who professed in 1651, was a 'native of Holland', the daughter of a merchant's family.

From very different backgrounds, therefore, their Lives give insight into devotional individuality within a common framework: when Mary Magdalen died, she was discovered in her bed surrounded by devotional paraphernalia, while Agnes Maria, ever since she almost drowned as a child, had been afraid of being sacramentally unprepared for death.

Sister Agnes' text, too, suggests the possibilities open to a woman in secular life during this period: following the death of her parents, she managed her own affairs and those of her brothers, using her business acumen to survive as 'her own woman', eventually joining an 'unregulated' religious community, typically referred to in these papers as *filles devotes*, before she became a Carmelite.

Margaret of Jesus (Margaret Mostyn: 1625–78; Chapter 31A), in the account of her own exorcism in 1651, claims that Sister Agnes was possessed by devils of melancholy, pride, luxury and despair, and that she had great esteem for her own sanctity: this allegation reflects Sister Margaret's antagonism towards Sister Agnes, an antipathy that possibly may have resulted from the latter's opposition to the election of Sister Ursula as Subprioress (see Hallett, 2007).

———————

[*L13.7*, 152–67]

… This deare sister of ours [Mary Magdalen of Jesus] had ye esteeme of a saint while she leaued [lived] in ye world. Her innosent puere soule was adorned wth meny moralle virtues, as was her body wth beautie, being called 'ye handsome Mrs Leuession' … As other Ladys ware wont in those times to carre [carry] glasses of essence [perfume] about them, she carred one of holy watter to wch she euer had a great reuerence & devotion … She adicted her selfe in her youth to ye practis of all sorts of virtues yt could be found in secular life, as prayer, fasting, allmes deedes & pillgermagise. Going once a ffoot to St

Winnifreds well [in Wales] … this saint … aperied to her in a blacke habett att ye head of ye well, from whome she receaiued many lights & consolations in her afflictions.

… When she was but 15 yeares old, haueing lost a brother yt she passinetly loued, ye greef for his death had licke to haue robed her of her life. This affliction was so great yt she could take no pleasur in anything of ye world, making a firme resolution neuer to weare any coullars but blacke, not so much a ribeng [ribbon], wch she contiewed tell her entrry into religione …

… She was very tender & sickly in ye world, so yt she thought (& ye docturs & her frinds declared) it was not possible for her to liue a yeare in religion, where as she liued 35 & for about twenty yeares, so strong & healthfull as to be able to upsarue exactly ye full rigoure of our holy roule …

… [By nature] she loued to be spokeng sweetly tow, & not contredicted, but Allmit God, for her greater merit, so permetted we are always more inclined to chide & contredict her then another, tho she did not deserue it. She was also very dellicate & nise [precise] in her dyet, both for ye goodnes & clenlynes of it, yet she was neuer knowne to complaine or haue any choys, saying all was tow good; & when it was in her power, made choys of the worst & hardest crousts [crusts] tho she had not a tooth in her head, and being in a dipe consumption, wch visally [usually] causeis a constant great stomeke … She had a great contrary [aversion] in ill smelles, or any durty fowle things, yet by her good will she would haue done all ye meanest druggery of ye house … & when she had fowle pottes to empty, or any thing to doe yt was desgustfull or lothsome as will offten happen amongst sicke [when she was Infirmarian], she was so officeius & deligent in all such accations & semed in her kindome [kingdom] …

… Uppon Sondays & other feastiall days, she was faithfull in hereing all ye Massis uppon her knees, upright wth out leaning against any thing for 3th or 4 howers in ye same possture … She offered all her labours up for ye reliue of ye soules in Purgatory, … siting up lat & reising early, both in heats & could, giueing yt body wch was more lick to an nottimie [corpse], only skine to couer ye bones … Infine, her continuwall labours, both exteriour & interiour, so wasted her body as yt she simed [seemed] a walkeing shadow, but her holy soule resembled an odorrifferus garding [sweet-smelling garden] of all sorts of fragerent flowers wch she culltifyed [cultivated] wth ye dayly exareyes [exercises] of all sorts of virtus & peyetie, haueing her thoughts uppon heauenly things … Reading was her delight wch, to make a right profitte of, she notted [noted] doune for her memory an innumerable nomber of holy sentence for her practis, as would fill a great volloume …

… She loued to discource of spirituall matters wth ye Sisters, & also wth seculares att ye grat[e], who war euer highly eddiffyed by her discret way of conuersation, in wch all yt treated wth her found ye marckes of a sainct … She had for meny yeares a great deffnes [deafness] & a rotten conssomsife [consumptive] cold wch caused her to cauffe & spiet [cough and spit] a great quantitie of loothsome fleames [phlegms], so very disgousfull yt she was forst to yous meny cloaths for that purposse, wch she contriued so as neuer to permet any one to tuch or wash them, but stole time early or latt to doe them her selfe alone, for feare of giueing disgust to any. This, & her deffnes, was her greatest suffarings, for she loued dearly to here & speake of heuenly thinges. She also, to her very last being Infermarion, had ye care of an ould religious, wch she sarued & tended most faithfully ...[1]

... Our doctur coming to visett Sister Agnes, who was also ill, he found fitt to giue her ye rights of church, & was wth Sister Magdelene ye same time & sayed she was not in any present danger ... She came wth ye rest to accompany Our Lord to ye sicke, & heelpe to gett the thinges ready, & made ye balles of flacks [flax] redy for ye holy oyles and remained there present all ye time & wth out dout made her intintion wth ye other, as she had seuerall times comunicatted condissinally [conditionally] for her viaticume [viaticum]. Abut 9 a clocke she went to bead & semed something better then ordinary, but ye Sister yt had care of her, coming early in ye morning as she uist to doe, found her dead, her boody in a possture most mouing as if she had layed her selfe for yt porposse – her eyse swetly cast done wth a smielling countance, wth her head raysed, tourning as if she answaring her spousses call ('I come'), and looked licke an angell, incompassed round about her parsone wth relects, medalles, beads & bages of picturs, her Crucifix in one hand, & a pare of beads in ye other & a holoued [hallowed] candell under her pillow, a sight so moueing yt we could not but condole our losse, & enuie her happines. A fewe howers affter deyed Sister Agnes so yt thay ware both lay'd out in ye quier together, & buered att the same time. Tho this deare sister of ouers dyed sudinly yet we are morally sartan not vnprouided; [she] made it for meny yeares her chiefest study & constant indeuours to be prepard for yt moment wch she continually longed for ...

Our dearly beloued sister Agnes Maria of St Joseph ... [had] all ye course of her life a great sence of offending God, haueing allways a filliall feare of God before her eyes – for att ye age of 4 yeare old, by misfortun, she fell in ye water & was in danger of being drowned, & remembered she did not so much feare death as she aprehended & was afrayd yt she was not in God Allmitys fauour because she had spocken some ill word and not confest it ...

[She] contriued with a lettle cosen [cousin] of her owne age to goe togethe[r] to liue an earametticall life [as a hermit] in ye proect [protection] of St Rosalyae whos life she had read & was resolued to imetat [imitate],[2] but there designe came to light & was hindered. Att 13 yeares old she made a sollume [solemn] vow of virginity and had from yt time great desiers of being religious, but her parence [parents] and ghostly Father would by no menes consent to it ... so yt she spent most of her time yt she liued in the world in a congreation [congregatiuon] of deuout wemen who liued a very orderly & pennetanicall [pious] life. Her parencets being dead, she toke uppon her the care of her three brothers, and ye manigment [management] of thers & her owne affaers, for she was notible in bussnes and good witt, a great memory, and very industtrus & skillful in ye law, & writt two or three hands admierable well. She was not longe her owne womane but her desiers of being religious increased & she resouled to be a Carmelitt in our monastary & she broath [brought] a considerable fortune wch heelpe us much (it being at ye begening of ye foundation) towards ye purchising of our house ...

---

1   Around one page of the original text is omitted here.
2   Presumably St Rose of Lima (Isabel de Flores y del Oliva: 1586–1671), canonized in 1671, who lived as a Dominican tertiary in a summerhouse/ hermitage in the garden of her home.

... wth continowall workeing on ye habbetts & new leenen, ye joynts of her fingers was gr   growne crooked, infine nobody could equall her in workeing of plaine worke ...[3]

... She was of a cold wattrish constution, very grosse & corpolent, wch made her unwelldy & not able to store [move] much, haueing gott a lamnis [lameness] in her legs wch put her much [in] paine euen to goe about ye house. Yet she was ingenius in finding out ways to healpe her self, yt she allways came to quier, reffectory and recreation, & could goe to bead & rise wth very lettle healpe, wch was a great blessing for our own monistarey for had she not bine so handy in assisting herselfe it would haue bine impossible for us to haue done it – as we experenced in her last 8 days sicknes before her death, when she could not sture her selfe. Halfe a dosene of ye strongest sisters in ye house had a noufe [enough] to doe only to draugd [drag] her in & out of her bead, for to lift or carry her was [an] impossible thing, she was so very fatt and big ...

[She] was subigct to cattars & vement colickes, wch made her fear she should dye soodenly, and being of a mallingcoly youmer [melancholy humour] she was offten much raught upon & affraid of ye last moment ... She was not so very sincible of death when it came to it, being taken wth a feauour and a kind of pallsise [palsy] in her tong[ue] yt we could hardly understand what she sayd, wch continewed 4 or 5 days ... Our Bd Lord ... gaue her speech suffissent [sufficient] to be understoode and made a parfect good confisson [confession], & also expressed a great desiere to haue ye rights of ye church, wth great peeace & tranquility received them all ... But her spich [speech] failed her imediately affter, she departed ye next day ...

When her boody was exposs'd in ye quire she looked so young & smoue, wth such a fresh coluer in her cheekes, yt you would haue thaught her a sleepe & we ware euen afraid of naylen [nailing] up ye coffen, tho ye corps had laine 24 howers & was as stife as a boord. This fallowing paper was found, a mongest her things, writen in her owne hand wch we can not leue to place her[e] ...

I desiere that when I am a dying this paper may be read to ye community whether I be present or noe;

I protest yt I will liue & dye a true child of our Mother, ye Catholick Roman Church; I confesse yt I will liue & dye a reliegius of Mont Carmeel, a true childe of our Bd Lord and of our Bd Mother Sainct Teresa;

I humbly aske pardon for all my disedification, & mortification & ye ill example I haue giuen;

I humblely thanke our Rd Mother for all he[r] Rce great charity & care of me, I allso humblely thank her Rce and all our dearest sisters, for ye fauour that thay haue bestooued upon me, in receauing me in my happy proffistion, & in licke maner I giue thankes to ye Rd Mother subprioress for her charity to me;

---

3   Around one page of the original text is omitted here.

I humblely thanke my Infirmarian for her loue & charity wher wth she hath sarued me, and I aske her pardon for all my disodedience & ill example I haue giuen her,

I desier yt this my protestation may be reade to ye community, and lastly I most humblely recomend my soule, when I shall be departed, to ye holy prayers of ye comunity, in a perticular manner yt I may quicklie enioy the pressence of Allmighty God.

This she writ some few yeares before her death, feareing it might be sodden, or yt she should not be able, by reasone of a lettence [hindrance] she had in her speech. Offten times she could not pronounce some words of English plaine, tho she understood it well, & could read it also, and silldome spooke Duch exceapt att ye grat[e] wth her fri[e]nds, who ware eddifyed to find her so happy a mungst strangers. Sweet Jesus grant we may emitate her virtus; Amen

Chapter 35

Mary Terease of Jesus:
Her Vision of Her Mother, All in White,
on Her Way to Heaven

Mary Terease Warren (1642–96) was niece to Margaret of St Teresa (Margaret Downs: Chapter 30), whose sister Anne is the focus of this extract. After Anne's death, Mary Terease was taken to Lierre, out of reach of her father's Protestant family; it was there that the young child had a vision of her mother on her way to Heaven. The impact of this, as well as a general concern for her upbringing, resulted in her being placed for education with a widow in Mechelen, after which she became a Carmelite. The extract provides a sense of an extended network of family care, not without its own complications; of education necessary for social and convent life; and of the nature of spiritual revelation. In January 1680 Mary Terease witnessed the recovery of Anna Maria of St Joseph (Chapter 39), attributed to the intercession of Margaret of Jesus (Margaret Mostyn; Chapter 31A).

[*L13.7*, 173–6]

… [She] was named in holy babtisme 'Mary Terease' by her pious mother, who dyed a fewe munths affter. She leaft ye care of this lettle orfine [orphan] to her sister Martha Downes, who liued a mayd [unmarried] a most virtus & holy life. Ye deceased, one her death bead, coniured [called upon] this sister of hers by all ye bonds of charitie & affection, to bring up her only daughter in ye fear of God & solled virtue, & yt, as soone as she was fitt to trauell, she should be sent to her sister beyon sees [over the sea], who was then our venarable Mother Margaret of Sta Tereasa, and was then Priorssis of our manastary, newly founded.

When this lettle one ariue to ye age of 6 yeares, it pleased God to call to a better life her deare aunt, Martha Downs, & leaft her to ye care of her mother's frinds to be bread up [raised] in ye Catholick faith. Her father, being then a Protistand [Protestant], uised all menes imaginable to take ye child from them, wch forst [forced] them to send her ouer before she was 7 yeares of age, & placed her in ye Englishe monastary of St Aug[u]stines order in Bruges, wher there was meny of her relations …

Our lettle angell was soon affer sent to her aunt who was then Superiore, & she ariued att our monastary the 24 of January 1651 wher she stayed for some time, tell her good aunt reflecting itt would be an aduantag [advantage], both for our house & ye child, to be placed abraud for her improuement, perticularly to learne ye languiss [language] of ye cuntrey, a quality most nessisary for our house, & ye childe being aptt & forward. It was resouled to put her in a Douch scoule [school], wher[e] in a short time she spooke Du[t]ch parfectly will ...

There was dificulty to remoue her from thence, tell a strang accident fill out. It was reuelled [revealed] to our most Venarable Mother Margeret of Jesus[1] yt ye mother of this child was still in Porgatory, & in want of Masies and other meritorious workes ... [Masses were therefore arranged for her]: ye last Mase being to be sayd att our Ladys of ye Clouse,[2] the child was to be present, but did not know for whome ye Mass was said. But of a sooden, towards ye end of ye Mass, she sounded [swooned] away being very much frighte[ne]d. Comeing to her selfe, she called out to ye deuots, 'I see my mother all in whit[e] goe up to heauen, & she says I shall come to her', & something of her being religious, wch she could not well relat[e]. Yt wch confirmed ye beliuef of this to be really so was ye child, haueing no memory of her mother, could describ[e] her parson & euery featur, wth other sircomestantis [circumstances] so very cliere as if she had knowne her, tho she had neuer seene her to her knowlidge, nor had she euer hard [heard] of her mothers being in Purgatory, or yt the Mass was sayd for her soule. Nor did ye maid of ye monastary, nor ye deuotts, know any thing why thay ware sent wth ye child, to heer Mass att our Ladys of ye Cloys, but to heer it for our Rd Mothers intention.

Ye lettle one was as one transported ye whole day, relatting [relating] to ye sisters what she had seen & hard. It raugh [wrought] so uppon her yt she got a great feaiure [fever] that neuer went off. Ye doctour feared it would be her death, but our Bd Lord desinged other ways [planned otherwise], tho she was neuer well affter, but locked licke [looked like] death ... so yt ye doctour conclouded [concluded] it was impossible for her to liue, or recouer, unless she did chainge eayre [air], & ware put in ye care of some discreat parson yt understod how to treat chilldren, & one so dangerusly ille, for unless she did keepe order & take remedies, she must dey.

It was a hard task to ef[f]ect: ye child was as fo[o]lishly fond of the deuots as thay ware of her, & all thaught it would break her hart to part wth them. But our Rd Mother resouled to remoue her, & placed her wth a discreat weddow [discreet widow] att Macklen, yt had daughters of her one [own], well bread & virtus [well bred and virtuous], & also to or thre others of her age. [There] she was so carfully tended yt in a short [time] she recouered to ye admiration of all yt know her, & was able to goe wth ye rest to scoule [school], & aplyed [applied] her selfe to lirne Duch and to read & writ & cast accounts – so yt she wholy forgot her mother ... & was as fond of Mrs Sherow as if she had bine her owne mother, obaing [obeying] in all she command her, & was of so sweet an tracttable a youmar [tractable humour] yt she gained ye harts of all yt had to doe wth her ...

She remained wth yt famely 5 or 6 years wth all ye sattisfaction imaiginable, att wch time her brother, ye Confessar of ye Poor Clares att Graluine [Gravelines], came on porposse [deliberately] to see her. [He] found her much emproued & well inclined to a religious course. He braught her a loing wth him to see his aunt ... but not being of age, [the child] could not be admetted wth out a dispence [dispensation]. But Holy Prouidence had so ordained yt our most Rd Lord Bishop was actually come to make our election, & our most Venarable Mother Margaret of Jesus was reelected, att wch time she beged ye fauour of his Lordship to dispenes wth her age, & admit of her to cloath. Calling for

---

[1] Margaret Mostyn (Chapter 31A).
[2] See Chapter 31, note 22.

her, he examned her vocation, and was much edifyed to find one so young haue so much kowlidge of religion & great desiers to pleace God. When she demaned uppon her knees ye holy habitt, my Lord wth a gracious countenance gaue her leaue[3] …

---

[3] She therefore entered on 24 July 1658, 'being but 15 years of age, & made her holy profession one ye 19th of March in ye yeare of our Lord 1660'.

Chapter 36

Anne Teresa of Jesus: A Colonel's Daughter, Scrupulous in Saving Time when She Met with her Brother; Mortified in Sleepiness, and a Lover of Poverty after whose Death from Leprosy Singing was Heard

Catherine Nelson's (1642–1700) mother's family were Catholic exiles; her father, a colonel with an English regiment in the region, was nursed by his daughter for some time after he received a severe head wound. The Life describes the nun as rather proud: her father encouraged her socially to aspire 'beyond her station' although she appears to have rejected this ambition when she joined the Carmel, though she remained meticulous and somewhat aloof. After she had entered the convent to join her sister, Anne Teresa met with her brother only once every two or three years and kept the meetings very short, not wishing to waste time on the matter. Her other habits, too, suggest a precise attention to the components of her profession: she maintained a strong spirit of poverty in her daily life, for example, not keeping unnecessary sewing materials. After her death, the nuns heard singing issuing from the dead-cellar and considered this to be a sign of her loving reception there by the deceased religious.

[*L13.7*, 203–11]

[Her mother, Ursula Collford, was a native of Brabant] tho her father, Gaberill Collford, gentillman, waer English and borne in England, but left ther estat, countrey and freinds upon the account of relegine in ye perticution [persecution] of Queen Elizabeth, choysing rather to liue pooer in a Chatholike countrey then to liue in plenty in a monge heriticts.

In this excile thay payst [passed] ther time so vertuesly as thay dyed in the oppioune of sainttety [the opinion of sanctity] … The eldest son inter'd into ye Sosietie of Jesus; the other became a Francescan Frier … The tow daughters wher religious in this couent: ye eldest, Str Mary of St Barned,[1] intr'd very young & when her sister was of age to imbrace

---

[1]   Marie Nelson (1635–68), took the habit at Lierre in 1653, aged 17, and professed in August 1654 (*L13.7*, 23). Her death, mentioned in this chapter, occurred soon after her sister entered the convent.

a stat, she arnistly deserd [earnestly desired] she might injoye ye same hapynis she ded ...
[But] our deare Sister contineud in the vanitiss of ye world, which her father, Correnall
Nellson, was cheifle cause of: being very fond of her, [he] gaue her dotter [daughter] a
much higher breeding then his estate & qualitie could well afford. She being natuerally
a lettle vaine & of a highe spirit toke much upon her in ye famelly. Even her father's
regement of shoulders [soldiers] stoude in awe of her, not dairing to shoot at publicke
rejoyccing because ye noyes offended her ... What I sayd just now of her lettle high and
proud incleantions was not in any wayes ment to lessen her, but rather to make her vertues
moer respendent, to see how after her inter in to religione, by mortification & other praties
of vertue, she wholy ouer came natuer.

She begane now to haue desiers of coming relegous, but her fat[her], by a wounde
he receiued in his head, was confind to his chamber for some years. She thought it her
obligation [to] assist him, but assane [as soon] as he was dead she left her mother, old &
lame, and toke the holy habett ...

... So soone as ever she was cloath, with what fereuer and corage she begane her taske,
striuing to ouer come natuer and dye to her selfe by continouell mortifien [continually
mortifying] her pasions, yt she soone brought ym under subiction [subjection]. For she
arnistly thursted to be nailed upon ye Crosse with her beloued spouse by her 3 vows ...
So it pleas his Deuine Maiesty to begene betimes to trye her constance, for she was noe
sooner in the monastrey but he calld to him self, 8 days affter, 2 of our relegous who dyed
of a violent feauer which rained much in ye towne. One of these was her owne sister, Mary
of St Barnard, whom she loued most passinetly allways[2] ...

... This affliction went very depe to our deare Sister's hart, and a lettle affter one of
her aunts (having but two) dyed sudingly ... but ye suffering of her body [under the
rigour of our Rule] wher nothing to thos of her interiouer ... being natuerly inclined to be
scupleouls, full of feares & depe aprehensions ... [Her Superior] allways cutt her short,
which cost her many a teare, for by her good will she would have bene continoually a
talking of her interouer trobles and scuples to her Superiouer and Confessor. Yett with
all [she was] so intyerly obedent & submissive to them yt affter ye death of these two of
hapy memory which she profest under, she never sturd (for 20 years that she survied them)
a hairs breath from ye admonishions, advics and orders thay had giuen her ... This she
declar'd to me one her death bed ...[3]

... Her holy brother, ye Francisan, whome she allways tenderly loued ... came once in
2 or 3 years to see her. She was not at all joyd ther with, nor would ever entertaine him
moer then halfe an houre at a time, nor omett any one singell acte of comunity to kepe
him company, tho had leaue to staye from all. She would tell us, when wee wonderd, she
kept him noe longer yt when she had inguierd [enquired] of his health, exspriesst her
owne content & sattisfection, recomend her self to his prayers, she had noe moer to say,

---

2   Marie of St Bernard died on 18 October 1668. The other religious referred to here is
    assumed to be Marie Martha of Jesus (Marie van Hetmisin, of Bois-le-duc), a lay sister
    who died on 16 October 1668 and whose Life accordingly appears immediately before
    Sister Marie of St Bernard's in the annals (*L13.7*, 22).

3   Around one page of the original text is omitted here.

therfoer wisht him gone for it was but losse of time … When ye sisters in recreation would be praiseg this brother of hers, sayen he had bene allways inployd in ye cheife offeris [offices] of his Order and was a most holy saintly man, she would be very mach disspleasd at such discou[r]ses, sayen it was a fooles [foolish] thing to talk so, her brother and she waer pooer creatuers before God Allmighty …

… This deare Sister of ours mortified in all perticular in sleepe – for ye time of ye divine offices she most allways use all ye forse & violents [violence] imaingable to kepe her eyes oppen, & often sayd ye whole Matins with one eye only, being not able to kepe ye other opaen … She was a great louer of holy pooerty & not only truly pooer in sprite but in ye practis and desier of possesing nothing – her books, medalls and pictuers pooer, and noe moer then what was presiuely necasesay. Nor would she kepe bye her moer thred, needles, sheuers [shears], thimbls, then what iust needful for hir present work …

… Her last sicknis, which was only 7 days duerince [endurance], she being much spent and worne a way with a violent humour in her head & forhead, wch was all of a scrufe[4] & some 2 months befoer her death became an intyer scab, & all downe her temples runing a vast quantety of theitk [thick] green and yellow matter, which ye doctors and surgings sayd was a sort of a leperos. Her face was suddingly well &, as wee sopose, [the disease] fell upone her hart, [and] put her into a highe feauer. Assune as ye docter came to her he sayd ther was noe hopes of life, which was joyefull news to our deare sister …[5]

… Ther happened a very remarkable passages at her buierall: as the corps waer sett before ye dead celler dore, ye relegous singen ye *Benedictus*, some 4 or 5 of our sisters heard very disstinckly severall from thence sing our quier tune with them. Thay allso thought yt thay perfectly disstingues [distinguished] perticular voyces of our dead sisters. When the cerimony was ended wee inquierd if ther waer noe singen in the church, street or turne. Thay assuerd us ther was noe singen & our mayd prottested ther cam noe body to the turne, for she was ther all the time, but a pooer old women; but she heard as she thought singin out of the ded celler. So wee may piouesly beleiue our deseased sisters, her compnyons, sung to wellcome her …

---

4 'Scurf', considered by the doctors in this case to be a form of leprosy, begins with spots and a thickening of the skin, then assumes a tubercular form.

5 Around one page of the original text is omitted here.

Chapter 37

Marie Teresa of St Albert:
A Lay Sister of Extraordinary Strength,
a Lover of Solitude who Sat in the Trees

Though she had the means to profess as a choir sister, Mary Teresa Beamont (1638–1701) of Somerset preferred to enter the Order as a lay sister. Her home and educational background had ill prepared her for the labour of such a position, though she overcame this deficiency because of her physical powers, on which, unusually in the Lives, this extract focuses.

[*L13.7*, 217]

[She professed on 21 November 1658, as a lay sister] which she choisse out of humeltie and devotion, otherways her father would haue giuen her ye portion of a quier nonne at Louean [Louvain] wher ther was one of her owne aunts relegous. But, receiuing the name of Teresa in holy baptisme, and from her childhood was a great louer of solitude, [she] would sett in trees and arborrs halfe days together, locking upon ye skies and sunn – so [she] thought being a Teresasin [Teresian] she should haue her delight of solitude and contemplation & becoming a laye sister should haue moer time for it. Her father had bene at ye charges of keping her at schole some years, to learne musick and fine works, so pooer thing had never bene uesst [used] to any labour of house afairs wch would haue bene mier proper for her station – tho [she was] of a strong natuerall strinth in liften [strength in lifting], carrien and, with ease, performe any labouerous work and willen to doe what she could. Our master work men waer wont to saye, when thay had any thing of wayte to remoue ore carry, thay would rather haue Sister Marie St Allbert to help then there owne men.

She made use of this strength and labowerd for some years, doen ye work of a laye sister according to her vocation. Yet [she] had noe very good health, offten trobled with violent colects [colic] and like an impostume [abscess] in her head. So, whether yt fell downe upon her inward parts, or whether with a suding force [sudden exertion she] had over reachd her selfe, so brouth downe ye Mother that, in fine, vement paines a bout her brast and other impedements renderd her uncapable of any labouer, ore so much as lefting up her armes. Thefoer [she] could only paer apells [peel apples] and … could doe lettle with her needle by reason of soer eyes: and when she first interd [she] could see but with one, yett wee never persaiud [knew] it till some years affter. She not knowen her selfe obligd to discouer it [reveal] & had noe want of it as long as she doe her house work. But now [she] could noe more performe ye office of Martha, she had her wish & incleantions to acte the part of Mary, in silence recolection and solitude …

Chapter 38

Teresa Maria of Jesus, Mary of St Joseph and Elizabeth Ursula of the Visitation: Three Religious of Extraordinary Humility – Who Ate Scraps, were Sparing in their Use of Candle and Pen, and who did Servants' Work

These three Lives have been arranged together here because they each feature an emphasis on the great humility of their subjects, clearly a matter for admiration and for particular note.

The first of the nuns in this chapter was by birth Bridget Kempe, originally from near Guildford in Surrey. She professed in 1651, the year in which Margaret of Jesus (Margaret Mostyn; Chapter 31A) wrote somewhat caustically about her that she 'was, by far, too formal in her [devotional] actions, doing them out of custom without any intention' (Hallett, 2007).

The second nun featured in this Chapter is Mary Vaughen [or Vaughan] of Monmouthshire, who died in 1709; and the third is Elizabeth Gerard who professed in 1706, one of a large family of whom several joined the convents at Antwerp and Lierre (see Chapter 17).

[*L13.7*, 31]

... [Teresa Maria of Jesus] seemed best pleassed when she could haue the scrapes and leauings of otheres, in so much that when she was Dispencer she left it for a maxceme [maxim] in the kichine [kitchen]: 'When there was any scrapes left ore what others did not eatt, give that to Sister Teresa Maria'. The same was her inclination in her cloathing, to haue the worst ore most pached and inconveniant. She was a person not only given to performe much corporiall penance, but on that could very well beare mortification ...

... For the spaces of 5 weekes she had a stronge vement fever, wch never left her till her death. She was never hard to complaine, but whatsoever medessyn [medicine] the docter ordayned, be it never so ungratfull [unpleasant], she sayed it was most delicatt. In her greatest sufferances, when we asked her how she did, she would reply 'Much better, very well'; and when she saw any of the sisters weepe she would saye 'Fye, fye, do not weep. I am not worth one teare of any of the sisters'; and to her Superiour she would say 'Deare Ma Mere, do not be troubled. Why should yu feare? Take courage there is nothinge to befeared' ...

*

[*L13.7*, 236]

... As to work, [Mary of St Joseph] was no less a rigorous then a laborious obseruer of it; not only diligent in those daily needle works wherein the sisters usually pass away their time after dinner and supers while they are together, but always ready to giue a helping hand towards all the burdensome actions of the whole house – namely carrying euen wood and weeding in the garden, and folding linnen and the like ... [though] not louing much that noise and hurry which does naturally attend great labours and stirring works ... For many years together she had the care of making the spargetts [sandals]. This work is really laborious and troublesome as all find by experience who are imployed in it ...[1]

... Nothing was so slight, poor and decayd which she would not find an use for: what others knew not what to do with, she would always bring to pass some thing or other, and bitts of old rotten fringes, laces, silks, purles which the sisters flung away, she would gather together and trime up beads and make them and everything serue some way or other for the use of poore and ordinary peeple. She was so sparing to her self of fire and candle that, during the whole time, namely 59 years, she was in religion, she spent but the quantity of one candle in going to bed at nights, using her self for the most part to go to rest in the dark. At leasure moments she writ a larger sort of book of priuate devotions, neuer spending more then a quarter of an hour at a time. This she writ with an old pen, and made use of the same pen for seven years together. In fine she exercised holy pouerty in her very diet ... she gave her self nothing but such bitts and scraps, which others would have giuen to the catts ...

*

[*L13.7*, 265]

[Of Elizabeth Ursula of the Visitation] justly it may be said she had made it her only concern from her infancy to bee faithful to God ... tho addicted hugely to play with those of her age, and to haue much pleasure in hauing others recreate, wherefore twas remarkable her humility and goodness to the servant maids. Upon holydays they had permission to deversions in the neighbourhood [and] she would of her own accord performe the fattiges of the kitchin, cooke the suppers and other labours, to the end they might not hesten from their innocent sports sooner than was nessary ...

---

[1]   Around three pages of the original text are omitted here.

Chapter 39

Anne Therese of the Presentation, Anna Maria of St Joseph and Joseph Teresa of the Purification: Three Lay Sisters who Learned the English Manner of Cooking

The Lives of these three lay sisters appear in close proximity in the annals, each account revealing interesting details about their relationship to the choir nuns of the convent. The first two in this chapter, Anne Lysens (who died in 1723) and Petronela van Dyck (1650–c.1724/5), both came from Brabant, whilst the third, Catherine Quinigham (1682–1738), was born in Ireland and moved to the Low Countries after visiting her uncle, a physician in Antwerp.[1]

All three women were required to adapt when they came into the service of the Carmel: Anne Therese tried to learn 'good English' as well as cooking; Anna Maria likewise acquired recipes, originally as Edmund Bedingfield's servant, and she was later believed to have been miraculously restored to health by the intercession of Margaret of Jesus (Mostyn); and Joseph Teresa, whose distressing medical condition is described here, could not bring herself to kill poultry for the kitchen.

———————

[*L13.7*, 266–7]

… [Anne Therese of the Presentation] she did the kitchen to great satisfaction by applyinge her self to the English manner of cookinge, and loued much more to speake English then her owne naturall language Dutch, being very attentive when ever she did but hear the sisters speake aney words wch sounded, as she imagin'd, fine and not common. Those she would carefully retaine in her mind to bring out in the first occasions, tho' maney times so improper to what she was sayeing, with which she hugely deuerted the community. She woud often say if she shou'd live to se a foundation goe from hence into England she shoud wish to be one of the number …

*

———————

[1]   Her mother was Joanna Trohy; a doctor of that surname, associated with the Antwerp Carmel, gave testimony concerning the preservation of Margaret Wake's body (see Chapter 29, notes 6 and 14).

[*L13.7*, 267–8]

... [Father Bedingfield] liuinge ouer against our monasterry,[2] [Anna Maria of St Joseph] was much edified [in his service]. In perceavinge the order and methods which pass'd the out side of the inclosure and the town, in treating with externes, and procuringe in provissions, all went so peaceably without any noise or what might be thought imperfect, seing the religiouse constantly vayled, not to be exposed when ye gate was open'd for the takeing in provissions, letting workmen in and out. Glad she was when twas thought necessary she should sometimes conferre with the touriours for instructions to the cooking some particulars for her masters table after the English way ...

[She expressed] ardent desiers to become a member [of the community]. She could not be easey till she had imparted her feruous [fervent] intentions to her Master and preuailed he would petition the Superioure for her admittance, which to her great joy his Reverence effected. She passed her nouiship piously ... performing the most seruile, laboriouse workes of ye monasterry with much feruour and dilligence ... exercising charity to the sisters euen when they had negligently spilt sauces in the Refectorie and other places of ye monasterry which had been newley scoured or not, and that she saw 'em takinge it up 'emselves she would fly to 'em and tell 'em 'twas her worke to cleane 'em. She had ye spirit of a feruorous lay sister ...

... [and was able] to find time, as she did, to beautifie our garden with stoaring it and settinge variety of flowers weeding and watteringe 'em and the tubbs of mirtle trees and potts ... Euen in her great age she would labour tho' yet had scarce vigour or strength to draw her limbs alonge.

She had seuerall sickneses, in particular a burninge feivor [3] ... She grew rather wors, leaving two of the sisters to watch her in the night who, perceavinge she grew extreame ill and as they thought in her agony ... She spoke to 'em, and sayed something of a great light she had seen. They, imagininge she was idle in the hight of the feivour, drew the curtains of the bede cloyse ... the sick sister was so quiet they knew no more of her till the conuent Mass was out, then she desired with great earnestness to speake with her Confessour and gave him this account: ... [that] on a suddain their appear'd a heauenly light and our Venerable Mother [Margaret of Jesus][4] bearing the divine infant Jesus in her armes upon a white cloth ... her blake vayle glitter'd as it were full of starres, and at that very moment [she] found her selfe perfectly well ... That very night she got out of her bedde, and the next morninge heard Mass...

... She liued maney yeares after ... [and] finish'd her life in the exercise of a laborious spouse of Jesus to her death ... [when] not being in quire at morning prayer [this] gaue feares she might be indisposd. The Sister who was sent found her faln upon the ground expired and half dressd ...

---

2 He purchased a house adjoining the convent, which he left to the Carmel in his will.
3 The events described here can be precisely dated (by reference to *L3.36*) to 20 January 1680 (see Hallett, 2007).
4 Margaret Mostyn, who died in 1679 (Chapter 31A).

*

[*L13.7*, 275–6]

... At her own desire [Joseph Teresa of the Purification] was receaued for a lay sister, but might have been one for ye quire had she choose it ... She was in ye outmost anxiety to see any of ye Sisters in pain; nor could she ever conquer her self so far as to kill a foul, tho she was in a station where it was hard to avoid it. She seem'd to feel the pain euen of an insect if it suffr'd any violence ...

[She had] great affection to all ye community in gen'ral wch discover'd it self to each member in particular so visibly yt, in Holy Cross or Innocence Day, when any of them came in to ye kitching, he[r] eyes sparkled with joy. With a chair in her hand, in ye most respectfull & affecyionate manner, she urged them to accept it, & if [it was] cold [she] placed it at ye fire in ye most obligeing terms. She had an education which made her Mrs of civility & good manners.

She came from Ireland to visit an uncle she had, who wa[s] a doc[to]r of physick in Antwerp, with whom she remain'd til she persued her resolution to become a Carmelite. She was naturaly of a hott temper, but constant vigilance gave her an intire conquest over it ... She was at last seas'd with a swelling in both her legs from which issu'd such a vast quantity of watter that, not withstanding all the necessary precations of dressing & cloaths used, it run even to ye very door ...

Chapter 40

Mary Rose of the Sacred Heart of Jesus: her dramatic journey from Maryland and Her Death, after which She Continued to Sweat

Mary Boon (1718–58) came to Lierre from 'Prince George's County', Maryland, one of several religious who travelled from America to the Low Countries in this period to join convents (see Chapters 23, 27). Her Life, the final extract from the annals included here, describes her journey to Lierre, amidst shipwreck and storm, via Wales and London; and it also gives intriguing details of her death, after which her body continued to give signs of life, to the alarm of the other religious, who subsequently disinterred her to check that she was indeed dead.

[*L13.7*, 299–301]

… She left America with an assurance of being addmitted to a tryal amongst us. She bid a finall adue [adieu] to her father & mother & c, put to sea & hop'd to be as speedy as possible … Whilst a prosporous sail flattered her, a storm arose so violent nothing cou'd be done but lowering ye masts & abandoning the vesal to the fury of the tempest. When it ceased, the pilot found it incompast with a chain of rocks from which he disintangled it & arrived safe on shore in the principality of Wales. This was an other disaster: not knowing the language of ye people which is that of true Britons [Bretons, Celts] & being a great way from London & ye trouble & expence of a land journey. When she gott there she was forced to rest much longer then she liked for a ships coming this way. Harass'd in mind and body, at length she came to Lier where after a proper time to recrute [recover], she put on our holy habett & at ye end of ye year profest …

…[She was ever busy] having allways some little work with her which she pul'd out when she stop'd to talk & when confind to her bed on account of ye swelling in her leg … We may say she was like ye industrious bee …

… from ye time of her profession she never enjoy'd any health … & by her looks one wou'd have thought her likely to goe into a consumtion; but her complaints took quite a different turn. What she complained of in her back ceased, & in a little time was with great violence in her belly & appear'd to have some contracted matter yt form'd a large hard lump ... She found herself suddainly quite well ... [then] a great pain fell into one of her legs ... Some time after [she had gott a suddan faltering in her speech] her whole body was seased [seized] & she had no sort of sence as cou'd be deserned, only she breathed. She lay in this condition some days. Neither bleeding, nor blistering, took any effect; she expired upon the 30 of November 1758.

... [Before she died, a strong smell continued until she lay one night in the quire, when it was gone, and her face was covered in sweat. The doctors could not find any sign of life and her funeral was held but, again, sweat was found on her face, to the consternation of the religious]. ... the dead bells having rung, they resolved yt ye people yt was come to her funeral shou'd see her carry'd into ye dead cellar, but as soon as they were gone she was brought up again in her coffin & carry'd to the Infirmary where methods was taken to bring her to life – but in vain. Att night she was carry'd to the dead cellar again. 3 days after ye mason went to stop up ye oven, when we found her fresh without ye least smell & her face with ye same drops of sweat on it, which was wiped of[f] several times & still came on again ...

APPENDICES

Appendix 1

The Constitutions and Rule of St Albert

This extract is included to illustrate the structures within which the Teresians lived. The constitutions provide the nuns with a framework for contemplative discipline, in aspiration if not actuality, and crucially inform the structure of daily life within the convent. The Lives should be read against their backdrop – and vice versa, for it is possible to see in the tension between Rule and Life how individual dilemmas and personal struggles were played out.

This text is a seventeenth-century copy of the Rule, originating most probably in Antwerp, though subsequently held at Lierre: on the cover it reads 'Constitutions wrote by one of our V[enerable] Dr Mothers, I think it is our first Dr Mothers hand', which suggests that it may have been compiled by Anne of the Ascension. The manuscript is now at Darlington (*L3.34*: 20cm × 15cm; pp. 31).

The Discalced Carmelite Order adopted the Rule of St Albert, formulated in *c.*1209, modified in 1247 by Pope Innocent IV (1243–54), and mitigated in 1432 by Pope Eugene IV (1431–47). In 1562, Teresa de Jesus was given papal authority to draw up statutes and ordinances, and she committed her new female Order to keep the Rule 'without mitigation' (*Book*, Chapter 36), not allowing ownership of private property and insisting on claustration. In 1581, the Congregation of Discalced Carmelites held their first Chapter General and approved constitutions for both sexes, within which Teresa de Jesus made provision for the nuns to be free to choose their own confessor, exempting her Prioresses from the authority of local Priors (McNamara, 1996, 500). This was an important precedent, and one embraced by her successors even in the face of much opposition from the friars: it was crucial for claims of autonomy made within various Lives and for the wider history of the female Carmelite Order.

The Teresian constitutions were widely translated and distributed as new foundations were established, understandably and necessarily modified over time in order to meet local needs and shifting social conditions. Nonetheless, the constitutions remained (and remain) essentially the same, offering 'a pattern of religious observance, at once gentle and austere in their discipline and an effective means of leading souls to the highest degree of religious perfection' (Teresa de Jesus, 1946 ed., III, 210).

The first section of the Rule as it appears below indicates the essence of the three vows and the type of accommodation considered suitable for the Order. This is followed by rules designed to facilitate the gradual process of admission and the conditions associated with this: a potential new nun must be healthy in body and mind to be acceptable to the other religious before clothing. If the community subsequently found her to be unsatisfactory, there was no obligation to allow her to proceed to profession. Such safeguards were clearly thought to be important so as to protect the community.

There is considerable emphasis in the Teresian constitutions on the importance of enclosure, with various rules designed to secure it – in both spatial and conceptual terms. The grates and gates were locked, and only designated key-holders (such as the Superior) and the 'Tourriers' could admit necessary outsiders, such as physicians or confessors, when the religious were too unwell to meet them at the grates. All meetings were to be chaperoned and all 'unnecessary' communication avoided. Those who broke these rules were severely reprimanded, given a series of warnings and even 'imprisoned' within the convent, which suggests just how important claustration was held to be. Though Protestant critics made much of such details, and exaggerated them in anti-Catholic publications promulgated as evidence of Popish oppression (Claydon and McBride, 1998; Haydon, 1993; Tumbleson, 1998; Marotti, 1999), from a devotional point of view, it was crucial to maintain the rhythm and seclusion afforded by enclosure so that the religious were not distracted from their contemplative goal by worldly concerns. The Rule builds in a protection, stating that both novices and professed nuns should be visited by authorised inspectors to whom they could make any legitimate complaints, ensuring that 'they may stay heere of their owne free will and accorde' (p. 246). Teresa de Jesus had written that 'A convent of unenclosed nuns seems to me a place of very great peril' (*Book*, Chapter 7), so she sought in her reforms to establish a space of quiet, 'to withdraw more from everything and live my profession and vocation with greater perfection and enclosure' (*Book*, Chapters 33, 36).

Faults are listed, and range from light (being late, forgetting a book, laughing in choir), to middling (speaking without permission in the Chapter House), grievous (lying, stealing, entering another's cell), to more grievous (hitting another religious, stirring up discontent) and most grievous (falling into sensuality, defaming the convent). These carry a range of punishments, including that for the serious fault of bearing false witness, which involved the penance of eating on the floor of the refectory wearing only a scapular. The list is designed to regulate behaviour at both a domestic and a more conceptual level.

Similarly, the stress laid on poverty and the lack of personal property, as well as on the reduction of individual relationships (with family and in particular friendships), was designed to avoid tensions within community life that might arise from material attachment or from one-to-one loyalties: within an Order that focussed on inner meditation there was naturally a concern to minimise 'outer' distraction, and this is reflected in contemplative techniques as well as in rules for daily life.

[*L3.34*, 1–31]

JHS[1]
The First Rule of Albert Patriarch of HJerusalem confirmed and corrected by our holy Father Innocent the fourth for the Religious of Mount Carmellus

To haue a Pryor[ess][2] and of the three vowes

Wee institute first and ordayne, that you haue amongst you for Pryor[ess], who shall be elected for this charge, by the common consent of all, ore of the greatest part, to whom each one of you shall promisse obedience and after haueing promissed it, shall haue care to keepe it in verity, by there workes, wth chastity and pouerty.

Of receauing places ore houses

You may haue places and houses in solitary places, ore other parts where they shall be giuen you comodious for the obseruation of your religioun as shall seeme conuenient …

Constitutions of the Religious Carmeletes of the First Obseruance called Discalced

Made and ordained wth diuine spirit by Mother Teresa of Jesus, first foundresse of the said Order; approued by the Superiours and Chapters Generall and Prouinciall. And afterwards approued and confirmed by the sea Apotolike; as appeereth by the Bulles and Breues graunted unto the said Order as well as by our holy Father, Pope Gregory the XIII, as by Sixtus the fifth and their successours unto the time of Clement the Eyght who also hath confirmed and approued the same with force of perpetuall memory.[3]

Chapter 2: Of Obedience and Election of Superiours

1 wee doe declare that the religious woemen of the Primitiue Rule bee subiect unto the right Reuerend Generall of the Order of Discalced Carmelites of the first Ruele, and to the Prouinciall, and that the right Rd Generall may visit them either by himselfe, ore by any other visiter, whom he shall please to nominate;

2 The Election [of religious and Superiors] shall be made by secret voyces [votes] … And the election being made the papers are to be burned presently in the place before them all, so that ye names of those who doe giue their voyces, be not published;

3 … neither the Prouinciall nor his company haue any voyce in the election of the religious … and the Prouinciall may disallowe ore confirme this election as shall seeme best unto him;

---

1   Abbreviation in Greek letters for '*[I]Jesus Hominum Salvator*': 'Jesus Saviour of Man'.
2   This first section of the original manuscript contains male references (to a Prior) that are adapted as the text proceeds. Arrangements for the election of a Superior apply equally to the female Discalced, so I have edited the text to reflect this.
3   Gregory XIII (1572–85); Sixtus V (1585–90); Clement VIII (1592–1605).

4 To receaue the voyces of the sick wch cannot come to the grate – he who proceedes [presides] shall in presence of all those who are to giue voyces, name two graue religious and not suspected to goe fetch the voyces, wch they shall bring without eyther opening, or chaunging the bill … upon perill of their soules …

5 moreouer because that monasteries of the first Rule are alltogeather new, and haue not as yet many fitt persons to gouerne, wee doe permit that they may chuse againe, and continue [re-elect] their Pryoresse in the same Conuent, prouided allwaies yt she who is chosen againe haue three partes of the voyces, wth out wch three partes their reelection shall bee of noe value …

6 Noe religious may giue, or receaue any thinge, nor aske it allthough it ware of her father ore mother without permission of the Pryoresse, to whom all thinges are to be showne, wch shall be giuen ore brought.

Chapter 2: Of the receauing of Nouices and thir professions and of the number of religious wch they may haue in euery conuent

1 Let great heed be taken yt such persons as are receaued be persones giuen to praier and such as only seeke perfection and contempt of the world … it is better to consider this before, then to dismisse them afterward. They must not be under the age of seauenteene they must be alsoe healthfull of bodie, haueing a good understanding and fitt also to say the diuine office, and to helpe in the quire … if any of the aforesaid be wanting yt they be not receaued …

2 Being satisfied of the person, although she haue not any thinge to bestow in almes upon ye house, yet ought she not for that to be refused according as untill this present hath bin practised; and yt if she haue wherewith, and will giue it, if afterwards upon some occation it be not giuen, though it might be asked in iustice, yet it is to be done with such moderation as that noe skandall come therby;

3 Great heed is to be taken that ye reception of Nouices be not for interrest, because yt couetousnes may by litle and litle enter, in such sort, as rather the almes come to be respected, then the goodnes and quality of the person … Let them also remarke that it is not ye substance wch must maintaine them, but their fayth, perfection and their confidence in God only …

4 The Prouinciall cannot receaue any religious to be either cloathed or professed wth out ye voyce of ye greater parts of ye Conuent …

5 The lay sisters wch are to be receaued ought to be strong … and they must be a yeare wth out the habitt, except their great vertue deserue that it should be sooner giuen them … They shall not weare the blacke vaile, neither is it to be giuen them, but they shall make their profession a yeare after they haue taken the habitt. They are to be used wth all loue and fraternall charity, and to be prouided for, both in cloathing and diet, like ye rest;

6 Wee doe ordaine yt henceforwarde ye professions be not made at ye grate, but in ye Chapter House, where none are to be present, but only the religious of ye house. Let it be

done by the aduise of the greatest part, of those who haue voyces in the conuent, giueing their voyces secretly by white, and blacke beanes;

7 Before the receauing of any to be cloathed, there must be made diligent inquirie of her health and what spirit she hath for to perform this holy obseruances because it is hard to remedy it after they are receaued. This notwithstanding doth not oblige, she not haueing careied her selfe during the yeare of her probation wth diligence required to receaue her to profession of whom there is not that hope wch is required ...

8 If an nouice hath bin once put out of one monastery, she shall not be receaued in another, unlesse by the voyce of all ye religious of yt conuent from whence she was dismissed, and she shall neuer be receaued in ye same againe;

9 Item wee doe declare yt ye Religious who haue found any monastery canot be out out of ye same, unlesse it be for some very urgent cause by ye aduise of the Prouinciall;

10 For as much as ye holy Councell of Trent[4] doth defend [forbid] that in noe monasterys there be greater number of religious than yt which it can comodiously maintaine, haueing regard to ye reuenue and almes ... Wee doe ordaine yt in the monasteryes yt are to be poore, and haue noe rent, there may not in anie sort be more then 13 or 14, and in those wch shall haue rent, noe more then 20 ... [and that] there be not more then three lay sisters;

9[5] And when it shall happen yt for any just occasion any religious goeth into another Conuent, if it be knowne yt she must stay long time, another may be receaued in her place;

11 ... in those monasteryes wch shall be founded to haue rent, there may be receaued noe more then fourteene religious untill such time as it hath reuenue sufficient to maintaine more, unlesse one be received to cloathing wch bringeth a sufficient portion to maintaine more ... and ye Superiour ore Prioresse cannot goe against it under paine of being put out of her office.

Chapter 3: of ye Inclosure

1 That they see noe body wthout a vaile unless it be their fathers or mothers, ore brothers ... wth such persons as may receaue rather edification and ayde as in our exercises of prayer ... and not for recreation; and that it be alwaies with a companion, except it be for the affaires of ye soule;

2 The Prioresse is to haue ye keyes of the grate, and also of ye gate. When ye Phisition or Surgeon enter, or other necessary persons, or ye Confessarious, there must allwaies be two companions; and when ye sicke is to confesse, there must allwaies be a companion,

---

4   The primary council of early modern Catholic reform, held between 1545 and 1563.
5   Misnumbered in the original text.

somewhat distant, but in sorte yt she may see ye Confessarious to whom she may not speake ... and one of ye companions shall ring ye bell to ye end yt ye rest of ye conuent may know there be strangers in ye house;

The religious may not in any sort goe fourthe to ye church or lodging of ye Touriers of ye first gate of ye house, but there but be a Sacristan or Tourier, to locke ye church doores ... to keepe ye inclosure ordained ...

4 The Nouices shall be visited, as well as ye professed, to ye end yt if they haue any discontentment it may be knowne, for we desire nothing else but yt they may stay heere of their owne free will and accorde ...

5 That they doe not regard or esteeme of ye affayres of ye world, nor treat of them, excepting in such thinges as may helpe or giue remedie unto thos who speake of them ... that ye companion be carefull yt this be obserued, and is obliged to aduertise [inform] ye Prioresse, if it be not kept: and when she shall omitt this she shall incurre ye same penalty yt she who ded comitt ye fault ... After haueing giuen twice warning, the third time, if she amend not, she shall haue nine dayes imprisonment, and euery third day she shall receiue a discipline in ye Refectory, for yt is a thinge yt greatly importeth the good of religion;

6 That they wth draw as much as conueniently they can dealing wth their parents, because besides ye affection to their affaires, it would be difficult not to inter medle wth worldy things;

7 They ought to be carefull in speaking to those abroad, all tho' they be their neere kindred, unlesse such persons as take pleasure in discourse of Godly thinges ...

Also ye Prouincial, vicare or visiter shall know yt ye Councell of Trent doth forbidd under paine of excomunication ... that noe persone of what age, estate, or quality soeuer, may enter in to ye monasterys of religious woemen, saue only in case of necessity ... saue only yt wch those of the monastery cannot put in execution wth out helpe of those abroad, as artificers for their worke, ye phisitian, surgen, or ye lik;

9 ... wee comand yt perticular care be had ye religious men goe not in to ye monasteries of religious woemen; and we doe forbidd unto ye Prouinciall and visiter yt in noe case they doe enter in to ye monasteries of religious woemen, except it be for some thing very necessary wch cannot be done at ye grat[6] ...

10 In noe case ye Confessour ought not to enter ... if it be not to confesse ye sicke when ye phision shall say yt it is necssary, and to minister unto her ye Bd Sacrement and extrem unction, when it tis time. And if ye sicke party, after she hath received the sacrements, hath any scruple ye Confessor may enter to reconcile her ... And if there be any sicke wch for a long time haue kept her bedd, and cannot by any meanes come to ye grate or confession seate, the Confessor in this case may enter sometimes to confesse her ...

---

[6] So, for example, a Dominican brother was permitted to enter, to carry a heavy image held in the care of his Order, taking it to the bedside of a nun who was ill (see p. 189).

Chapter 4: Of Dinner and Refection

1 ... They shall ringe to dinner at a leauen of ye clocke and a halfe [at 11.30], when it shall be fasting day of the church, and att a leauen [11.00] when it shall be fasting day of ye Order; and in sommer dinner shall be att tenn aclocke;

2 ... if before they sitt to dinner, our Lord shall inspire any of ye religious to do any mortification, she shall aske leaue to do it ...

3 out of ye houre of dinner and supper, noe religious shall eate or drinke without permission;

4 ... [Afterwards] all may speake togeather [providing it is] discourse wch good religious ought to haue ...

5 That gameing or such sporte be not in any sort permitted ...

6 That they haue care not to be troublesome or tedious one to another ... This houre of coming togeather being ended, in ye somer they shall sleepe an houre, and they wch will not sleepe, shall keepe silence;

7 That none of ye sisters imbrace one another, or touch face or hands or haueing particular friendshipe, but yt they loue one another all in genarall as our Sauiour Jesus Christ often comanded his Apostles, and seeing thay are so few in number it will be easy to doe it, indeauouring to imitate their spouse who hath giuen his life for us all. This point of louing one another in generall is of great importance.

Chapter 5: Of the Canonicall Hours and Spirituall Thinges

1 They shall say Mattins after nine ... and not before ...

2 They shall be rung to this examination, and she whom ye Mother Pryoress comandeth shall read a litle of ye mistery;

3 In somer, they shall rise at fiue ... and be in prayer till sixe, and in winter they shall rise at six and remaine in prayer untill seuen ...

4 On Sondayes and feastiuall dayes, they shall sing Masse, Vesperas and Mattines ...

5 A litel before dinner they shall ring to ye examen of what they haue done untill then, and purpose to amend ye greatest fault ...

6 Vespers shall be said at ye strooke of two, and affter Vespers, ye lecture shall be made ...

7 ... ye religious ought to keepe silence after Compline untill Prime of ye day following ...

Chapter 6: of Comucation and Confession

1 They shall comunicate ye Sondays and feasts ...

2 ... The Pryoress and ye Prouinciall or visiter shall seeke a Priest of such life, age and manner as shall bee to their satisfaction ...

Chapter 7: of Pouerty and Temporalls[7]

They ought to liue of almes wth out any reuenues where ye community are in rich and wealthy cittyes ... in places where they can not be sustayned by almes only, they may haue reuenues ...

2 ... They ought to helpe themselfes wth ye labour of their hands ...

3 That in noe sort ye sisters possesse any thing in perticular ... neither for dyett, nor for cloathing, and yt they haue neither coffer, nor deske, or cubbert ... but yt all be in common ... because in litle thinges ye Diuell may seeke to hender ye perfection of true pouerty ...

4 The almes wch our labour shall giue, in money, shall be presently put in to the coffer of three keyes[8] ...

Chapter 8: Of Fasting and Habitts

1 She must fast from ye day of ye Exultation of ye Holy Crosse in September untill Easter ... They ought neuer to eate flesh, unlesse it be for necissity ...

2 ... one ye fast dayes ... ye ordinary meate of Refectory shall neither be eggs, nor whitt meates ... ye Pryoresse may dispence wth this ... wth ye sicke and those wch haue neede and wth whom fish doth not agree ...

3 The habitt must be of course stament of a darke brownish couler wthout dye, called in Spanish xerga [serge] or sayall ... that ye sleeues be straite and no langer at ye one end then at ye other. That ye habitt be round wth out pleats, noe longer before, then behinde and downe to ye feet;

---

7   The issue of poverty was of deep concern to Teresa de Jesus when she was establishing her first convent: 'Since I knew it was in the rule and saw that observing poverty would be more perfect, I couldn't persuade myself that the monastery should have an income. ... I found so many disadvantages in having an income and saw it would be so great a cause of disquiet and even distraction ...' (*Book*, 304).

8   The chest of three keys is mentioned often in the papers: having three separate locks and keyholders ensured that money or important papers could be secured with three witnesses responsible for their safe keeping. The text states who should hold the keys (p. 252).

The scapular[9] shall be ye same, four fingers shorter then ye habitt; the mantle of ye quire as long as ye scapular and yt as litle stuffe be spent as may be ... The tuckes or head cloaths shall be hempe or corse linnen, not playted [pleated], and ye scapular a boue it. The tunicks shall be stamett[10] ... The shoes of breaded hempe and cordes, called alspargates and for decency ye stockings shall be of some course linen ...

... The beddes shall be without mattresses and only canuesse filled wth strawe ...

4 That euery one haue her bedd apart ...

5 That there neuer be eyther in their habitts or on there bedds any couloured thing ...

6 They shall haue their haire cutt yt they may not loose time in koming it: they ought neuer to haue looking glasses nor any curious thinge, but all contempt of themselues.

Chapter 9: Of Labour and Handy Workes

1 That they shall neuer doe any curious [over-decorative] worke ...

2 ... lett euery one endeauour to worke yt ye others may be nourished ...

Chapter 10: Of Silence and Retyring to their Celles

1 Silence shall be kept from Compline ... [until] Prime ye next morning; ... The religious may not speake to one another wthout leaue ...

2 That ye Pryoresse haue care yt there be good bookes, especially ye Charereux, ye Liues of Saints, ye Oratery of Religions, the Contempt of ye World, those of Fa Leruis Granada[11] and Father Pecter of Alcantard[12] ...

3 ... [When not in community or offices] euery one shall remaine apart by her self in ye cell or hermitage wch ye Pryoresse haue permitted her ...

4 Noe religious may enter into ye cell of another without leaue of the Mother Pryoresse;

There ought neuer to be a place where they assemble to worke togeather, fearing yt this might giue occasion of breaking silence in being together.

---

9   A long strip of cloth with an opening for the head, worn hanging in front and behind, over the habit.
10   Presumably 'stammel', a kind of woollen cloth, often of a reddish colour.
11   Luis of Granada (1505–88), a favourite writer of Teresa de Jesus. His works had been placed on the Valdés Index in 1559 (Teresa de Jesus, 1976 ed., 30).
12   Peter of Alcántara (1499–1562), canonized in 1669, a Franciscan penitent and reformer. A confessor and mentor of Teresa de Jesus, he wrote a *Treatise on Prayer and Meditation* that was translated into many languages (see Teresa de Jesus, 1976 ed., 482).

Chapter 11: Of Humility and Penaunce

1 The table [rota] yt is made for those yt are to sweepe shall begin wth ye Mother Pryoresse to ye end she giue good example in all. There must be great care that yt those who are in offices of ye Community, and Dispencers, prouide with charity according to all necessity of ye sisters, as well for ye Nouviture as for ye rest. There is no more due to ye Pryoeress and ye ancienter then to ye others as ye Rule ordayneth, but only haue regarde to ye necessity and ye age, and more to ye necessity then ye age, because yt oftentimes those who haue more yeares haue lesse neede …

2 That they neuer use to ye Pryoresse nor any of ye rest these words, 'Dame' or 'Mada[m]e', nor 'Ladyshipe'; but lett them use humble tearmes: ye Pryoress and Subpryoresse and those wch haue bin Pryoresses shall be called 'Mothers' and ye rest 'Sisters';

3 The house shall be built wthout any curiosity, unlesse it be ye Church; there ought to be nothinge yt is curious, ye stuffe and timber shall be rude, and grosse, ye house litle, ye peeces low, so yt it may suffice necessity and haue nothinge superfluous. It is good to haue nothinge superfluous. It is good to haue as stronge, and lasting, as conueniently may be. As for ye inclosure, yt ye walles be high, and yt there be a field where hermitages may be made, for ye religious to retire themselues to meditation as our holy fathers did;

4 yt noe one reprehend another of ye faults which she shall see her comitt, and if ye faults be great yt she aduertise [advise] her wth charity alone; and if she doth not amend being aduertised thrice, lett her tell ye Pryoresse, but none of ye other sisters. And being yt there be zealatrices[13] who haue charge to obserue ye faults, ye others ought not to trouble themselues, but lett those passe wch they see, and take care of their owne defects, and not medle if those yt are in offices … doe faile therein …

5 for soe much as all is ordayned and conformable to our Rule, ye correction of faults wch shall be comitted in yt wch hath bin sayd shall be done by ye penaunces wch shall be sett in ye end of these Constitions, touching both ye great and litle faults. The Mother Pryoresse may, wth charity and discretion, ordaine all this, and shall not oblige any for ye obseruance of this under sine but under corporall paine;

6 Besides ye discipline of rodds, wch ought to be taken because ye seremoniall doth ordaine some, as when they say serry in Lent, ore in Aduent;

… This discipline shall be taken in ye quire after Mattines, and none ought to take any discipline or doe any act of penaunce wthout leaue of the Mother Pryoresse.

Chapter 12: Of ye Sicke

1 The sicke shall be treated wth much loue and compassion … They [shall] be visited and comforted by ye sisters;

2 Ther is to be apointed an Infirmarion who hath charity required for such an office …

---

[13] Monatrices, responsible for observing the faults of others.

... [Ensure] that they haue linen, good bedds, wth mattresses and sheets and lett them be treated very neatliy and charitably;

3 That non of ye religious speake whether there be litle meate or too much, or whether it be well drissed or noe. The Pryoresse and Dispencer shall haue care yt what God sendeth be well drissed ...

4 The sisters are bound to tell ye Mother Pryoresse, and ye Nouices there Mistrese, ye need they haue, be it for cloathing ore dyet ...

Chapter 13: Of ye Dead

1 The sacraments ought to be adminsitered as it is said in ye bookes of ye ceremonies, and ye obsequies and buriall of those who dye in ye conuent wth ye vigills and high masse and, if it be possible, they shall haue ye Masse of St Gregory said[14] ...

2 ... Euery one shall say an office of ye dead, or altogether in ye quire, and if it be possible there shall be said a High Masse for them, and those that are not of ye quire shall say 30 Pater Nosters and so many Aue Maries ...

Chapter 14: Exhortations to what are obliged as well as ye Mother Pryoresse as ye others in there offices

Pryoresse ... haue care yt ye Rules and Constitutions be in all thinges entyrely obserued, and is to haue great zeale of ye decency and inclosure of ye house ... and yt they bee prouided of all thinges necessary be it for ye spirituall or temporall, and yt wth a motherly loue, and yt shee endeauoir to be beloued, yt she may bee obeyed;

2 The Pryoress shall giue ye charge of ye Porteresse and Sacristine to persons in whom she hath confidence, and may chaunge them when she thinketh good, to ye end it may be avoyded yt none in any wise tye or engage themselues to offices; and she shall also prouid all the others, excepting ye Subpryoresse and ye Depositarie, ye wch shall be sett by election ...

Subpryoresse ... haue care of ye quire, and yt ye office be well said and song leasurely to wch she ought to looke diligently. When ye Pryoresse shall be absent, she shall preceed in her place, and ought to bee allwaies in ye comunity and reprehend ye faults wch shall be comitted in ye quire and in ye refectory when ye Pryoresse shall not be present.

The Depositaryes ... ought euery monith to take an account of her wch is the Receaur in ye presence of the Pryoresse ...

---

14 According to legend, whilst celebrating Mass in Rome, Pope Gregory had experienced a vision of Christ displaying his wounds. Subsequent Popes gave indulgences to those who prayed before such an image or used this form of the Mass (see Mâle, 1986 ed., 94–100; Duffy, 1992, 238–40).

2 There ought to be a coffer wth three keyes for to put in ye registers, writings and almes of ye conuent. The Pryoresse shall haue one of ye keyes and ye two ancient depositaryes ye other tow.

Sacristan … is to haue all thinges of ye church, and to take care yt God be serued with all reuerence and neatness;

2 She ought to haue care yt euery one goe to Confession in order, and not permitt any one to goe to ye Confession seat wth out leaue, under paine of a great fault if it be not to confesse to him who is ordained.

The Receauer and she yt hath charge of ye torne

1 The office of ye Receauer and great Tourrier, who ought to be but one, is to haue care and cause to be bought to yt wch shall bee necessiary for ye house …

2 She ought to speake lowe at ye tourne, and wth edification, and to haue regarde wth charity to ye necesity of ye sisters;

3 She is to haue care to wright [write] ye expences and receipts, not contest or use many wordes when she shall buy any thinge, but either take or leaue it after she hath sayd … what she shall giue for it;

4 She shall not permitt any of ye sisters to come to ye tourne wth out leaue, and she shall presently call a companion if she goe to ye great;

5 She shall not giue account unto any body of yt wch shall passe, but to ye Pryoresse only;

6 She shall giue letters to noe body but to ye Pryoresse, who shall first redde them; neither shall she bringe any message unto any one wth out hauing related it fi[r]st to ye Pryoresse, and shall neither report any thinge to those yt are abroad under paine of the grieuious fault.

Monatrice[s] … are to haue care to obserue ye faults they see in things of importance, and to relate them to ye Superiour;

2 Sometimes, by her comaundements they shall reprehend them in publike, be it ye least to ye ancienter, to ye end they exercise humility, and those who shall be reprehended shall not reply unto any thinge allthough they find themselues without fault.

Mistress[es] of Nouices … ought to be of great prudence, prayer and spiritt, and to haue great care to read ye Constitutions to ye nouices, and to teach them all they haue to doe, be it ceremonyes or morifications. She shalle looke more to ye interiour then exteriour, making them giue an account euery day how they haue profited in prayer and how they carrye themselues in ye mistery wch they ought to meditate of, and what profitt they draw out of it. She shall instruct them how they ought to gouerne themselues in time of gust and aridity, and how to breake their wills euen in smale thinges. Lett her who hath this office bee carefull she forgett her self in nothinge, for her charge is to bring up soules in which Allmighty God may dwell. That she gouerne them wth compassion and loue, not wondering at their faults ... litle mortifying euery one according as she perceaueth their spiret can beare; and yt she make greater account of ye impediments wch they haue to vertue then of ye rigour of penance ...

2 when ye Pryoresse shall see yt she hath noe body yt can performe ye charge of Mistresse of Nouices, she shall doe it her selfe ...

3 All ye religious shall giue an account once a month to ye pryoresse of ye profitt wch they haue made in prayer ... And to doe this in great humility and mortification ...

4 ... wee forbidd ye Pryoresse and Mistresse of Nouices to presse ther religious much in this point [of rendering a monthly account]. And lett ye religious know yt neither this, nor ye rest of these Constitutions, doe not oblige them to sinne ...

Chapter 15: of ye Chapter of Faults

1 The Chapter of Faults ought to be made once a weeke ... ye sisters shall be corrected wth charity and [it] shall be held at an hour most comodious and most conuenient for them;

2 ... all assembled in Chapter, at ye signe wch ye Superiours shall giue, yt ye sisters wch hath ye office of Lectrice shall shall read some thinge of these Constitutions and of ye Rules ... Then, if ye Pryoresse desire to say any thing upon ye lecture or correction of ye sisters ... [they shall be] prostrating themselues till they be comanded to rise, and being risen they shall sitt downe againe. The discourse being ended, ye Superiour haueing giuen ye signe, they shall rise to recite there faults, begining wth ye nouices, afterwards ye lay sisters, and then followes ye most ancient. They shall come to ye midest of ye Chapter House, tow and tow, and their tell ye Superiour their manifest faults but furst ye nouices, lay sisters and those wch haue noe voyces must be appoynted to retire;

3 ye religious ought not to speake in ye Chapter only for tow thinges, saying thire faults, or simply those of their sisters, and answering ye Superiour ... She yt shall be accused, lett her take heed of accusing another out of suspition only which she hath of her; and if some time it happen to any to doe it, she shall receaue ye saime punishment of ye crime yt she hath accused another ... To ye end yt ye vices and faults be not couered, ye religious may tell ye Mother Pryoresse yt wch she hath seene ore heard, and also ye Prouinciall or visiter;

4 She also who shall relate anything falsly of another shall receaue ye same chastisment, and shall be lickwise obliged to restitute as much as she can ye faime of her whom she hath defaimed. And she wch shall be accused shall not answere, if she be not commaunded, and then shall humly say, 'Benedicite', and if she answere impatiently she shall then be more seuerely punished, according to ye discretion of the Superiour, but ye chasticement shall be giuen her when ye passion is appeased;

5 That ye religious take heed yt they doe not diuulge or publish ye sacretts of ye Chapter;

6 All yt ye Mother hath corrected or resolued in Chapter, noe religious shall repeate it out of ye same by way of murmuring because from thence proceeds discords. This troubleth ye peace of ye conuent and produces partialityes …

7 The Mother Pryoresse or Superiour shall correct wthout dissimulation, wth zeale of charity and loue of justice, ye faults wch shall be openly acknowledged, or of wch ye sisters shall be accused, according to yt wch shall be related to heerafter;

8 The Mother Pryoresse may mitigate or lesson ye paine due to ye fault when it was not cometted of malices, at ye least for ye first, second and third time, but those whom she shall see to offend of malice, or of a vicious custome she ought to augment their former punishment and not to remitt or deminish it, wth out authority of ye Prouinciall or visiter;

9 Those wch haue acustome to comitt light faults shall haue ye penaunce giuen to ye greater faults, and so shall former pennances be augmented to others if it be by custome they faile;

10 The faults being said and ye corrections giuen, they shall say ye Psalme 'Deus misereatur nostri'[15] wth ye surplus of yt wch is ordayned by ye booke of ye Cirmonyes.

Psalmes for ye Chapter[16]

Chapter ye 16: of ye Light Faults

1 A light fault is if, after ye sound of ye bell, a religious shall be slowe in preparing her selfe to come to ye quire in good order and handsome;

2 If any one enter after ye office is begun, or readeth or singeth ill, and if she faile in saying, and doth not humble herselfe in kissing ye ground in ye presence of all;

3 If any doe not prouide for ye lecture in due time;

4 If any one through negligence hath not in ye quire ye booke in wch she ought to say her office;

5 If any one laugh in ye quire, or causeth others to laugh;

6 If any one come slowe to spirituall busines or worke;

7 If any one contemneth and doth not duly obserue ye prosternations, inclinations and other ceremonies;

8 If any one make any noyse or disquiet others in ye quire, dormitary or in ye cells;

---

15   Psalm 67: 'God be merciful to us, and bless us …'
16   These are listed as Psalm 46, 47 and half of 48.

9 If any one be slowe to come at due houre to ye Chapter, Refectory or to ye worke;

10 If any one speake idle words;

11 If she handle or breake by negligence, or loose any thinge wch serueth to ye conuent;

12 If any one drinke or eate wthout leaue.

Those wch shall accuse themselues of theese fauts, or such licke, they shall haue imposed or giuen in pennance one prayer or more prayers according to ye quality of ye faults or some worke of humilty, or silence, especially for haueing broaken ye silence of ye Order; or abstinence of some meate, or some refection, or meale.

Chapter 17: Of ye Midle Fau[l]ts

1 A midle fault is if any one doth not come to ye quire wth in ye first Psalme, and when she cometh late she ought to prostrate untill ye Mother Prioress or Superiour comand her to rise;

2 If any one doe undertake to read ore sing otherwise then is accoustomed to be done;

3 If any one being not attentive to ye deuine office shall by lifting up her eyes make appeere ye lightnes of her spiret;

4 If any one shall handle irreuerently ye ornaments of ye Alter;

5 If any one be wanting at Chapter or handy worke, at sermon, or be not found at comon refectory;

6 To omitt wittingly yt wch is comaunded in gennerall;

7 If she be found neglegent in ye offece wch is in her charge;

8 To speake in Chapter wth out leaue;

9 if being accused she excuse herselfe in speakin alowde;

10 if for reuenge she goeth about to accuse another of some things whereof she herselfe hath ben accused by ye other ye same day;

11 if any one carry her selfe disorderly ether in her habitt or head dressing;

12 If any one sweareth, or speaketh irreuerently, or wch is more grieueously if she make a custome of it;

13 If any one Sister dispute against another or speake any thinge wherat ye sister m[a]y be offended;

14 If any one refuse to pardon her wth whome she is offended if she do aske it;

15 If any one enter in to ye offices of ye conuent without leaue;

16 The chasticement of ye forsayde faults and ye licke shall be by a discipline in ye Chapter, which is to be giun by ye Superiour, or by her whom she shall comaund.

17 She wch hath accused shall not giue a discipline to her wch hath failed, nor ye younger to the ancienter.

Chapter 18: Of the Grieuous Faults

1 Grieuous faults is if any one be found speaking iniurious to another … saying disordinate words of choller [out of anger] and not religiously;

2 If any one curse or reproach any of ye Sisters to make her asshamed of ye fault wch is passed, for wch she hath satisfyed, or doth reproach her of her natural defects, or those of her parents;

3 If any defend her owne fault or yt of anothe[r];

4 If any one be found of purpose to tell a lye;

5 If any one be accustomed to breake silence;

6 If any one, wth out just cause or leaue, doe breake the fasts appoynted by ye Order especially those ordayned by the Church;

7 To take any thing from another, or yt wch belongeth to ye community, or to change her cell, or habit, wth another;

8 To enter in ye hour of sleepe, or at other time, in to ye cell of another wth out leaue, or euident necessity;

9 To be wth out leaue of ye Pryoresse at ye tourne, speak house, or any other places where seculars be;

10 If any of ye Sisters doe threaten another wth anger, lifting up her hand or any other thinge, to strike her, ye paine of ye grieuous fault shall be doubled upon her.

11 Those who shall aske pardon for ye faults of this kind, or such as haue bene accused of them, they shall haue two corrections in ye Chapter and shall fast two dayes wth bread and water and shall eat in ye presence of all at ye end of ye table, without either table or table cloath, but for each as shall be accused they shall haue one correction more, and one dayes fast more.

Chapter 19: Of ye more Grieuous Fault

1 The more grieuous fault is if any one be so bold as irreuerently to contend against ye Mother Pryoress or Superiour, or speake any thing in any discurtious manner ore unto her;

2 If any one maliciously striche [hits] any of ye Sisters, they doe incurr by yis act sentence of excommunication and all ought to fly from her;

3 If any body be found breeding discordes [discontent] amongst ye Sisters, or custoime to detract in their absence or muermering of another;

4 If any one undertake to speake wth those abroad wth out leaue of Mother Pryoresse, or wth out a companion wch may be wittnes and heere her playnely.

If she hath been accused and conuinced of such faults, she shall prostrate upon ye ground, beging deuoutly pardon, and uncouering her shoulders she shall receaue ye sentence accordng to her meritts, wth a disicplene so long as it shall please ye Mother Pryoresse; and after she is comaund to rise she shall goe to ye cell wch ye Mother Pryoresse shall apoynt her, and none shall be so hardy or bold as to goe speake to her, nor send her any thinge; to the end yt by this meanes she may know yt she is seperated from ye conuent, and drpriued of ye company of angells, and during ye time she doth this pennance she shall not communicat, neither shall she haue any office, nor any obedience enjoyned, neither shall she be comaund any thinge: but contrary shall be depriued of the office she had before. She shall haue no voyce nor inttrrest in ye Chapter, unlesse for her owne accusation, she shall be ye least of all untill she hath made full and entire satisfaction. She shall not sitt wth ye others, but sitt herselfe in midle of ye Refectory upon ye bare boards wth her mantle; and shall haue but bread and water, unlesse for pitty she hath some other thinge giuen her, by comaund of ye Mother Pryoresse who shall behaue herselfe towards her wth compassion and shall send one of ye Sisters to comfort her. If she haue humility of hart, lett her intention be furthered to wch all ye conuent shall giue fauour and ayd …

5 If any rise manyfestly against ye Mother Pryoresse or against her Superiours, or if against them she imagine or doth something wch is not lawfull or decent, she shall doe ye afiresayd penneance during forty days and shall be depriued of voyce and interest in ye Chapter, and of ye office she had what soeuer it was;

If by any conspiracy of this sort, or any malitious plott, it happen yt seculare persons intermedle wth these matters of ye confusion, discreditt and domage of ye Sisters, or of ye monastery, ye religious whoe haue done this shall be put in prison, and shall be there detayned according to ye greatnes of ye scandall wch there shall arriue. And if, by occasion of this, there shall come diuision or parciallityes in ye Monastery, those who shall make them and also those who shall fauour them, shall incurre sentence of excommunication and shall be imprisonned;

6 If any one shall hinder ye pacifycation or correction of faults, alleadging yt ye Superiour proceeds of hatred or fauour or such like thinges, she shall be punished wth ye same peannance as those who shall conspire against ye Mother Pryoresse;

7 If any one be so bold as to giue or receaue letters wthout ye leaue of ye Mother Pryoresse, or send out any thinge or receaue for herselfe yt wch is giuen her. Likewise if any worldly or seculare person be scandalised by ye fault or ye sister, beside ye pennance ordayned by these constitutions, when they shall goe to say conoicall hours and ye grace after dinner, she shall remayne prostrate before ye dore of ye quire whilst ye sisters passe.

Chapter 20: Of the Most Grieuous Fault

1 The most grieuous fault is ye incoriged blenes [incorrigible-ness] of her who doth not feare to come to faults and refuseth ye pennance;

2 If any one be apostata [renegade from religion], and goeth fourth out of ye Monastary ore limites of ye conuent, she incureth sentence of excomunication;

3 If one be disobedient, and by a manyfest rebellion shall not obey ye comaundedment wch ye Pryores or Superiour shall giue ether to her in perticular or to all in generall;

4 If any one fall into ye sinne of sensuality (which God permitt not who is ye strenght of all those yt hope in him);

5 If any one be proprietary [proprietorial, keeping property], or confesse to be so, and if at her death she be found so, she shall not haue ecclesiasticall buriall;

6 If any one lay violent hands upon the Mother Pryoresse or any other Sister, or any sote whatsoeuer shall discouer unto strangers any crime of ye sisters, or of ye conuent, whence ye religious or conuent may be defamed, or shall open other secret act of ye conuent;

7 If any one seeke for her selfe or for others any ambitious thinge or office, or going against ye Constetitions of ye religion, such religious shall be put in preson, wth fast and abstinence more or less, according to ye quality and quantity of fault, and according to ye discretion of ye Mother Pryoresse, or of Prouinciall, ore Visiter. The Sisters shall leade her to ye prison presently upon ye comaund of ye Mother Pryoresse under paine of rebellion, whosoeuer it be of ye religious yt hath comitted such faults, and none shall speake unto her so longe as she shall be in prison, unlesse it be they who keepe here, and non of them shall send her any thinge under ye same pennance. If ye imprisoned religious goe fourth of the prison, she who looketh unto her, or she by whose meanes she went fourth, being conuensed of it, shall be put in ye same prison and shall stay there so longe as ye fault of ye imprisoned merited;

8 There must be a prison ordayned where they may be who comett those things, and being prisonners for these scandalous faults they canot be deliuered but by ye Prouinciall or Visiter;

9 She who shall be an Apostata shall be put in to prison, and she who falleth into ye sine of ye flesh, and she who shal comitt such crimes as deserue death in ye world, and those who will not humble themselues to acknowleg their fault, whence they shall neuer be deliuered, except their amendment and patience haue ben noted in thse times to be such, as by ye counsell of those yt pray for them, they mirett to be deliuered out of ye sayd prison, by ye Prouenciall, wth ye consent of ye Mother Pryoresse.

Each one of them who shall be in this prison must know yt they haue lost there voyce, actiue and passiue, and likwise their place, and shall be depriued of all legitimall act and of all offices; and allthough she be deliuered out of prison, she shall not be for all yt restored to ye aforsaid things, if it be not by an expresse benefett granted at her deliuery out of prison. And though she hath her place rendred, yet for all yt she shall not haue a voyce in Chapter, and allthough she haue ye actiue voyce unto her, yet she hath not ye passiue, unless it be exprisly granted her as hat ben sayed. But for all this she yt falleth into these falts shall not be established againe to be permeted to any office, not cannot accompany ye sisters to ye tourne, nor other where. If she fall into ye sine of sensuality, allthough she being sorry, shall come of her owne accord to aske mercy and pardon, she cannot be by any meanes receaued, but by ye permission and counsell of ye Prouenciall, or if there doe not fall out some reasonable cause;

20 If any one be conuinced before [the] Pryoresse to haue giuen false wittnes, or been accustomed to defame others, she shall doe her pennance at ye time of reflection being wthout a cloake, haueing nothing but her scapular, upon wch there shall be sewed tow tounges of white cloath before and behinde in different manners[17]; and being in ye midest of ye Refectory she shall eate bread and drinke water upon ye ground, to shew yt this pennance was giuen her for ye great vice of touching and thence she shall be brought to prison; and if any time she be deliuered, she shall haue no voyce, nor place;

21 If ye Pryoresse (wch God forebidd) fall in to any of these sayd faults, she shall be presently deposed to be very grieuously punished.

The end of ye Rule and Constitution.

---

[17] Presumably for modesty, the scapular being 'four fingers shorter then ye habitt' (p. 249).

Appendix 2

How the Prioress is to Exercise the Religious in Mortifications

This extract is from a two-page seventeenth-century manuscript originating at Lierre (*L3.5*). It indicates how the Prioress should effect obedience through imposing mortifications on the religious. Within a contemplative discipline, obedience was considered to free the nun from attachment to worldly concerns so that she might focus inwardly. Whilst the Lives suggest that some religious were proficient in this, other nuns consider it to be the aspect of profession with which they had most difficulty.

These notes suggest a variety of ways to instil and test obedience – ranging from frequently changing instructions (a technique employed by Mary Xaveria's confessor, see pp. 138–9), to sending a nun on senseless errands, to leaving objects around to see if anyone is curious enough to look at them, thereby breaking codes concerning modesty, about which Anne of the Ascension had also written: '… no chasting [casting] the eye curiusly about. no ernest nor lowde speaking … the hands but iuned [joined] to gether or held in some composed manar a gate desontly [decently] fast with out any affectui motion …' (*L1.6.I*, 1). Clearly such disciplines were intended to strengthen the alignment between bodily and mental demeanour.

[*L3.5*, 1–2]

A Gennerall Practies how the Prioriss is to excercisse the religious in mortyfycations, euery one according to ye spirittuall proffet they make of it, wth zeall & charrity

Mortyfication being the grownde & presse of all vertue, & yt wch makes mentall prayer … of value …

… ye gennarall Rulle, for memory sake, in what ye Prioriss should exerciss ye religious in are thees following:

… Often times to change suddenly thinges yt be conuiniant as theer habbets, cells, bockes, ore what elces may be conuiniant …

… Sometimes to giue sudenly a penances wth out seeming to haue thought upon it, [such] as to kesse ye growned, ye feet of otherese present ore abssent, to keesse a post ore a pane in the kitchen & this not only in occations of defects but when it is well knowen theer is none;

... To a[p]point one to keepe sillances whyle otheres speake, euen in time of recreation;
...

... Unexpectedly to cause others, wth whome they are in offices, to reprehend them ...

... To lay things upon downe ye housse, to see whether any one will be so curious as to locke upon them; & for yt curiosity of ye ey[e]s, giue some lettle reprehention in ye Community or to weer a bynder ouer theer ey[e]s;

... Att an on uisiall [unusual] time to send them to speake theer faults of something wch they neuer thought of, as in time of ye 2 reffetory, ore in ye ketchen, ore ye like;

... To giue occation sometimes to a religious to excuse her selfe and then emediattly to reprehend them for it;

... Sometimes to shew them [a] letter receaued & not giue them; & sometimes giue them & forbed [forbid] them to read them; & sometimes causs them to writt letters and find some faults wth them & tear them; & so in theer workes allso, when they thinke it tis very well & haue them taken much time about it, to slight it;

... To cause them sometimes to be accused wth out cause ore truth ...

... To giue lettle employments more then one can perform, [such] as offices in ye quire yt are incompattable ... Sende them to helpe an nothere wheer theer is noe great neessery, to try theer semple obedience;

...To send a religious [on senseless errands]; ... To cause them to sweept a gaine what hath ben sweept ...

Appendix 3A

A Letter to Anne of the Ascension, Warning her of Indiscretion and Promising New Novices

This letter from 1623 is now in the Lierre Carmel archive at Darlington (*L1.1*) though it is addressed to Anne of the Ascension, Prioress at Antwerp. The author has been identified most probably as Father Simon Stock, the religious name of Thomas Doughty (alias Dawson; *c*.1574–1652), who was a Carmelite in Belgium and, from 1631–52, chaplain to the Roper family in Canterbury (Hardman, 1936, 13–14).

The letter illustrates the dangers which Catholics faced in England at this time, and admonishes the Prioress for having sent a letter openly to an individual who would have been 'undone' had Protestant authorities intercepted the post (see Hallett, 2002b). The writer proceeds to give details of the income and demeanour of two young women who desire to 'come over', presumably to join the convent, in one case only if their father can be persuaded to allow them to do so. The identity of the women involved is unclear – if they ever arrived at the convent – and hardly matters, since in so many ways the letter reflects the situation which several Lives illustrate: reluctant parents resist the requests of their daughters to join the convent, and the daughters, as presumably in this case, are abetted by priests who facilitate their journey.

The letter also shows how money was sent to the convent from England via merchants who regularly traded – suggesting how useful such a 'cover' was, and how for this purpose the nuns' location in a city like Antwerp would have been especially helpful.

[*L1.1*]

1623

Deare Mother, I haue receaued tow letters from you, the one sent by one that come ouer. I desire you to haue great care in the letters you write, & neuer send any but by the post: you indorse the letter to mee & put the name of a gentleman, my frend, upon the back also, so yt if the letter had fallen in to the handes of Protestants you had undon him. So I desire you to be verie warie in sending letters, & what you write, the persequetion [persecution] is great, & is lyke to be greater.

She hath the 50 … the yeare, as I am informed, [and] may haue the tenne poundes from her own lyf so I will hould her in suspence untill I heare more from you … She that is but 13 years old & hath £20 a year untill £200 be payd unto her together, is very desirous to come and it is a very handsome gentlewomen, & of very good nature. The other shall haue £40 a yeare, is willing & her mother is willing: but her father is not, & though he loue me much, yet I cannot bring him unto it. She is 16 but little, & wthout any deformitie & of good wit, a gentlewoman & fit for any course.

The young gentleman I sent ouer is her kinsman: by his letters, her father may be woonne [persuaded] after a wyhle. The tow sisters are to come from there fathers unto an other place, where I may come more easyly unto them. They are gentlewomen of a good house. They haue also a brother that will come if I will send him & was very desirous to haue come … and I repent me that I did not send him. I stayed only upon his fathers good will. Then he had £30 in his purse, & now his father hath got itt from him.

I would get you some almes agaynst this Christenmas, if I did know how to send it, so fynd out some marchant there who hath correspondenc here, by whome I may now & then send you some litle thing.

… If you take that Duch woman, make her promise you under her hand that she will not seeke to bring in others.

Appendix 3B

Anne of the Ascension's Letter to Catherine of the Blessed Sacrament

This letter is addressed to Catherine of the Blessed Sacrament (Chapter 6), a religious who professed at Antwerp then transferred to Lierre in 1648. The letter, dated to c.1632, derives from the Lierre archive and is now at Darlington (*L1.1*).

In 1632, when consent was given to establish a Carmel at Alost, Sister Catherine was one of a small group (with Teresa of Jesus Maria and Margaret of St Teresa: Chapters 3, 30) sent to prepare the house (Hardman, 1936, 45). It was probably during such an absence that her Antwerp Prioress, Anne of the Ascension, wrote to her. The affectionate, supportive tone reflects the strong community bonds that continued to be forged across time and space (as Anne of the Ascension's own Life demonstrates in describing her relationship with Anne of St Bartholomew). In her Life, Catherine of the Blessed Sacrament expressed particular respect for Anne of the Ascension, and this letter and the scapular the Prioress prepared for Sister Catherine (Appendix 3C) indicate the mutuality of this regard.

[*L1.1*]

To my loving Sister Katren of ye Bsed Sacrament Carmelit[1]

My deer sister, I ame very sory to heer you are greued [grieved]. I praye be not soe bot teak corage [but take courage] for ye loue of God and be mery, for I doe promes yu it is bot a shet [short] tyme yt yu are to be frome us as I would haue told yu befor wee parted bot that I fered to greue yu so much tyme soeuer. Soe, good sister, be shoer [sure] I and all doe desier yr confort and loue yu very deerly, soe I know yu doe us and I haue so much confidense in yu as yt yu will pas thes mortificasion [mortifications] with corege, being I doe desier it of yu and cheafly because it is for Gods seruise to be parteaker [partaker] in so good a worke which all yu are. I praye remember my commendasions to Sister Terese,[2] Sister Elsebeth[3] ... and all the rest.

---

[1]   These words appear on the reverse of the letter.
[2]   Presumably Teresa de Jesus Maria (Worsley), her own sister.
[3]   Presumably Elizabeth of the Visitation (Emery).

Tell Sister Elsebeth I ame edefied to heer shee doth beheaue her self soe meryly [merrily] to recreat others, which I teak very kindly.

I, and all our Sisters heer, are in good health and wee shall all be as glad to see yu as yr self will be to see us, which shall be very shortly. Therfor I desier yu agan not to greeu: yu are my litle sister Katren, so doe not think I mean to leaue my litle une. Praye hard, good sister, yt all mea sucside [may succeed] to Gods glory, so good nicht dear sister.

[4]All ye sisters remember theyr loue to yu all. I ame euer yours Anne of ye Ascension.

---

4   This appears sideways across the paper.

Anne of the Ascension: 'A Scappuler of our Most Deare and Rd Mother … for Sister Catharine of the Bd Sacrament'

There are three copies of this paper in the Lierre archive, one of which bears the inscription of the title. A scapular would be worn in the same manner as an item of monastic dress of the same name (described p. 249) over the head and down the front of the chest, generally underneath clothing, sometimes containing an image, prayer or meditation, the wearing of which often had indulgences attached to it.

This is a copy of the whole text (*L1*.6). Written in two columns, it can be dated by reference to personal details to between 1623, when Catherine of the Blessed Sacrament, for whom it was written, professed, and 1644, when Anne of the Ascension, who wrote it, died. It seems likely that Anne of the Ascension composed or transcribed this piece for the other nun's personal devotion, perhaps in Sister Catherine's absence from Antwerp (as in the letter in Appendix 3B). It was presumably taken to Lierre by Sister Catherine when she transferred there in 1648; and since it appears to draw on Rodríguez's *Short and Sure Way to Heaven* (1630), a text which seems to have influenced Anne of the Ascension elsewhere in her writing (see pp. 41–43), a composition date between 1630 and 1644 seems plausible.

Anne of the Ascension's advice also echoes that of Teresa de Jesus when she wrote about the interior recollection and contemplative 'self-detachment' designed to bring about union of the soul with God, a process in which the soul 'seems to want to withdraw within, away from the outside noise' inducing 'a sleep of the faculties' (*Spiritual Testimonies*, 1976 ed., 426; see p. 40).

[*L1.6*]

Jesus Maria[1]

Being ons in discurs [once in discourse] with on that was much illumi nated by God, I was tould by them acecure [a secure] and short way and short way[2] to per fection, which is a continuall upholding of ye spiritt and an adheerig to God, which is to be don more by leeuing then working. I mean by [this] a continuall leauing and denying our selves in all things which natuer desiereth. This must be don with great sweettnes and repose of mind, as not as if wee wear to undertak a terible hard and laborius exersys, for it is nothing but a continuall scinking in to our senter, for the more wee incres in being unknowne and estraned to exterior sence and feelling, the more shall wee be drowned and loost in that replenishing fullnes which filleth[3] all placis with his greatnes. But this wee must not think to obtaine with out taking paines, for wee must put our selus ernestly to it without permitting natuer to take content in any thing, for if wee ar not resoluedd [resolved] to suffer the continuall want of all feelling sattisfaction, it is but in vaine to undertak this maner of proceeding. Moreouer, wee must all ways cary our selues with an upright and simple hart, remaining steadfast lyck a walle, neuer declining at what so euer may happen, no more heeding the repugnance of natuer in contradiction and aduercity [adversity] then if it belonged not unto us. In this maner wee must proceed with great care and whach fullnes ouer our interior desiers and affection and exterior actions, for the eye of our soule sayk that must allways[4] be fexed on God in that maner as if thar wear no other in the woreld but God and she alone, being both dome, deefe and blind to all things which tend not to ye per formance of our oblygation toward God, and charitable corispondence with our neabore [neighbour] – as allso quick and spidy in actes of obedience and charity, mild and affable in conversation, acomodating our selfes in all things to each other, well composed in our exterior cariage. For thay sayd that it was not possible fo[r] the mind to remaine in pese and quiet, except the iestuers and cariage of the body wear acording, for by only leening or going to on side or other, or in seecking our eas, or following sence in the least maner that can be, hindareth yt interior recolection of ye mind, which ye continuall mortification and faithfullness to God sett downe in this paper doth ordinarily bring with it.

1　　1r, Column 1.
2　　Repeated in the original, and echoing Rodríguez's title.
3　　Followed by 1r, column 2.
4　　Followed by 1v, column 1 (column 2 is blank).

Bibliography

Manuscript Sources

Darlington Carmelite Convent, County Durham (Lierre archive)

L1.1:	Letters to and from Anne of the Ascension (Anne Worsley)
L1.5:	Anne of the Ascension: prayers and appreciations
L1.6:	Anne of the Ascension: papers
L3.27:	Life of Margaret of Jesus (Margaret Mostyn)
L3.29:	Life of Margaret of Jesus (Margaret Mostyn)
L3.30:	Life of Ursula of All Saints (Elizabeth Mostyn)
L3.31:	Life of Margaret of Jesus (Margaret Mostyn)
L3.34:	Constitutions and the Rule of St Albert
L3.36:	The cure of Sister Anna Maria (Petronela van Dyck)
L3.39:	Life of Margaret of Jesus (Margaret Mostyn)
L3.5:	'How a Prioress is to exercise the religious in mortifications'
L4.39:	Life of Margaret of St Teresa (Margaret Downs)
L4.40:	Instructions on making silk flowers
L4.41:	A note on the eyes of Mary Margaret of the Angels (Margaret Wake)
L5.52:	Plans of the convent
L13.7:	Lierre Annals (recording deaths from 1652–1776)
L13.8:	Lierre Annals (recording deaths from 1779–1877)

St Helens Carmelite Convent, Merseyside (previously at Lanherne Carmelite Convent, Cornwell) (Antwerp archive)

A1: Antwerp Annals, Volume 1
A2: Antwerp Annals, Volume 2
A3: The Life of Mary Xaveria of the Angels (Catherine Burton)
A4: The Life of Mary Margaret of the Angels (Margaret Wake)

Printed and Unpublished Primary Sources

Baker, Augustine (1927 ed.) *Contemplative Prayer: Ven. Father Augustine Baker's Teaching Thereon from 'Sancta Sophia'*, ed. Benedict Weld-Blundell (Exeter: Catholic Records Press)
———, (1998 ed.) *A Secure Stay in All Temptations*, ed. John Clark (Salzburg: University of Salzburg)

———— (1999 ed.) *Directions for Contemplation*, ed. John Clark (Salzburg: University of Salzburg)

———— (2001 ed.) *A Spiritual Treatise Called ABC*, ed. John Clark (Salzburg: University of Salzburg)

Bedingfield, Edmund (1884) *The Life of Margaret Mostyn (Mother Margaret of Jesus): Religious of the Reformed Order of Our Blessed Lady of Mount Carmel (1625–1679)*, ed. H.J. Coleridge (London: Burns, Oates and Washbourne)

Hamilton, Adam (1904) *The Chronicle of the English Augustinian Canonesses Regular of the Lateran, at St Monica's in Louvain, 1548 to 1625* (Edinburgh and London: Sands)

Hardman, Anne (1932) *Life of the Venerable Anne of Jesus, Companion of St Teresa of Avila* (London: Sands)

———— (1937) *Mother Margaret Mostyn, Discalced Carmelite, 1625–1679* (London: Burns, Oates and Washbourne)

———— (1939) *Two English Carmelites: Mother Mary Xaveria Burton (1668–1714) and Mother Mary Margaret Wake (1617–78)* (London: Burns, Oates and Washbourne)

Hunter, Thomas (1876) *An English Carmelite: The Life of Catharine Burton, Mother Mary Xaveria of the Angels, of the English Teresian Convent at Antwerp*, ed. H.J. Coleridge (London: Burns, Oates and Washbourne)

Jerdan, W., ed. (1845) *Letters from James Earl of Perth, to his Sister, The Countess of Erroll* (London: Camden Society)

John of the Cross (1906 ed.) *The Ascent of Mount Carmel*, trans. David Lewis, ed. Benedict Zimmerman (London: Thomas Barker)

Linden, Erik van der (1984) *The Former Convent of the English Teresians at Lierre*, unpublished thesis for a degree in architecture, St Lukas Hoyer Institute for Architecture, Brussels

McCann, Justin and Connolly, Hugh (1933) *Memorials of Father Augustine Baker and Other Documents Relating to the English Benedictines* (Leeds: Catholic Record Society)

More, Gertrude (1658) *The Spiritual Exercises of the Most Vertuous and Religious D. Gertrude More of the Order of S. Bennet and English Congregation of Our Ladies of Comfort in Cambrai* (Paris: Lewis de la Folle)

———— (1910 ed.) 'The Apology of Dame Gertrude More', in *The Writings of Dame Gertrude More*, Benedict Weld-Blundell, ed. (London, Manchester and Glasgow: R. and T. Washbourne)

———— (1910 ed.) *The Inner Life of Dame Gertrude More*, ed. Benedict Weld-Blundell (London, Manchester, Glasgow: R. and T. Washbourne)

O'Neill, George (1909) *Blessed Mary of the Angels. Discalced Carmelite, 1661–1717, A Biography* (London, Manchester, Glasgow: R. and T. Washbourne)

Petre, Edward (1849) *Notices of the English Colleges and Convents Established on the Continent After the Dissolution of Religious Houses in England*, ed. F.C. Husebeth (Norwich: Bacon and Kinnebrook)

Puccini, Vincenzo (1687) *The Life of St Mary Magdalene of Pazzi, a Carmelite Nun* (London: R. Taylor)

Ribera, Franciso de (1669 repr. 1671) *The Life of the Holy Mother S. Teresa, Foundress of the Reformation of the Discalced Carmelites, According to the Primitive Rule, Divided into Two Parts, The 2nd Containing Her Foundations* (London: publisher n.s.)

Robinson, Thomas (1622 repr. 1630) *The Anatomie of the English Nunnery at Lisbon in Portugall* (London: George Purslowe)

Rodríguez, Alfonso (1627) *A Treatise of Mentall Prayer with Another of the Presence of God, translated out of Spanish into English* (St Omer: English College Press)

———— (1630) *A Short and Sure Way to Heaven and Present Happiness. Taught in a Treatise of Our Conformity with the Will of God, in His Worke Intituled The Exercise of Perfection and Christian Vertue, translated out of Spanish* (Ilkley and London: The Scolar Press)

Teresa de Jesus (1946 ed.) *Life of the Holy Mother Teresa of Jesus; Spiritual Relations Addressed by St Teresa of Jesus to her Confessors*, in *Complete Works of St Teresa*, Volume I, E. Allison Peers, trans. and ed. (London and New York: Sheed and Ward)

———— (1946 ed.) *Book Called Way of Perfection; Interior Castle; Conceptions of the Love of God; Exclamations of the Soul to God*, in *Complete Works of St Teresa*, Volume II, E. Allison Peers, trans. and ed. (London and New York: Sheed and Ward)

———— (1946 ed.) *Book of the Foundations; Minor Prose Works; Poems; Documents*, in *Complete Works of St Teresa*, Volume III, trans. and ed. E. Allison Peers (London and New York: Sheed and Ward)

———— (1957) *The Life of Saint Teresa of Avila by Herself*, trans. J.M. Cohen (Harmondsworth: Penguin) [Referred to here as: *Book*]

———— (1976) *The Book of Her Life; Spiritual Testimonies; Soliloquies,* in *The Collected Works of St Teresa of Avila*, Volume I, trans. Kieran Kavanaugh and Otilio Rodriguez (Washington DC: Institute of Carmelite Studies)

Secondary Sources

Ackerman, Jane (2000) 'Teresa and Her Sisters', in Robert Boenig, ed., *The Mystical Gesture: Essays on Medieval and Early Modern Spiritual Culture in Honor of Mary E. Giles* (Aldershot and Burlington: Ashgate), 107–40

Aers, David and Staley, Lynn (1996) *The Powers of the Holy: Religion, Politics and Gender in Late Medieval English Culture* (University Park, Pennsylvania: Penn State University Press)

Ahlgren, Gillian T.W. (1996) *Teresa of Avila and the Politics of Sanctity* (Ithaca and London: Cornell University Press)

———— (2000) 'Ecstasy, Prophecy and Reform: Catherine of Siena as a Model for Holy Women of Sixteenth-Century Spain', in Robert Boenig, ed., *The Mystical Gesture: Essays on Medieval and Early Modern Spiritual Culture in Honor of Mary E. Giles* (Aldershot and Burlington: Ashgate), 53–66

Anson, Peter F. (1949) *The Religious Orders and Congregations of Great Britain and Ireland* (Worcester, Massachusetts: Stanbrook Abbey Press)

Arnstein, Walter L. (1982) *Protestant vs. Catholic in Mid-Victorian England* (Columbia, Missouri and London: University of Missouri Press)

Aughterson, Kate (1995) *Renaissance Woman: A Sourcebook. Constructions of Femininity in England* (London and New York: Routledge)

Ballaster, Ros (1994) '"The Vice of Old Rome Revived": Representations of Female Same-sex Desire in Seventeenth- and Eighteenth-Century England', in Suzanne Raitt, ed., *Volcanoes and Pearl Divers: Essays in Lesbian Feminist Studies* (London: Onlywomen Press), 13–36

Barratt, Alexandra, ed. (1992) *Women's Writing in Middle English* (London and New York: Longman)

Bartlett, Anne Clark, ed. (1995) *Vox Mystica: Essays on Medieval Mysticism in Honor of Valerie M. Logorio* (Cambridge: D.S. Brewer)

Beilin, Elaine V (1987) *Redeeming Eve: Women Writers of the English Renaissance* (Princeton, New Jersey: Princeton University Press)

Bell, David N. (1995) *What Nuns Read: Books and Libraries in Medieval English Nunneries* (Kalamazoo, Michigan and Spencer, Massachusetts: Cistercian Publications)

Bireley, Robert (1999) *The Refashioning of Catholicism, 1450–1700. A Reassessment of the Counter-Reformation* (Basingstoke: Macmillan)

Boenig, Robert (2000), ed. *The Mystical Gesture: Essays on Medieval and Early Modern Spiritual Culture in Honor of Mary E. Giles* (Aldershot and Burlington: Ashgate)

Bolles, Edmund Blair (1997, repr. 2000) *Galileo's Commandment. An Anthology of Great Science Writing* (London: Abacus)

Booy, David (2002) *Personal Disclosures. An Anthology of Self-writings from the Seventeenth Century* (Aldershot and Burlington: Ashgate)

Bossy, John (1975) *The English Catholic Community, 1570–1850* (London: Darton, Longman and Todd)

Bowerbank, Sylvia (1986) 'Gertrude More and the Mystical Perspective', *Studia Mystica*, 9, 34–46

Brennan, Margaret (1985) 'Enclosure: Institutionalising the Invisibility of Women in Ecclesiastical Communities', *Concilium*, 182, 38–48

Briggs, Robin (2001) 'Circling the Devil: Witch-Doctors and Magical Healers in Early Modern Lorraine', in Stuart Clark, ed., *Languages of Witchcraft. Narrative, Ideology and Meaning in Early Modern Culture* (Basingstoke: Macmillan Press), 161–78

Burckhardt, Jacob (1860, repr. 1960) *The Civilisation of the Renaissance in Italy*, ed. Irene Gordon (New York: Mentor)

Burke's Peerage, Baronetage and Knightage, 14th edition (London, 1967)

Burke, Peter (1997) 'Representations of the Self from Petrarch to Descartes', in Roy Porter, ed., *Rewriting the Self: Histories from the Renaissance to the Present* (London and New York: Routledge), 17–28

Bynum, Caroline Walker (1991) *Fragmentation and Redemption: Essays on Gender and the Human Body in Medieval Religion* (New York: Zone Books)

Carlson, Cindy L. and Weisl, Angela Jane (1999) 'Introduction', in Cindy L. Carlson and Angela Jane Weisl, eds, *Constructions of Widowhood and Virginity in the Middle Ages* (Basingstoke and London: Macmillan), 1–21

Catherine of Siena (1980 ed.) *Catherine of Siena: The Dialogue*, ed. and trans. Suzanne Noffke (New York: Paulist Press)

Catholic Enclopaedia: http://www.newadvent.org

Clare, Janet (1996) 'Transgressing Boundaries. Women's Writing in the Renaissance and Reformation', *Renaissance Forum*, 1,1 (March 1996), 1–28

Clarke, Danielle (1996) 'The Iconography of the Blush: Marian Literature of the 1630s', in Kate Chedgzoy, Melanie Hansen and Suzanne Trill, eds, *Voicing Women. Gender and Sexuality in Early Modern Writing* (Edinburgh: Edinburgh University Press), 111–28

Clarke, Danielle and Clarke, Elizabeth, eds (2000) *'This Double Voice': Gendered Writing in Early Modern England* (Basingstoke: Macmillan)

Claydon, Tony and McBride, Ian, eds (1998) *Protestantism and National Identity, Britain and Ireland c.1650–c.1850* (Cambridge: Cambridge University Press)

Cook, Harold J. (1994) *Trials of an Ordinary Doctor: Joannes Groenevelt in Seventeenth Century London* (Baltimore and London: Johns Hopkins University Press)

Crawford, Patricia (1993) *Women and Religion in England, 1500–1700* (London and New York: Routledge)

Crawford, Patricia and Gowing, Laura, eds (2000) *Women's Worlds in England, 1580–1720: A Sourcebook* (London and New York: Routledge)

Crewe, Jonathan (1994) 'The Garden State: Marvell's Politics of Enclosure', in Richard Burt and John Michael Archer, eds, *Enclosure Acts. Sexuality, Property and Culture in Early Modern England* (Ithaca and London: Cornell University Press), 270–89

del Rio, Martin (2000) *Investigations into Magic*, ed. and trans. P.G. Maxwell-Stuart (Manchester and New York: Manchester University Press)

D'Monté, Rebecca and Nicole Pohl, eds (2000) *Female Communities 1600–1800. Literary Visions and Cultural Realities* (Basingstoke and London: Macmillan Press)

Descartes, René [1637] (1968, repr. 1975) *Discourse on Method and the Meditations*, trans. F.E. Sutcliffe (Harmondsworth: Penguin)

Dinshaw, Carolyn (1999) *Getting Medieval. Sexualities and Communities, Pre- and Postmodern* (Durham, North Carolina and London: Duke University Press)

Docherty, Thomas (1996) *Alterities, Criticism, History, Representation* (Oxford: Clarendon Press)

Duffy, Eamon (1992) *The Stripping of the Altars. Traditional Religion in England, 1400–1580* (New Haven and London: Yale University Press)

Faderman, Lillian (1981, repr. 1985) *Surpassing the Love of Men: Romantic Friendship and Love between Women from the Renaissance to the Present* (London: The Women's Press)

Friedman, Susan Stanford (1988) 'Women's Autobiographical Selves: Theory and Practice', in Shari Benstock, ed. *The Private Self, Theory and Practice of Women's*

Autobiographical Writings (Chapel Hill, North Carolina and London: University of North Carolina Press), 34–62

Galen (1997) *Selected Works*, trans. P.N. Singer (Oxford: Oxford University Press)

Geyl, Pieter (1936) *The Netherlands in the Seventeenth Century, 1609–1648* (London: Ernest Behn)

Gilchrist, Roberta (1994) *Gender and Material Culture: The Archaeology of Religious Women* (London and New York: Routledge)

Graham, Elspeth (1996) 'Women's Writing and the Self', in *Women and Literature in Britain, 1500–1700* (Cambridge: Cambridge University Press), 209–33

Grundy, Isobel (1992) 'Women's History? Writings by English Nuns', in Isobel Grundy and Sue Wiseman, eds, *Women, Writing, History, 1640–1740* (London: B.T. Batsford), 126–38

Guilday, Peter (1914) *The English Catholic Refugees on the Continent 1558–1795. Volume I: The English Colleges and Convents in the Catholic Low Countries, 1558–1795* (London: Longmans, Green and Co.)

Gusdorf, G (1980) 'Conditions and Limits of Autobiography', in James Olney, ed., *Autobiography: Essays Theoretical and Critical* (Princeton, NJ: Princeton University Press), 28–48

Hadland, Tony (1992/2001) *Thames Valley Papists. From Reformation to Emancipation, 1534–1829*, http://www.users.globalnet.co.uk/~hadland/tvp

Hallett, Nicky (2002a) '"as if it had nothing belonged to her": The Lives of Catherine Burton (1668–1714) as Discourse on Method in Early Modern Life-writing', *Early Modern Literary Studies*, 3 (January), 1–30

—— (2002b) 'Anxiously Yours: the Epistolary Self and the Culture of Concern', *Journal of European Studies: Literature and Ideas from the Renaissance to the Present*, 32 (June/September 2002), 107–18

—— (2007) *Witchcraft, Exorcism and the Politics of Possession in a Seventeenth Century Convent: 'How Sister Ursula was once bewiched and Sister Margaret twice'* (Aldershot and Burlington: Ashgate)

—— (forthcoming) '"as if some other had done it for me": Issues of Gender and Authority in the Lives of Early Modern Carmelite women', in Johan Bergström-Allen, ed., *Mystics from the Mountain: Spirituality, Gender and Authority in the Carmelite Order in Medieval and Early Modern Europe* (Faversham, Kent: St Albert's Press)

Hannay, Margaret Patterson, ed. (1985) *Silent but for the Word: Tudor Women as Patrons, Translators and Writers of Religious Works* (Kent State, OH: Kent State University Press)

Hanson, Elizabeth (1998) *Discovering the Subject in Renaissance England* (Cambridge: Cambridge University Press)

Hardman, Anne (1936) *English Carmelites in Penal Times* (London: Burns, Oates and Washbourne)

Harline, Craig (1995) 'Actives and Contemplatives: The Female Religious of the Low Countries Before and After Trent', *Catholic Historical Review*, 81, 541–67

—— (2000) *The Burdens of Sister Margaret. Inside a Seventeenth-Century Convent* (abridged ed.; New Haven and London: Yale University Press)

Harline, Craig and Eddy Put (2000) *A Bishop's Tale. Mathias Hovius Among His Flock in Seventeenth-Century Flanders* (New Haven and London: Yale University Press)

Haydon, Colin (1993) *Anti-Catholicism in Eighteenth Century England, c.1714–80, A Political and Social Study* (Manchester and New York: Manchester University Press)

———— (1998) ' "I love my King and my Country, but a Roman Catholic I hate": Anti-Catholicism, Xenophobia and National Identity in Eighteenth Century England', in Tony Claydon and Ian McBride, eds, *Protestantism and National Identity, Britain and Ireland c.1650–c.1850* (Cambridge: Cambridge University Press), 33–52

Hegel, G.W.F. (1977 ed.) *The Phenomenology of Spirit*, trans. A.V. Miller (Oxford: Clarendon Press)

Hill, Bridget (1987) 'A Refuge for Men: The Idea of a Protestant Nunnery', *Past and Present*, 117, 107–30

Hobby, Elaine (1988) *Virtue of Necessity: English Women's Writing 1649–88* (London: Virago)

Hsai, R. Po-chia (1998) *The World of Catholic Renewal, 1540–1770* (Cambridge, New York and Melbourne: Cambridge University Press)

Hull, Suzanne W. (1982, repr. 1988) *Chaste, Silent and Obedient. English Books for Women, 1475–1640* (San Marino: Huntington Library)

Hutchison, Ann M (1995) 'What the Nuns Read: Literary Evidence from the English Bridgettine House, Syon Abbey', *Mediaeval Studies*, 57, 205–22

Israel, Jonathan (1995) *The Dutch Republic. Its Rise, Greatness and Fall, 1477–1806* (Oxford: Clarendon Press)

Jantzen, Grace M. (1995) '"Cry Out and Write": Mysticism and the Struggle for Authority', in Lesley Smith and Jane H.M. Taylor, eds, *Women, the Book and the Godly* (Cambridge: D.S. Brewer), 67–76

———— (1998) *Becoming Divine. Towards a Feminist Philosophy of Religion* (Manchester: Manchester University Press)

Jordan, Constance (1990) *Renaissance Feminism: Literary Texts and Political Models* (Ithaca: Cornell University Press)

King, Margaret L. (1991) *Women of the Renaissance* (Chicago and London: University of Chicago Press)

Krontiris, Tina (1992) *Oppositional Voices. Women as Writers and Translators of Literature in the English Renaissance* (London and New York: Routledge)

Latz, Dorothy L. (1989) *Glow-worm Light: Writings of Seventeenth-Century English Recusant Women: from Original Manuscripts (Elizabethan and Renaissance Studies)* (Salzburg: University of Salzburg)

Laven, Mary (2002) *Virgins of Venice. Enclosed Lives and Broken Vows in the Renaissance Convent* (London: Viking)

Luongo, Thomas (1995) 'Catherine of Siena: Rewriting Female Holy Authority', in *Women, the Book and the Godly*, ed. Lesley Smith and Jane H.M. Taylor (Cambridge: D.S. Brewer), 89–104

Magray, Mary Peckham (1998) *The Transforming Power of the Nuns. Women, Religion and Cultural Change in Ireland, 1750–1900* (New York and Oxford: Oxford University Press)

Malcolmson, Cristina (1994) 'The Garden Enclosed/The Woman Enclosed: Marvell and the Cavalier Poets', in Richard Burt and John Michael Archer, eds, *Enclosure Acts. Sexuality, Property and Culture in Early Modern England* (Ithaca and London: Cornell University Press), 251–69

Mâle, Emile (1986 repr.) *Religious Art in France: The Late Middle Ages* (Princeton, New Jersey: Princeton University Press)

Marcus, Laura (1994) A*uto/biographical Discourses. Theory, Criticism, Practice* (Manchester and New York: Manchester University Press)

Marotti, Arthur F. (1999) 'Alienating Catholics in Early Modern England: Recusant Women, Jesuits and Ideological Fantasies', in Arthur Marotti, ed., *Catholicism and Anti-Catholicism in Early Modern English Texts* (Basingstoke: Macmillan), 1–34

Mascuch, M. (1997) *Origins of the Individualistic Self: Autobiography and Self-Identity in England, 1591–1791* (Cambridge: Polity Press)

Mason, Mary (1980) 'The Other Voice: Autobiographies of Women Writers', in ed. James Olney, ed., *Autobiography: Essays Theoretical and Critical* (Princeton, New Jersey: Princeton University Press), 207–35

McNamara, Jo Ann Kay (1996) *Sisters in Arms. Catholic Nuns Through Two Millennia* (Cambridge, MA and London: Harvard University Press)

Medwick, Cathleen (1999) *Teresa of Avila. The Progress of a Soul* (London: Duckworth)

Mooney, Catherine M. (1999) 'Voice, Gender and the Portray of Sanctity', in *Gendered Voices. Medieval Saints and Their Interpreters,* ed. Catherine M. Mooney (Philadelphia: University of Pennsylvania Press), 1–15

Noffke, Suzanne, ed. and trans. (1980) *Catherine of Siena: The Dialogue* (New York: Paulist Press)

Norman, Edward (1986) *Roman Catholicism in England from the Elizabethan Settlement to the Second Vatican Council* (Oxford and New York: Oxford University Press)

Norman, Marion (1975/76) 'Dame Gertrude More and the English Mystical Tradition', *Recusant History* 13, 196–211

O'Brien, Susan (1988) '*Terra Incognita*: The Nun in Nineteenth-Century England', *Past and Present*, 121, 110–40

Oxford English Dictionary (1989, 2nd ed.; Oxford: Clarendon Press)

Olney, James, ed. (1980) *Autobiography: Essays Theoretical and Critical* (Princeton, New Jersey: Princeton University Press)

Parish, Debra L. (1992) 'The Power of Female Pietism: Women as Spiritual Authorities and Religious Role Models in Seventeenth-Century England', *The Journal of Religious History*, 17, 1 (June 1992), 33–46

Peers, E. Allison (1951) *Studies of the Spanish Mystics*, 3 volumes (London and New York: Macmillan)

Porter, Roy (1997) 'Introduction', in Roy Porter, ed., *Rewriting the Self: Histories from the Renaissance to the Present* (London and New York: Routledge), 1–16

Ranft, Patricia (1996) *Women and the Religious Life in Premodern Europe* (Basingstoke and New York: Macmillan)

———— (2000) *A Woman's Way: The Forgotten History of Women Spiritual Directors* (Basingstoke and New York: Palgrave Macmillan)

Raymond, Janice G. (1986, repr. 1991) *A Passion for Friends. Toward a Philosophy of Female Affection* (London: The Women's Press)

Rhodes, Elizabeth (2000) 'What's in a Name: On Teresa of Avila's *Book*', in Robert Boenig, ed., *The Mystical Gesture: Essays on Medieval and Early Modern Spiritual Culture in Honor of Mary E. Giles* (Aldershot and Burlington: Ashgate), 79–106

Robinsheaux, Thomas (2001) 'Witchcraft and Forensic Medicine in Seventeenth-Century Germany', in Stuart Clark, ed., *Languages of Witchcraft. Narrative, Ideology and Meaning in Early Modern Culture* (Basingstoke: Macmillan Press), 197–216

Rogers, John (1994) 'The Enclosure of Virginity: The Poetics of Sexual Abstinence in the English Revolution', in Richard Burt and John Michael Archer, eds, *Enclosure Acts. Sexuality, Property and Culture in Early Modern England* (Ithaca and London: Cornell University Press), 229–50

Roper, Lyndal (1991) 'Witchcraft and Fantasy in Early Modern Germany', *History Workshop Journal*, 32, 19–43

Rose, Mary Beth (1986) 'Gender, Genre and History. Seventeenth-Century English Women and the Art of Autobiography', in Mary Beth Rose, ed., *Women in the Middle Ages and the Renaissance* (Syracuse: Syracuse University Press), 245–78

Rowlands, Margaret (1985) 'Recusant Women 1560–1640', in *Women in English Society 1500–1800*, ed. Mary Prior (London: Methuen), 149–80

Rubin, M. (1991) *Corpus Christi* (Cambridge: Cambridge University Press)

Sackville-West, Vita (1943) *The Eagle and the Dove: A Study in Contrasts. St Teresa of Avila and St Thérèse of Lisieux* (London: Michael Joseph)

Sawday, Jonathan (1995) *The Body Emblazoned. Dissection and the Human Body in Renaissance Culture* (London and New York: Routledge)

Schutte, Anne Jacobson (1996) *Cecilia Ferrazzi. Autobiography of an Aspiring Saint* (Chicago and London: University of Chicago Press)

Scott, Karen (1999) 'Mystical Death, Bodily Death. Catherine of Siena and Raymond of Capua on the Mystic's Encounter With God', in Catherine M. Mooney, ed., *Gendered Voices. Medieval Saints and Their Interpreters* (Philadelphia, Pennsylvania: University of Pennsylvania Press), 136–67

Seguin, Colleen M. (2003) 'Cures and Controversy in Early Modern Wales: The Struggle to Control St Winifred's Well', *North American Journal of Welsh Studies*, 3, 2 (Summer 2003), 1–17

Sharpe, Pamela (1999) 'Dealing with Love: The Ambiguous Independence of the Single Woman in Early Modern England', *Gender and History*, 11, 2 (July 1999), 209–32

Shell, Alison (1999) *Catholicism, Controversy and the English Literary Imagination, 1558–1660* (Cambridge: Cambridge University Press)

Stallybrass, Peter (1986) 'Patriarchal Territories: The Body Enclosed', in Margaret W. Ferguson and Maureen Quilligan, eds, *Rewriting the Renaissance. The Discourses*

278   *Lives of Spirit*

278   *Lives of Spirit*

278   *Lives of Spirit*

of Sexual Difference in Early Modern Europe (Chicago and London: University of Chicago Press), 123–44

Stanley, Liz (1992) 'Romantic Friendship? Some Issues in Researching Lesbian History and Biography', *Women's History Review*, 1, 2, 193–216

Stimpson, Catharine R. (1991) 'Foreword', in Margaret L. King, *Women of the Renaissance* (Chicago and London: University of Chicago Press)

Strien, C.D. van (1991) 'Recusant Houses in the Southern Netherlands as Seen by British Tourists, *c*.1650–1720', *Recusant History*, 20, 295–511

Tausiet, Marie (2001) 'Witchcraft as Metaphor: Infanticide and its Translations in Aragon in the Sixteenth and Seventeenth Centuries', in Stuart Clark ed., *Languages of Witchcraft. Narrative, Ideology and Meaning in Early Modern Culture* (Basingstoke: Macmillan Press), 179–96

The Complete Peerage of England, Scotland, Ireland, Great Britain and the United Kingdom, Extant Extinct or Dormant (1916; London: St Catherine's Press)

Traub, Valerie (2002) *The Renaissance of Lesbianism in Early Modern England* (Cambridge, New York and Melbourne: Cambridge University Press)

Travitsky, Betty S. and Cullen, Patrick, eds (2000), *Recusant Translators: Elizabeth Cary and Alexia Grey*, in *The Early Modern Englishwoman: A Facsimile Library of Essential Works*, 13 (Aldershot: Ashgate)

Tumbleson, Raymond D. (1998) *Catholicism in the English Protestant Imagination* (Cambridge: Cambridge University Press)

Walker, Claire (2003) *Gender and Politics in Early Modern Europe. English Convents in France and the Low Countries* (Basingstoke: Palgrave Macmillan)

Walsh, Barbara (2002) *Roman Catholic Nuns in England and Wales, 1800–1937* (Dublin and Portland Oregon: Irish Academic Press)

Warnicke, Retha M. (1983) *Women of the English Renaissance and Reformation* (Westport, Connecticut and London: Greenwood Press)

Watt, Diane, ed. (1997) *Medieval Women in their Communities* (Cardiff: University of Wales Press)

Weber, Alison (1990) *Teresa of Avila and the Rhetoric of Femininity* (Princeton, NJ: Princeton University Press)

——— (1992) 'Saint Teresa, Demonologist', in Anne J. Cruz and Mary Elizabeth Perry, eds, *Culture and Control in Counter-Reformation Spain* (Minneapolis: University of Minnesota Press), 171–95

Weller, B. and Margaret W. Ferguson, eds (1994) *The Tragedy of Mariam The Fair Queen of Jewry and The Lady Falkland: Her Life by One of her Daughters* (Berkeley, CA: University of California Press)

Whelan, Basil (1936) *Historic English Convents of To-day: The Story of the English Cloisters in France and Flanders in Penal Times* (London: Burns Oates and Washbourne)

Wiesner, Merry E. (1993, repr. 1995) *Women and Gender in Early Modern Europe* (Cambridge: Cambridge University Press)

Wogan-Browne, Joceyln (1994) 'Chaste Bodies: Frames and Experiences', in Sarah Kay and Miri Rubin, eds, *Framing Medieval Bodies* (Manchester: Manchester University Press), 13–28

Wolffe, John (1991) *The Protestant Crusade in Great Britain, 1829–60* (Oxford: Clarendon Press)

Wright, Wendy (2000) 'Inside My Body is the Body of God: Margaret Mary Alacoque and the Tradition of Embodied Mysticism', in Robert Boenig, ed., *The Mystical Gesture: Essays on Medieval and Early Modern Spiritual Culture in Honor of Mary E. Giles* (Aldershot and Burlington: Ashgate), 185–92

Yates, Julian (1999) 'Patristic Geographies: Manifesting Catholic Identity in Early Modern England', in Arthur F Marotti, ed., *Catholicism and Anti-Catholicism in Early Modern English Texts* (Basingstoke: Macmillan Press), 63–84

Zarri, Gabriella (1998) 'Gender, Religious Institutions and Social Discipline: The Reform of the Regulars', in Judith C.Brown and Robert C. Davis, eds, *Gender and Society in Renaissance Italy* (London: Longman)

Index